Preservation and Place

Preservation and Place

*Historic Preservation by and of
LGBTQ Communities in the United States*

Katherine Crawford-Lackey and Megan E. Springate

berghahn
NEW YORK · OXFORD
www.berghahnbooks.com

First published in 2019 by
Berghahn Books
www.berghahnbooks.com

Library of Congress Cataloging-in-Publication Data

Names: Crawford-Lackey, Katherine, editor. | Springate, Megan E.,
    editor.
Title: Preservation and Place: Historic Preservation by and of LGBTQ
    Communities in the United States / Katherine Crawford-Lackey and
    Megan E. Springate.
Description: New York: Berghahn Books, 2019. | Includes
    bibliographical references and index.
Identifiers: LCCN 2019014384 (print) | LCCN 2019017822 (ebook) | ISBN
    9781789203073 (ebook) | ISBN 9781789203066 (hardback:alk. paper)
Subjects: LCSH: Sexual minority community—United States—History. |
    Historic sites—Conservation and restoration—United States.
Classification: LCC HQ73.3.U6 (ebook) | LCC HQ73.3.U6 P74 2019
    (print) | DDC 306.760973—dc23
LC record available at https://lccn.loc.gov/2019014384

British Library Cataloguing in Publication Data

A catalogue record for this book is available from the British Library

ISBN 978-1-78920-306-6 hardback
ISBN 978-1-80073-642-9 paperback
ISBN 978-1-78920-307-3 ebook

https://doi.org/10.3167/9781789203066

Contents

Illustrations

Cover Image. The Pauli Murray Family Home in Durham, North Carolina, is associated with groundbreaking civil rights activist, lawyer, educator, writer, and Episcopal priest Pauli Murray. She served as a bridge figure between social movements through her advocacy for both women's and civil rights. Her efforts were critical to retaining "sex" in Title VII, a fundamental legal protection for women against employment discrimination. She was known as a mother to the feminist legal strategy and acknowledged as such by Justice Ruth Bader Ginsberg. After decades of work for black civil rights, her vision for a civil rights association for women became the National Organization for Women (NOW). As a young person, Murray struggled with her gender identity and sexual orientation. She later found loving, same-gender relationships foundational to her life. Discrimination based on her sexual orientation informed her work in civil rights. The Pauli Murray Family Home was designated a National Historic Landmark on 23 December 2016. Photo of the Pauli Murray Family Home before and after exterior rehabilitation courtesy of the Pauli Murray Center for History and Social Justice.

Preface

Katherine Crawford-Lackey

Preservation and Place: Historic Preservation by and of LGBTQ Communities in the United States was born out of a previous publication, *LGBTQ America: A Theme Study of Lesbian, Gay, Bisexual, Transgender, and Queer History*, edited by Megan E. Springate for the National Park Foundation and the National Park Service (2016). The theme study, only available online, covers a range of topics and issues related to two-spirit, lesbian, gay, bisexual, transgender, and queer (LGBTQ) history. This volume contains several revised and updated chapters from the theme study, as well as one new addition by Ty Ginter. The chapters in this volume were selected for their focus on topics relating to the historic preservation of LGBTQ historic sites, histories, and communities.

This volume includes activities not published in the theme study. Intended for advanced college undergraduate and graduate students, these were designed to allow educators the flexibility to adapt them to course curriculum. These materials can also be used by community leaders and activists seeking to engage with LGBTQ history and to undertake their own preservation projects. Designed specifically with the topic of preservation in mind, the activities offer opportunities to practically apply the book's content in the classroom and in communities.

Preservation and Place explores both the tangible and intangible aspects of place-making through the processes of preservation and interpretation. This volume (and the series as a whole) provides a unique focus on the historic sites affiliated with lesbian, gay, bisexual, transgender, and queer Americans, which afforded opportunities to gather, socialize, protest, mourn, and celebrate. The content discussed in the following pages reveals the power of place in shaping individual identities, in forming relationships, and in engaging with a broader community of citizens. Not only are sites associated with queer communities important for contemporary self-expression and collective bonding, they are also essential forms of documentation in that they speak to how LGBTQ Americans have historically created nonheteronormative spaces. Preserving and studying the built environment, by extension, can provide information about how queer people moved through and interacted with the world.[1]

American history, broadly taught in our public and private institutions, is too often decentered from the physical geography, displacing historical people and events from context. This form of historical amnesia makes these histories, particularly those of marginalized communities, vulnerable to those who would hijack these narratives for their own gain, a practice that has been normalized in contemporary political discourse. In addition, urban renewal has progressed at an alarming rate since the mid-twentieth century, leading to the destruction of countless historical places, particularly those of nonheteronormative Americans. Recording these properties is imperative in preserving the stories of queer Americans and revealing their significance within the broader framework of American history. Preserving historic properties facilitates the interpretation and commemoration of significant events, people, and communities in American history, embedding them in collective memory. The recognition of historically significant places is particularly important to underrepresented identities who too often remain voiceless in the historic record.

The silencing of certain perspectives from the historical narrative is an ongoing (and often intentional) process. Haitian anthropologist Michel-Rolph Trouillot examined the process of historical production, identifying how and why certain histories are selected for collective remembrance over others. His book *Silencing the Past: Power and the Production of History* interpreted the creation and preservation of historical records as a form of power as they inevitably result in the erasure of voices, leaving contemporary scholars with a limited glimpse of the past. These silences can occur when primary sources are created, when these sources are archived, during the research process, and in "the making of history" when information is disseminated.[2] The ability to study the past—through the recording of events, the management of the primary sources, the retrieval of sources, and the creation of interpretation based on the sources—implies a certain authority. Those who control the means of historical production control the past, and those who have the power to access the historic records (whether in the form of documents, oral stories, material culture, or the built environment) choose the history that is made available to the public through historic scholarship, interpretive programs, and preserved structures and sites.[3] Historic places are also primary sources that can be used to interpret certain stories while silencing others. In the words of Trouillot, historians "imagine the lives under the mortar, but how do [they] recognize the end of a bottomless silence?"[4] Along this line of inquiry, practitioners should consider the exclusionary aspects of historic preservation and how the stories of underrepresented communities can more fully be recognized though this process.

One of the challenges in recognizing the spaces of LGBTQ Americans entails how to document and preserve these sites in a way that warrants their survival for the next generation. As human geographers Kath Browne and Gavin Brown note, even if not acknowledged, gender and sexuality influence the geography of the landscape and how space is constructed and mapped. The built environment has historically been laid out to reinforce hierarchies of power by creating gendered spaces that are based on the assumption that heterosexuality is "normal." The relationships of power inherent in both public and private spaces was (and continues to be) used to legitimize the history and heritage of the privileged.[5]

Despite the power of historical spaces in shaping our collective consciousness, Americans have not always valued preservation as a means to study the past. When the historic preservation movement did take root in the early to mid-nineteenth century, it was generally concerned with preserving the history of white, heterosexual, cisgender men of privilege. Notable for its grassroots origin, the movement was galvanized by middle- and upper-class white women's organizations that recognized the intrinsic value of historic structures. Viewed as "guardians of the society's culture and morals," women such as Ann Pamela Cunningham played a prominent role in safeguarding the history of the young nation by restoring and preserving the historic homes of great American figures.[6] Cunningham founded the Mount Vernon Ladies Association (MVLA) and led efforts to restore and preserve George Washington's homestead in northern Virginia.[7] The establishment of the MVLA inspired other women's organizations, including the Ladies Hermitage Association, responsible for the preservation of Andrew Jackson's Hermitage near Nashville, Tennessee.[8] While the movement was empowering to affluent white women who wanted to preserve (and control) the narrative of the American past, the early preservation movement is problematic as it excluded people of color from participating, and it ignored the places of those who did not fit within the definition of "respectable" citizens.[9]

Private efforts to save America's (white) historic sites continued into the twentieth century with the establishment of Henry Ford's Greenfield Village and the restoration of Colonial Williamsburg by John D. Rockefeller.[10] While these examples of private rehabilitation speak to the direction of the movement, they were rooted in a colonial mentality that portrayed the lifestyles of upper-class society while ignoring the oppression of eighteenth- and nineteenth-century America in regard to gender, race, sexuality, and class. At this time, the federal government also began to take a more active role in the preservation of America's natural and cultural sites. The National Park Service (NPS) was established in 1916 to protect America's natural landscapes.[11] At its founding, the NPS was "primarily focused on nature and scenery";[12] however, its role began to expand in the 1930s when it assumed responsibility for over sixty historic sites and monuments.[13] When the United States government became further entrenched in the preservation movement in the 1930s, due in part to the Great Depression, it used the themes of natural and cultural conservation to encourage a sense of patriotism and camaraderie among its citizens, leading to an increased appreciation of the nation's history. President Franklin Delano Roosevelt also became wary of the effects of industrialization and modernization on historic structures.[14] In response, the federal government passed the Historic Sites Act of 1935, which designated policies to preserve historic places for the public.[15]

In the decades that followed, the federal government's involvement in the preservation of historic sites continued to expand. According to National Park Service historian John H. Sprinkle Jr., "From 1935 through 1966, the National Park Service adopted criteria to identify and classify nationally significant sites with an eye towards acquisition, management, and interpretation."[16] As America continued to urbanize and expand in the second half of the twentieth century, the government passed the National Historic Preservation Act of 1966. A milestone for the preservation movement, this act established the National Register of Historic Places (NRHP), created State Historic Preservation Offices (SHPOs),[17] and set a standard for assessing potential outcomes when developing federal land or using federal funds in development under Section 106.[18] The creation of the National Register, with its broader recognition of historically significant sites, freed the National Park Service from having to review countless park proposals.[19] Today, the NRHP continues to aid the NPS, functioning as a "national program to coordinate and support public and private efforts to identify, evaluate, and protect America's historic and archeological resources."[20]

As "the official list of the Nation's historic places worthy of preservation," the National Register of Historic Places recognizes historic and archaeological sites with local, state, and national importance.[21] In contrast, National Historical Landmarks (NHL) recognize places of exceptional national significance, emphasizing "a common bond between all Americans."[22] Properties listed on the National Register as well as those designated as National Historic Landmarks are not necessarily owned or cared for by the National Park Service (even though the NPS manages the NRHP and NHL programs). A historic site's inclusion in one or more of these programs, however, signifies its importance in the broader story of American history. Federally recognizing a site's historical significance is one way to legitimize its role and contribution in American history. Such designations are also important to the communities they represent. A site can possess historical significance and not be listed on the National Register; however, this program provides certain benefits for property owners. In addition to tax benefits, property owners can also apply for select grants.[23] The National Park Service also uses the history of these places in its official interpretation, which brings greater public awareness about the importance of the properties.

The National Register guidelines, however, can be limiting and exclusionary and have in the past favored the histories of wealthy, white, heterosexual American men.[24] A number of factors, including a lack of financial capital, discriminatory zoning laws and practices, and an increased likelihood of transiency, often cause the spaces associated with those with marginalized identities to go unrecognized. The National Register criteria does not take into account the added challenges when considering the places of minority communities, and this should cause professionals to reevaluate how "historical significance" is determined.[25]

The authors of this book series frequently refer to queer places listed on the National Register and emphasize the need to have LGBTQ historic sites federally designated as National Historic Landmarks. Both programs are managed by the National Park Service, and, as this book series originally began as an online publication for the NPS, there is a notable emphasis on using the National Register and National Historic Landmark programs to recognize and preserve queer spaces. Despite this volume's emphasis on NRHP listings and NHL designations, there are many other ways to recognize historically significant properties. In December 2017, the Metro Nashville Historical Commission recognized the significance of a local lesbian activist named Penny Campbell, adding a marker at her former home to the city's Historic Marker Program. A local LGBT activist who was instrumental in organizing the city's first pride parade, Campbell is also remembered as the lead plaintiff in a court case challenging the state's "homosexual acts" statute. Due to the efforts of Dr. Pippa Holloway, a professor of history at Middle Tennessee State University, and Jessica Reeves, a member of the Metro Historical Commission, the city of Nashville dedicated its first marker to a queer rights activist. The commemoration of the Campbell house by the Metro Historical Commission serves as an example of the importance of local and regional designation programs in preserving the history of sexually variant and gender nonconforming Americans.[26]

Other avenues of preservation include greater stakeholder participation and community involvement. Practitioners such as urban historian Andrew Hurley have called for a more flexible approach to historic preservation policy. While Hurley acknowledges positive aspects of the National Historic Preservation Act, and specifically historic district designation, he notes the nature of private investment in architecturally significant buildings creates "minimal yields on the nation's poorest quarters."[27] A more holistic approach to preservation is needed in order to ensure that preservation efforts are beneficial to all. Historic properties can also be used as educational tools and perhaps even more so as beacons of empowerment and inspiration. It is through federal and grassroots cooperation that we as citizens can work together to be educators of our youth, leaders in our communities, and advocates for the irreplaceable sites that are a testament to our history as a complex yet united America. One way to achieve this is to foster a stronger relationship between professionals and the public, which is what we attempted to accomplish with this book series.

Shared authority between practitioners and members of the community allows for a more authentic and sustainable preservation model. But studying and preserving LGBTQ history and spaces requires an understanding of the language used when referring to queer individuals and communities. Today, sexually nonconforming and gender-variant people are often labeled as belonging to LGBTQ communities. While people who identify as lesbian, gay, bisexual, transgender, or queer are often referred to as a collective, lived experiences are inherently different depending on categories of difference (such as race, class, gender, sexual orientation, ability, and religion). Knowing who identifies as part of these communities is necessary when studying the construction of queer identity. Lesbian and gay Americans are defined by an attraction to the same gender. While "lesbian" refers to women, the term "gay" often refers to men, but can be used when speaking of multiple genders. Bisexuals have "the capacity to be attracted to and love more than one gender."[28] The term transgender refers to "the ways people can live lives that depart from the conventional patterns according to which all bodies are assigned a sex at birth (male or female) and enrolled in a social gender (girl or boy)."[29]

Many have debated the use of the term "queer" when referring to nonheteronormative people and behavior. Originally used as a derogatory term beginning in the late nineteenth century, the word queer has recently been reclaimed by a younger generation of Americans. This term is now used to refer to those of us who do not identify as lesbian, gay, bisexual, or transgender but who are also not exclusively heterosexual. The use of the term today recognizes that there are many identities within lesbian, gay, bisexual, and transgender communities. In the spirit of inclusivity, this book series uses the term when referring broadly to nonheteronormative Americans in the past and present.[30]

Over the past several years, the National Park Service has played a leading role in raising greater awareness to historic sites affiliated with LGBTQ history. As America's storyteller, the National Park Service is responsible for identifying, preserving, and interpreting the history of all U.S. citizens. Recently, the NPS and its programs, such as the National Register of Historic Places and National Historic Landmarks Program, have begun to care for and interpret more diverse historic sites that represent the broader spectrum of American experiences. The NPS is, by extension, addressing the underrepresentation of certain communities, including Latinos/Latinas, Asian Americans, Pacific Islanders, women, and LGBTQ communities.[31] *LGBTQ America: A Theme Study of Lesbian, Gay, Bisexual, Transgender, and Queer History*, released by the National Park Foundation and the National Park Service in 2016, is a prime example of the growing diversity represented within the National Park Service. Over twelve hundred pages in length and with contributions from dozens of authors, the study is intended to help historians, preservationists, and members of the public identify potential properties for nomination to the National Register of Historic Places and as National Historic Landmarks. The listings, designations, and amendments to existing listings resulting from the LGBTQ theme study further demonstrate the significance of LGBTQ sites to the overall American story.[32]

At the time the NPS released *LGBTQ America*, the impetus for this book series, I was a public history Ph.D. student completing my residency with the National Park Service's Cultural Resources Office of Interpretation and Education. Editor Megan E. Springate and I were invited by Berghahn Books to propose a publication based on *LGBTQ America*. As editor of the theme study, Megan's familiarity with the topic material and her working relationships with the authors were instrumental when conceptualizing and executing the series. To make the material more accessible to young professionals, community leaders, and members of the public, we created a series of activities for the practical application of topics and theories discussed in the chapters. With a background in civic engagement and public interpretation, I took on the challenge of creating activities to complement the content, with the target audience being college undergraduate and graduate students in fields relating to LGBTQ history, public history, and historic preservation. This project was meaningful not only as a way to guide people in the field; I was also grappling with how to identify myself as someone attracted to multiple genders. Accordingly, the project took on a special significance to me, and I was excited to have the opportunity to make the content accessible to a broader readership in a way that was deeply personal.

Megan and I were also eager to make the chapters of the LGBTQ theme study available in print (as the original is only accessible online) and to disseminate this information widely to a new generation of scholars. As we attempted to identify sections of the theme study to include in the book, we began to recognize the centrality of all the chapters in depicting the LGBTQ experience in America. In *LGBTQ America*, the contributing authors addressed unique facets of queer communities and imparted how affiliated historic sites are interconnected with the larger historical narrative. As a result, our proposal to Berghahn Books was expanded to include a series of three volumes encompassing the themes of identity, community, and historic preservation.

The book series takes an all-encompassing approach to the study of queer history and culture. Due to their backgrounds as historians, public historians, preservationists, and community leaders, each author brings a different voice to the table. The series is also unique as it offers an interactive element designed to engage undergraduate and graduate students. Each chapter is accompanied by worksheets and activities to prompt readers to think critically and immerse themselves in the subject matter. Designed with the belief that learning should be an interactive process that inspires continued quest for knowledge, the activities were created to spark the imagination and reveal larger connections between LGBTQ history and American history. Intended to be read as a series or individually, the books examine the history of LGBTQ communities in the United States, explore the complexities of LGBTQ identities, and provide guidance on how to identify, preserve, and interpret affiliated properties.

Katherine Crawford-Lackey is a Ph.D. candidate in public history at Middle Tennessee State University in Murfreesboro, Tennessee.

Notes

1. Scholars such as architectural historian Dell Upton and American studies professor Bernard L. Herman examine the intentionality of the built landscape in influencing human behavior and perceptions. Their work reveals how landscapes and structures are designed to reinforce hierarchies of power. For more information about the topic, see Dell Upton, "White and Black Landscapes in Eighteenth-Century Virginia," in *Material Life in America 1600–1860*, edited by R. B. S. George (Boston: Northeastern University Press, 1988); and Bernard L. Herman, "The Embedded Landscapes of the Charleston Single House, 1780–1820," *Perspectives in Vernacular Architecture* 7 (1997): 41–57.
2. Michel-Rolph Trouillot, *Silencing the Past: Power and the Production of History* (Boston: Beacon Press, 1995), 24.
3. Ibid, 26.
4. Ibid, 30.
5. Kath Browne and Gavin Brown, "An Introduction to the Geographies of Sex and Sexualities," in *The Routledge Research Companion to Geographies of Sex and Sexuality*, edited by Gavin Brown and Kath Browne (New York: Routledge, 2016); Dolores Hayden, *The Power of Place: Urban Landscapes as Public History* (Cambridge: MIT Press, 1995).
6. Barbara Howe, "Women in Historic Preservation: The Legacy of Ann Pamela Cunningham," *Public Historian*, 12, no. 1 (1990): 31–61, 32.
7. Ibid.
8. Virginia O. Benson and Richard Klein, *Historic Preservation for Professionals* (Kent, OH: Kent State University Press, 2008), 13.
9. The early preservation movement originated from the concept of the "cult of domesticity" where middle- and upper-class white women, beacons of morality, were expected to uphold and pass on American values and traditions. Preserving the great places that embodied the best of the American experience, these women shaped the early history of the nation. Historian Barbara J. Howe elaborates on the role of women in the historic preservation movement in her chapter "Women in the Nineteenth-Century Preservation Movement," in *Restoring Women's History through Historic Preservation*, ed. Gail Lee Dubrow and Jennifer B. Goodman (Baltimore: Johns Hopkins University Press, 2003); but Fath Davis Ruffins reminds us that the role of women in the movement was limited to the elite. Speaking in reference to the historic sites featured by the National Park Service at the end of the twentieth century, Davis Ruffins notes that there are "rare examples in which the memory of Black women is present 'on the ground,' that is, on the national landscape of historic preservation." Fath Davis Ruffins, "Four African American Women on the National Landscape," in *Restoring Women's History through Historic Preservation*, ed. Dubrow and Goodman (Baltimore: Johns Hopkins University Press, 2003), 59.

10. For more information on the preservation endeavors of John D. Rockefeller and Henry Ford, see Michael Wallace, "Visiting the Past: History Museums in the United States," in *Presenting the Past: Essays on History and the Public*, ed. Susan Porter Benson, Stephen Brier, and Roy Rosenzweig (Philadelphia: Temple University Press, 1986), 137–61; Steven Conn, "Objects and American History: The Museums of Henry Mercer and Henry Ford," in *Museums and American Intellectual Life, 1876–1926* (Chicago: University of Chicago Press, 1998), 151–92.

11. Norman Tyler, Ted J. Ligibel, and Ilene R. Tyler, *Historic Preservation: An Introduction to Its History, Principles, and Practice* (New York: W.W. Norton & Company, 2009), 30.

12. Anne Mitchell Whisnant, Marla R. Miller, Gary B. Nash, and David Thelen, *Imperiled Promise: The State of History in the National Park Service* (Bloomington, IN: Organization of American Historians, 2011), 20.

13. John H. Sprinkle Jr., *Crafting Preservation Criteria: The National Register of Historic Places and American Historic Preservation* (New York: Routledge, 2014), 7.

14. Ibid, 9–10.

15. Tyler, Ligibel, and Tyler, *Historic Preservation*, 61.

16. Sprinkle, *Crafting Preservation Criteria*, 2.

17. In 1992, the National Historic Preservation Act was amended, and tribal governments were permitted to establish Tribal Historic Preservation Officer (THPO) programs. Operating on tribal land, THPOs provide similar services as the State Historic Preservation Officers. NATHPO, "THPO Funding," National Association of Tribal Historical Preservation Offices website, accessed 1 January 2018, http://nathpo.org/wp/thpos/history-of-funding/.

18. Department of the Interior, *Federal Historic Preservation Laws: The Office of Compilation of U.S. Cultural Heritage Statutes* (Washington, DC: Department of the Interior, 2006), 60.

19. Sprinkle, *Crafting Preservation Criteria*, 17.

20. "National Register of Historic Places," website homepage, National Park Service, https://www.nps.gov/nr/.

21. *National Register of Historic Places*, Brochure/poster, National Park Service, https://www.nps.gov/nr/publications/bulletins/NR_Brochure_Poster/NR_Brochure_Poster.pdf.

22. Tyler, Ligibel, and Tyler, *Historic Preservation*, 150.

23. Sprinkle, *Crafting Preservation Criteria*, 1–4.

24. In the past, the National Register and National Historic Landmarks programs placed an emphasis on architecturally significant structures, and resulting nominations often ignored the human stories of those who lived and worked in these buildings. Additional challenges in nominating LGBTQ-affiliated properties arise when considering physical integrity. Current NPS bureau historian John H. Sprinkle Jr. gives an overview of requirements for listing properties to these programs in his book *Crafting Preservation Crite-*

ria, and he acknowledges that properties often lose integrity over time, especially those in urban areas. The National Register's "50 Year Rule" further complicates LGBTQ-affiliated nominations as the period of significance for many of the properties associated with queer history is relatively recent. Sprinkle, *Crafting Preservation Criteria*.

25. Critics of the National Register have cautioned against its arguably narrow interpretation of the concept of "historic preservation." Urban historian Dolores Hayden, for example, studies how women and ethnic minorities are often erased from the public landscape. She argues that these spaces can be reclaimed even without an intact physical structure. Similarly, architectural historian and cultural geographer Michael R. Allen contends that symbolical spaces are worth preserving. He uses the former site of the QuikTrip in Ferguson as one such example. The structure was set on fire during riots that erupted after the murder of Michael Brown in 2014. The work of Hayden and Allen explores how to memorialize past people and events even when the built environment has been disturbed. Hayden, *The Power of Place*; Michael R. Allen, "What Historic Preservation Can Learn from Ferguson," in *Bending the Future: 50 Ideas for the Next 50 Years of Historic Preservation in the United States*, ed. Max Page and Marla R. Miller (Amherst: University of Massachusetts Press, 2016); For more information about the spaces of transient communities, see Jen Jack Gieseking, "The Geographies of LGBTQ Lives: In and Beyond Cities, Neighborhoods, and Bars," in *Communities and Place: A Thematic Approach to the Histories of LGBTQ Communities in the United States*, ed. Katherine Crawford-Lackey and Megan E. Springate (New York: Berghahn Books, forthcoming).

26. Chris St. Clair, "Metro Historical Commission Approves First Marker to Honor LGBT Struggle," Nashville Public Radio, 8 October 2017, accessed 27 August 2018, http://www.nashvillepublicradio.org/post/metro-historical-commission-approves-first-marker-honor-lgbt-struggle#stream/0.

27. Andrew Hurley, *Beyond Preservation: Using Public History to Revitalize Inner Cities* (Philadelphia: Temple University Press, 2010), 114.

28. Loraine Hutchins, "Making Bisexual Visible," in *Identities and Place: Changing Labels and Intersectional Communities of LGBTQ and Two-Spirit People in the United States*, ed. Katherine Crawford-Lackey and Megan E. Springate (New York: Berghahn Books, 2019).

29. Susan Stryker, "Transgender History in the United States and the Places That Matter," in *Identities and Place: Changing Labels and Intersectional Communities of LGBTQ and Two-Spirit People in the United States*, ed. Katherine Crawford-Lackey and Megan E. Springate (New York: Berghahn Books, 2019).

30. It should be noted that some gay individuals and communities still associate the term "queer" with very negative connotations due to the word's charged history. Authors in this study use this term to be more inclusive of identities that do not fit within lesbian, gay, bisexual, or transgender com-

munities. Popular LGBT media outlets such as the *Advocate* and *Go Magazine* have published articles about the benefits and potential detriments of using this word given its historical context. Mark Segal, "The Problem with the Word 'Queer,'" *Advocate*, 11 February 2016, accessed 31 August 2018, https://www.advocate.com/commentary/2016/2/11/problem-word-queer; Dayna Troisi, "I'm A Lesbian and I'm Not Offended by the Word Queer," *Go Magazine*, 17 January 2018, accessed 31 August 2018, http://gomag.com/article/im-a-lesbian-and-im-not-offended-by-the-word-queer/.

31. Whisnant, *Imperiled Promise*.
32. The Pauli Murray Family Home (Durham, NC) and Earl Hall, located on the campus of Columbia University, are examples of National Register listings and National Historic Landmark designations that have been recognized since the publication of the LGBTQ theme study. *LGBTQ America* has also led to the amendment of existing listings, including Whiskey Row, located in Louisville, KY. View the nominations: Pauli Murray Family Home, https://www.nps.gov/places/pauli-murray-family-home.htm; Earl Hall, http://www.nyclgbtsites.org/wp-content/uploads/2017/03/NY_NewYorkCounty_Earl Hall.pdf; and Kentucky's Whiskey Row, https://www.nps.gov/nr/feature/pla ces/pdfs/AD89000385_03_13_2017.pdf.

Bibliography

Allen, Michael R. "What Historic Preservation Can Learn from Ferguson." In *Bending the Future: 50 Ideas for the Next 50 Years of Historic Preservation in the United States*, edited by Max Page and Marla R. Miller. Amherst: University of Massachusetts Press, 2016.

Benson, Virginia O., and Richard Klein. *Historic Preservation for Professionals*. Kent, OH: Kent State University Press, 2008.

Browne, Kath, and Gavin Brown. "An Introduction to the Geographies of Sex and Sexualities." In *The Routledge Research Companion to Geographies of Sex and Sexuality*, edited by Gavin Brown and Kath Browne. New York: Routledge, 2016.

Conn, Steven. "Objects and American History: The Museums of Henry Mercer and Henry Ford." In *Museums and American Intellectual Life, 1876–1926*, 151–92. Chicago: University of Chicago Press, 1998.

Davis Ruffins, Fath. "Four African American Women on the National Landscape." In *Restoring Women's History through Historic Preservation*, edited by Dubrow and Goodman. Baltimore: Johns Hopkins University Press, 2003.

Department of the Interior. *Federal Historic Preservation Laws: The Office of Compilation of U.S. Cultural Heritage Statutes*. Washington, DC: Department of the Interior, 2006.

Gieseking, Jen Jack. "The Geographies of LGBTQ Lives: In and Beyond Cities, Neighborhoods, and Bars." In *Communities and Place: A Thematic Approach to the Histories of LGBTQ Communities in the United States*, edited by Katherine Crawford-Lackey and Megan E. Springate. New York: Berghahn Books, forthcoming.

Hayden, Dolores. *The Power of Place: Urban Landscapes as Public History*. Cambridge: MIT Press, 1995.

Herman, Bernard L. "The Embedded Landscapes of the Charleston Single House, 1780–1820." *Perspectives in Vernacular Architecture* 7 (1997): 41–57.

Howe, Barbara. "Women in the Nineteenth-Century Preservation Movement." In *Restoring Women's History through Historic Preservation*, edited by Gail Lee Dubrow and Jennifer B. Goodman. Baltimore: Johns Hopkins University Press, 2003.

Hurley, Andrew. *Beyond Preservation: Using Public History to Revitalize Inner Cities*. Philadelphia: Temple University Press, 2010.

Hutchins, Loraine. "Making Bisexual Visible." In *Identities and Place: Changing Labels and Intersectional Communities of LGBTQ and Two-Spirit People in the United States*, edited by Katherine Crawford-Lackey and Megan E. Springate. New York: Berghahn Books, 2019. NATHPO [National Association of Tribal Historical Preservation Offices. "THPO Funding," NATHPO website. Accessed 1 January 2018, http://nathpo.org/wp/thpos/history-of-funding/.

National Register of Historic Places Registration Form: Earl Hall (New York, New York), http://www.nyclgbtsites.org/wp-content/uploads/2017/03/NY_NewYorkCounty_EarlHall.pdf.

National Register of Historic Places Registration Form: Pauli Murray Family Home (Durham, North Carolina), https://www.nps.gov/places/pauli-murray-family-home.htm.

National Register of Historic Place Registration Form: Whiskey Row Historic District (Louisville, Kentucky), https://www.nps.gov/nr/feature/places/pdfs/AD89000385_03_13_2017.pdf.

National Register of Historic Places. Brochure/poster. National Park Service. https://www.nps.gov/nr/publications/bulletins/NR_Brochure_Poster/NR_Brochure_Poster.pdf.

"National Register of Historic Places." Website homepage. National Park Service. https://www.nps.gov/nr/.

Segal, Mark. "The Problem With the Word 'Queer.'" *The Advocate*, 11 February 2016. Accessed 31 August 2018, https://www.advocate.com/commentary/2016/2/11/problem-word-queer.

Springate, Megan E., ed. LGBTQ America: *A Theme Study of Lesbian, Gay, Bisexual, Transgender, and Queer History*. Washington, DC: National Park Foundation, 2016.

Sprinkle, John H., Jr. *Crafting Preservation Criteria: The National Register of Historic Places and American Historic Preservation*. New York: Routledge, 2014.

St. Clair, Chris. "Metro Historical Commission Approves First Marker to Honor LGBT Struggle." Nashville Public Radio, 8 October 2017. Accessed 27 August 2018, http://www.nashvillepublicradio.org/post/metro-historical-commission-approves-first-marker-honor-lgbt-struggle#stream/0.

Stryker, Susan. "Transgender History in the United States and the Places That Matter." In *Identities and Place: Changing Labels and Intersectional Communities of LGBTQ and Two-Spirit People in the United States*, edited by Katherine Crawford-Lackey and Megan E. Springate. New York: Berghahn Books, 2019.

Troisi, Dayna. "I'm A Lesbian and I'm Not Offended by the Word Queer." *Go Magazine*, 17 January 2018. Accessed 31 August 2018, http://gomag.com/article/im-a-lesbian-and-im-not-offended-by-the-word-queer/.

Trouillot, Michel-Rolph. *Silencing the Past: Power and the Production of History*. Boston: Beacon Press, 1995.

Tyler, Norman, Ted J. Ligibel, and Ilene R. Tyler. *Historic Preservation: An Introduction to Its History, Principles, and Practice*. New York: W.W. Norton & Company, 2009.

Upton, Dell. "White and Black Landscapes in Eighteenth-Century Virginia." In *Material Life in America 1600–1860*, edited by R. B. S. George. Boston: Northeastern University Press, 1988.

Wallace, Michael. "Visiting the Past: History Museums in the United States." In *Presenting the Past: Essays on History and the Public*, edited by Susan Porter Benson, Stephen Brier, and Roy Rosenzweig, 137–61. Philadelphia: Temple University Press, 1986.

Whisnant, Anne Mitchell, Marla R. Miller, Gary B. Nash, and David Thelen. *Imperiled Promise: The State of History in the National Park Service*. Bloomington: Organization of American Historians, 2011.

Acknowledgments

This book and the series it is part of is the product of the collaborative efforts of many individuals. Their dedication and support throughout this process has made this publication possible.

This series comes out of *LGBTQ America: A Theme Study of Lesbian, Gay, Bisexual, Transgender, and Queer History*, which was edited by Megan Springate for the National Park Foundation and the National Park Service (2016). We are grateful to the Gill Foundation for funding it, and to all of the National Park Service and National Park Foundation staff, scholars, community members, authors, peer reviewers, and production folks who made that project—and therefore also this one—possible. Many thanks to the authors and peer reviewers who worked with us on this volume for your thoughtful contributions. Your work is the heart of this book.

We would like to extend special thanks to Dr. Barbara J. Little at the National Park Service, who provided encouragement and guidance throughout this process, and to Dr. Caryn M. Berg, our editor at Berghahn Books, for suggesting this series and working with us to bring it to fruition.

We are grateful for the support and feedback of our colleagues in the Cultural Resources Office of Interpretation and Education and in the Cultural Resources, Partnerships and Science Directorate at the National Park Service.

Of course we could not have done this without the support of friends and colleagues. Katherine would like to thank Dr. Pippa Holloway and Dr. Carol Van West for reviewing her contributions, and her parents, Leo and Kathleen, for their continued support. She would also like to recognize her partner, Jonathan Eizyk, for reading (and rereading) the prologues and activities. Megan is grateful for the support of her family and friends, including Chelsea Blackmore and Danielle Easter.

The views and conclusions contained in this volume are those of the authors and should not be interpreted as representing the opinions or policies of the U.S. government. Mention of trade names or commercial products does not constitute their endorsement by the U.S. government.

CHAPTER 1

Invisibility and Representation

An Introduction to LGBTQ Historic Preservation

Gail Dubrow

Introduction

The LGBTQ Theme Study released by the National Park Service in June 2016 is the fruit of three decades of effort by activists and their allies to make historic preservation a more equitable and inclusive sphere of activity. The LGBTQ movement for civil rights has given rise to related activity in the cultural sphere aimed at recovering the long history of same-sex relationships, understanding the social construction of gender and sexual norms, and documenting the rise of movements for LGBTQ rights in American history. This work has provided an intellectual foundation for efforts to preserve the tangible remains of LGBTQ heritage and make that history publicly visible at historic sites and buildings, in museum exhibits, and on city streets. This essay traces the history of the movement to identify, document, designate, interpret, and preserve elements of the built environment and cultural landscape associated with LGBTQ heritage.

Undocumented LGBTQ History at National Historic Landmark Properties and Those on the National Register of Historic Places

Sites with queer associations made their way onto the National Register of Historic Places (NRHP) and roster of National Historic Landmarks (NHL) not long after the passage of the 1966 Historic Preservation Act; however, their connections to LGBTQ heritage almost always went undocumented in inventory-nomination forms and the subject went unmentioned—or was referred to only in euphemisms—when visitors toured places open to the public. Only in recent years, with rising public acceptance of differences in sexual orientation and gender expression, wider public support for LGBTQ civil liberties, and the creation of a robust body of scholarship in LGBTQ studies, has it become possible to document and convey the full significance of these "lavender landmarks." Yet much work remains to be done to fully integrate the histories of lesbian, gay, bisexual, transgender, and queer people into local, state, and federal cultural resources management programs.

Not all historic places are open to the public. Among those that are, many—including historic house museums—were established at a time when any discussion of sexuality and gender nonconformity was impermissible in public venues, but especially in the context of LGBTQ issues.[1] Historic houses associated with individuals noted for their literary or political achievements constitute the majority of listed properties with untapped potential to address LGBTQ themes. Because gay-positive public attitudes have evolved more quickly in major metropolitan areas, historic house museums that lie outside of urban centers have been slower to broadcast their LGBTQ associations.

In some cases, those charged with managing historic properties have been aware of relevant LGBTQ content, but have suppressed it within their interpretive programs. Despite persistent inquiries about LGBTQ connections to the properties, they have resisted taking action, sometimes hesitant to "out" historical figures who worked overtime to hide their sexual orientation. Some managers of historic properties have been mired in uncertainty about how to make sense of documented same-sex affections that do not neatly fit into contemporary categories of sexual orientation and identity. Others are grappling with residual social stigma and shame attached to homosexuality, bisexuality, and gender nonconformity, fearing these labels might color the reputation of notable individuals at the sites they manage. Finally, in the context of the nation's culture wars, in which the rights of gay, lesbian, bisexual, and transgender people became one of the most divisive issues in American politics, few mainstream organizations relished the idea of actively courting controversy by bringing LGBTQ content to the fore at historic places. For all of these reasons, there are many designated NHLs and properties listed on the NRHP whose connections with LGBTQ history are just beginning to be articulated, including historic properties associated with Walt Whitman, Willa Cather, Eleanor Roosevelt and her associates, and Frances Perkins.

The small two-story, wood-framed house in Camden, New Jersey, that Whitman occupied from 1884 until his death in 1892, is open to the public, managed by the New Jersey Division of Parks and Forestry.[2] Whitman's homosexuality is neither mentioned in the NHL nomination for his home, nor on the museum's website, despite the homoeroticism in his work, including his masterpiece, *Leaves of Grass* (the final version of which he wrote at this location), and evidence of his relationships with other men.[3] Likewise, although the NHL nomination for Willa Cather's childhood home in Red Cloud, Nebraska, recognized the home as a source of inspiration for her fiction, it was silent on Cather's transgressive gender expression in adolescence and her adult romantic and sexual ties with women (figure 1.1).[4] Existing interpretation at the historic house museum, as well as the official website, also skirts these aspects of her life history, referring only briefly to Cather cropping her hair short, calling herself Willie or William, and adopting male attire as examples of her unusual degree of independence, rather than her defiance of social norms regarding sexual orientation and gender expression.[5] Changing ideas about Cather's place in American literature are mirrored in the evolving interpretation of her Red Cloud childhood home, except for the treatment of her personal life—and its implications for her work—which remain outdated by three decades.

As scholars have uncovered evidence of same-sex intimacies in connection with some of the most prominent figures in American history, including Eleanor Roosevelt and her circle, the managers of landmark destinations such as the Eleanor Roosevelt National Historic Site in Hyde Park, New York, known as Val-Kill, have had to weigh competing

Figure 1.1. Willa Cather's childhood home in Red Cloud, Nebraska, 2010. Photo by Ammodramus (public domain: Wikimedia Commons).

pressures to tackle the subject head-on or deflect potential controversy by addressing it only when visitors make inquiries.[6]

Eleanor Roosevelt was close friends with many influential and powerful women who were likely lesbians, including couples Nancy Cook and Marion Dickerman, and Esther Lape and Elizabeth Read. Roosevelt credited Lape and Read as playing an important role in her development as a political activist; Cook and Dickerman were frequent visitors to Val-Kill, ultimately residing in a stone cottage there for three decades.[7] Eleanor herself had a lengthy and intimate relationship with journalist Lorena Hickok (whom she called "Hick"): they vacationed together, Hickok had a bedroom in the White House, and the two wrote extensive and sensual letters to each other daily.[8] Evidence of this passionate relationship challenges long-standing stereotypes of Eleanor as "cold, remote . . . ugly, terminally insecure, dry-as-dust."[9]

As to whether Eleanor Roosevelt and "Hick" were physically intimate, historian Blanche Wiesen Cook writes, "We can never know what people do in the privacy of their own rooms. The door is closed. The blinds are drawn. We don't know. I leave it up to the reader. But there's no doubt in my mind that they loved each other, and this was an ardent, loving relationship between two adult women."[10] Neither the NHL nomination for Val-Kill nor the NPS website mentions the same-sex relationships of either Eleanor Roosevelt or Cook and Dickerman. Concerns about the erasure of these aspects of Val-Kill's history have been long-standing, dating to Paula Martinac's 1997 observations in *The Queerest Places* that, despite the evidence, "you won't hear even a hint about Eleanor's lesbianism [or bisexuality] in the official Park Service interpretation and film, in which Nancy and Marion are painted as 'good friends,' and Hick—one of the major relationships of her life—isn't mentioned at all."[11] In this case and many others, the ambiguity of evidence surrounding same-sex sexual intimacy, as opposed to intense emotional or romantic attachments, frequently has been used as a rationale for avoiding the issue. Established as a National Historic Site in 1977, Val-Kill would benefit from refreshed interpretation that brings insights from the past twenty-five years of scholarship into the presentation of Eleanor Roosevelt's life and legacy.

Likewise, nominations and interpretations of places associated with Frances Perkins, another major figure in Franklin and Eleanor Roosevelt's New Deal circle, neglect to mention her same-sex relationships.[12] The first woman to serve in a presidential cabinet, Frances Perkins was Secretary of Labor from 1933 to 1945. While married to Paul Caldwell Wilson, Perkins maintained a long-standing romantic relationship with

Mary Harriman Rumsey, who had founded the Junior League in 1901. Both women made their mark advancing the Progressive movement's labor and consumer reform agenda and subsequent New Deal initiatives. They lived together in DC until Rumsey's death in 1934, after which Perkins shared her life and home in DC with Caroline O'Day, a Democratic congresswoman from New York.[13] Building on her many accomplishments, Perkins went on to fight for the Social Security Act.

The interpretation and understanding of these places—and all of the others with silenced LGBTQ history—would benefit from representing the full complexity and histories of those who lived there. Part of this process is making amendments to the existing nominations, and ensuring that LGBTQ history is incorporated into future nominations. Since anyone can prepare and submit an NHL nomination, the coverage of LGBTQ-related content depends on the author's awareness, comfort level, and facility. Review of draft nominations by NHL and NRHP program staff is therefore key to ensuring quality control. But these programs have, for many years, been chronically understaffed. One way to help ensure successful representation of LGBTQ places in these programs is by more fully engaging LGBTQ scholars in the review process at the state, regional, and federal levels.[14]

Strategies for Improving the Documentation and Interpretation of LGBTQ History at Existing Landmarks

Similar to past efforts to improve the presentation of American women's history at historic properties and museums, designated landmarks open to the public might benefit from a coordinated program of consultation with experts in LGBTQ history to develop more accurate and complete interpretive programs. At the federal level, planning grants to museums, libraries and cultural organizations from the National Endowment for the Humanities are an underutilized source of support to plan for re-interpretations of historic sites and districts that improve the coverage of previously neglected aspects of history and expand the diversity of public history audiences.[15] A 1992 project by the Pennsylvania Humanities Council, aimed at improving the interpretation of women's history at the state's historic sites and buildings, offers one model for bringing the staff at multiple historic properties into an extended dialogue with scholars to mine the possibilities for improved interpretation.[16] As LGBTQ sites are identified in systematic surveys and theme studies, it is important to designate overlooked properties and improve both the documentation and interpretation of places already listed on landmark registers.

Scaling Up: Illuminating LGBTQ Presence in National Register Districts

Individual buildings—often historic houses—constitute the vast major-ity of properties listed on landmark registers with unexplored connec-tions to LGBTQ history. But many historic districts also have unrealized potential to address LGBTQ themes, including those designated at the local, state, and federal levels. Greenwich Village was designated a local historic district by the New York City Landmarks Preservation Commis-sion in 1969.[17] Completed in the same year as the Stonewall uprising, the designation report for Greenwich Village reflects the preservation movement's contemporary emphasis on documenting the architectural significance of buildings in field surveys, rather than elaborating on their social history. To the extent that the district's historical significance was addressed directly, attention focused on its vibrant role as a cultural in-cubator for theater, literature, and the arts, evidencing no awareness of its overarching national significance as a haven for LGBTQ people over the long arc of the twentieth century, which has been documented in numerous scholarly works in recent decades.

Districts such as Greenwich Village have been protected by what-ever land use tools are available at the local level, but in many cases their original nominations and related preservation plans need to be updated from a LGBTQ perspective. Among the missing elements in Greenwich Village are apartment buildings that were not only home to bohemians generally, but also havens for lesbians specifically in the in-terwar years. One co-op building, for example, was home to two power couples in Eleanor Roosevelt's circle: Molly Dewson and Polly Porter, and Marion Dickerman and Nan Cook, who lived across the hall from one another.[18] The property was proposed for NHL designation under the Women's History Landmark Project in 1991, but rejected by NHL program staff because they had an internal practice of only designat-ing apartment houses when the whole building was deemed signifi-cant, rather than selected apartments.[19] Beyond recognizing multifamily housing associated with major political figures, even the well-covered theme of Greenwich Village as a creative cauldron merits updating with respect to the lesbian and gay literary figures who made it their home, including luminaries such as Lorraine Hansberry and James Baldwin.[20]

The places associated with them present opportunities to reflect on the confluence of gender, race, and sexuality in the life and work of two pivotal writers in the mid-twentieth century. Beyond individual properties, district boundaries and determinations about which places constitute contributing elements might change when considered from a queer perspective.

The interpretive silences and distortions that overshadow LGBTQ lives at historic properties extend more broadly to historical figures whose circumstances and choices carried them beyond normative expectations of their gender. This is particularly true of women who chose not to engage in intimate relationships with anyone; those who married, but were unable or chose not to have children; free spirits who defied normative expectations of monogamy; or the minority who preferred communitarian living to the relative isolation of a nuclear family. Normative expectations about men's and women's proper roles affect the interpretation of all lives—gay, straight, and beyond the usual binaries—making insights from feminist and queer theory relevant to the interpretation of many historic properties.

Historic resources associated with the modernist poet Marianne Moore illustrate some of the possibilities for challenging visitors' assumptions about gender norms and preconceptions about sexual orientation and identity in a domestic setting. Marianne Moore's parents were only married for two years, separating before her 1887 birth in Kirkwood, Missouri.[21] Marianne and her brother John Warner were raised by their mother Mary, with help from her female lover, Mary Norcross, until the relationship ended. One of Moore's childhood homes is pictured below (figure 1.2). Photographs from around 1904, showing one Mary sitting affectionately on the other's lap, and the two adults and children on a trip to the shore, are stunning reminders of lesbian family life more than a century ago.[22]

Gay and lesbian individuals and couples figured prominently in the Moore household's social circle. After crushes on other women in her youth, however, the poet is not known to have entered into any intimate relationships, either with men or women. She thought it necessary to choose between dedication to her craft and the social expectations that accompanied romantic relationships, marriage, or parenting. Though Marianne's brother married and established an independent home, the poet ended up living with her mother in various apartments in New York City for almost all of her adult life, first moving to Greenwich Village in 1918. Her mother, Mary, provided nearly all of the supports needed for her daughter to focus on writing, although by all accounts it was a

Figure 1.2. Front elevation of the John V. Gridley House, 37 Charlton Street, New York, New York, 1936. Also one of the childhood homes of Marianne Moore. Photograph by Arnold Moses, Historic American Buildings Survey, Library of Congress, HABS NY,31-NEYO,31--1 (public domain).

complicated mutual dependency. As Marianne Moore rose to prominence as a pioneer of modernist poetry, she enjoyed a rich social life
that included the most notable literary figures of the time who were gay
or lesbian: Elizabeth Bishop, H.D., H.D.'s lover Winnifred Ellerman (a.k.a.
Bryher), William Carlos Williams, and more. The first time Marianne lived
on her own was at the age of sixty, after her mother's death in 1947. In all
of these respects, the Moores' lives did not follow the standard narrative
for women who came of age in the late nineteenth and early twentieth
centuries.[23]

Philadelphia's Rosenbach Museum and Library was the recipient of
the poet's papers, photographs, and personal possessions, including the
contents of her apartment at 35 West Ninth Street, in Greenwich Village,
New York City, after her death in 1972.[24] Exhibited on the third floor of
the townhouse that contains the Rosenbach's collections, Moore's literary works are displayed in a reconstruction of her living room, allowing
visitors to contemplate Marianne Moore's creative accomplishments in
the social and spatial context of her unconventional upbringing and
adult lives that defied social expectations for two generations of women.

Indeed, the reconstruction of Moore's living room is a rare example of alternative constructions of family on display in a museum. With
the exception of communitarian settlements such as Shaker villages or
historic properties associated with Catholic religious orders of men and
women, there are exceedingly few places where visitors can glimpse
the private lives of people who in past times opted out of the mainstream. The recent NRHP designation of the DC home of the lesbian-
feminist collective the Furies boldly points to the ways that places originally designed to be single-family dwellings could be reappropriated for
collective living.[25] The NRHP designation of Bayard Rustin's home signals
the beginnings of a more racially inclusive LGBTQ agenda for historic
preservation, but is also notable for marking a distinguished American
political figure whose home life was based in one unit within a larger
urban apartment building—a breakthrough in its own right.[26] Occupied
by private owners, neither the Furies' home nor Rustin's apartment are
open to the public.

While the Rosenbach's reconstruction of Moore's apartment offers
a welcome view of bohemian lives, dislocation from its physical context increases the risk that gays, lesbians, bisexuals, uncoupled people,
and even those who chose celibacy will appear to have been more
isolated from community than they were in actuality. Women who led
unconventional lives, such as Mary and Marianne Moore, felt at home
in Greenwich Village precisely because they contributed to shaping a

public literary, artistic, and social culture that was their own. From the 1920s on, according to New York City's Landmarks Preservation Commission (LPC),

> The South Village emerged as one of the first neighborhoods in New York that allowed, and gradually accepted, an open gay and lesbian presence. Eve Adams' Tearoom at 129 MacDougal Street was a popular after-theater club run in 1925–26 by Polish-Jewish lesbian émigré Eva Kitchener (Clothier), with a sign that read, 'Men are admitted but not welcome.' Convicted of "obscenity" (for *Lesbian Love*, a collection of her short stories) and disorderly conduct, she was deported. Later popular lesbian bars were: Louis' Luncheon (1930s–40s), 116 MacDougal Street; [and] Tony Pastor's Downtown (1939–67), 130 West 3rd Street, which was raided on morals charges in 1944 for permitting lesbians to 'loiter' on the premises, but survived with mob backing until the State Liquor Authority revoked its license in 1967.[27]

Because these and other welcoming public places provided a community context for women whose sexual orientation, identity, or choice of living arrangements set them apart from the mainstream, the most powerful approach to presenting the domestic lives of LGBTQ people is likely to be *in situ*, where the inextricable connections between public and private lives are evident.

Fortunately, the Greenwich Village Society for Historic Preservation (GVSHP) has taken the lead in efforts to remedy these sorts of oversights and omissions in preservation planning.[28] In 2006, the Society commissioned a report supporting the establishment of a new South Village Historic District; its author, Andrew Dolkart, noted that the section of MacDougal Street within the proposed district was "'the most important and the best known locus of gay and lesbian commercial institutions'" by the 1920s.[29] A cluster of new local landmark nominations advanced by GVSHP also brings attention to individual properties significant in LGBTQ heritage, such as Webster Hall, a popular working-class gathering space that included lesbians and gays in the African American culture of drag at costumed balls.[30] The New York City LPC increasingly has addressed LGBTQ history within its designation reports for individual historic properties, as well as proposed historic district designations. Its 2003 and 2004 reports for houses on MacDougal Street detailed the block's importance to lesbians and gays in the 1920s, and reports for the Gansevoort Market (2003) and Weehawken Street Historic Districts (2006) called attention to the cluster of bars and nightclubs serving LGBTQ patrons from the 1970s to the present.[31] The long-term presence of historian Jay Shockley on the LPC's research staff, from 1979 until his retirement in 2014, was key to incorporating LGBTQ history into designation reports.[32] There is no substitute for expertise in LGBTQ heritage among staff and consultants working for advocacy groups and cultural resources management agencies.

Greenwich Village is one of many historic districts designated at the local, state, or national level that have overlooked LGBTQ heritage in their documentation. Similarly, the historical significance of Chicago's Boystown, which lies within the eastern section of the Lakeview Historic District, was not articulated in the original NRHP nomination.[33] One consequence is that contributing resources are defined mostly in terms of their architectural distinction as opposed to their connections with LGBTQ themes or other aspects of significance, particularly in relation to marginalized groups. Without documenting important aspects of social history within historic districts, gaps remain in the knowledge base used to make decisions about planning, preservation, and future development.

New York City's Greenwich Village and Chicago's Boystown are just two examples of neighborhoods with enormous potential for enriched public interpretation. There are many other places between the Atlantic and Pacific coasts that are significant in LGBTQ heritage. One example is the German Village Historic District in Hamilton (Columbus), Ohio, recognized for its association with German settlement, anti-German sentiment during World War I, the impact of urban renewal on near-downtown neighborhoods, and the power of preservation to revitalize them. A recently developed tour offered by the German Village Society calls attention to the role of gay men in the neighborhood's preservation and revitalization from the 1960s on, efforts which led to listing the district on the NRHP.[34] A new walking tour, "Gay Pioneers of German Village," explains that

> one commonality for many men that came to German Village in the early years was their sexuality[;] they were gay. While this fact was not broadcasted in the open for most of them, it was integral part to whom they were and why they chose to move to German Village in the first place. The Gay Pioneers of German Village tour is intended to interpret the lives of individuals that impacted the community and whose stories just happen to be intertwined by their sexual orientation.[35]

German Village has become an influential model for historic district restoration, winning recognition from the American Planning Association as one of its Great Places in America in 2011. Similarly, the role of gay men in preserving other historic places, such as Pendarvis in Mineral Point, Wisconsin, has been a topic of renewed interpretive interest.[36] In his 2005 book, *A Passion to Preserve*, Will Fellows made a compelling case for recognizing the instrumental role that gay men have played in the historic preservation movement. It is now time to recognize their contributions, as well as those of lesbian, bisexual, and transgender Americans at the historic buildings, landscapes, and districts they have so lovingly restored and saved.

Considering New National Register Districts Associated with LGBTQ Communities

Many urban neighborhoods with clusters of properties significant in LGBTQ history await survey, documentation, recognition, and protection. In Seattle, Washington, for example, two historic neighborhoods have unrealized potential to be recognized for their association with LGBTQ heritage: Pioneer Square, which was central to LGBTQ activity during the pre–World War II period; and Capitol Hill, which became important in the post-Stonewall era.[37] Specific Seattle landmarks of LGBTQ history remain to be designated—for example, the Double Header Tavern in Pioneer Square, which laid claim to being the oldest continually operating gay bar in the city (and possibly the United States), having opened in 1934 and closed on 31 December 2015.[38]

Largely framed by neighborhoods as units of study, official surveys of Seattle's historic resources have generally emphasized architecture at the expense of social history, including LGBTQ themes.[39] Even the Harvard-Belmont Historic District, which lies in the heart of Capitol Hill, presents its character-defining features in terms of "fine homes built by the city's leading financiers, industrialists, merchants, and businessmen in the early years of the twentieth century," overlooking the role of the LGBTQ community in shaping neighborhood character.[40] But it is not just a matter of adding the missing information. The way that district boundaries have been framed from neighborhood and architectural perspectives may not align with the social geography of the LGBTQ community.[41]

Signature urban "gayborhoods" too often have been overlooked by preservation planners. However, geographers Michael Brown and Larry Knopp, who mapped Seattle's LGBTQ heritage, including historic places within the Pioneer Square and Capitol Hill neighborhoods, caution that concentrated neighborhoods are also paralleled by more diffuse patterns of queer settlement: "we are everywhere."[42] Historical patterns of residential segregation by race also complicate the geography of LGBTQ settlement. This pattern made San Francisco's Castro District a center for white gay men beginning in the 1960s, while across the Bay, the color line combined with a richness of community institutions to make Oakland the locus of African American LGBTQ settlement. Building on the work of Omi and Winant, and Oliver and Shapiro, respectively, Charles Nero offers a reminder of the critical role housing has played as a site of racial formation, constraining African Americans' residential opportunities in American cities. It has framed the racialized geography of LGBTQ communities in ways that have largely unexplored implications for preservation planning.[43]

Moreover, geographic differences among and between cities have implications for varying patterns of spatial development in LGBTQ communities. For example, Los Angeles covers more geographic area than Manhattan and San Francisco put together, necessitating "a mobility of daily life that scatters ethnic, racial, religious, and other culturally defined communities," including LGBTQ communities. As a result, instead of concentrated "gayborhoods," like those found in the Castro and Greenwich Village, "gay and lesbian communities exist at all scales and levels of visibility ... simply put, the complexity of Los Angeles's social and physical geography is the basis for a different narrative."[44] These observations point to the need for more conceptually and methodologically sophisticated approaches to conducting surveys of places significant to LGBTQ communities, designating their landmarks, framing prospective historic districts, and assessing the relative significance of cultural resources.

From Los Angeles's West Hollywood and Las Vegas's so-called Fruit Loop, heading east to gay-friendly enclaves such as Lambertville, New Jersey, and New Hope, Pennsylvania, and reaching north to the lesbian haven of Northampton, Massachusetts, the commercial and residential spaces claimed by LGBTQ people in America, while often recognized at the local level, have yet to be fully acknowledged as nationally significant in the context of the NHL and NRHP programs.[45] The tendency to conceptualize urban historic districts as dense, contiguous, and rooted in the downtown core may make it easier to designate neighborhoods historically populated by those white gay men whose relative economic, social, and racial privileges have allowed them to come together in dense urban residential and commercial zones, as opposed to the places where queer women and people of color have tended to make their homes.

Addressing Overlooked Property Types in Federal, State, and Local Preservation Programs

The abundance of historic houses on the NRHP and the predominance of this building type among listings with potential to interpret LGBTQ lives reflect a prior generation's emphasis on extraordinary individuals as agents of change and underlying biases that favored preserving the architecturally distinguished heritage of property-holding classes. The rise of the New Social History in the 1960s and 1970s brought greater attention to places associated with the collective struggles, accomplishments, and experiences of the American people. Beyond the questions it raised about whose history is remembered, this paradigm shift in historical scholarship has pointed to the need to preserve a wider array of property types beyond historic houses and districts. Historic resort destinations that established a welcoming climate long before it was a consistent feature of everyday life—such as Provincetown, Massachusetts; Fire Island, New York; and Palm Springs, California—offered unusual degrees of freedom precisely because of the vast scope of the public landscape queer folks claimed as their own: hotels, guest houses, beaches, groves, entertainment venues, and streets.[46] When a single property with a high degree of integrity is designated as emblematic of a larger landscape, such as the Cherry Grove Community House and Theater on Fire Island, it skews the overall picture of LGBTQ community life in past times and places.[47]

Private residences of various types served as safe spaces for launching homophile and gay rights organizations. Henry Gerber's Chicago residence was the organizational base for the short-lived Society for Human Rights from 1924 and 1925. The Society was the first chartered organization in the United States dedicated to advocacy for the rights of homosexuals, and published *Friendship and Freedom*, the first known publication of a homosexual organization in the United States. While the Society dissolved in 1925 when Gerber and several other members were arrested, Gerber continued to advocate for the rights of homosexuals throughout his lifetime.[48] The brick row house, built in 1885, is a contributing element in the Old Town Triangle Chicago Landmark District, which was listed on the National Register of Historic Places in 1984. The property associated with Gerber was first designated a Chicago City Landmark based on its significance in LGBTQ history in 2001 and became a National Historic Landmark in 2015. Similarly, Harry Hay's various residences in Los Angeles played a role by hosting formative meetings of the Mattachine Society in the late 1940s and early 1950s, the Gay Liberation Front at the end of the 1960s, and the Radical Faeries a decade later.[49]

Once these sorts of groups gained organizational momentum, expanded membership, and adopted a more confident public posture, the next step was to rent storefronts and office space. Any organization that survived more than a few years, such as the Daughters of Bilitis, moved multiple times, since they were tenants rather than property owners.[50] Other commercial property types historically associated with the formation of LGBTQ communities include bathhouses, bars, and social halls. Ephemeral events often are tied to place without necessarily leaving a permanent imprint, including sites of protests and demonstrations, marches, riots, gatherings, and celebrations. The random accrual of NHL and NRHP listings without intentionally planning for the protection of LGBTQ cultural resources has skewed queer lives in ways that render them as more isolated than they were in actuality. In years to come, as the historic context for LGBTQ heritage is fleshed out and a wider range of property types are documented, a far richer picture will emerge of the LGBTQ dimensions of American history.

Mapping LGBTQ Historic Places

Beginning in the mid-1990s, grassroots efforts were launched simultaneously in several cities to identify and map places of significance in gay and lesbian history. One notable project was *A Guide to Lesbian and Gay New York Historical Landmarks*, prepared in 1994 by preservationists involved with the Organization of Lesbian and Gay Architects and Designers (OLGAD) in honor of the twenty-fifth anniversary of the Stonewall rebellion in New York City.[51] This project drew on original research by OLGAD members, including Ken Lustbader's 1993 Columbia University graduate thesis on preserving lesbian and gay history in Greenwich Village.

Community-based mapping projects, driven largely by volunteer energy, have been intertwined with two related developments to support LGBTQ preservation: the emergence of archives with collections and exhibition programs, and a growing body of scholarship—particularly studies of local history—highlighting LGBTQ individuals, organizations, events, and aspects of everyday life potentially linked to historic places.[52] Mapping projects have reflected this convergence of archival collecting, public history projects, and local scholarship.

Founded in 1994 by Mark Meinke, José Gutierrez, Charles Johnson, Bruce Pennington, and James Crutchfield, the volunteer organization

Rainbow History Project initially took on the task of archiving DC's gay history, driven by an overarching concern about the loss of community memory due to the AIDS epidemic and Meinke's specific interest in documenting local drag culture. As the oral histories and archival sources pointed to places of significance, Rainbow History established a database of historic places. As Meinke has explained, "By the end of the first year, the Places and Spaces database of sites, compiled from oral histories, newspaper advertising, and extant community guides, had reached 370 sites."[53]

By its second year, the organization used the information it had amassed to begin preparing an NRHP nomination for the Dr. Franklin E. Kameny home and office in the Palisades area of Washington, DC.[54] Between 2003 and 2010, Meinke generated a series of eight self-guided walking tours of LGBTQ historic places in DC, available to the public in brochure form, with members of Rainbow History periodically leading groups on tours. Similar volunteer initiatives that generated public exhibits, maps, and walking tours in Boston, Los Angeles, and Seattle, among other cities, brought new attention to the status of LGBTQ historic sites and buildings long before the mainstream of the preservation movement was ready to extend its embrace.[55] Although it was not necessarily the case at the time, they were originally identified for maps and walking-tour itineraries. Some of these extant historic buildings eventually became the object of focused preservation activity.

A number of urban design, streetscape improvement, and street naming interventions have amplified an LGBTQ presence in public places. Yearly Pride celebrations to mark the anniversary of the Stonewall rebellion have built an audience for relevant programming at the local level and offered an impetus for new projects to increase the public visibility of LGBTQ communities, simultaneously presenting opportunities for local, state, and federal government entities to signal their commitment to diversity and inclusion. The City of Philadelphia added rainbows to its Twelfth and Thirteenth Street signs in recognition of its vitality as a so-called "gayborhood," and the cities of West Hollywood and Seattle, in 2012 and 2015 respectively, decorated crosswalks in a rainbow design in conjunction with Pride celebrations.[56] As a strategy to promote LGBTQ tourism, West Hollywood ultimately made its rainbow crosswalks permanent. Related initiatives have popped up in cities including Key West, Philadelphia, Northampton, San Francisco, and Sacramento.[57] Recognizing that progress in LGBTQ rights has also been matched by a backlash, Seattle, like some other cities and towns, has used rainbow crosswalks to call attention to the consequences of virulent homophobia. The city marked eleven spots where people had been the victims of homo- and transphobic assaults.[58] This raises the larger question of whether there is room within commemorative programs to address some of the most pernicious and troubling aspects of LGBTQ history—discriminatory firings and evictions, unjust incarceration in prisons and mental hospitals, hate speech, and violence—subjects not readily embraced by the tourist industry, which tilts toward substantially more upbeat and heroic narratives.

This introduction reviewed the history of efforts to identify, document, designate, interpret, and preserve elements of the built environment and cultural landscape associated with LGBTQ heritage. Increasingly, advocates for preserving queer histories are adding sites to the National Register of Historic Places and the roster of National Historic Landmarks with the intention of translating recognition into long-term protection of key cultural resources. Yet even places of exceptional significance—across the broad range of LGBTQ identities—remain to be documented or interpreted in ways that do justice to the historical experience of people who did not conform to narrow societal expectations about gender identity and expression. This applies to individual properties as well as larger historic districts whose queer associations remain to be articulated in plans for preservation and public interpretation. Beyond the most obvious property types, such as gay bars or bathhouses, a wider range of property types associated with LGBTQ heritage might be considered for designation. While the tools of cultural resource management are useful for increasing public awareness of these aspects of the nation's history, grassroots efforts to inventory and map sites, and engage the public in walking and driving tours, continue to expand the knowledge base and advocacy network critical to establishing LGBTQ history as a vital part of America's heritage.

Dr. Gail Dubrow is a professor of architecture, landscape architecture, public affairs and planning, and history at the University of Minnesota.

Notes

1. For more on interpreting LGBTQ historic sites, see Susan Ferentinos, "Interpreting LGBTQ Sites" (this volume).
2. The Walt Whitman home is located at 330 Dr. Martin Luther King, Jr. Boulevard (formerly Mickle Street), Camden, New Jersey. It was listed on the NRHP on 15 October 1966 and designated an NHL on 29 December 1962. It

is a key contributing element of the Walt Whitman Neighborhood Historical District, listed on the NRHP on 20 January 1978.

3. See, for example, Justin Kaplan, *Walt Whitman: A Life* (New York: Harper Perennial, 2003), 287; John Stokes, *Oscar Wilde: Myths, Miracles and Imitations* (New York: Cambridge University Press, 1996), 194n7.

4. Willa Cather's childhood home is located at 241 North Cedar, Red Cloud, Nebraska. It was added to the NRHP on 16 April 1969 and designated an NHL on 11 November 1971. As an adolescent, Cather developed a masculine alter ego she called William J. that prefigured her unorthodox adult life as a lesbian and woman writer. Photographs of Cather as William exist, and her gender-bending persona is well documented by scholars. By the 1980s, literary scholars such as Phyllis C. Robinson and Shannon O'Brien, who integrated biographical and literary analysis, were openly addressing the issue of Cather's lesbianism and identifying the specific women she loved over a lifetime. More recently, scholars have analyzed her fiction through the lens of queer theory, finding in her male protagonists and female love objects a coded expression of same-sex attachments, developed at a time when open expressions of lesbian desire were unacceptable among adult women. Phyllis C. Robinson: *Willa: The Life of Willa Cather* (New York: Doubleday, 1983); and Shannon O'Brien, *Willa Cather: The Emerging Voice* (New York: Oxford University Press, 1986). For a brief review of Cather's treatment within queer literary theory, see Phyllis M. Betz, "Willa Cather," in *Readers Guide to Lesbian and Gay Studies*, ed. Timothy F. Murphy (Chicago: Fitzroy Dearborn Publishers, 2013), 119–20. See also Marilee Lindemann, *Willa Cather: Queering America* (New York: Columbia University Press, 1999).

5. See "Will Cather's Biography: The Early Years, 1873–1890," Willa Cather Foundation website, https://www.willacather.org/willa-cathers-biography.

6. Val-Kill is part of the Eleanor Roosevelt National Historic Site in Hyde Park, New York, established as an NPS unit on 27 May 1977. It was listed on the NRHP on 20 March 1980 and designated an NHL on 27 May 1977.

7. Eleanor rented an apartment from Lape and Read in New York City's Greenwich Village, staying there on her many trips into the city. Eleanor also visited Salt Meadow, the country retreat of Lape and Read on several occasions. Esther Lape donated Salt Meadow to the U.S. Fish and Wildlife Service in 1972. Located at 733 Old Clinton Road, Westbrook, Connecticut, it now forms the core of the Stewart B. McKinney National Wildlife Refuge. Refuge staff are working on an NRHP for the former Salt Meadow estate that will recognize the same-sex relationship of Lape and Read. See "Elizabeth Fisher Read (1872–1943)," Eleanor Roosevelt Papers Project, George Washington University website, https://www.gwu.edu/~erpapers/teachinger/glossary/read-elizabeth.cfm; and Susan Wojtowicz, "Esther Lape and Elizabeth Read: Pioneers for Women's Rights and Conservation," U.S. Fish and Wildlife Ser-

vice website, https://usfwsnortheast.wordpress.com/2016/03/21/esther-la pe-and-elizabeth-read-pioneers-for-womens-rights-and-conservation.

8. Leila J. Rupp, "'Imagine My Surprise': Women's Relationships in Historical Perspective," *Frontiers: A Journal of Women Studies* 5, no. 3 (1980): 61–70; Blanche Wiesen Cook, *Eleanor Roosevelt*, vol. 1, *1884–1933: The Early Years* (New York: Viking, 1992); and *Eleanor Roosevelt*, vol. 2, *1933–1938: The Defining Years* (New York: Viking, 1999); and Judith C. Kohl, "Eleanor Roosevelt," in *Lesbian Histories and Cultures: An Encyclopedia*, ed. Bonnie Zimmerman (New York: Garland Publishing, 2000), 651–52.

9. The furor that accompanied publication of Blanche Wiesen Cook's biography of Eleanor Roosevelt is captured in her reply to Geoffrey Ward, "Outing Mrs. Roosevelt," *New York Review of Books*, 25 March 1993, http://www .nybooks.com/articles/1993/03/25/outing-mrs-roosevelt. Among the interpretive issues Cook highlights is the inability of Ward to consider the possibility that women who exercised power in the public realm also had sexual passions, pointing to the combination of sexism and homophobia that have influenced past interpretations of Eleanor Roosevelt's life.

10. See "Interview: Blanche Wiesen Cook," *The American Experience*, PBS, 1999, http://www.pbs.org/wgbh/americanexperience/features/interview/el eanor-cook.

11. Paula Martinac, *The Queerest Places* (New York: Henry Holt, 1997); also see Paula Martinac, "ER at Val-kill," *The Queerest Places: A Guide to LGBT Historic Sites* (blog), 16 January 2009, https://queerestplaces.com/2009/01/16/ er-at-val-kill.

12. The Frances Perkins House in northwestern Washington, DC secured NHL status under the Women's History Landmark Study. Perkins lived here in the mid-1930s. It was added to the NRHP and designated an NHL on 17 July 1991. The Perkins Homestead at 478 River Road, Newcastle, Maine, was first listed on the NRHP on 13 February 2009 as the Brick House Historic District for its archaeological significance. The property was added to the NRHP and designated an NHL on 25 August 2014. This NHL nomination, prepared by a board member of the Frances Perkins Center (dedicated to preserving the homestead and her legacy) explains the complications of Perkins's marriage (her husband suffered from a mental illness that had him in and out of hospitals and boarding houses), but attributes her shared living arrangements in DC during the mid-1930s to economy measures, skirting entirely the evidence of her intimate same-sex relationships.

13. Kirstin Downey, *The Woman Behind the New Deal: The Life and Legacy of Frances Perkins* (New York: Anchor Books, 2009), 250.

14. One source of subject experts is the pool of academic and community historians who contributed to the LGBTQ Theme Study.

15. See "NEH Grants," National Endowment for the Humanities website, "Museums, Libraries, and Cultural Organizations: Planning Grants" http://www

.neh.gov/grants/public/museums-libraries-and-cultural-organizations-planning-grants.

16. Kim Moon, "'Raising Our Sites': A Pilot Project for Integrating Women's History into Museums," in *Restoring Women's History through Historic Preservation*, ed. Gail Dubrow and Jennifer Goodman (Baltimore: Johns Hopkins University Press, 2003), 248–62.

17. New York City Landmarks Preservation Commission, *Greenwich Village Historic District Designation Report*, vols. 1 and 2 (1969). For more on historic preservation in New York City, see Jay Shockley, "Preservation of LGBTQ Historic and Cultural Sites: A New York City Perspective" (this volume).

18. References to this apartment building and its lesbian residents, located at 171 West 12th Street, is found in Roger Streitmatter, ed., *Empty Without You: The Intimate Letters of Eleanor Roosevelt and Lorena Hickok* (Boston: Da Capo Press, 1998), 74. It was included in Andrew Dolkart, *The Guide to New York City Landmarks* (New York: John Wiley & Son, 1992) and in subsequent editions. The Porter family's summer cottage, Moss Acre, in Castine, Maine, is another significant property associated with Dewson and Porter, who summered there annually and made it their permanent residence in retirement. It was designed by the Chicago architectural firm of Handy and Cady in 1892 for the Porter family and was still standing as of 2016. Castine Historical Society, *Images of America: Castine* (Charleston, SC: Arcadia Publishing, 1996), 119.

19. Gail Dubrow and Carolyn Flynn, "Molly Dewson Residence," proposed NHL Nomination, 1991. A proposed nomination for the tenement apartment in New York City's East Village where Emma Goldman lived and published *Mother Earth News* also was rejected by staff at the time for similar reasons. In both cases, issues of sexuality tainted the proposals, and in Goldman's case, her anarchist politics were regarded by reviewers as controversial.

20. LPC Staff Christopher D. Brazee, Gale Harris, and Jay Shockley, "James Baldwin and Lorraine Hansberry Residences, Greenwich Village Historic District and Upper West Side/Central Park West Historic District, Manhattan," in *150 Years of LGBT History*, PowerPoint presentation prepared for LGBT Pride 2014, http://www.nyc.gov/html/lpc/downloads/pdf/LGBT-PRIDE_2014.pdf.

21. Her father, who suffered from mental illness, played no role in parenting his children.

22. These photographs are in the Rosenbach's collection. See for example, "Marianne Moore, Mary Warner Moore, and Mary Jackson Norcross on rocks, Monhegan Island, Maine," (1904), Moore XII: 02:33f, Marianne Moore Collection. One of the childhood homes of Marianne Moore was the John V. Gridley House, 37 Charlton Street, New York City, New York.

23. Details of Marianne Moore's life and critical appraisals of her literary works are contained in Linda Leavell, Cristanne Miller, and Robin G. Schulze, eds., *Critics and Poets on Marianne Moore: "A Right Good Salvo of Barks"* (Lewisburg, PA: Bucknell University Press, 2005); and Linda Leavell, *Holding On*

Upside Down: The Life and Work of Marianne Moore (New York: Farrar, Straus and Giroux, 2013).

24. See "Marianne Moore Collection," Rosenbach Museum and Library website, https://www.rosenbach.org/learn/collections/marianne-moore-collection. The Rosenbach Museum and Library is located at 2008–2010 Delancey Place, Philadelphia, Pennsylvania.

25. The Furies Collective house in Washington, DC's Capitol Hill neighborhood, was listed on the NRHP on 2 May 2016.

26. Bayard Rustin's residence in the Chelsea neighborhood of New York City, New York was listed on the NRHP on 8 March 2016.

27. "20th Century Lesbian Presence, South Village Historic District (1920s)," in LPC, 150 Years of LGBT History. For more information on LGBTQ sites in New York City, see Shockley, "Preservation of LGBTQ Historic and Cultural Sites" (this volume).

28. For an overview of the GVSHP's LGBTQ-positive initiatives, see "LGBT History of Greenwich Village," Greenwich Village Society for Historic Preservation website, http://www.gvshp.org/lesbianandgayhistory.htm.

29. Andrew S. Dolkart, *The South Village: A Proposal for Historic District Designation* (New York: Greenwich Village Society for Historic Preservation, 2006), 58.

30. Webster Hall is located at 119–125 East 11th Street, New York City, New York. See "Webster Hall 402, Pl and Annex Designation List, LP-2273," New York City Landmarks Preservation Commission website, http://www.nyc.gov/html/lpc/downloads/pdf/reports/websterhall.pdf.

31. Jay Shockley, *Weehawken Street Historic District Designation Report* (New York: New York City Landmarks Preservation Commission, 2 May 2006), 19; and Jay Shockley, *Gansevoort Market Historic District Designation Report* (New York: New York City Landmarks Preservation Commission, 2003), 19. The Gansevoort Market Historic District was added to the NRHP on 30 May 2007.

32. Shockley was an original member of the 1994 Organization of Lesbian and Gay Architects and Designers (OLGAD) mapping group, a coauthor of the Stonewall nomination, and is now co-director of a project to document the city's LGBTQ landmarks.

33. Robert Wagner, "National Register of Historic Places Nomination: Lakeview Historic District," National Register of Historic Places, National Park Service, Washington, DC, 1976. The Lakeview Historic District was added to the NRHP on 15 September 1977; boundary increase on 16 May 1986.

34. Gretchen Klimoski, "German Village: National Register Inventory-Nomination Form," July 1974. The boundaries of the district later were amended to include eleven adjacent acres of historic houses. Nancy Recchie, "German Village Amendment: National Register of Historic Places Inventory-Nomination Form," 1980. The German Village Historic District was added to the NRHP on 7 February 1991.

35. Sarah Marsom, "Gay Pioneers Tour Aligns with Preservation Message," German Village Society website, https://germanvillage.com/gay-pioneers-tour-aligns-with-preservation-message.

36. Will Fellows, *A Passion to Preserve: Gay Men as Keepers of Culture* (Madison: University of Wisconsin Press, 2004), 194–98. Pendarvis, located at 114 Shake Rag Street, Mineral Point, Wisconsin, was listed on the NRHP on 25 January 1971.

37. For key sites of significance in Seattle's LGBTQ history, see *A Historical Map of Lesbian and Gay Seattle* (Seattle: Northwest Lesbian and Gay History Museum Project, 1996). NLGHMP's projects can be found at http://home.earth link.net/~ruthpett/lgbthistorynw/index.htm. An expanded and updated version of the 1996 map, *Claiming Space: Seattle's Lesbian and Gay Historical Geography*, published in 2004, is available online at http://cdm16118.con tentdm.oclc.org/cdm/ref/collection/p16118coll2/id/35. See also Richard Freitas, "'The Land at Our Feet': Preserving Pioneer Square's Queer Landscape." Master's thesis, University of Washington, 2017. Seattle's Pioneer Square-Skid Road Historic District was added to the NRHP on 22 June 1970 with boundary increases on 7 July 1978 and 16 June 1988.

38. The Double Header was located at 407 Second Avenue Extension S, Seattle, Washington. See Yani Robinson, "One Last Inning for the Double Header," *Jetspace Magazine*, 31 December 2015, http://jetspacemagazine.com/last-inning-for-the-double-header.

39. See, for example, Seattle Department of Neighborhoods, "Narrative Statement of Significance for the Pioneer Square—Skid Road National Historic District." For a complete list of context statements completed for Seattle neighborhoods, see http://www.seattle.gov/Documents/Departments/Nei ghborhoods/HistoricPreservation/HistoricResourcesSurvey/context-pioneer-square.pdf.

40. Seattle Department of Neighborhoods, "Harvard-Belmont," Seattle Department of Neighborhoods, City of Seattle website, http://www.seattle.gov/neighborhoods/programs-and-services/historic-preservation/historic-distr icts/harvard-belmont. The Harvard-Belmont Historic District was listed on the NRHP on 13 May 1982.

41. While early scholarship addressed the role of gay men in gentrification, a recent body of work interrogates the impact of a new wave of gentrification on LGBTQ communities. See Petra Doan and Harrison Higgins, "The Demise of Queer Space? Resurgent Gentrification and the Assimilation of LGBT Neighborhoods," *Journal of Planning Education and Research* 31, no. 1 (2011): 6–25.

42. Nancy Wick, "Geographer Puts Gays, Lesbians on the Map," *UW Today*, 22 July 2004, http://www.washington.edu/news/2004/07/22/geographer-puts-gays-lesbians-on-the-map.

43. For more about community formation, see Christina B. Hanhardt, "Making Community: The Places and Spaces of LGBTQ Collective Identity Forma-

tion," in *Communities and Place: A Thematic Approach to the Histories of LGBTQ Communities in the United States*, ed. Katherine Crawford-Lackey and Megan E. Springate (New York: Berghahn Books, forthcoming); and Jen Jack Gieseking, "The Geographies of LGBTQ Lives: In and Beyond Cities, Neighborhoods, and Bars," in *Communities and Place*. For more about the intersection of LGBTQ identity and race, see also Jeffrey A. Harris, "'Where We Could Be Ourselves': African American LGBTQ Historic Places and Why They Matter," in *Identities and Place: Changing Labels and Intersectional Communities of LGBTQ and Two-Spirit People in the United States*, ed. Katherine Crawford-Lackey and Megan E. Springate (New York: Berghahn Books, 2019); Will Roscoe, "Sexual and Gender Diversity in Native America and the Pacific Islands," in *Identities and Place*; Amy Sueyoshi, "Remembering Asian Pacific American Activism in Queer History," in *Identities and Place*; and Deena J. González and Ellie D. Hernández, "Latina/o Gender and Sexuality," in *Identities and Place*.

44. Moira Rachel Kenney, *Mapping Gay L.A.: The Intersection of Place and Politics* (Philadelphia: Temple University Press, 2001); especially chap. 1: "Locating the Politics of Difference," 5–6. For other examples of geographic differences in LGBTQ communities, see Donna J. Graves and Shayne E. Watson, "San Francisco: Placing LGBTQ Histories in the City by the Bay" (this volume); Julio Capó Jr., "Locating Miami's Queer History," in *Communities and Place*; John Jeffrey Auer IV, "Queerest Little City in the World: LGBTQ Reno," in *Communities and Place*; Shockley, "Preservation of LGBTQ Historic and Cultural Sites: A New York City Perspective" (this volume); and Jessica Herczeg-Konecny, "Chicago: Queer Histories at the Crossroads of America," in *Communities and Place*.

45. Ann Forsyth, "'Out' in the Valley," *International Journal of Urban and Regional Research* 21, no. 1 (1997): 36–60.

46. For more about LGBTQ resort communities, see Katherine Schweighofer, "LGBTQ Sport and Leisure," in *LGBTQ America: A Theme Study of Lesbian, Gay, Bisexual, Transgender, and Queer History*, ed. Megan E. Springate (Washington, DC: National Park Foundation and National Park Service, 2016), https://www.nps.gov/articles/lgbtqtheme-sport.htm. The Provincetown Historic District was added to the NRHP on 30 August 1989 (but does not include mention of LGBTQ history).

47. Carl Luss, "Cherry Grove Community House and Theater," 180 Bayview Walk, Cherry Grove, New York, National Register of Historic Places Registration Form, 12 February 2013. The Cherry Grove Community House and Theater was added to the NRHP on 4 June 2013.

48. University of Michigan Public History Initiative, "Henry Gerber House: National Register of Historic Places Registration Form," Chicago, Illinois, 12 December 2014. The Henry Gerber House is a contributing element in the Old Town Triangle Chicago Landmark District, which was listed on the NRHP on 8 November 1984. The property associated with Gerber was first desig-

nated a Chicago City Landmark based on its significance in LGBTQ history in 2001 and designated an NHL on 19 June 2015.

49. Hay's residence in the Silver Lake neighborhood of Los Angeles was the site of meetings of the group called Bachelors Anonymous beginning in the summer of 1948. By 1950, they formally named the organization the Mattachine Society. The Margaret and Harry Hay House in the Hollywood Hills neighborhood of Los Angeles was listed as Los Angeles Historic-Cultural Monument #981. Hay commissioned architect Gregory Ain to design this split-level, international style house for his mother Margaret in 1939. Margaret was supportive of her son's causes and hosted meetings at her home. The property is regarded as Los Angeles's first gay landmark, as well as the first location that the FBI identified as a known gathering place in California for homosexuals.

50. Recent efforts to designate a historic property associated with Daughters of Bilitis, established in 1955 in San Francisco, have been complicated by its many locations over the years. Originally located in the Williams Building at 693 Mission Street, it moved to at least three other Mission Street addresses and others on O'Farrell, Grove, and Hyde Streets.

51. Organization of Lesbian and Gay Architects and Designers, *A Guide to Lesbian & Gay New York Historical Landmarks* (New York: Organization of Lesbian and Gay Architects and Designers, 1994). For a digitized version, see http://www.gvshp.org/LGBTguide.htm.

52. See Gerard Koskovich, "The History of Queer History: One Hundred Years of the Search for Shared Heritage" (this volume).

53. Mark Meinke, email communication to author, 14 April 2016.

54. The Dr. Franklin E. Kameny Residence was added to the NRHP on 2 November 2011.

55. See for example, the Northwest Lesbian and Gay History Museum Project, *Claiming Space*; or the History Project, dedicated to documenting LGBTQ Boston, which was established in 1980 by historians, activists, and archivists, http://www.historyproject.org. Among its earliest initiatives were the exhibit *Public Faces/Private Lives* at the Boston Public Library (1996) and the book *Improper Bostonians: Lesbian and Gay History from the Puritans to Playland* (Boston: Beacon Press, 1998).

56. Andrew Thompson, "The Success of Philly's Gayborhood May Be Its Undoing," *NBC10.com*, 17 September 2013, http://www.nbcphiladelphia.com/news/local/The-Success-of-Phillys-Gayborhood-May-be-its-Undoing-224067791.html.

57. Jorge Rivas, "America's Crosswalks are Getting Gayer," *Fusion*, 3 June 2015, http://fusion.net/story/143596/the-gay-crosswalks-are-coming-gay-crosswalks-are-coming.

58. Lauren Lloyd, "West Hollywood's Permanent Rainbow Crosswalk to Color Streets Come October," *Hollywood LAist*, 3 September 2012, http://laist.com/2012/09/03/west_hollywoods_permanent_rainbow_crosswalks.php;

Katia Hetter, "Rainbow Sidewalks and Other LGBT Pride Celebrations," *CNN*, 29 June 2015, http://www.cnn.com/2015/06/24/travel/lgbt-gay-pride-celebrations-2015-feat. In an even bolder move, Reykjavik Pride 2015 painted an entire central street in rainbow colors.

Bibliography

Auer, John Jeffrey, IV. "Queerest Little City in the World: LGBTQ Reno." In *Communities and Place: A Thematic Approach to the Histories of LGBTQ Communities in the United States*, edited by Katherine Crawford-Lackey and Megan E. Springate. New York: Berghahn Books, forthcoming.

Betz, Phyllis M. "Willa Cather." In *Readers Guide to Lesbian and Gay Studies*, edited by Timothy F. Murphy, 119–20. Chicago: Fitzroy Dearborn, 2013.

Brazee, Christopher D., Gale Harris, and Jay Shockley. *150 Years of LGBT History*. PowerPoint presentation prepared for LGBT Pride 2014, http://www.nyc.gov/html/lpc/downloads/pdf/LGBT-PRIDE_2014.pdf.

Capó, Julio, Jr. "Locating Miami's Queer History." In *Communities and Place: A Thematic Approach to the Histories of LGBTQ Communities in the United States*, edited by Crawford-Lackey and Springate. New York: Berghahn Books, forthcoming.

Castine Historical Society. *Images of America: Castine*. Charleston, SC: Arcadia Publishing, 1996.

Cook, Blanche Wiesen. *Eleanor Roosevelt*. Vol. 1, *1884–1933: The Early Years*. New York: Viking, 1992.

———. *Eleanor Roosevelt*. Vol. 2, *1933–1938: The Defining Years*. New York: Viking, 1999.

Doan, Petra, and Harrison Higgins. "The Demise of Queer Space? Resurgent Gentrification and the Assimilation of LGBT Neighborhoods." *Journal of Planning Education and Research* 31, no. 1 (2011): 6–25.

Dolkart, Andrew S. *The Guide to New York City Landmarks*. New York: John Wiley & Son, 1992.

———. *The South Village: A Proposal for Historic District Designation*. New York: Greenwich Village Society for Historic Preservation, 2006.

Downey, Kirstin. *The Woman Behind the New Deal: The Life and Legacy of Frances Perkins*. New York: Anchor Books, 2009.

Dubrow, Gail, and Carolyn Flynn. "NHL Nomination: Molly Dewson Residence" (proposed), 1991.

Eleanor Roosevelt Papers Project. "Elizabeth Fisher Read (1872–1943)." Eleanor Roosevelt Papers Project, George Washington University, https://www.gwu.edu/~erpapers/teachinger/glossary/read-elizabeth.cfm.

Fellows, Will. *A Passion to Preserve: Gay Men as Keepers of Culture*. Madison: University of Wisconsin Press, 2004.

Forsyth, Ann. "'Out' in the Valley." *International Journal of Urban and Regional Research* 21, no. 1 (1997): 36–60.

Freitas, Richard. "The Land at Our Feet: Preserving Pioneer Square's Queer Land-scape." Master's thesis, University of Washington, 2017.

Gieseking, Jen Jack. "The Geographies of LGBTQ Lives: In and Beyond Cities, Neighborhoods, and Bars." In *Communities and Place: A Thematic Approach to the Histories of LGBTQ Communities in the United States*, edited by Crawford-Lackey and Springate. New York: Berghahn Books, forthcoming.

González, Deena J., and Ellie D. Hernández. "Latina/o Gender and Sexuality." In *Identities and Place: Changing Labels and Intersectional Communities of LGBTQ and Two-Spirit People in the United States*, edited by Katherine Crawford-Lackey and Megan E. Springate. New York: Berghahn Books, 2019.

Greenwich Village Society for Historic Preservation. "LGBT History of Greenwich Village." Greenwich Village Society for Historic Preservation. http://www.gvshp.org/lesbianandgayhistory.htm.

Hanhardt, Christina B. "Making Community: The Places and Spaces of LGBTQ Collective Identity Formation." In *Communities and Place: A Thematic Approach to the Histories of LGBTQ Communities in the United States*, edited by Crawford-Lackey and Springate. New York: Berghahn Books, forthcoming.

Harris, Jeffrey A. "'Where We Could Be Ourselves': African American LGBTQ Historic Places and Why They Matter." In *Identities and Place: Changing Labels and Intersectional Communities of LGBTQ and Two-Spirit People in the United States*, edited by Crawford-Lackey and Springate. New York: Berghahn Books, 2019.

Herczeg-Konecny, Jessica, "Chicago: Queer Histories at the Crossroads of America." In *Communities and Place: A Thematic Approach to the Histories of LGBTQ Communities in the United States*, edited by Crawford-Lackey and Springate. New York: Berghahn Books, forthcoming.

Hetter, Katia. "Rainbow Sidewalks and Other LGBT Pride Celebrations." *CNN*, 29 June 2015. http://www.cnn.com/2015/06/24/travel/lgbt-gay-pride-cele brations-2015-feat.

History Project: Documenting LGBTQ Boston (homepage). *History Project*. http://www.historyproject.org.

———. *Improper Bostonians: Lesbian and Gay History from the Puritans to Play-land*. Boston: Beacon Press, 1998.

"Interview: Blanche Wiesen Cook." *American Experience*, PBS, 1999. http://www.pbs.org/wgbh/americanexperience/features/interview/eleanor-cook.

Kaplan, Justin. *Walt Whitman: A Life*. New York: Harper Perennial, 2003.

Kenney, Moira Rachel. *Mapping Gay L.A.: The Intersection of Place and Politics*. Philadelphia: Temple University Press, 2001.

Klimoski, Gretchen. "National Register of Historic Places Nomination: German Village." National Register of Historic Places, National Park Service, Washington, DC, 1974.

Kohl, Judith C. "Eleanor Roosevelt." In *Lesbian Histories and Cultures: An Encyclopedia*, edited by Bonnie Zimmerman, 651–52. New York: Garland Publishing, 2000.

Koskovich, Gerard. "The History of Queer History: One Hundred Years of the Search for Shared Heritage." In *Preservation and Place: Historic Preservation by and of LGBTQ Communities in the United States*, edited by Katherine Crawford-Lackey and Megan E. Springate. New York: Berghahn Books, 2019.

Leavell, Linda. *Holding On Upside Down: The Life and Work of Marianne Moore*. New York: Farrar, Straus and Giroux, 2013.

Leavell, Linda, Cristanne Miller, and Robin G. Schulze, eds. *Critics and Poets on Marianne Moore: "A Right Good Salvo of Barks."* Lewisburg, PA: Bucknell University Press, 2005.

Lindemann, Marilee. *Willa Cather: Queering America*. New York: Columbia University Press, 1999.

Lloyd, Lauren. "West Hollywood's Permanent Rainbow Crosswalk to Color Streets Come October." *Hollywood LAist*, 3 September 2012. http://laist.com/2012/09/03/west_hollywoods_permanent_rainbow_crosswalks.php.

Luss, Carl. "National Register of Historic Places Nomination: Cherry Grove Community House and Theater." National Register of Historic Places, National Park Service, Washington, DC, 2013.

Marsom, Sarah. "Gay Pioneers Tour Aligns with Preservation Message." *German Village Society*, https://germanvillage.com/gay-pioneers-tour-aligns-with-preservation-message.

Martinac, Paula. *The Queerest Places*. New York: Henry Holt, 1997.

———. "ER at Val-kill." *The Queerest Places: A Guide to LGBT Historic Sites*, 16 January 2009. https://queerestplaces.com/2009/01/16/er-at-val-kill.

Moon, Kim. "'Raising Our Sites': A Pilot Project for Integrating Women's History into Museums." In *Restoring Women's History through Historic Preservation*, edited by Gail Dubrow and Jennifer Goodman, 248–62. Baltimore, MD: Johns Hopkins University Press, 2003.

National Endowment for the Humanities. "NEH Grants: Museums, Libraries, and Cultural Organizations: Planning Grants." *National Endowment for the Humanities*. http://www.neh.gov/grants/public/museums-libraries-and-cultural-organizations-planning-grants.

New York City Landmarks Preservation Commission. *Greenwich Village Historic District Designation Report*, vols. 1 and 2. New York: New York City Landmarks Preservation Commission, 1969.

———. "Webster Hall 402, Pl and Annex Designation List, LP-2273." New York City Landmarks Preservation Commission. http://www.nyc.gov/html/lpc/downloads/pdf/reports/websterhall.pdf.

Northwest Lesbian and Gay History Museum Project. *A Historical Map of Lesbian and Gay Seattle*. Seattle: Northwest Lesbian and Gay History Museum Project, 1996. http://home.earthlink.net/~ruthpett/lgbthistorynw/index.htm.

———. *Claiming Space: Seattle's Lesbian and Gay Historical Geography*. Seattle: Northwest Lesbian and Gay History Museum Project, 2004. http://cdm16118.contentdm.oclc.org/cdm/ref/collection/p16118coll2/id/35.

O'Brien, Shannon. *Willa Cather: The Emerging Voice*. New York: Oxford University Press, 1986.

Organization of Lesbian and Gay Architects and Designers. *A Guide to Lesbian & Gay New York Historical Landmarks*. New York: Organization of Lesbian and Gay Architects and Designers, 1994. http://www.gvshp.org/LGBTguide.htm.

Recchie, Nancy. "National Register of Historic Places Nomination: German Village Amendment." National Register of Historic Places, National Park Service, Washington, DC, 1980.

Rivas, Jorge. "America's Crosswalks are Getting Gayer." *Fusion*, 3 June 2015. http://fusion.net/story/143596/the-gay-crosswalks-are-coming-gay-crosswalks-are-coming.

Robinson, Phyllis C. *Willa: The Life of Willa Cather*. New York: Doubleday, 1983.

Robinson, Yani. "One Last Inning for the Double Header." *Jetspace Magazine*, 31 December 2015. http://jetspacemagazine.com/last-inning-for-the-double-header.

Roscoe, Will. "Sexual and Gender Diversity in Native America and the Pacific Islands." In *Identities and Place: Changing Labels and Intersectional Communities of LGBTQ and Two-Spirit People in the United States*, edited by Crawford-Lackey and Springate. New York: Berghahn Books, 2019.

Rosenbach Museum and Library. "Marianne Moore Collection." *Rosenbach Museum and Library*, https://www.rosenbach.org/learn/collections/marianne-moore-collection.

Rupp, Leila J. "'Imagine My Surprise': Women's Relationships in Historical Perspective." *Frontiers: A Journal of Women Studies* 5, no. 3 (1980): 61–70.

Schweighofer, Katherine. "LGBTQ Sport and Leisure." In *LGBTQ America: A Theme Study of Lesbian, Gay, Bisexual, Transgender, and Queer History*, edited by Megan E. Springate. Washington, DC: National Park Foundation and National Park Service, 2016. https://www.nps.gov/articles/lgbtqtheme-sport.htm.

Seattle Department of Neighborhoods. "Harvard-Belmont." Seattle: Seattle Department of Neighborhoods, City of Seattle. http://www.seattle.gov/neighborhoods/programs-and-services/historic-preservation/historic-districts/harvard-belmont.

———. "Narrative Statement of Significance for the Pioneer Square—Skid Road National Historic District." Seattle: Seattle Department of Neighborhoods, City of Seattle. http://www.seattle.gov/neighborhoods/programs-and-services/historic-preservation/historic-districts/pioneer-square.

Shockley, Jay. *Gansevoort Market Historic District Designation Report*. New York: New York City Landmarks Preservation Commission, 2003.

———. *Weehawken Street Historic District Designation Report*. New York: New York City Landmarks Preservation Commission, 2006.

———. "Preservation of LGBTQ Historic & Cultural Sites: A New York City Perspective." In *Preservation and Place: Historic Preservation by and of LGBTQ*

Communities in the United States, edited by Crawford-Lackey and Springate. New York: Berghahn Books, 2019.

Stokes, John. *Oscar Wilde: Myths, Miracles and Imitations*. New York: Cambridge University Press, 1996.

Streitmatter, Roger, ed. *Empty without You: The Intimate Letters of Eleanor Roosevelt and Lorena Hickok*. Boston: Da Capo Press, 1998.

Sueyoshi, Amy. "Remembering Asian Pacific American Activism in Queer History." In *Identities and Place: Changing Labels and Intersectional Communities of LGBTQ and Two-Spirit People in the United States*, edited by Crawford-Lackey and Springate. New York: Berghahn Books, 2019.

Thompson, Andrew. "The Success of Philly's Gayborhood May Be Its Undoing." *NBC10.com*, 17 September 2013. http://www.nbcphiladelphia.com/news/local/The-Success-of-Phillys-Gayborhood-May-be-its-Undoing-224067791.html.

University of Michigan Public History Initiative. "National Register of Historic Places Nomination: Henry Gerber House." National Historic Landmarks Program, National Park Service, Washington, DC, 2014.

Wagner, Robert. "National Register of Historic Places Nomination: Lakeview Historic District," National Register of Historic Places, National Park Service, Washington, DC, 1976.

Ward, Geoffrey. "Outing Mrs. Roosevelt." *New York Review of Books*, 25 March 1993. http://www.nybooks.com/articles/1993/03/25/outing-mrs-roosevelt.

Wick, Nancy. "Geographer Puts Gays, Lesbians on the Map." *UW Today*, 22 July 2004. http://www.washington.edu/news/2004/07/22/geographer-puts-gays-lesbians-on-the-map.

Willa Cather Foundation. "Will Cather's Biography: The Early Years, 1873–1890." *Willa Cather Foundation*, https://www.willacather.org/willa-cathers-biography.

Wojtowicz, Susan. "Esther Lape and Elizabeth Read: Pioneers for Women's Rights and Conservation." U.S. Fish and Wildlife Service, 21 March 2016. https://usfwsnortheast.wordpress.com/2016/03/21/esther-lape-and-elizabeth-read-pioneers-for-womens-rights-and-conservation.

CHAPTER 2

The History of Queer History
One Hundred Years of the Search for Shared Heritage

Gerard Koskovich

Searching for the history of lesbian, gay, bisexual, and transgender history may seem a particularly queer conceit—and searching for meaningful places associated with efforts to document, preserve, interpret,
and share that history may seem queerer still. After all, every individual
has a past, so at first glance it may appear that every social group must
have a heritage. Those who benefit from a position of power and respect
indeed share a heritage that can take the form of historical knowledge
elaborated over the course of centuries and conveyed via institutions
of state and culture such as schools, museums, and monuments. Those
marginalized by hierarchies of class, race, language, or immigrant status
are often ignored in such settings, yet they nonetheless manage to create a shared heritage through more informal means, with elders telling
their children or grandchildren stories of earlier times that succeeding
generations pass along as a vital family inheritance.

LGBTQ people, by contrast, customarily are born into families that
have little or no connection with lesbian, gay, bisexual, and transgender
life. While growing up, they have not benefited from hearing stories at
home that reflect their emerging same-sex desires or their sense of a
gender that differs from the one assigned to them at birth. As historian
and theorist of sexuality David Halperin observes, "Unlike the members of
minority groups defined by race or ethnicity or religion, gay men cannot
rely on their birth families to teach them about their history or culture."[1]
Although Halperin focuses on the experience of gay men, the statement
applies equally well to lesbian, bisexual, and transgender individuals.

Traditionally, history as a formal discipline and a cornerstone for
national heritage likewise has represented little or nothing of LGBTQ
lives. What were seen as the homoerotic misdeeds of the occasional an-

cient Roman emperor or Renaissance monarch might have surfaced in passing in a history volume or a college course, but historians customarily ignored evidence of same-sex desires and nonnormative gender identities—or regarded such evidence as inconsequential or as a sign of immoral, criminal, or deviant behavior best forgotten. LGBTQ people similarly saw scant reflection of their own past in museums, public monuments, local historical societies, and the popular history distributed by mainstream media, let alone at officially recognized historic sites. As Paula Martinac notes in her 1997 book *The Queerest Places*, "One thing that historic sites and travel guides never taught me was about a most important part of myself—my heritage as a gay person in this country."[2]

As a movement to defend homosexual men and women established itself in the United States in the second half of the twentieth century, the silence—and the silencing—did not go unremarked. Around 1979, the San Francisco Lesbian and Gay History Project described the situation in these stark terms: "Our letters were burned, our names blotted out, our books censored, our love declared unspeakable, our very existence denied."[3] The sense that LGBTQ people had been deprived of their heritage likewise echoes in the title of an anthology that provided a foundational text for the remarkable growth of LGBTQ history in the 1990s: *Hidden from History: Reclaiming the Gay and Lesbian Past* (1989).[4] Beyond the disregard or outright disapproval of society in general, however, evidence of a desire for history among people with same-sex attractions and nonnormative gender identities in the United States extends back at least to the late nineteenth century.[5]

Scholars have yet to produce comprehensive studies on the emergence and development of queer history as a cultural practice, but we can trace a few of the outlines through the one hundred years before the consolidation of an academic discipline of LGBTQ history in the 1990s.[6] The narratives that emerge are necessarily fragmentary given the gaps in the record of a practice that—much like its practitioners— was marginalized during most of the period under consideration. Even within the networks of LGBTQ people, variations of relative social and economic status mean that more evidence exists for the pursuit of history by middle-class cisgender white homosexual men living in urban centers than by working-class and poverty-class individuals, cisgender women, transgender people, people of color, and inhabitants of rural areas. Particularly for the decades before the 1970s, ongoing research will be required to more fully document and analyze the production and uses of history by those whose experience of LGBTQ life intersected with further experiences of exclusion.

The Prehistory of Queer History

Despite the strictures imposed by kin and the silence of formal history, at least some LGBTQ Americans caught glimpses of their own heritage in an era when the topic was not addressed in family settings or public discourse. Before the emergence of print media produced by and for LGBTQ people in the United States, stories of the queer past no doubt circulated confidentially between individuals and within local queer social networks.[7] For those who gained access to such networks, conversations among the members could include personal memories recounted by those who experienced same-sex desires or whose sense of gender did not match social expectations, as well as recollections they had heard from elders whose stories extended further back in time. Such folk interest in queer history is difficult to trace before the late nineteenth century, both because evidence is scarce and because the shifting meanings, forms, and interrelations of gender, same-sex desire, and homosexual acts over a longer period make the task increasingly complex.

One telling incident of oral transmission of memory from around 1900 appears in *The Stone Wall*, the autobiography of Ruth Fuller Field (1864–1935), published in 1930 under the pseudonym Mary Casal.[8] The author describes her introduction to a circle of lesbian friends in Brooklyn, including a somewhat older but much more worldly woman whose short hair is "tinged with gray" and who tells stories of her many same-sex affairs over the years. Hearing these memories had a powerful effect on Field: "How much suffering would have been saved me and what a different life I would have led if I had known earlier that we are not all created after one pattern."[9] The knowledge of the past produced by contacts of the sort Field experienced was thus invaluable, yet most often it also would have been personal, fragmentary, and fragile—subject not only to the variations inevitable in stories told and retold but also to the vagaries of memory embodied in stories passed from one individual to another and gradually distorted or lost.

Looking further, individuals with the cultural capital of literacy and the means to buy or borrow print materials could come upon tantalizing evidence, although finding it often required enduring the trauma of repeated assertions that same-sex desires and nonnormative gender are by nature signs of moral impairment, criminal intent, or mental illness. Notably, medical, psychological, and legal publications dealing with sex not infrequently featured historical details of what was characterized as sexual and gender irregularity over the centuries or of the supposed prevalence of homosexuality among noted figures of the past.[10] One

American example is *Human Sexuality: A Medico-Literary Treatise on the History and Pathology of the Sex Instinct for the Use of Physicians and Jurists* (1912) by J. Richardson Parke (1858–1938), a physician of dubious background whose practice was located near Washington Square Park in Philadelphia.[11] Borrowing from earlier English, French, German, and Italian writers, his comments on the past range from "Sexual Depravity in Early Rome" through "Sexual Inversion among Artists" to the "'Freda Ward' Case" (a lesbian murder case in Memphis, twenty years before the book was published).[12] Obscenity laws restricted the sale of such publications to the professional class, yet as Parke acknowledges in his preface, they nonetheless found their way into the hands of avid laypeople.[13]

A more comprehensive synthesis of sources similar to those used by Parke forms the basis for the first book extensively addressing the history of homosexuality and bisexuality authored by an American known to have been homosexual: Edward Irenaeus Prime-Stevenson (1858–1942) wrote *The Intersexes: A History of Similisexualism as a Problem in Social Life* during sojourns in Europe in the last years of the nineteenth century, set the manuscript aside in 1901, then revised it for private printing under the pseudonym "Xavier Mayne" in 1909 (figure 2.1).[14] Born in Madison, New Jersey, and trained in classics and the law, Prime-Stevenson became a music critic for such publications as *Harper's Weekly*, traveling widely, learning several languages, and living in Europe for the last four decades of his life.[15] *The Intersexes* draws on anthropological, psychological, sociological, and cultural analyses as well as historical evidence to defend homosexuality and bisexuality, citing examples from Biblical stories, ancient Greece and Rome, the Middle Ages, and Europe of the eighteenth and early nineteenth centuries.[16] Produced in Italy in an

Figure 2.1. Edward Irenaeus Prime Stevenson, 1909; portrait photograph inscribed to American music critic James G. Hunecker. Courtesy Dartmouth College Library.

edition of just 125 copies, Prime-Stevenson's pioneering work remained little known in Europe and essentially unknown in his home country, although one bookstore in New York City apparently offered copies for sale.[17] A German article critiquing *The Intersexes*—the only substantial review that appeared when the book was published—suggests one reason it remained out of view: "The laws in England and the United States impose unfortunate obstacles to such a publication."[18] A half-century later, *The Intersexes* was finally discovered by the emerging homophile movement in the United States.[19]

Discussions of the history of homosexuality and nonnormative gender of the sort presented by Parke and Prime-Stevenson would begin reaching a wider public in the United States only in the 1920s and 1930s with the gradual emergence of popularized sexology books. Examples include O. P. Gilbert's *Men in Women's Guise: Some Historical Instances of Female Impersonation* (1926), LaForest Potter's *Strange Loves: A Study in Sexual Abnormalities* (1933), Dr. Caufeynon's *Unisexual Love: A Documentary Study of the Sources, Manifestations, the Physiology and Psychology of Sexual Perversion in the Two Sexes* (1934), and Maurice Chideckel's *Female Sex Perversion: The Sexually Aberrated Woman as She Is* (1935).[20] None of these books offers anything resembling critical historiography, but all made it possible for readers at the time to learn that the past had been well populated with individuals whose sexual desires and senses of their own gender diverged from the expectations of contemporary society.

Biographies, autobiographies, and memoirs are another genre of readily available publications where stories of the recent past for homosexual and bisexual women and men and for gender-variant individuals occasionally turned up. Books of this sort usually required close attention to decipher hints, coded references, and strategic silences. In *The Intersexes*, Prime-Stevenson provides an example of the practice in his reading of Morris Schaff's *The Spirit of Old West Point, 1858–1862*, a volume of memoirs published in 1907:

> In its author's pen-portraits of early friends in the famous military academy . . . are to be noted many delicate suggestions of the uranian emotion in young and soldierly comrades. Indeed the accent of a manly similisexualism of psychic quality pervades the record. To many Anglo-Saxons it will make a peculiarly subtle appeal, even if its sub-uranistic accent may not be intelligently appreciated. Especially in its elegiac passages, it is eloquent of the homosexual thrill in young hearts that beneath uniforms can beat so passionally for each other.[21]

In contrast, a few such books addressed the subject directly and in ways that questioned or countered dominant narratives of depravity and pathology. Field's *The Stone Wall* is a striking example: living in retirement in California, she recorded both her own memories and the memories of the somewhat older lesbian she had met in Brooklyn decades before, thus ensuring that further generations of LGBTQ people could learn these stories of the past.[22] Similarly exceptional are two volumes, *The Autobiography of an Androgyne* (1918) and *The Female-Impersonators* (1922), that look back to queer life in New York City in the 1890s, both written by the pseudonymous Earl Lind (ca. 1874–?), also known as Ralph Werther and Jennie June, a feminine-identified man whom some might now see as a precursor to contemporary transgender and genderqueer individuals.[23] Published by specialized small presses, Field's and Lind's books received limited circulation, yet knowledge of their existence reached those on the lookout for such titles.[24] Long after publication, new readers continued discovering them through copies passed hand to hand or sold in shadowy zones of the used book market.

The fragments of the queer past found scattered in published nonfiction and fiction in this early period enabled LGBTQ individuals and social networks to constitute alternative cultural histories that were missing from the textbooks and that helped sustain them in the face of social opprobrium and marginalization. The result was not critical scholarship, but a folk historiography demonstrating that queer and gender-variant people had always existed, had been accepted in some cultures distant in time and place, had been persecuted for centuries, and were not always admirable individuals but often were capable of greatness. The phenomenon even found its way into at least two American novels of the period: an obscure title portraying the lives of the international elite in Europe and a mass-market volume focused on everyday Americans.

In Edward Irenaeus Prime-Stevenson's novel *Imre: A Memorandum*, privately printed in an edition of five hundred copies in Italy in 1906, the expatriate English narrator, Oswald, addressing his Hungarian love object, Imre, describes in high Edwardian prose how reading led him to recognize that men throughout time had shared his same-sex attractions:

> So often in books, old ones or new, nay, in the very chronicles of the criminal courts, I came face to face with the fact that . . . tens of thousands of men in all epochs, of noblest natures, of most brilliant minds and gifts, of intensest energies, scores of pure spirits, deep philosophers, bravest soldiers, highest poets and artists, had been such as myself in this mystic sex-disorganization.[25]

He adds that many homosexuals also could be classed among "the worthless or the wicked," but that history "whether Greek, Latin, Persian or English" nonetheless suggests the intrinsic "righteousness" of same-sex love.[26]

Another novel, Blair Niles's *Strange Brother* (1931), brings the story back to the United States. The young white protagonist, Mark Thornton, has moved to New York City to live as a homosexual.[27] Before Mark left his small hometown, an older friend had sent him a copy of Walt Whitman's nineteenth-century masterwork *Leaves of Grass* with its homoerotic "Calamus" poems. In New York, Mark discovers English sex reformer and homosexual emancipationist Edward Carpenter's *Love's Coming of Age* (1902) "by chance in a second-hand book shop on Fifty-Ninth Street."[28] When another friend asks him to ship some books to a doctor, he encounters a volume of English sexologist Havelock Ellis's *Studies in the Psychology of Sex* (1900–1905), where he reads about "the history of abnormal love" and learns that it "had existed always, everywhere . . . everywhere from the beginning."[29] Finding self-affirmation in his discoveries and inspired by Alain Locke's influential anthology *The New Negro* (1925), Mark even dreams of editing a book of historic texts defending "manly love."[30]

As the fictional Mark Thornton's discovery of homosexual history through happenstance and personal contact suggests, creating an alternative queer heritage was not a simple matter. In *The Intersexes*, Prime-Stevenson directly took note of a major obstacle Americans searching for queer-themed publications faced: "The author or publisher of a homosexual book, even if scientific, not to speak of a belles-lettres work, will not readily escape troublesome consequences."[31] Many publishers, bookstores, and libraries wanted little or nothing to do with the most forthright books, and no readily available bibliographies existed to guide interested readers—yet the effort to discover themselves and their past in print remained vital for many LGBTQ people. As Donald Webster Cory (pseudonym of Edward Sagarin, 1913–1986) notes in his 1951 book *The Homosexual in America: A Subjective Approach*, scouring the historical record for heroes "is characteristic of any minority having an inferior social status"; he adds that homosexual men and women in particular were "anxious to find in literature justification and clues to happiness."[32]

A well-documented example is offered by Jeannette Howard Foster (1895–1981). In the mid-teens of the twentieth century, when she was an undergraduate at Rockford College (now Rockford University) in Rockford, Illinois, she began a lifelong search for books referring to romantic and erotic relationships between women, including women portrayed as bisexual or favoring men's clothing.[33] By the 1920s she was collecting such books and by the 1930s was giving much of her free time to bibliographical research, including travel to libraries holding otherwise inaccessible titles. During both of these decades, she lived for periods of time in her parents' Chicago home and kept her growing collection there.[34] After obtaining a Ph.D. in library science at the University of Chicago and holding a series of posts as a librarian, Foster ultimately produced a groundbreaking study reflecting both her search for a personal heritage and her academic training: *Sex Variant Women in Literature: A Historical and Quantitative Study* (1956). She courageously published the book under her own name and at her own expense in the midst of the anti-homosexual panic of the 1950s.[35] Foster's publication provided a foundation for work on the cultural history of lesbianism that would appear in the subsequent two decades.[36]

Homophile Organizers and History Enthusiasts

With the emergence in the 1950s of the earliest enduring American homosexual organizations and periodicals—a phenomenon often referred to as the homophile movement—the search for a shared heritage began to shift from largely private and fragmentary pursuits to more public and structured ones. The first national groups were the Mattachine Society, founded in 1950, which focused on the concerns of homosexual men; One Incorporated, founded in 1952, which primarily concentrated on men but also took an interest in women's issues; and the Daughters of Bilitis (DOB), founded in 1955, which brought together lesbian women.[37] Both One Incorporated and the Mattachine Society were initially based in Los Angeles, with Mattachine moving to San Francisco late in 1956; DOB was headquartered in San Francisco from the start. All three published long-running periodicals that usually appeared monthly: the *Mattachine Review* (1955–1966); *One* (1953–1967, with a brief reappearance in 1972); and the *Ladder* (1956–1972).[38] In addition, One Incorporated later launched a scholarly publication, *One Institute Quarterly: Homophile Studies* (1961–1970).

The earlier informal knowledge of queer history produced by individual effort and disseminated through social networks reached a nascent public readership via these new periodicals, with homosexual history buffs contributing articles on a fairly regular basis.[39] As John D'Emilio notes, "Through bibliographies, books reviews, and essays on history and literature, the publications filled an informational void and became valuable tools for self-education."[40] He adds that such articles reflected the groups' effort "to legitimate homosexuality as a significant and pervasive component of human experience."[41] Despite their broad attention to evidence of the past, however, homophile history enthusiasts expressed virtually no interest in historic preservation, likely because publicly marking places meaningful to queer memory would have attracted traumatic reactions in an era when LGBTQ territories remained clandestine, policed, and contested.[42]

A survey of the initial five years of each of the three major national homophile magazines suggests the extent to which history in general held an important place in the movement. The *Mattachine Review*, for instance, ran approximately twenty substantial articles with a historical focus during its first five years. These include brief biographies of figures from the past, such as the Roman emperor Hadrian; lengthy reviews of popular books, such as G. Rattray Taylor's *Sex in History* (1954); a two-part series on what the author characterized as homosexuality among Native Americans, drawing on observations from European explorers and colonists; the tale of Civil War hero Jennie Hodges, portrayed as a woman who passed as a man to serve in the Union Army; and a ten-year retrospective of the Mattachine Society's own history.[43] The magazine also published a multipart bibliography with more than one thousand listings for fiction and nonfiction books dealing with homosexuality, including out-of-print titles dating back decades.[44]

The *Ladder* also played its part in bringing alternative homosexual histories into print, publishing approximately twelve substantial history-related articles in its first five years. Mostly dealing with literary and cultural history, the articles include a succinct biography of British novelist Radclyffe Hall (1886–1943), a survey of cross-dressing by women, a synopsis of films with lesbian themes produced from the early 1930s on, and a discussion of lesbianism and the law from ancient Rome to twentieth-century America.[45] In addition, the magazine contributed to lesbian bibliography by publishing a standing "Lesbiana" column of capsule book reviews, primarily of recent fiction, but also of fiction from the first half of the twentieth century and occasionally nonfiction titles touching in some way on lesbian history. Initially written by Marion Zimmer Bradley (1930–1999), the column ran unsigned before being taken over by Barbara Grier (1933–2011) under the pseudonym Gene Damon in September 1957.[46]

The third national homophile group, One Incorporated, merits particular notice for working to develop alternative understandings of homosexuality into a structured field of study with history as a key com-

ponent. Much like the Mattachine Society and the DOB, the organization started out with a periodical that included substantial articles dealing in whole or part with history—approximately seventeen in the first
five years of One magazine.[47] In 1956, the leaders of the organization
went beyond publishing the occasional history article: they moved to
elaborate a systematic approach to thinking and teaching about homosexuality by establishing the One Institute for Homophile Studies. The
Institute described itself as "an adult education facility offering courses
of undergraduate and graduate levels. Classes in history, literature and
social studies centered upon homosexuality and its relation to world
cultures, religion, law, morals, psychology, medicine, and the arts."[48]
Among the instructors from the beginning was Harry Hay (1912–2002),
a founder of the Mattachine Society who had devoted himself in particular to the ethnohistory of homosexuality and gender variation in
American Indian cultures.[49]

In an era when academic historians and university history departments ignored not only the history of homosexuality but also the
history of sexuality in general, developing a cross-cultural history curriculum on homosexuality from ancient times to the modern era was
an objective of the One Institute from the outset.[50] Going beyond the
inward-looking, self-affirming search for a personal heritage that LGBTQ
people had pursued informally for decades, the Institute argued that
learning about the history of homosexuality also served an important
purpose for society as a whole. One of the instructors, James Kepner
(1923–1997), put it in these terms: "The task of countering majority bias
is in the long run as vital to the majority itself as it is for the homophile
or other social deviants. Does anyone seriously think he can really understand the history, not only of ancient Greece or modern Germany,
but of any era or country, while ignoring the homosexual pieces in the
puzzle?"[51]

Both course lectures and student papers from this enterprise provided content for the organization's scholarly journal, One Institute Quarterly: Homophile Studies. The full run includes approximately twenty-two
substantial history articles. Taken together, they provide a sweeping
view of Western history of the ancient, Renaissance, early modern, and
nineteenth-century periods, along with considerations of Asian history
and ethnohistory. The contributors drew largely on published primary
and secondary sources in English, generally emphasizing intellectual
and cultural history. With no trained historians involved and no access
to outside fellowships or significant funding, the Institute's early participants evidently found archival research beyond their means.[52] The his-

torical articles in the quarterly mostly discuss male homosexuality, with lesbian and transgender topics more often featured in essays employing sociological, medical, and psychological frameworks.[53] The One Institute lasted well beyond the period of the homophile movement, ultimately receiving accreditation from the State of California in 1981 to issue graduate degrees; it ceased operation as a teaching institution in 1994.[54]

Community Archivists, Independent Scholars, and Academic Pioneers

The gay liberation and lesbian-feminist movements of the late 1960s and the 1970s produced a wave of highly visible organizing across the United States that quickly surpassed the reach of the much smaller homophile organizations.[55] As the movement garnered members and allies, it also encountered widespread and at times harsh opposition. As with other groups that embraced identity politics at the time, gay and lesbian people responded in part by looking for support from a shared past they could publicly assert as their own.[56] Given the generational and political divides between older homophile activists and younger liberationists, many among the latter group may have been unaware that they were carrying on a search that itself had a long history.[57] At least a few of the younger history enthusiasts, however, eagerly found guidance in the bibliographies developed in the homophile period.[58] Others turned to bibliographical resources inspired by the gay liberation movement itself, such as "A Gay Bibliography," which longtime activist Barbara Gittings (1932–2007) produced for the American Library Association's Task Force on Gay Liberation; six editions appeared from 1971 to 1980.[59]

Starting with the era of gay liberation in the 1970s and continuing through the 1980s, three interlinked phenomena demonstrate the growing interest in the United States in the histories of gay men and lesbians—and to a lesser extent transgender and bisexual people:

- the founding of the first organizations devoted primarily or entirely to documenting, researching, interpreting, and disseminating these histories;
- the contributions of a growing number of independent scholars; and
- the emergence of the first scholars to address the history of homosexuality in the setting of university humanities and social sciences departments.

To some extent, these developments reflected the decades-old desire for self-affirmation and a common heritage among people with same-sex attractions and nonnormative gender identities. As Jeffrey Escoffier notes, lesbian and gay scholars in this period initially "looked for antecedents as a way of claiming ancestors, of validating themselves through the achievements of great and famous queers and dykes."[60] In addition, they advanced and transformed the historical project of the homophile period, sharpening its assertion of a shared past not only into a tool for the formation of identity and community, but also into a political strategy for influencing internal and external debates about lesbian and gay communities and for demanding respect from society as a whole.[61] The resulting production of community-based historical institutions, resources, and scholarship laid the groundwork for the establishment of LGBTQ history as a seriously regarded subject of academic study and for the emergence of queer heritage initiatives in the traditional field of historic preservation.

The effort to create LGBTQ archives and libraries as independent entities starting in the 1970s brought focus to a less noticed enterprise of the three national homophile groups: all had collected relevant books and periodicals—and in the case of One Incorporated, the holdings had grown considerably to support the educational initiatives of the One Institute.[62] Academic libraries and archives, by contrast, had taken little interest in documenting the history of homosexuality and nonnormative gender expression—a situation that persisted into the 1990s. The rare exceptions proved the rule: the Kinsey Institute at Indiana University, founded in 1947, had gathered such materials as part of its wider focus on human sexuality, but the collection remained largely inaccessible to outside researchers in the field of history until the 1980s.[63] Another forerunner was the Joseph A. Labadie Collection at the University of Michigan, Ann Arbor, with holdings focused on the history of radical social movements. The collection expanded to include sexual reform movements under the leadership of Edward C. Weber (1922–2006), a gay man who served as director from 1960 to 2000 and who began accessioning homophile materials in the early 1960s.[64]

Starting in the 1970s, the void left by academic libraries was filled by community-based LGBTQ archives and libraries, many of which not only collected books, periodicals, and papers, but also responded to the equivalent exclusion from museum collections by gathering works of art and artifacts. Furthermore, most of the organizations assumed additional functions of traditional public history institutions by documenting historic places associated with LGBTQ life and by offering exhibitions and public programs. As scholar Ann Cvetkovich notes, by gathering and interpreting this array of LGBT historical materials outside traditional academic frameworks, such groups play a vital role in addressing

> the traumatic loss of history that has accompanied sexual life and the formation of sexual publics, and they assert the role of memory and affect in compensating for institutional neglect. Like other archives of trauma, such as those that commemorate the Holocaust, slavery or war, they must enable the acknowledgment of a past that can be painful to remember, impossible to forget, and resistant to consciousness.[65]

The first such formally established organization in the United States was the Lesbian Herstory Archives (LHA), conceived in 1974 during discussions at a lesbian-feminist consciousness-raising group in Manhattan of which writer, activist, and self-defined "white Jewish fem lesbian" Joan Nestle was a member.[66] As the LHA notes in the history posted on its website, "At one meeting in 1974, Julia Stanley and Joan Nestle, who had come out before the gay liberation movement, talked about the precariousness of lesbian culture and how so much of our past culture was seen only through patriarchal eyes"; with others responding to the observation, "a new concept was born—a grassroots lesbian archives."[67]

In 1975, the organization installed its collections in the apartment on Ninety-Second Street in the Upper West Side of Manhattan that was shared by Nestle and her then-partner, Deborah Edel (figure 2.2). Volunteers, researchers, and visitors frequented the space for the next seventeen years, after which the institution relocated to its current home, a brownstone in the Park Slope neighborhood of Brooklyn.[68] Nestle's apartment also provided a home to Mabel Hampton (1902–1989), a working-class African American lesbian elder who had donated her own collection to LHA and was a mainstay among the volunteers. She lived there part-time starting in 1976 and full-time for the last three years of her life.[69] Hampton was one of a number of women of color who played significant roles in the early years of LHA; others have provided ongoing leadership as members of the governing collective.[70]

The other major queer archives and library founded in the United States in the 1970s started as the Western Gay Archives, the name that Los Angeles homophile movement pioneer James Kepner gave his personal collection. In the first half of the 1970s, he began inviting researchers to his apartment one afternoon a week to use the materials he had amassed in the previous three decades. Kepner transformed his private collection into a formal nonprofit association and renamed it the Natalie Barney/Edward Carpenter Library of the National Gay Archives in 1979,

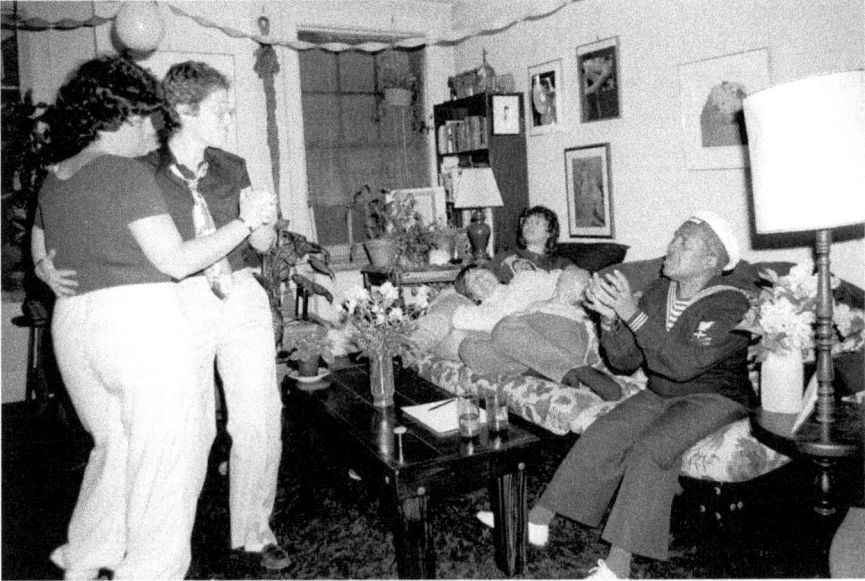

Figure 2.2. Birthday party for Mabel Hampton at the Lesbian Herstory Archives in the Manhattan apartment of Joan Nestle, ca. 1979. *Left to right:* Joan Nestle and Deborah Edel; LHA volunteers Judith Schwarz and Judy Reagan; and Mabel Hampton. Photo copyright Morgan Gwenwald.

at which time the collection moved to a Hollywood storefront where it was regularly open to the public.[71] In contrast to the lesbian-feminist orientation of the LHA with its emphasis on recuperating the history of women loving women, the Southern California institution adopted a comprehensive approach from the outset, looking to gather historical and contemporary materials reflecting in any way on homosexuality, bisexuality, and gender variation.[72] Through name changes, moves, and a merger with One Incorporated, the archives and library remained in the hands of community-based organizations until 2010, when the group donated the materials to the University of Southern California.[73]

These two groundbreaking institutions embodied in several ways the organizational outlines for the LGBTQ archives and libraries that would be established around the United States throughout the 1980s, into the 1990s, and beyond.[74] Some would grow out of community organizing efforts, as did the LHA. This group includes the Gerber/Hart Library and Archives in Chicago, founded in 1981, and the Gay and Lesbian Historical Society in San Francisco, founded in 1985.[75] Others would grow from private collections, as did the National Gay Archives. This group includes the Quatrefoil Library, created in 1983 in Minneapolis from the personal library that David Irwin (1920–2009) and Dick Hewetson started in the mid-1970s, and the Stonewall Library, created in 1987 in Fort Lauderdale, Florida, from a private collection launched in 1973 by Mark Silber.[76]

All of those organizations developed wide-ranging holdings embracing lesbian, gay, bisexual, and transgender materials, limited in some cases only by a regional focus. Furthermore, all were committed to documenting the racial and ethnic diversity of LGBTQ communities. In practice, however, evidence of the experience of cisgender white gay men often constituted a majority of the collections, in part because systems of privilege meant that more such material had been produced and preserved in the first place.[77] Other community-based archives followed the model of the LHA, seeking to address such challenges by focusing specifically on underrepresented groups. Institutions in this category include the National Transgender Library and Archive, which Dallas Denny created as a personal collection in 1990 in Tucker, Georgia, then donated in 1993 to the American Educational Gender Information Service, which in turn transferred it to the Labadie Collection at the University of Michigan in 2000.[78] Another example is the Historical Archive of the Latino GLBT History Project, started as a personal collection by José Gutierrez in Washington, DC, in 1993 and incorporated as a nonprofit in 2007.[79]

The 1970s and 1980s also saw the emergence of independent scholars working individually and in collaboration to research the history of homosexuality and nonnormative gender expression.[80] These historians drew not only on a depth and range of published primary sources that surpassed those employed by the homophile movement, but also on the production of oral histories and sustained archival research, often gathering the materials directly from LGBT elders or working in association with the new community-based archives. As Susan Ferentinos notes,

> The field of LGBT history owes a great debt to these mostly amateur community historians, for they saw the need to collect the history long before mainstream archives, and these early efforts form essential contributions to the historical collections of today. In a similar vein, many of the earliest books on LGBT history in the United States were written by historians (professionally trained or otherwise) who were unaffiliated with universities.[81]

A major independent scholar whose work emerged in this milieu is historian Jonathan Ned Katz, who conducted much of his early research at the Bobst Library at New York University in the years before LGBTQ community libraries and archives were established.[82] He found support for his efforts at weekly meetings of the Gay Socialist Action Project, active from 1975 through 1977; the gatherings rotated among the members' apartments, including the Morningside Heights home of Columbia University graduate student John D'Emilio, who would himself go on to claim a place as a leading gay historian.[83] "My work on gay history began with my play *Coming Out*, produced by the Gay Activists Alliance, NYC, in June 1972, and reproduced the following year," Katz recalls. "There was also a Boston production, I guess in 1973. The play used documents of LGBT history for dramatic purposes. The attention the play got led to my being offered a contract for a book on gay history, which turned into *Gay American History* in 1976. I always say that my work on gay history comes directly out of the political movement."[84] Katz adds, "I started out by trying to find out everything that was already known about LGBT history. I collected all the existing bibliographies on homosex and cut them up and put them in chrono order on 3 x 5 cards. It was revelatory."[85]

Katz's 1976 book, *Gay American History: Lesbians and Gay Men in the U.S.A.—A Documentary*, brought together an array of primary sources from the sixteenth through the twentieth centuries, along with Katz's historical commentaries and an eighty-three page bibliography.[86] As with the play that preceded it, the book included histories of white people and people of color, women and men, and individuals with diverse desires and gender expressions, many reflecting the experience of eras well before the conception of gay, lesbian, bisexual, or transgender identities.[87] *Gay American History* was the first volume in the field brought out by a major New York publishing house. This connection helped give the book unprecedented reach, drawing the attention of many LGBTQ individuals and not a few academic historians to the potential depth and range of this area of history. Katz also helped develop basic resources for gay and lesbian studies by serving as general editor of "Homosexuality: Lesbians and Gay Men in Society, History, and Literature," a series of some one hundred books from Arno Press in New York City that reprinted scarce and long-out-of-print titles and brought unpublished original scholarship into print.[88]

At a time when American universities remained almost entirely unwelcoming to the history of homosexuality, the period from 1972 to 1980 nonetheless saw the first three graduate students successfully complete doctoral dissertations dealing with the subject: Rictor Norton, Salvatore Licata, and Ramón Gutiérrez.[89] With a new assertiveness reflecting the impact of gay liberation politics, these young researchers took on the sustained intellectual labor and constrained economic circumstances of graduate school, even though they had every reason to believe they would face considerable challenges establishing careers in academia.[90] As Gayle Rubin notes, advisors of graduate students doing such work at the time not infrequently "told them bluntly that they were committing academic suicide, and these warnings were not unrealistic."[91] In their overall approach to queer history, the early dissertations at once look back to the traditions of folk and homophile histories and look forward to future thinking about LGBTQ people and their place in the past. Their pioneering authors opened the way for three more Ph.D.s in the field in the 1980s, earned by John D'Emilio, Michael Lombardi, and George Chauncey.[92]

The first individual in the United States to receive a Ph.D. for work dealing with the history of homosexuality was Rictor Norton, a graduate student in English at Florida State University in Tallahassee from 1967 to 1972.[93] His dissertation traces literary representations of male homosexuality through pastoral mythology from the ancient world to the Renaissance, with an afterword on modern European and American authors. Norton's work brought scholarly rigor to the queer tradition of alternative cultural and literary histories, but having come out publicly, he found that his advisor opposed his search for an academic post.[94] In 1973, he moved to London, where he worked in journalism and publishing, and has produced numerous publications on gay history as an independent scholar.[95]

The second Ph.D. in the United States on the history of homosexuality went to Salvatore Licata (1939–1990), a graduate student in history at the University of Southern California in Los Angeles from 1971 to 1978. In part recalling the early efforts of the Mattachine Society to record its own history, his dissertation focused on the American gay movement from the early twentieth century to 1974.[96] Licata taught an early course section titled "Sexual Nonconformity in America" as part of a freshman American history seminar at USC in 1976.[97] He later taught gay history and served as associate editor of the *Journal of Homosexuality* at San Francisco State University, but did not obtain a permanent academic post; when he died of AIDS in 1990, he had worked for the New York Transit Authority, then as a journalist and community educator focusing on HIV.[98]

The third American doctoral dissertation that discusses the history of homosexuality is the work of Ramón Gutiérrez, a graduate student in the History Department at the University of Wisconsin, Madison, from

1974 to 1980.[99] Although in part addressing the ethnohistory of American Indians that previously had attracted the attention of homophile organizers, Gutiérrez dropped the homophiles' approach to same-sex desire and nonnormative gender expression as isolated entities; instead, he integrates these phenomena into his analysis of larger systems of sex, gender, marriage, and family in colonial New Mexico from the late seventeenth century to the mid-nineteenth century.[100] Guitiérrez subsequently published an essay in part critiquing Harry Hay's homophile approach to American Indian sexuality—an example of queer historiography, which was developing into a critical discipline cognizant of its own intellectual past.[101] In contrast to Norton and Licata, Gutiérrez built an academic career and now holds an endowed chair in history at the University of Chicago.[102]

Creating links between the community and the university, independent scholars and academics also worked together in several initiatives during this period. One such effort was the Buffalo Women's Oral History Project, founded in 1978 by Elizabeth Lapovsky Kennedy, Madeline D. Davis, and Avra Michelson.[103] They jointly conceived an initiative to record oral histories of the Buffalo lesbian community, develop a public collection of the interviews and supporting documents, and write a book based on the materials. With other collaborators over time, including Wanda Edwards (1955–1995), an African American graduate student, the project continued for fourteen years, capturing memories reflecting the diversity of gender expression, race, and urban territories among the city's working-class lesbians before 1970.[104] Kennedy and Davis ultimately produced a book drawn from the work of the project: *Boots of Leather, Slippers of Gold: The History of a Lesbian Community* (1993). Their introduction sums up the project in these words: "Uncovering our hidden history was a labor of love, and restoring this history to our community was a political responsibility."[105]

Another such initiative was the San Francisco Lesbian and Gay History Project, which had a wide-ranging national impact over time. Founded in summer 1978, the project provided a network of support and intellectual exchange for participants who were carrying out research, writing, and public history initiatives.[106] Meeting initially in the apartment of founding member Allan Bérubé (1946–2007) in a Victorian house in the Haight-Ashbury District and occasionally sponsoring public presentations in community settings such as the Women's Building of San Francisco, the History Project remained active into the mid-1980s.[107] John D'Emilio and Estelle Freedman, both of whom were members, recall that "remarkably, given the strong tendencies toward lesbian separatism in the 1970s, the project remained a mixed-sex group, although lesbians met separately as well as with the male participants. While almost entirely white, it also was a mixed-class group and one that defined itself as politically activist."[108]

Many of those involved in the History Project went on to produce significant work. Independent scholars who were active with the group include Bérubé, recipient of a MacArthur Fellowship for his historical research; Academy Award-winning filmmaker Rob Epstein; author and editor Jeffrey Escoffier; historian and bibliographer Eric Garber (1954–1995); and activist and writer Amber Hollibaugh.[109] The History Project also was the setting where Garber and independent scholar Willie Walker (1949–2004) launched a database of San Francisco LGBTQ historic sites that has subsequently supported the work of numerous researchers on the history of queer places in the city.[110] The group likewise nurtured Walker's proposal that led to the creation in 1985 of the GLBT Historical Society, now a renowned LGBTQ archives and museum.[111]

The careers of academics who were involved with the Lesbian and Gay History Project suggest the extent to which universities remained a challenging setting for LGBTQ scholarship during this period: several produced exceptional work, yet endured long struggles to achieve full university appointments in their chosen fields. For instance, D'Emilio was a graduate student at the time he joined the project. After completing his Ph.D., he initially taught at the University of North Carolina, Greensboro, then took a position at the National Gay and Lesbian Task Force Policy Institute. Ultimately, in 1989 he was hired as a professor by the history department at the University of Illinois, Chicago, from which he retired in 2015.[112] When Freedman joined the project, she was already teaching at Stanford University, where she was awarded tenure in 1983 only after a lengthy public battle. She established a distinguished career as a feminist historian and now holds an endowed professorship at Stanford.[113] A third member, Gayle Rubin, was an anthropology graduate student who went on to publish highly influential essays in feminist theory, sexuality studies, and the history of leather and SM. After many years of short-term posts at various institutions, she obtained tenure in 2011 at the University of Michigan, Ann Arbor, where she is now an associate professor.[114]

Coda: The Queer 1990s and Beyond

The 1990s and beyond have seen LGBTQ history widely recognized as both a valid field of academic study and a subject of popular interest. Several developments demonstrate this shift away from the long period in which individuals and communities searching for stories of the LGBTQ past encountered the barriers of shaming, pathologizing, silence, and silencing; the struggle to find and share sources for production of knowledge; and the risk of disapproval and opposition when possibilities for scholarship began to emerge. Since the beginning of the 1990s, academics working in LGBTQ history have been active around the United States, with an increasing number of universities supporting research, acquiring library special collections, and offering courses related to the subject.[115] One marker of the establishment of the field is the production of Ph.D.s in history, art history, American studies, geography, and related fields: in the bibliography established by the Committee on LGBT History of the American Historical Association, the count jumps from three in the 1970s and three in the 1980s to thirty-seven in the 1990s followed by sixty-seven in the 2000s and thirty-eight from 2010 to 2017.[116] Doctorates in the 1990s include the first focused on lesbian history and the first substantially dealing with transgender history.[117] Among the institutions awarding these degrees were Harvard, Stanford, the University of California, the University of Iowa, the University of Louisiana, the University of New Mexico, the University of North Carolina, and Yale.[118]

Drawing on the boom in dissertations as well as the ongoing research and writing of professors and independent scholars, the 1990s and 2000s also saw university presses and commercial publishers bring out a significant number of titles in the field of LGBTQ history. Reflecting insights from feminist studies, sexuality studies, ethnic studies, and queer studies, these publications often emphasize the extent to which the forms and meanings of sexuality and gender change through time; the intersectionality of experiences of sexuality, gender, race, immigration, and class; questioning the concept of stable sexual and gender identities that form unitary communities; and understanding same-sex desire, same-sex sexual activity, and nonnormative gender as aspects of broader systems of sex, gender, and power that structure society as a whole. In addition, the 1990s brought the first books from major commercial publishers addressing bisexual and transgender history: *Vice Versa: Bisexuality and the Eroticism of Everyday Life* (1995) by Marjorie Garber, a professor of English at Harvard, and *Transgender Warriors: Making History from Joan of Arc to RuPaul* (1996) by transgender activist, journalist, and grassroots historian Leslie Feinberg (1949–2014).[119] Garber's book notwithstanding, the history of bisexuality has remained one of the least documented areas of the LGBTQ past.[120]

Beyond the academy, LGBTQ people continue looking for the self-affirmation offered by a shared heritage.[121] Individuals fascinated by the queer past are creating history projects and archives well beyond the metropolises customarily recognized as centers of LGBTQ culture.[122] In addition, they widely echo James Kepner's prescient warning of almost six decades ago that "ignoring the homosexual pieces in the puzzle" of history deprives society in general of vital knowledge. Advocacy for inclusion of LGBTQ history in public school curriculums highlights one setting where this approach is evident.[123] Another place where it is literally on display is exhibitions at LGBTQ and non-LGBTQ institutions such as libraries, historical societies, and museums.[124] A number of museums, ranging from the Leslie Lohman Museum of Gay and Lesbian Art, to the Schomburg Center for Research in Black Culture at the New York Public Library, to the National Museum of American History, also have been building permanent collections devoted in whole or part to aspects of queer history.[125] And the field of historic preservation is bringing the queer past to the attention of the wider public, a development forcefully demonstrated by the National Park Service, which published a monumental national LGBTQ theme study with nearly thirty contributing authors in October 2016.[126] Queer academic historians, public historians, independent scholars, and history activists today insist that the LGBTQ past forms a meaningful part of history as a whole and emphasize that creating a shared heritage for LGBTQ people also means honoring a past that rightfully belongs to all Americans in all its diversity.

Mr. Gerard Koskovich is a public historian, curator, rare book dealer, and founding member of the GLBT Historical Society in San Francisco, California.

Acknowledgments

I am grateful to the many individuals who responded to my queries and requests for leads in the course of my work on this chapter; a number are cited in the footnotes. I also wish to acknowledge the following for their assistance: Alan Miller, Canadian Lesbian and Gay Archives, Toronto; Raimondo Biffi, Kristen Franseen, James Gifford, and Tom Sargant, all of them scholars of the work of Edward Irenaeus Prime-Stevenson; Joan E. Biren; Joanna Black and Alex Barrows, GLBT Historical Society, San Francisco, California; Lora Martinolich, Glendale Public Library, Glendale, California; Desiree Yael Vester, Lesbian Herstory Archives, Brooklyn, New York; Ralf Dose, Magnus-Hirschfeld-Gesellschaft, Berlin; Loni Shibuyama, One Archives, and the staff at the USC University Archives, both at the University of Southern California Libraries, Los Angeles, California; and the staff of the San Francisco Public Library. For commenting on drafts, I thank Marcelo DeSousa, Marcia Gallo, Alexander Gray, and Gayle Rubin.

Notes

1. David M. Halperin, *How to Be Gay* (Cambridge, MA: Harvard University Press, 2012), 7.
2. Paula Martinac, *The Queerest Places: A National Guide to Gay and Lesbian Historic Sites* (New York: Henry Holt & Co., 1997), xi.
3. "San Francisco Lesbian and Gay History Project," flyer (circa 1979); GLBT Historical Society (San Francisco), San Francisco LGBT Groups Ephemera Collection (collection no. GRP EPH), folder: "San Francisco Gay and Lesbian History Project, 1979–1983."
4. Martin Bauml Duberman, Martha Vicinus, and George Chauncey Jr., eds, *Hidden From History: Reclaiming the Gay and Lesbian Past* (New York: New American Library, 1989).
5. The phrase "desire for history" is borrowed from the title of a posthumous collection of essays by the gay community-based historian Allan Bérubé, edited with an introduction by John D'Emilio and Estelle B. Freedman, *My Desire for History: Essays in Gay, Community and Labor History* (Chapel Hill: University of North Carolina Press, 2011). Bérubé discusses the complexity of his own desires—homosexual, intellectual, historical—in "Intellectual Desire," a talk he gave in 1992, reprinted in the collection, pages 161–81.
6. The history of queer history has attracted scholarly attention primarily in discussions of theory that draw on aspects of intellectual history, notably historiography and rhetoric. For a useful brief bibliography of works published from 1979 through 2007, see Rictor Norton, "Bibliography of Gay and Lesbian History: Theory" (updated 13 July 2008), Gay History & Literature: Essays by Rictor Norton, http://rictornorton.co.uk/bibliog/bibtheor.htm. At least three significant publications can be added to Norton's list: Elizabeth A. Armstrong and Suzanna M. Crage, "Movements and Memory: The Making of the Stonewall Myth," *American Sociological Review* 71, no. 5 (October 2006): 724–51; Scott Bravmann, *Queer Fictions of the Past: History, Culture, and Difference* (Cambridge: Cambridge University Press, 1997); and Marc Stein, "Theoretical Politics, Local Communities: The Making of U.S. LGBT Historiography," *GLQ: A Journal of Gay and Lesbian Studies* 11, no. 4 (2005): 605–25. For further examples focusing on rhetoric, see Jean Bessette, *Retroactivism in the Lesbian Archives: Composing Pasts and Futures* (Carbondale: Southern Illinois University Press, 2017); Charles E. Morris III, ed., *Queering Public Address: Sexualities in American Historical Discourse* (Columbia: University of South Carolina Press, 2007); and Thomas R. Dunn, *Queerly Remembered: Rhetorics for Representing the GLBTQ Past* (Columbia: University of South Carolina Press, 2016).

7. On the shift from oral and confidential networks of communication to wider and more public communication via print media, see Martin Meeker, *Contacts Desired: Gay and Lesbian Communications and Community, 1940s–1970s* (Chicago: University of Chicago Press, 2006).

8. Mary Casal [pseudonym of Ruth Fuller Field], *The Stone Wall: An Autobiography* (Chicago: Eyncourt Press, 1930), 178–80. On the identity of the pseudonymous author, see Sherry A. Darling, "A Critical Introduction to *The Stone Wall: An Autobiography*," Ph.D. diss., Tufts University, Department of Drama, 2003, 2. For a brief overview of Field's life, excerpts from *The Stone Wall*, and a bibliography of works by and about Field, see "Mary Casal, Pseudonym of Ruth Fuller Field: The Autobiography of an American Lesbian," introduction by Jonathan Ned Katz, Outhistory.org, http://www.outhistory.org/exhibits/show/casal.

9. Casal, *The Stone Wall*, 178–80. The woman is referred to in *The Stone Wall* only as "the Philosopher" or "Phil." Darling, "A Critical Introduction," 91–92, identifies her as Vittoria Cremers, an early follower of Theosophy. Darling does not give Cremers's date of birth, but various authors indicate 1859 or 1860, based on records indicating Cremers was 26 when she married in 1886. See, for instance, Richard Kaczynski, *Perdurabo: The Life of Aleister Crowley* (Berkeley, CA: North Atlantic Books, 2012), 221. Neither Field nor Darling provide a date for Field's first encounter with Cremers, but it was before the death in 1906 of Johnstone Bennett, another member of the group whom Field met at the same time; for Bennett's death, see Darling, "A Critical Introduction," 87.

10. For a discussion of homosexual men drawing on such materials to create folk histories in the late nineteenth and early twentieth centuries, see George Chauncey, *Gay New York: Gender, Urban Culture, and the Making of the Gay Male World, 1890–1940* (New York: Basic Books, 1994), 282–86.

11. J. Richardson Parke, *Human Sexuality: A Medico-Literary Treatise on the History and Pathology of the Sex Instinct for the Use of Physicians and Jurists* (Philadelphia: Professional Publishing Company, 1912). Parke had been found guilty of counterfeiting patent medicines in 1887; see "Legal Reports: Imitating Patent Medicines in America," *Chemist and Druggist*, 16 April 1887, 473. For Parke's birth and death dates, see Susan G. Kennedy-Ajax, "My Genealogy Home Page: Information about Joseph Richardson Parke," Genealogy.com, http://www.genealogy.com/ftm/k/e/n/Susan-G-Kennedy-Ajax/WEBSITE-0001/UHP-0109.html.

12. Parke, *Human Sexuality*, viii (list of subheads for chap. 6, "Inversion of the Sexual Impulse"). On the Freda Ward case, see Lisa Duggan, *Sapphic Slashers: Sex, Violence, and American Modernity* (Durham, NC: Duke University Press, 2000); also see Lisa J. Lindquist, "Images of Alice: Gender, Deviancy, and a Love Murder in Memphis," *Journal of the History of Sexuality* 6, no. 1 (July 1995): 30–61.

13. Parke, *Human Sexuality*, 11–12. Parke himself had been arrested in 1909 on

a complaint of obscenity for sending an earlier edition of *Human Sexuality* through the mail, but no charges were brought; see Theodore Schroeder, *"Obscene" Literature and Constitutional Law: A Forensic Defense of Freedom of the Press* (New York: privately printed, 1911), 71–72.

14. Xavier Mayne [pseudonym of Edward Iranaeus Prime-Stevenson], *The Intersexes: A History of Similisexualism as a Problem in Social Life* (n.pl.: privately printed, n.d.). Note that Prime-Stevenson more or less interchangeably uses a variety of terms as a synonym for *homosexual*, including *intersexual*, *similisexual*, and *uranian*. On the history of the writing and printing of the book, see Mayne, *The Intersexes*, xi, xii; and Edward Prime-Stevenson, letter to Paul Elmer Moore (10–12 March 1906), published in Xavier Mayne, *Imre: A Memorandum*, ed. James J. Gifford (Peterborough, Canada: Broadview Literary Texts, 2003), Appendix A, "On the Origin of *Imre*." Also see James Gifford, "What Became of *The Intersexes*?" *The Gay & Lesbian Review Worldwide* 18, no 5 (September–October 2011), http://www.glreview.org/article/what-became-of-the-intersexes. Most sources give the printing date of *The Intersexes* as 1908, the year indicated at the end of the introduction, but the book clearly was printed no earlier than 1909, as the text refers to events that occurred as late as April of that year; see Mayne, *The Intersexes*, 521, 526.

    Locating exact details on sites closely associated with Prime-Stevenson is no simple task given his peripatetic life and the paucity of biographical information available. One well-documented location is the row house he apparently shared with his mother and sister at 143 East Fifty-Fifth Street between Lexington and Third avenues in the Midtown neighborhood of Manhattan from 1889 or earlier until at least 1893. The lot is now part of the site of an eleven-story co-op block at 139–141 East Fifty-Fifth Street; the Lychee House restaurant at no. 141 is on the ground floor of the lot where the house stood. For Prime-Stevenson's address and years of occupation, see Mayne, *Imre*, Appendix E, "From Life to Fiction," as well as the author's 1889 passport application, National Archives and Records Administration (NARA), Washington, DC, NARA Series: Passport Applications, 1795–1905; Roll # 332: 08 Jun 1889–12 Jun 1889. The 1892 Sanborn map shows 143 East Fifty-Fifth Street as a row house directly adjacent to a Baptist church; see Sanborn-Perris Map Company, *Insurance Maps of the City of New York* (New York: Sanborn-Perris Map Co., 1892): Manhattan, vol. 6, plate 107: New York Public Library Digital Collections, http://digitalcollections.nypl.org/items/94a1adcb-e63b-7f2b-e040-e00a18060d94.

15. On Prime-Stevenson's life, see James J. Gifford, "Introduction" in Mayne, *Imre*, 13–26. Also see Séan Henry, "Mayne, Xavier," in *Who's Who in Gay and Lesbian History from Antiquity to World War II*, ed. Robert Aldrich and Gary Wotherspoon (London: Routledge, 2001), 302–4, and John Lauritsen, "Edward Irenaeus Prime-Stevenson (Xavier Mayne) (1868–1942)," in *Before Stonewall: Activists for Gay and Lesbian Rights in Historical Context*, ed. Vern L. Bullough (Binghamton, N.Y.: Harrington Park Press, 2002), 35–39. Note

that the incorrect year of birth given in Henry and Lauritsen reflects the false year that Prime-Stevenson himself routinely provided in the final decades of his life.

16. See Mayne, *The Intersexes*, in particular chap. 4, "Similisexual Love in the Brute World; in Primitive, Barbarous and Semi-Civilized Man; in Ancient Civilizations and Religions; and under Ancient and Modern Statutory Law" and chap. 7, "The Uranian and the Uraniad in the Military and Naval Careers; in the Athletic Professions, and in Royal, Political and Aristocratic Social Life: Types and Biographies."

17. The only in-depth contemporaneous review of *The Intersexes* I have been able to locate is Eduard Bertz, "Xavier Mayne (Author of 'Imre, a Memorandum'): The Intersexes: A History of Similisexualism as a Problem in Social Life," *Vierteljahresberichte des Wissenshaftlich-humanitären Komitees* 3, no. 1 (October 1911), 78–91. Published in a journal from Magnus Hirschfeld's Scientific-Humanitarian Committee in Berlin, this article sparked a handful of inconsequential subsequent references, including mentions in Hirschfeld's magnum opus, *Die Homosexualität des Mannes und des Weibes* (Berlin: Louis Marcus Verlag, 1914), 11, 1020, and a comment in post-1909 editions of British sexologist Havelock Ellis's *Sexual Inversion* (originally published in England in 1897), where a footnote suggests that Ellis had consulted the Bertz review, but not the book itself. The Ellis reference led to a brief notice in Montgomery Belgion, *Our Present Philosophy of Life* (London: Faber & Faber, [1929]), 195–96, and likely to the citation of Mayne in the definition for the word *intersex* in James A. Murray, *The Oxford English Dictionary: Supplement and Bibliography* (Oxford: Clarendon Press, 1933), 507. *The Intersexes* also received a positive mention of one sentence in the first French literary journal focused on homosexuality: J.A.F. [Jacques d'Adelswärd-Fersen], "P.S. Je tiens à signaler . . . ," *Akademos: revue mensuelle d'art libre et de critique* 12 (1909): 974.

    In the United States, the two-sentence footnoted mention of *The Intersexes* in American editions of Havelock Ellis appears to be the only early reference in print; for an example, see *Studies in the Psychology of Sex*, Vol. 2: *Sexual Inversion* (Philadelphia: F. A. Davis & Company, 1915), 71–72. On the book being offered for sale in New York, see Gifford, "What Happened to The Intersexes?" Gifford notes that a tipped-in label in "a recently discovered copy" identifies the shop, but he does not give the name or address and doesn't state who owns the copy. In an email to the author, 14 June 2017, Gifford indicates that he was unable to locate the details in his research files.

18. Bertz, 78; translated by the author: "Lieder stellen jedoch die Gesetze in England und den Vereinigten Staaten einer solchen Publication unübersteigliche Hindernisse entgegen."

19. Mayne's work first drew significant attention in the United States with a biographical overview in the only scholarly journal of the homophile movement: Noel I. Garde [pseudonym of Edgar Leoni], "The Mysterious Father

of American Homophile Literature: A Historical Study," *One Institute Quarterly: Homophile Studies* 1, no. 3 (Fall 1958): 94–98. Garde devotes only four paragraphs to *The Intersexes*, which he characterizes on page 94 as a "masterwork"; he adds on page 97 that he "will summarize and discuss this encyclopaedic and thought-provoking work in a later article"—but no such publication has been traced. *The Intersexes* subsequently was reprinted in 1975 as part of the Arno Press series "Homosexuality: Lesbians and Gay Men in Society, History, and Literature"; for details on the series, see below, note 88.

20. O. P. Gilbert, *Men in Women's Guise: Some Historical Instances of Female Impersonation*, trans. Robert B. Douglas (New York: Brentano's, 1926); La-Forest Potter, *Strange Loves: A Study in Sexual Abnormalities* (New York: Robert Dodsley, 1933); Dr. Caufeynon, *Unisexual Love: A Documentary Study of the Sources, Manifestations, the Physiology and Psychology of Sexual Perversion in the Two Sexes* (New York: New Era Press, 1934); and Maurice Chideckel, *Female Sex Perversion: The Sexually Aberrated Woman as She Is* (New York: Eugenics Publishing Company, 1935). Although not stated by the publisher, *Unisexual Love* is an adaptation from a French book by a prolific author of trashy fiction and putative nonfiction with sexual themes: Dr. Caufeynon [pseudonym of Jean Fauconney], *L'Homosexualité chez l'homme et chez la femme: physiologie et psychologie de l'inversion sexuelle—étude documentaire sur ses origines et ses manifestations dans les deux sexes* (Paris, France: Librairie Offenstadt, 1909).

21. Mayne, *The Interexes*, 210. I have corrected the typographical errors and nonstandard capitalization that appear in the original text. For the memoirs, see Morris Schaff, *The Spirit of Old West Point, 1858–1862* (Boston: Houghton Mifflin, 1907). The United States Military Academy at West Point was listed on the National Register of Historic Places on 15 October 1966, and designated a National Historic Landmark on 19 December 1960.

22. Field lived in California for the last twenty years of her life; at the time of her death, her address was the Gailmore Apartments, 500 North Glendale Avenue (demolished) in Glendale, a city near Los Angeles; see Darling, "A Critical Introduction," 24. The site is now the location of a Chase Bank branch built in 1965. For the apartment building, see *Glendale City Directory 1928* (Glendale, CA: Glendale Directory Co., 1928), 78; for the bank building, see City of Glendale Property Information Portal website, record for 500 North Glendale Avenue, https://csi.glendaleca.gov/csipropertyportal. Field's publisher, Eyncourt Press, was based in Chicago at 440 South Dearborn Street; see the display ad for *Jonathan Meeker, Pioneer Printer of Kansas* by Douglas McMurtrie, the owner of the press, and Albert H. Allen in *The Rotarian* (August 1930): 52. The site is now a parking lot.

23. Earl Lind [Ralph Werther, Jennie June], *Autobiography of an Androgyne* (New York: Medico-Legal Journal, 1918), and Ralph Werther–Jennie June [Earl Lind], *The Female-Impersonators* (New York: Medico-Legal Journal,

1922); the publisher's office was located in an existing apartment building on West Eighty-Third Street near Central Park in New York City. The identity of the author behind the pseudonyms has not been established; his year of birth can only be estimated based on internal evidence from his books, and his date of death is unknown; see Scott Herring, "Introduction" in Ralph Werther, *Autobiography of an Androgyne*, edited and with an introduction by Scott Herring (New Brunswick, NJ: Rutgers University Press, 2008), xvi. For the complexities of the author's sexuality and gender identity in the context of his times, see Herring, "Introduction," xxiv–xxvi.

24. Herring, "Introduction," xviii, notes that the books by Earl Lind/Ralph Werther/Jennie June were offered by a "small-scale, specialized scientific press 'by mail only.'" He adds that the titles received no reviews and soon vanished from sight; see page x. Both volumes were, however, reprinted in 1975 by Arno Press (New York City) in the "Homosexuality: Lesbians and Gay Men in Society, History, and Literature" series. *The Stone Wall* also had a traceable afterlife. For example, the first nationally circulated lesbian periodical in the United States published a retrospective review three decades after the book appeared: Gene Damon [pseudonym of Barbara Grier], "Books: *The Stonewall: An Autobiography*," *Ladder* 4, no. 8 (May 1960): 18–19. The title also was reprinted in the 1975 Arno Press series.

25. Mayne, *Imre*, 86. James Gifford notes that although the character of Oswald is described as an Englishman, many aspects of his story reflect the experience of Prime-Stevenson himself. See Gifford, "Introduction," in Mayne, *Imre*, 18–20.

26. Mayne, *Imre*, 88–89.

27. Blair Niles, *Strange Brother* (New York: Liveright, 1931). The novel had a long afterlife, with a new hardback edition released in 1949 by Harris; a pocket paperback with lurid cover art published in 1952 by Avon; and a hardback published in the 1975 Arno Press reprint series. All the publishers were based in New York City.

28. Niles, *Strange Brother*, 78. For the used bookstore where Mark Thornton finds *Love's Coming of Age*, the novelist likely had in mind the storefront at 107 East Fifty-Ninth Street near Park Avenue, which had been the bookshop of Edward A. Custer from circa 1900 until his death in 1919. The space remained a bookshop under other owners and names into the mid-1920s at least. Custer's store is described in Bruno Guido, *Adventures in American Bookshops, Antique Stores and Auction Rooms* (Detroit: Douglas Book Shop, 1922), 40–43. The address appears in "Books Wanted," *Publisher's Weekly*, 21 April 1917, 1284. For Custer's death and the years he was in business, see "Old Book Dealer Dies," *Bridgewater Courier News*, 22 May 1919, 7. In 1921, a classified ad shows 107 East Fifty-Ninth Street as the location of Meltzer's Book Store; see "Fair and Liberal Valuation" under "Books Wanted," *New York Times*, 20 November 1921, 55. In 1922, the shop was sold and became a branch of the Empire State Book Co.; see "Business Notes," *Publish-

er's Weekly, 29 July 1922, 419. The shop advertised in the *New York Times* until late 1923; the last appearance was a display ad on page X9 of the 2 September 1923 issue. The site at 107 East Fifty-Ninth Street is now the location of a later multistory building with a leather goods shop in the storefront at number 107.

29. Niles, *Strange Brother*, 299–309, ellipses in the original. The publication dates for the books mentioned in this paragraph are for the American first editions: Edward Carpenter, *Love's Coming of Age* (Chicago: Stockham, 1902); and Havelock Ellis, *Studies in the Psychology of Sex*, 6 vols. (Philadelphia: F.A. Davis, 1900–1905). Presumably the character was reading vol. 2, *Sexual Inversion* (1901).

30. Niles, *Strange Brother*, 234–35. Mark's inspiration was Alain Locke, ed., *The New Negro: An Interpretation* (New York: Albert and Charles Boni, 1925). Locke's home on R Street NW, Washington, DC, is a contributing resource to the Fourteenth Street Historic District, added to the National Register of Historic Places on 9 November 1994.

31. Mayne, *The Intersexes*, 376.

32. Donald Webster Cory [pseudonym of Edward Sagarin], *The Homosexual in America: A Subjective Approach* (New York: Greenberg, 1951), 157, 167. The author likely drew on personal observations of these phenomena going back to the 1930s. On Edward Sagarin, see Gerard Sullivan, "Cory, Donald Webster," in *Who's Who in Contemporary Gay and Lesbian History from World War II to Today*, ed. Robert Aldrich and Gary Wotherspoon (London: Routledge, 2001), 92–93.

33. Jeannette H. Foster, *Sex Variant Women in Literature: A Historical and Quantitative Study* (New York: Vantage Press, 1956); in the unpaginated "Foreword," the author dates the start of her bibliographical search to learning about a student expelled for lesbianism when she was in college (circa 1915). For further details on the incident, see Joanne Ellen Passet, *Sex Variant Woman: The Life of Jeannette Howard Foster* (New York: Da Capo Press, 2008), 44–45. Rockford College is located at 5050 East State Street, Rockford, Illinois. It opened in 1847 as Rockford Female Seminary, becoming Rockford College in 1892 and Rockford University in 2013; see "Our History," Rockford University website (n.d.), https://www.rockford.edu/about/history.

34. On the scope of Foster's research, see Passet, *Sex Variant Woman*, especially pages 121 and 129. As an adult building her collection and researching lesbian literature, Foster spent two periods living with her parents in the home where she had grown up: in 1922–23 while studying for her master's degree, and in 1933–34 as a doctoral student; see Passet, *Sex Variant Woman*, 16, 68–75, 114–17. Located on Pleasant Avenue in the Beverly neighborhood of Chicago, Illinois, the house is extant, although a comparison with the 1906 photograph reproduced in Passet, *Sex Variant Woman*, 16, shows that it has undergone extensive modifications, notably with an addition including a garage constructed on one side of the house in 2016.

35. Marion Zimmer Bradley, "Variant Women in Literature," *Ladder* 1, no. 8 (May 1956): 8–10, observes that Foster was reduced to publishing through a vanity press due to trade publishers' refusal to take on serious books of limited interest. Also see Marcia M. Gallo, *Different Daughters: A History of the Daughters of Bilitis and the Rise of the Lesbian Rights Movement* (New York: Carroll & Graf, 2006), 38. On the postwar anti-homosexual panic, see David K. Johnson, *The Lavender Scare: The Cold War Persecution of Gays and Lesbians in the Federal Government* (Chicago: University of Chicago Press, 2004).

36. For example, Gallo, *Different Daughters*, 37–38, notes Foster's influence on the bibliographical efforts of Marion Zimmer Bradley. For an instance from the subsequent generation of lesbian scholars, see note 58 below.

37. A fairly extensive scholarly literature has been produced on the politics and organizational strategies of the homophile period. For a founding study in the field, see John D'Emilio, *Sexual Politics, Sexual Communities: The Making of a Homosexual Minority in the United States, 1940–1970* (Chicago: University of Chicago Press, 1983). For monographs on individual organizations, see Gallo, *Different Daughters*, which focuses on the Daughters of Bilitis; James T. Sears, *Behind the Mask of Mattachine: The Hal Call Chronicles and the Early Movement for Homosexual Emancipation* (Binghamton, NY: Harrington Park Press, 2006); and C. Todd White, *Pre-Gay L.A.: A Social History of the Movement for Homosexual Rights* (Urbana: University of Illinois Press, 2009), which focuses on One Incorporated.

38. Sites associated with the periodicals include the Williams Building at 693 Mission Street in San Francisco, where the Mattachine Society rented offices for most of its existence and where the Daughters of Bilitis shared the space starting early in 1957 before moving in 1958 to its own office in the Department Store Center Building at 165 O'Farrell Street in San Francisco; the Williams Building also housed the Pan-Graphic Press, a small-press publishing and offset printing firm established by Mattachine members that printed the *Mattachine Review* and the *Ladder*. For the Mattachine Society, 693 Mission Street appears for the first time in "Mattachine Review: Where to Buy It," *Mattachine Review* 1, no. 5 (September–October 1955): 35; it remained the address through the final issue, "Organizational Directory," *Mattachine Review* 11, no. 1 (July 1966): 14–15. For Pan-Graphic Press, see Hal Call, "Mattachine Review" in *Homosexuals Today 1956*, ed. Marvin Cutler [pseudonym of W. Dorr Legg] (Los Angeles: One Incorporated, 1956), 58–60. For DOB, see the masthead of the *Ladder* 1, no. 5 (February 1957), which gives the address as 693 Mission Street for the first time; for the move to 165 O'Farrell St., see Del Martin, "We've Moved," *Ladder* 2, no. 6 (March 1958): 4–5. For sites associated with *One*, see notes 48 and 54 below.

39. The homophile movement's use of history has yet to receive in-depth scholarly attention; the discussion here is based largely on the author's review of the organizations' periodicals. Also note that the first documented

homosexual advocacy group in the United States was the Society for Human Rights in Chicago in 1924–25. It published two newsletter issues, but no copies are known to survive; a few paragraphs of content preserved in French translation make no mention of historical topics. See Clarens, "Friendship and Freedom," *L'Amité*, no. 1 (April 1925): 13, posted at Séminaire Gay, http://semgai.free.fr/doc_et_pdf/L_amitie.pdf. The article also is available in reprint in Lucien Mirande, *Inversions 1924–1925, L'Amitié 1925: Deux revues homosexuelles françaises* (Lille, France: GayKitschCamp, 2006), 228–29. The Society for Human Rights operated out of the rooming house where Henry Gerber lived in the Old Town Triangle neighborhood of Chicago, Illinois. It was designated a National Historic Landmark on 19 June 2015; see Diana Novak Jones, "Old Town Site of Nation's First Gay Rights Group Designated National Landmark," *Chicago Sun-Times*, 19 June 2015, http://chicago.suntimes.com/news/7/71/705597/old-town-site-nations-first-gay-rights-group-designated-national-landmark.

40. D'Emilio, *Sexual Politics, Sexual Communities*, 110.
41. D'Emilio, *Sexual Politics, Sexual Communities*, 111.
42. The only article mentioning recognition of an LGBTQ historic site recorded in my survey of national homophile journals suggests how fraught the topic could be: an article reprinted from the Canadian weekly *Macleans* describes London celebrations in 1954 marking the centenary of Oscar Wilde's birth. Reporting on the unveiling of a plaque at Wilde's former home identifying him as a "dramatist and wit," the text also disparages homosexuality as a "crime or disease" and a "dreadful cult." For the author of the article, Wilde merits a historic site as a great writer, yet still deserves nothing but scorn as a homosexual. See Beverly Baxter, "London Letter: Has Oscar Wilde's Crime Been Redeemed?" *Mattachine Review* 1, no. 4 (July–August 1955): 22–25.
43. See the following, all in the *Mattachine Review:* Mack Fingal, "Hadrian and Antinous: The Love-Life of an Emperor," 1, no. 6 (November–December 1956): 21–22; "Books: *Sex in History* by G. Rattray Taylor," 3, no. 3 (March 1957): 8–10; Omer C. Stewart, "Homosexuality among American Indians and Other Native Peoples of the World," 6, no. 1 (January 1960): 9–15, and 6, no. 2 (February 1960): 13–18; "Mattachine Society Inc.: First Decade, 1950–1960," 6, no. 4 (April 1960): 2, 26–30; and Joseph Charles Salak, "Civil War Heroine," 6, no. 11 (November 1960): 5–6. Apparently none of the authors were professional historians, but one was an academic: Omer C. Stewart was a professor of anthropology at the University of Colorado; see "Mattachine Breaks through the Conspiracy of Silence," *Ladder* 4, no. 1 (October 1958): 18.
44. See D'Emilio, *Sexual Politics, Sexual Communities*, 111. For the first installment of the bibliography, see "Bibliography of Books on the Homosexual (and Related) Subjects," *Mattachine Review* 3, no. 8 (August 1957): 24–29.
45. See the following, all in the *Ladder:* Gene Damon, "Radclyffe Hall," 3, no. 3 (December 1958): 8–9; Gene Damon and Lee Stuart, "Transvestism in

Women," 3, no. 5 (February 1959): 11–13; LauraJean Ermayne, "The Sapphic Cinema," 4, no. 7 (April 1960): 5–9; and David Hamblen, "Lesbianism and the Law," 5, no. 2 (November 1960): 6–9.

46. See Gallo, *Different Daughters*, 36–37. The first installment of "Lesbiana" ran in the *Ladder* 1, no. 6 (March 1957): 12. It included reviews of a 1955 edition of the collected works of Pierre Louÿs, the French poet whose *Songs of Bilitis* (1894; English translation 1926) inspired the name of the Daughters of Bilitis; Radclyffe Hall's *The Well of Loneliness* (1928); and a new edition of a "long out-of-print classic," Colette's *Claudine at School* (1900; English translation 1930). "Lesbiana" continued appearing regularly through the end of the run. For reprints of the columns from the final six years of the magazine, see Barbara Grier, also known as Gene Damon, *Lesbiana: Book Reviews from The Ladder, 1966–1972* (Reno, NV: Naiad Press, 1976).

47. In the case of *One*, the count is less clear than for the *Mattachine Review* and the *Ladder* for two reasons: the run on microfilm from the New York Public Library consulted by the author lacks scattered issues, so an article or two may be missing; in addition, the editors of the publication tended to run think-piece essays that draw only in passing on historical evidence and arguments, so determining which to count as substantial history articles is a somewhat subjective matter.

48. "One Institute of Homophile Studies," *One Institute Quarterly: Homophile Studies* 1, no. 1 (Spring 1958): inside front cover. Classes were held at the offices of One Incorporated, located at 232 South Hill Street in downtown Los Angeles from 1953 to 1962, then at 2256 Venice Boulevard in the Arlington Heights neighborhood from 1962 to 1983; see "History," One Archives at the USC Libraries website, http://one.usc.edu/about/history. The Hill Street building no longer exists. The Venice Boulevard structure is extant and is listed as a "known resource" in GPA Consulting, Carson Anderson, and Wes Joe, *SurveyLA: LGBT Historic Context Statement* (Los Angeles: Office of Historic Resources, Department of City Planning, City of Los Angeles, 2014), 30.

49. See W. Dorr Legg, *Homophile Studies in Theory and Practice* (Los Angeles: One Institute Press & San Francisco: GLB Publishers, 1994), 27, note 15. For an example of Hay's ethnohistorical analysis that provided a basis for his work with the One Institute, see Harry Hay, "The Homosexual and History: An Invitation to Further Study," in *Radically Gay: Gay Liberation in the Words of Its Founder*, ed. Will Roscoe (Boston: Beacon Press, 1996), 94–119; written in 1953, the essay draws on talks Hay had presented at a Mattachine Society discussion group in 1952–53. In his introduction to the text, Roscoe, pages 92–93, provides a brief assessment of the sources of Hay's historiography.

50. See White, *Pre-Gay L.A.*, chap. 4, "The Establishment of One Institute." As White notes on page 74, a report prepared by One Incorporated that led up to the founding of the institute underscored the failure of higher education to address the subject of homosexuality with the exception of approaches involving "medical, psychoanalytic, and other biases." On the early history

classes at the institute, see Legg, *Homophile Studies*, 27–28, 31–32, and chap. 5, "Homosexuality in History."

51. Jim Kepner, "Editorial," *One Institute Quarterly: Homophile Studies* 1, no. 1 (Spring 1958): 3.

52. Only one academic was involved in the early years of the One Institute for Homophile Studies: Merritt Thompson (under the pseudonym Thomas R. Merritt), an emeritus dean of the School of Education at the University of Southern California; see White, *Pre-Gay L.A.*, 74–76. The leader of the institute, W. Dorr Legg, had bachelor's degrees in landscape architecture and music from the University of Michigan, Ann Arbor, and had briefly taught at the State University of Oregon, Eugene; see Wayne R. Dynes, "Legg, W. Dorr (1904–94)," in *Who's Who in Contemporary Gay and Lesbian History from World War II to Today*, ed. Aldrich and Wotherspoon, 244–45.

53. For examples, see Harry Benjamin, "Transvestism and Transsexualism," *One Institute Quarterly: Homophile Studies* 1, no. 3 (Fall 1958): 102–4, written by an endocrinologist; and Virginia Arman, "Some Facts about Lesbians: Introduction," *One Institute Quarterly: Homophile Studies* 2, no. 4 (Fall 1959): 111–12, written by a psychologist.

54. See "History," One Archives. On the authorization to grant degrees, also see White, *Pre-Gay L.A.*, 206. In its final years from 1983 to 1994, One Incorporated was based at the Millbank Estate, a large villa in the Arlington Heights neighborhood of Los Angeles. The only Ph.D. awarded to a student in the institute's program went to Michael Lombardi for his German history dissertation, "The Translation of the Works by Karl Heinrich Ulrichs with Special Emphasis on Research on *The Riddle of Man-Manly Love*," Ph.D. diss., One Institute for Homophile Studies, 1984; see Michael Lombardi-Nash, email to the author, 10 June 2015. Lombardi-Nash went on to publish translations of foundational documents in LGBTQ studies, including Karl-Heinrich Ulrichs, *The Riddle of Man-Manly Love: The Pioneering Work on Male Homosexuality* (Buffalo, NY: Prometheus Books, 1994); and Magnus Hirschfeld, *The Homosexuality of Men and Women* (Amherst, NY: Prometheus Books, 2000).

55. The scholarly literature on the gay liberation and lesbian-feminist movements is considerable. For an overview, see Marc Stein, *Rethinking the Gay and Lesbian Movement* (New York: Routledge, 2012), chap. 3–4.

56. Susan Ferentinos notes the link between identity politics and interest in community history in this period; see her book *Interpreting LGBT History at Museums and Historic Sites* (Lanham, MD: Rowman & Littlefield, 2015), 22.

57. Gayle Rubin comments on the gaps and links in the production of "queer knowledge" between the homophile and gay liberation eras in "Geologies of Queer Studies: It's Déjà Vu All Over Again," in Gayle S. Rubin, ed., *Deviations: A Gayle Rubin Reader* (Durham, NC: Duke University Press, 2011), 347–49. Also see "Sexual Traffic: Interview with Gayle Rubin by Judith Butler," in ibid., 301–2.

58. For instance, Gayle Rubin describes her delight when discovering around 1970 that lesbian bibliographies already existed from the homophile period; see "Geologies of Queer Studies," in Rubin, *Deviations*, 348–49. Both the Daughters of Bilitis and DOB member Marion Zimmer Bradley had published such bibliographies as stand-alone publications in the years from 1958 to 1967; see Maida Tilchen, "The Legendary Lesbian Treasure Map," in *The Lesbian in Literature*, ed. Barbara Grier (Tallahassee, FL: Naiad Press, 1981), xi–xii. For a bibliography focused on male homosexuality by an author who was associated with the One Institute, see Noel I. Garde [pseudonym of Edgar Leoni], *The Homosexual in Literature: A Chronological Bibliography, Circa 700 B.C.–1958* (New York: Village Books, 1959).

59. See Cait McKinney, "'Finding the Lines to My People': Media History and the Queer Bibliographic Encounter," *GLQ* 24, no. 1 (January 2018): 55–83; citation pages 56–58.

60. Jeffrey Escoffier, *American Homo: Community and Perversity* (Berkeley: University of California Press, 1998), 110.

61. On uses of lesbian and gay history in the context of political debates in the 1980s, see Escoffier, *American Homo*, 169–70.

62. See Gerard Koskovich, "Libraries and Archives," in *LGBTQ America Today: An Encyclopedia*, vol. 2, ed. John C. Hawley (Westport, CT: Greenwood Press, 2009), 684–92. On the One Incorporated library, also see Leslie Colfax, "Library," in *Homosexuals Today 1956*, ed. Marvin Cutler [pseudonym of W. Dorr Legg] (Los Angeles: One Incorporated, 1956), 83–84; and White, *Pre-Gay L.A.*, 78.

63. See *The Kinsey Institute for Research in Sex, Gender, and Reproduction* (Bloomington, IN: Kinsey Institute, 1984), especially pages 19–21. Also see Judith A. Allen, Hallimeda E. Allison, Andrew Clark Huckstep, et al., *The Kinsey Institute: The First Seventy Years* (Bloomington, IN: Well House Books, 2017). The Institute has been located on the Indiana University campus in Bloomington, Indiana, since its founding: in Biology Hall (Swain Hall East) from 1947 to 1950, in Wylie Hall from 1950 to 1955, in Jordan Hall from 1955 to 1967, and subsequently in Morrison Hall. See "The Kinsey Institute: Chronology of Events and Landmark Publications," The Kinsey Institute website, archived at https://web.archive.org/web/20160304161639/http://www.kinseyinstitute.org/about/chronology.html. Wylie Hall was listed on the National Register of Historic Places as part of the Old Crescent Historic District on 8 September 1980.

64. See Tim Retzloff, "Edward Weber, Retired Labadie Collection Curator at U of M, Dies at 83," *Pride Source*, 20 April 2006, http://www.pridesource.com/article.html?article=18419. Also see Rubin, *Deviations*, 15–16. The Labadie Collection is housed in the Harlan Hatcher Graduate Library at 913 South University Avenue on the University of Michigan campus in Ann Arbor. From the construction of the library in 1920 until 1970, the collection was

located in the original building, now known as the North Building; in 1970, Ed Weber oversaw the move to its current home in the Special Collections Library in the then-new South Building. See Julie Herrada, curator, Joseph A. Labadie Collection, email to the author, 19 June 2015.

65. Ann Cvetkovich, *An Archive of Feelings: Trauma, Sexuality and Lesbian Public Cultures* (Durham, NC: Duke University Press, 2003), 241.

66. On the founding, see "Lesbian Herstory Archives: History and Mission," Lesbian Herstory Archives website, http://www.lesbianherstoryarchives.org/history.html; on Nestle's self-definition, see Joan Nestle, *A Fragile Union: New and Collected Writings* (San Francisco: Cleis Press, 1998), "Introduction." posted on JoanNestle.com, July 1998, http://www.joannestle.com/fragileu.html. For a history of the institution through the late 1990s, see Polly J. Thistlethwaite, "Building 'A Home of Our Own': The Construction of the Lesbian Herstory Archives," in *Daring to Find Our Names: The Search for Lesbigay Library History*, ed. James V. Carmichael Jr. (Westport, CT: Greenwood Press, 1998), 153–73.

67. Lesbian Herstory Archives, "Lesbian Herstory Archives: History and Mission." Julia Stanley (1941–2013) was better known as Julia Penelope, an early openly lesbian academic and a lesbian-separatist author and theorist; see Tracy Baim, "Passages: Author Julia Penelope Dead at 71," *Windy City Times*, 24 January 2013, http://www.windycitymediagroup.com/lgbt/PASSAGES-Author-Julia-Penelope-dead-at-71/41298.html.

68. The LHA purchased the brownstone, where it is still located at 484 Fourteenth Street in the Park Slope Historic District of Brooklyn, in 1990 and opened to the public there in 1993. See Lesbian Herstory Archives, "Lesbian Herstory Archives: History and Mission." According to Deborah Edel, the collection was moved from Nestle's apartment in the first half of 1992; email from Edel to the author, 15 June 2015. Thistlethwaite, "Building 'A Home of Our Own,'" 155, likewise dates the move to 1992. The Park Slope Historic District was listed on the National Register of Historic Places on 21 November 1980.

69. Joan Nestle, emails to the author, 22 May 2015 and 8 June 2015. For an overview of Hampton's life, see Joan Nestle, "I Lift My Eyes to the Hill: The Life of Mabel Hampton," published in *A Fragile Union* (1998) and as a seven-part series on the author's blog, *Don't Stop Talking 2*, 27 October 2011, http://joannestle2.blogspot.com/2011/10/in-memory-on-october-26-i-lift-my-eyes.html.

70. Thistlethwhaite, "Building 'A Home of Our Own,'" 161.

71. On the Western Gay Archives and its transformation into the National Gay Archives, see James Kepner, "An Accidental Institution: How and Why a Gay and Lesbian Archives?" in *Daring to Find Our Names*, ed. Carmichael, 179. Also see One Archives, "History"; this page gives 1971 as the year in the introduction and 1975 in the chronological timeline that follows. White, *Pre-Gay L.A.*, 78 and 202, gives the year as 1975. For a brief summary of Kepner's

life, see One National Gay and Lesbian Archives, "Finding Aid of the Jim Kepner Papers, Coll. 2011.002," http://www.oac.cdlib.org/findaid/ark:/13030/kt8d5nf4c6/admin. The National Gay Archives storefront was located at 1654 North Hudson Avenue in Hollywood (demolished) from 1979 to 1988; see One Archives, "History."

72. Notably, Kepner reported that early purchases for his collection starting in 1942 included both nonfiction and fiction and books dealing with both gay and lesbian themes. See Kepner, "An Accidental Institution," 176.

73. See One Archives, "History."

74. A precise count of the community-based archives created during this period is difficult to establish, as many were small, local, and ephemeral, with collections that ultimately merged with those of larger organizations or were placed at university libraries or general historical societies; see "Introduction," in Lesbian and Gay Archives Roundtable, "Lavender Legacies Guide" (updated 2012), Society of American Archivists website, http://www2.archivists.org/groups/lesbian-and-gay-archives-roundtable-lagar/lavender-legacies-guide-introduction.

75. On the Gerber/Hart Library, see Michael McCaslin, "A Brief History of Gerber/Hart Library," *Illinois Libraries* 81, no. 4 (Fall 1999): 228–31; posted on Illinois Periodicals Online, http://www.lib.niu.edu/1999/il9904228.html; the article notes that Gerber/Hart's first location was in the offices of Gay Horizon at 3225 North Sheffield Avenue, Chicago, Illinois. On the Gay and Lesbian Historical Society (now known as the GLBT Historical Society), see Gerard Koskovich, "Displaying the Queer Past: Purposes, Publics, and Possibilities at the GLBT History Museum," *QED: A Journal in GLBTQ Worldmaking* 1, no. 2 (2014): 61–78; the article indicates that the society's collections initially were housed in the apartment of cofounder Willie Walker on Seventeenth Street near Sanchez Street in San Francisco's Castro District.

76. On the Quatrefoil Library, see Adam G. Keim, *History of the Quatrefoil Library* (Golden Valley, MN: Friends of the Bill of Rights Foundation, 2009), posted on the library's website, http://www.qlibrary.org/wordpress/wp-content/uploads/2014/04/QUATRE_FINAL_E-BOOK.pdf; Keim notes that the library was housed from its founding until 1986 in Irwin and Hewetson's condominium on Grand Avenue near Dale Street in St. Paul, Minnesota. On the Stonewall Library (now known as the Stonewall National Museum and Archives), see "About Us: History," Stonewall National Museum and Archives website, http://www.stonewall-museum.org/about-us/history. The Stonewall Library collections initially were located in founder Mark Silber's house on Jefferson Street near South Sixteenth Avenue in Hollywood, Florida; see David Jobin, executive director, Stonewall National Museum and Archives, email to the author, 19 May 2015.

77. For a brief discussion of gaps in LGBT archives and the systems that produce them, see Amy L. Stone and Jamie Cantrell, eds, *Out of the Closet, Into*

the Archives: Researching Sexual Histories (Albany: State University of New York Press, 2015): 8–9.

78. See Dallas Denny, emails to the author 25 May 2015, 11 June 2015, and 13 June 2015. Also see the catalog record for the holdings at the University of Michigan Library website, http://mirlyn.lib.umich.edu/Record/00436 6562. According to Denny, the collection was located in her home on Chisholm Court in Tucker, Georgia, from 1991 until it was transferred to the University of Michigan.

79. See "About Us: Our History" and "Historical Archive," Latino GLBT History Project website, http://www.latinoglbthistory.org. The collections have been housed in Gutierrez's apartment on S Street NW at the corner of Seventeenth Street in Washington, DC, since he began gathering the materials; José Gutierrez, message to the author, 26 October 2015.

80. For a discussion of the efforts of lesbian and gay independent scholars in this period, see Escoffier, American Homo, 104–10.

81. Ferentinos, Interpreting LGBT History, 22.

82. See Jim Downs, Stand by Me: The Forgotten History of Gay Liberation (New York: Basic Books, 2016), chap. 4, "Gay American History." On the Bobst Library, see Jonathan Ned Katz, email to the author, 22 May 2015. On the cultural and intellectual significance of Katz's work in the 1970s, see Escoffier, American Homo, 109, 126–27.

83. See Downs, Stand by Me, 92–95. Also see John D'Emilio, private Facebook message to the author, 12 June 2017. In contrast to the meeting details given in Downs, D'Emilio recalls that the Gay Socialist Action Project gatherings took place only occasionally at his apartment; he adds that Katz also frequented the weekly dinners that he and his housemate hosted for forty or more gay men on Saturday evenings throughout this period. D'Emilio notes that his apartment was located at 400 Riverside Drive at the corner of West 112th Street.

84. Jonathan Ned Katz, email to the author, 7 May 2015. Also see Jonathan Katz, Coming Out! A Documentary Play about Gay Life and Liberation in the U.S.A. (New York: Arno Press, 1975), which includes an introduction by the author recounting the productions of the play, along with a selection of reviews and news coverage, and Jonathan Ned Katz, "Recalling My Play 'Coming Out!' June 1972," OutHistory.org, last modified 3 September 2013, http://outhistory.org/oldwiki/Jonathan_Ned_Katz,_Recalling_My_Play_ "Coming_Out!"_June_1972; and Downs, Stand by Me, 101–9. These sources note that Coming Out! was first presented at the Gay Activist Alliance Firehouse at 99 Wooster Street. The building now houses a watch store on the ground floor. It is located in the SoHo-Cast Iron Historic District, listed on the National Register of Historic Places and designated a National Historic Landmark on 29 June 1978.

85. Jonathan Ned Katz, email to the author, 22 May 2015.

86. Jonathan Katz, *Gay American History: Lesbians and Gay Men in the U.S.A.—A Documentary* (New York: Thomas Y. Crowell Company, 1976).

87. Katz's analysis of sexual and gender variation among Native Americans and among "passing women" (individuals assigned female at birth who lived part or all of their adult lives as men) later attracted comments from authors and activists who faulted what they saw as his focus on same-sex erotic and romantic contacts supposedly presaging modern gay and lesbian identities. The critics qualified this approach as an erasure of transgender historical experience. For an example, see Pat Califia, *Sex Changes: The Politics of Transgenderism* (San Francisco: Cleis Press, 1997), chap. 4, "The Berdache Wars and 'Passing Women' Follies: Transphobia in Gay Academia." Katz's work certainly was a reflection of its time: in the first half of the 1970s when he was researching and writing *Gay American History*, transgender visibility, politics, and theory had not yet taken the form they would develop more than two decades later.

88. See Escoffier, *American Homo*, 109. Also see the preliminary announcement for the series, which was subsequently expanded to include additional titles: *Homosexuality: Lesbians and Gay Men in Society, History, and Literature. A Collection of 54 Books and 2 Periodicals. First Announcement* (New York: Arno Press, 1975). In addition to Katz as general editor, the editorial board consisted of two university professors, Louis Crompton of the University of Nebraska, Lincoln, and Dolores Noll of Kent State University; a graduate student at Cornell University, James Steakley, who went on to a career as a professor at the University of Wisconsin, Madison; and another independent scholar who was a veteran of the homophile movement, Barbara Gittings.

89. On the lack of welcome for lesbian and gay history—and for lesbian and gay studies in general—in universities in the 1970s, see Escoffier, *American Homo*, 104–10. For an overview of the production of doctoral dissertations on LGBTQ history, see "Dissertations and Theses," Committee on Lesbian, Gay, Bisexual and Transgender History website, http://clgbthistory.org/resources/dissertations.

90. For the development of careers in the field, see Marc Stein, "Committee on Lesbian and Gay History Survey on LGBTQ History Careers," Committee on Lesbian, Gay, Bisexual and Transgender History website, June 2001, http://clgbthistory.org/resources/reports/lgbtq-history-careers.

91. See "Blood under the Bridge: Reflections on 'Thinking Sex,'" in Rubin, *Deviations*, 198. Brenda Marston reports that such obstacles continued into the next decade: when she was a graduate student hoping to study lesbian history at the University of Wisconsin, Madison, in the early 1980s, an advisor told her, "It will ruin your career." See Brenda Marston, "Archivists, Activists, and Scholars: Creating a Queer History," in *Daring to Find Our Names*, ed. Carmichael, 137.

92. Committee on Lesbian, Gay, Bisexual and Transgender History, "Dissertations and Theses"; John D'Emilio, "Out of the Shadows: The Homosexual Emancipation Movement in the United States," Ph.D. diss., Columbia University, 1982; Lombardi, "The Translation of the Works by Karl Heinrich Ulrichs," 1984; George Chauncey, "Gay New York: Urban Culture and the Making of the Gay Male World, 1890–1940," Ph.D. diss., Yale University, 1989.

93. On Norton's graduate school experiences, see Rictor Norton, emails to the author, 3 June 2015 and 4 June 2015.

94. Rictor Norton, "The Homosexual Literary Tradition: An Interpretation," Ph.D. diss., Florida State University, Tallahassee, 1972; the dissertation formed the basis for Norton's book *The Homosexual Literary Tradition: An Interpretation* (New York: Revisionist Press, 1974). Norton notes that he spent much of his time as a grad student at FSU's Strozier Library, located on campus at 116 Honors Way, Tallahassee, Florida; Norton, email to the author, 4 June 2015.

95. For a brief biography of Norton, a list of his publications, and links to many of his articles, see Gay History & Literature: Essays by Rictor Norton, updated 13 August 2017, http://rictornorton.co.uk.

96. Salvatore John Licata, "Gay Power: A History of the American Gay Movement, 1908–1974," Ph.D. diss., University of Southern California, 1978.

97. See "Schedule of Classes and Registration Instructions, Spring Semester 1976," *Bulletin of the University of Southern California* 71, no. 9 (15 November 1975): 30. The course was held in Room 206 of Waite Phillips Hall of Education at 3470 University Avenue (now Trousdale Parkway) on the USC campus; for the building, see "Schedule of Classes and Registration Instructions," 2. Currently known as Phillips Hall, the structure remains in use as the home of USC's Rossier School of Education.

98. See "Salvatore J. Licata: Helped Found Gay Academic Union," *Los Angeles Times*, 12 January 1990, A30, and "Salvatore J. Licata, 50, an Educator on AIDS," *New York Times*, 4 January 1990, http://www.nytimes.com/1990/01/04/obituaries/salvatore-j-licata-50-an-educator-on-aids.html. Also see Sarah Schulman, "ACT UP Oral History Project: Interview of Amy Bauer" (New York: New York Lesbian & Gay Experimental Film Festival, 7 March 2004), 2, http://www.actuporalhistory.org/interviews/images/bauer.pdf.

99. Ramón A. Gutiérrez, email to the author, 15 June 2015.

100. Ramón A. Gutiérrez, "Marriage, Sex, and the Family: Social Change in Colonial New Mexico, 1690–1846," Ph.D. diss., University of Wisconsin, Madison, 1980. The dissertation formed the basis for a subsequent book: Ramón A. Gutiérrez, *When Jesus Came, the Corn Mothers Went Away: Marriage, Sexuality, and Power in New Mexico, 1500–1846* (Stanford, CA: Stanford University Press, 1991). While working on his dissertation, Gutiérrez spent nine months in 1979–1980 conducting research at the New Mexico State

Records Center and Archives, then located in a former post office at 404 Montezuma Avenue in Santa Fe; Ramón A. Gutiérrez, email to the author, 15 June 2015. The structure is extant and apparently is still owned by the State of New Mexico, but no longer houses the Records Center and Archives.

101. Ramón Gutiérrez, "Must We Deracinate Indians to Find Gay Roots?" *OUT/LOOK* 1, no. 4 (Winter 1989): 61– 67. See note 6 for further sources documenting the development of LGBTQ historiography.

102. See the faculty homepage of Ramón A. Gutiérrez, University of Chicago website, https://history.uchicago.edu/directory/ramón-gutiérrez.

103. Kennedy was a professor of women's studies at the State University of New York, Buffalo; Davis was a librarian and lesbian activist who had returned to school to obtain a master's degree but did not pursue an academic career; Michelson had received a master's in American studies in 1976 but went on to work as an archivist. On Kennedy and Davis and on the Buffalo Women's Oral History Project in general, see Elizabeth Lapovsky Kennedy and Madeline D. Davis, *Boots of Leather, Slippers of Gold: The History of a Lesbian Community* (New York: Routledge, 1993), xvi; and Elizabeth Lapovsky Kennedy, email to the author, 20 July 2015. On Michelson's training and career, see Avra Michelson, "Description and Reference in the Age of Automation," *American Archivist* 50 (Spring 1987): 192. Kennedy lived in a rambling shingled house on a corner lot in the 300 block of Bryant Street in Buffalo at the time; see Kennedy, email to the author, 15 June 2015. The structure is extant. Other sites associated with the project remain to be identified.

104. Edwards went on to work as a musician, editor, and legal assistant; see Kennedy and Davis, *Boots of Leather, Slippers of Gold*, xvi, and "Wanda D. Edwards, Musician, Artist," *Buffalo News*, 22 December 1995, A12.

105. Kennedy and Davis, *Boots of Leather, Slippers of Gold*, xvi.

106. See "Blood under the Bridge," in Rubin, *Deviations*, 199–200; and John D'Emilio and Estelle B. Freedman, "Allan Bérubé and the Power of Community History," in *My Desire for History*, ed. D'Emilio and Freedman, 10–12. For the date the project was founded, see "San Francisco Gay History Project," typescript funding proposal (1978), 1; GLBT Historical Society (San Francisco), San Francisco Lesbian and Gay History Project Records (collection no. 1988-05), box 1, folder 1: "SFGHP Project Proposal 1978." Published sources based on the authors' recollections, by contrast, variously give the year as 1978 or 1979; see Rubin, *Deviations*, 362, note 57, and Escoffier, *American Homo*, 169. Note that the group originally called itself the San Francisco Gay History Project; the name was changed to add the word "lesbian" sometime between 1 June 1979 and 4 March 1980; see the dated promotional materials in GLBT Historical Society (San Francisco), San Francisco Lesbian and Gay History Project Papers (collection no. 1988-05), box 1, folder 2: "Publicity: Flyers, Articles, Events."

107. Bérubé's apartment was located on Lyon Street just south of the Panhandle of Golden Gate Park (extant); see GLBT Historical Society (San Francisco), Allan Bérubé Papers (collection no. 1995-17), box 1, folder 7: "125 Lyon Street Apartment Papers." The first public program sponsored by the project was a presentation of the slide show "Lesbian Masquerade" on 21 June 1979 at the Women's Building of San Francisco, located at 3543 Eighteenth Street in the Mission District (extant). See "Dear Friends," promotional letter signed by Amber Hollibaugh and Allan Bérubé (1 June 1979); GLBT Historical Society (San Francisco), San Francisco Lesbian and Gay History Project Papers (collection no. 1988-05), box 1, folder 2: "Publicity: Flyers, Articles, Events."

108. D'Emilio and Freedman, eds, *My Desire for History*, 10–11.

109. For examples of the members' work, see Allan Bérubé, *Coming Out under Fire: The History of Gay Men and Women in World War Two* (New York: Free Press, 1990); Rob Epstein, dir., *The Times of Harvey Milk* (Black Sand Productions, 1984); Jeffrey Escoffier, *Bigger than Life: The History of Gay Porn Cinema from Beefcake to Hardcore* (Philadelphia: Running Press, 2009); Eric Garber and Lynn Paleo, *Uranian Worlds: A Guide to Alternative Sexuality in Science Fiction, Fantasy, and Horror* (Boston: G.K. Hall, 1990); and Amber Hollibaugh, *My Dangerous Desires: A Queer Girl Dreaming Her Way Home* (Durham, NC: Duke University Press, 2000).

110. On the sites database, see Damon Scott, interview with the author, 19 May 2015. Scott indicates that Garber and Walker passed the database along to the GLBT Historical Society, where Scott himself later incorporated further data, including sites identified by Elizabeth A. Armstrong in research for her book *Forging Gay Identities: Organizing Sexuality in San Francisco, 1950–1994* (Chicago: University of Chicago Press, 2002). The database is now available to researchers at the society's reading room in San Francisco.

111. See Diana Kiyo Wakimoto, "Queer Community Archives in California since 1950," Ph.D. diss., Queensland University of Technology, Brisbane, Australia, 2012, 93–94. Also see Wyatt Buchanan, "Willie Walker: Archivist for the Bay Area Gay Community," *San Francisco Chronicle*, 22 October 2004, http://www.sfgate.com/bayarea/article/Willie-Walker-archivist-for-Bay-Area-gay-2679957.php. Note that the obituary erroneously refers to the San Francisco Lesbian and Gay History Project as the "San Francisco History Project." On the GLBT Historical Society and its GLBT History Museum, see Koskovich, "Displaying the Queer Past"; Don Romesburg, "Presenting the Queer Past: A Case for the GLBT History Museum," *Radical History Review* 120 (2014): 131–44; and Jennifer Tyburczy, *Sex Museums: The Politics and Performance of Display* (Chicago: University of Chicago Press, 2016), 115–24.

112. See D'Emilio's curriculum vitae, posted on his emeritus faculty page on the University of Chicago website, http://hist.uic.edu/history/people/emeriti/john-d'emilio.

113. See "Curriculum Vitae: Estelle B. Freeedman," Stanford History Department website, http://ebf.stanford.edu/cv.html; and Nancy Williams, "Estelle Freedman Wins Long Battle for Tenure," *Stanford Daily* 184, no. 1 (26 September 1983): 1, 15; http://stanforddailyarchive.com/cgi-bin/stanford?a=d&d=stanford19830926-01.2.3.

114. Gayle Rubin, email to the author, 2 February 2016; and Rubin curriculum vitae, 15 November 2015, copy in possession of the author.

115. For research, see Committee on Lesbian, Gay, Bisexual, and Transgender History, "Dissertations and Theses." For a sampling of LGBTQ history courses offered at more than fifty institutions of higher education in the United States from 1997 to 2016, see "Syllabi," Committee on LGBT History website, http://clgbthistory.org/resources/syllabi. For the growth of LGBT special collections and archival holdings in academic libraries, see Stone and Cantrell, eds, *Out of the Closet*, 7; also see Lesbian and Gay Archives Roundtable, "Lavender Legacies Guide."

116. Committee on Lesbian, Gay, Bisexual, and Transgender History, "Dissertations and Theses." The totals exclude dissertations produced at institutions outside the United States. Although Ramón Gutiérrez submitted his dissertation in 1980, I include it in the count for the 1970s because virtually all of his doctoral work took place during that decade. Note that the wide recognition of LGBTQ history should not be taken as an indication that universities have prioritized hiring in the field: most of those who receive Ph.D.s focused on LGBTQ history do not find work in history departments, and many do not find work in any academic setting. See Stein, "Committee on Lesbian and Gay History Survey," and Allison Miller, "Historians on the Edge: The LGBTQ Historians Task Force Report and the AHA," *Perspectives on History* (February 2016), http://historians.org/publications-and-direc tories/perspectives-on-history/february-2016/scholars-on-the-edge-the-lgbtq-historians-task-force-report-and-the-aha.

117. See Lisa Duggan, "The Trials of Alice Mitchell: Sex, Science, and Sensationalism in Turn of the Century America," Ph.D. diss., University of Pennsylvania, 1992, which deals with the Freda Ward lesbian murder case; and David Serlin, "Built for Living: Imagining the American Body through Medical Science, 1945–65," Ph.D. diss., New York University, 1999, which focuses substantially on transgender and genderqueer history, including the lives of Christine Jorgensen (1966–1989), one of the first highly visible American transgender women, and Gladys Bentley (1907–1969), an African American blues singer who spent much of her life as a butch who dressed in men's clothing. As best I can document, no dissertations focusing entirely or substantially on the history of bisexuality have been produced to date in the United States.

118. Committee on Lesbian, Gay, Bisexual and Transgender History, "Dissertations and Theses."

119. Marjorie Garber, *Vice Versa: Bisexuality and the Eroticism of Everyday Life* (New York: Simon & Schuster, 1995) draws on cultural, literary, medical,

and other histories as part of a wider work of contemporary cultural and social criticism. Leslie Feinberg, *Transgender Warriors: Making History from Joan of Arc to RuPaul* (Boston: Beacon Press, 1996) offers an intellectual autobiography tracing the author's creation of an alternative history that highlights nonnormative gender. On Feinberg, also see Bruce Weber, "Leslie Feinberg, Writer and Transgender Activist Dies at 65," *New York Times*, 24 November 2014, http://www.nytimes.com/2014/11/25/nyregion/leslie-feinberg-writer-and-transgender-activist-dies-at-65.html.

120. On the erasure of bisexuals from queer history, see Loraine Hutchins, "Making Bisexuals Visible," in *Identities and Place: Changing Labels and Intersectional Communities of LGBTQ and Two-Spirit People in the United States*, ed. Katherine Crawford-Lackey and Megan E. Springate (New York: Berghahn Books, 2019). Establishing the history of American bisexual history poses further challenges beyond those outlined by Hutchins, notably because the bisexual movement in its formative years did not produce its own national publications equivalent to the homophile journals. Furthermore, the homophile journals themselves largely ignored bisexual history, in contrast to their occasional discussion of transgender figures from the past. My review of more recent bisexual periodicals and anthologies suggests that compared to homophile, gay-liberation, and lesbian-feminist movements, the bisexual movement may have taken less interest in using history as a political and cultural tool—or bisexual organizers may have faced more obstacles in uncovering historical evidence and in producing and transmitting historical knowledge.

For instance, the complete run of *Bi-Monthly*, published by the Bisexual Center in San Francisco from 1976 to 1985, includes just four articles devoted in whole or part to history: Sally R. Binford, "Anthropological Perspectives on Bisexuality," *Bi-Monthly* 3, no. 3 (March–April 1979): 1, 3–4; Jim Barnes, "Casanova: Some Bi-ographical Notes," *Bi-Monthly* 3, no. 4 (May–June 1979): 3–4; Jim Barnes, "Options Unlimited: Bisexuality in Science Fiction (Part 1)," *Bi-Monthly* 6, no. 4 (July–August 1982): 5–6; and Jim Barnes, "Options Unlimited: Bisexuality in Science Fiction (Part 2)," 6, no. 6 (November–December 1982): 3–6. Likewise, the complete run of *Anything That Moves*, published by the Bay Area Bisexual Network from 1991 to 2001, shows only two such articles: Lisa Jean Moore, "The Native American Berdache," *Anything That Moves* 1 (Winter 1991): 27–30, and Liz Highleyman, "History of the Bi Movement: How We Got Here and Where We're Going," *Anything That Moves* 8 (Summer 1994): 24–25.

121. For a striking example that echoes the search for heroes common to early LGBTQ folk historiography, see Sarah Prager, "Every LGBTQ+ Person Should Read This," *Huffington Post*, 2 February 2016, http://www.huffingtonpost.com/sarah-prager/every-lgbtq-person-should_b_8232316.html; see also Sarah Prager, *Queer, There, and Everywhere: 23 People Who Changed the World* (New York: Harper, 2017).

122. See Steven L. Brawley, "The Emergence of America's LGBT History between the Coasts," Boom website, 15 February 2016, updated 22 February 2016, http://www.boom.lgbt/index.php/equal/126-our-tribe/851-the-emergence-of-america-s-lgbt-history-between-the-coasts. For community-based archives, also see the roster in Lesbian and Gay Archives Roundtable, "Lavender Legacies Guide," which shows that such collections are now available to the public in all regions and in many major cities of the United States.

123. For instance, the Fair, Accurate, Inclusive and Respectful (FAIR) Education Act went into effect in 2012 in California, mandating inclusion of LGBTQ history in lessons in the state's public K–12 schools; see FAIR Education Act: Resources for Educators and Families, a website maintained by the Our Family Coalition, http://www.faireducationact.com/. Another initiative, History UnErased, provides national teacher trainings at the Lowell National Historical Park in Lowell, Massachusetts (established as a unit of the National Park Service on 5 June 1978); see Scott Malone, "History UnErased Aims to Cast Light on Gay Americans in School," Reuters, 2 June 2017, http://www.reuters.com/article/us-usa-lgbt-education-idUSKBN18T1AP; and the History UnErased website, https://unerased.org. On both History UnErased and organizing to implement the FAIR Education Act, also see Casey Quinlan, "The History of LGBTQ People Isn't Being Taught in Our Schools," *ThinkProgress*, 1 September 2017, https://thinkprogress.org/understanding-lgbtq-history-931fe0779aad/.

124. Ferentinos, *Interpreting LGBT History*, 110–14, notes numerous instances of libraries, history museums, house museums, historical societies, and LGBTQ community archives in the United States sponsoring LGBT exhibitions since the mid-1990s. For examples of published catalogs from such exhibitions for the same time period, see Jill Austin and Jennifer Bryer, *Out in Chicago: LGBT History at the Crossroads* (Chicago: Chicago History Museum, 2013); Ryan Conrad, *Future of the Past: Reviving the Queer Archives* (Portland, ME: Maine College of Art/Moth Press, 2009); David Frantz and Mia Locks, eds, *Cruising the Archive: Queer Art and Culture in Los Angeles, 1945–1980* (Los Angeles: One National Gay and Lesbian Archives at USC, 2012); Dan Luckenbill, *With Equal Pride: Gay and Lesbian Studies at UCLA—Catalog of an Exhibit at the University Research Library, January–March 1993* (Los Angeles: Department of Special Collections, University Research Library, University of California, 1993); Molly McGarry and Fred Wasserman, *Becoming Visible: An Illustrated History of Lesbian and Gay Life in Twentieth Century America* (New York: New York Public Library/Penguin Group, 1998); Don Romesburg and Amy Sueyoshi, eds, "Passionate Struggle: Dynamics of San Francisco's GLBT History," *Fabulas: The Journal of the Gay, Lesbian, Bisexual, Transgender Historical Society* (Winter 2008): 1–17; Stephanie Snyder, ed., *Out at the Library: Celebrating the James C. Hormel Gay and Lesbian Center* (San Francisco: San Francisco Public Li-

brary, 2005); and Stuart Timmons, *Out West: L.A.'s Influence on the Lesbian and Gay Movement* (Los Angeles: Doheny Memorial Library, University of Southern California, 2003).

125. The Leslie-Lohman Museum opened in 1987; see Hugh Ryan, "What It Took to Create the World's First Gay Art Museum," *Smithsonian*, 7 July 2015, https://www.smithsonianmag.com/arts-culture/what-it-took-create-worlds-first-gay-art-museum-1-180955840. The Schomburg Center for Research in Black Culture has several LGBTQ holdings which are often discussed on their blog series; see, for example, K. Menick, "Schomburg Treasures: The StoryCorps Black LGBTQ Archive," 10 June 2015, https://www.nypl.org/blog/2015/06/10/storycorps-black-lgbtq-archive. At the National Museum of American History, according to Katherine Ott, curator of the Division of Medicine and Science, "collecting 'out' objects (with a publicly known association) probably began in the 1980s and has steadily increased since then"; email to the author, 13 November 2017. Franklin Robinson, archivist for the museum's Archives Center, adds that the center "began more aggressively collecting from the LGBTQ community" in the early 2000s, with the holdings constituting more than 156 cubic feet in late 2017; email to the author, 13 November 2017, and "LGBT+ in the Archives Center at a Glance 2017, National Museum of American History," unpublished information sheet (Washington, DC: National Museum of American History, 2017). Also see "National Museum of American History Collects History Related to Lesbian, Gay, Bisexual, and Transgender History," National Museum of American History media release, 19 August 2014, http://americanhistory.si.edu/press/releases/museum-collects-lesbian-gay-bisexual-transgender-history.

126. Megan Springate, ed., *LGBTQ America: A Theme Study of Lesbian, Gay, Bisexual, and Transgender History* (Washington, DC: National Park Foundation and National Park Service, 2016), https://www.nps.gov/subjects/tellingallamericansstories/lgbtqthemestudy.htm.

Bibliography

Allen, Judith A., Hallimeda E. Allison, Andrew Clark Huckstep, Brandon J. Hill, Stephanie A. Sanders, and Liana Zhou. *The Kinsey Institute: The First Seventy Years*. Bloomington, IN: Well House Books, 2017.

Arman, Virginia. "Some Facts about Lesbians: Introduction." *One Institute Quarterly: Homophile Studies* 2, no. 4 (Fall 1959): 111–12.

Armstrong, Elizabeth A. *Forging Gay Identities: Organizing Sexuality in San Francisco, 1950–1994*. Chicago: University of Chicago Press, 2002.

Armstrong, Elizabeth A., and Suzanna M. Crage, "Movements and Memory: The Making of the Stonewall Myth," *American Sociological Review* 71, no. 5 (October 2006): 724–51

Austin, Jill, and Jennifer Bryer. *Out in Chicago: LGBT History at the Crossroads.* Chicago: Chicago History Museum, 2013.

Baim, Tracy. "Passages: Author Julia Penelope Dead at 71." *Windy City Times,* 24 January 2013. http://www.windycitymediagroup.com/lgbt/PASSAGES-Author-Julia-Penelope-dead-at-71/41298.html.

Barnes, Jim. "Casanova: Some Bi-ographical Notes." *Bi-Monthly* 3, no. 4 (May–June 1979): 3–4.

———. "Options Unlimited: Bisexuality in Science Fiction (Part 1)." *Bi-Monthly* 6, no. 4 (July–August 1982): 5–6.

———. "Options Unlimited: Bisexuality in Science Fiction (Part 2)." *Bi-Monthly* 6, no. 6 (November–December 1982): 3–6.

Baxter, Beverly. "London Letter: Has Oscar Wilde's Crime Been Redeemed?" *Mattachine Review* 1, no. 4 (July–August 1955): 22–25.

Belgion, Montgomery. *Our Present Philosophy of Life.* London: Faber & Faber, [1929].

Benjamin, Harry. "Transvestism and Transsexualism." *One Institute Quarterly: Homophile Studies* 1, no. 3 (Fall 1958): 102–4.

Bertz, Eduard. "Xavier Mayne (Author of 'Imre, a Memorandum'): The Intersexes, a History of Similisexualism as a Problem in Social Life." *Vierteljahresberichte des Wissenshaftlich-humanitären Komitees* 3, no. 1 (October 1911), 78–91.

Bérubé, Allan. *Coming Out under Fire: The History of Gay Men and Women in World War Two.* New York: Free Press, 1990.

———. "Intellectual Desire." In *My Desire for History: Essays in Gay, Community, and Labor History,* edited by John D'Emilio and Estelle B. Freedman, 161–81. Chapel Hill: University of North Carolina Press, 2011.

Bessette, Jean. *Retroactivism in the Lesbian Archives: Composing Pasts and Futures.* Carbondale: Southern Illinois University Press, 2017.

Binford, Sally R. "Anthropological Perspectives on Bisexuality." *Bi-Monthly* 3, no. 3 (March–April 1979): 1, 3–4.

Bradley, Marion Zimmer. "Variant Women in Literature." *Ladder* 1, no. 8 (May 1956): 8–10.

Bravmann, Scott. *Queer Fictions of the Past: History, Culture, and Difference.* Cambridge: Cambridge University Press, 1997.

Brawley, Steven L. "The Emergence of America's LGBT History between the Coasts." *Boom,* 15 February 2016. http://www.boom.lgbt/index.php/equal/126-our-tribe/851-the-emergence-of-america-s-lgbt-history-between-the-coasts.

Buchanan, Wyatt. "Willie Walker: Archivist for the Bay Area Gay Community." *San Francisco Chronicle,* 22 October 2004. http://www.sfgate.com/bayarea/article/Willie-Walker-archivist-for-Bay-Area-gay-2679957.php.

Buffalo News. "Wanda D. Edwards, Musician, Artist." *Buffalo News,* 22 December 1995.

Califia, Pat. *Sex Changes: The Politics of Transgenderism.* San Francisco: Cleis Press, 1997.

Call, Hal. "Mattachine Review." In *Homosexuals Today 1956*, edited by Marvin Cutler [pseudonym of W. Dorr Legg],, 58–60. Los Angeles: One Incorporated, 1956.

Carpenter, Edward. *Love's Coming of Age*. Chicago: Stockham, 1902.

Casal, Mary [pseudonym of Ruth Fuller Field]. *The Stone Wall: An Autobiography*. Chicago: Eyncourt Press, 1930.

Caufeynon, Dr. [pseudonym of Jean Fauconney]. *L'Homosexualité chez l'homme et chez la femme: physiologie et psychologie de l'inversion sexuelle—étude documentaire sur ses origines et ses manifestations dans les deux sexes*. Paris: Librairie Offenstadt, 1909.

———. *Unisexual Love: A Documentary Study of the Sources, Manifestations, the Physiology and Psychology of Sexual Perversion in the Two Sexes*. New York: New Era Press, 1934.

Chauncey, George. *Gay New York: Gender, Urban Culture, and the Making of the Gay Male World, 1890–1940*. New York: Basic Books, 1994.

———. "Gay New York: Urban Culture and the Making of the Gay Male World, 1890–1940." Ph.D. diss., Yale University, 1989.

Chemist and Druggist. "Legal Reports: Imitating Patent Medicines in America." *Chemist and Druggist*, 16 April 1887, 473.

Chideckel, Maurice. *Female Sex Perversion: The Sexually Aberrated Woman as She Is*. New York: Eugenics Publishing Company, 1935.

City of Glendale, California. City of Glendale Property Information Portal. https://csi.glendaleca.gov/csipropertyportal.

Clarens. "Friendship and Freedom." *L'Amite* 1 (April 1925): 13. Available online at http://semgai.free.fr/doc_et_pdf/L_amitie.pdf.

Colfax, Leslie. "Library." In *Homosexuals Today 1956*, edited by Marvin Cutler [pseudonym of W. Dorr Legg], 83–84. Los Angeles: One Incorporated, 1956.

Committee on Lesbian, Gay, Bisexual, and Transgender History. "Dissertations and Theses." Committee on Lesbian, Gay, Bisexual, and Transgender History, http://clgbthistory.org/resources/dissertations.

———. "Syllabi." Committee on Lesbian, Gay, Bisexual, and Transgender History. http://clgbthistory.org/resources/syllabi.

Conrad, Ryan. *Future of the Past: Reviving the Queer Archives*. Portland: Maine College of Art/Moth Press, 2009.

Cory, Donald Webster [pseudonym of Edward Sagarin]. *The Homosexual in America: A Subjective Approach*. New York: Greenberg, 1951.

Courier News. "Old Book Dealer Dies." *Courier News*, 22 May 1919, 7.

Cvetkovich, Ann. *An Archive of Feelings: Trauma, Sexuality, and Lesbian Public Cultures*. Durham, NC: Duke University Press, 2003.

Damon, Gene [pseudonym of Barbara Grier]. "Books: *The Stonewall: An Autobiography*." *Ladder* 4, no. 8 (May 1960): 18–19.

———. *Lesbiana: Book Reviews from The Ladder, 1966–1972*. Reno: Naiad Press, 1976.

———. "Radclyffe Hall." *Ladder* 3, no. 3 (December 1958): 8–9.

Damon, Gene [pseudonym of Barbara Grier] and Lee Stuart. "Transvestism in Women." *Ladder* 3, no. 5 (February 1959): 11–13.

Darling, Sherry A. "A Critical Introduction to *The Stone Wall: An Autobiography*." Ph.D. diss., Tufts University, Department of Drama, 2003.

D'Emilio, John. Curriculum Vitae, University of Chicago. http://hist.uic.edu/history/people/emeriti/john-d'emilio.

———. "Out of the Shadows: The Homosexual Emancipation Movement in the United States." Ph.D. diss., Columbia University, 1982.

———. *Sexual Politics, Sexual Communities: The Making of a Homosexual Minority in the United States, 1940–1970*. Chicago: University of Chicago Press, 1983.

D'Emilio, John, and Estelle B. Freedman. "Allan Bérubé and the Power of Community History." In *My Desire for History: Essays in Gay, Community and Labor History*, edited by John D'Emilio and Estelle B. Freedman, 10–12. Chapel Hill: University of North Carolina Press, 2011.

D'Emilio, John, and Estelle B. Freedman, eds. *My Desire for History: Essays in Gay, Community and Labor History*. Chapel Hill: University of North Carolina Press, 2011.

Downs, Jim. *Stand by Me: The Forgotten History of Gay Liberation*. New York: Basic Books, 2016.

Duberman, Martin Bauml, Martha Vicinus, and George Chauncey Jr., eds. *Hidden from History: Reclaiming the Gay and Lesbian Past*. New York: New American Library, 1989.

Duggan, Lisa. *Sapphic Slashers: Sex, Violence, and American Modernity*. Durham, NC: Duke University Press, 2000.

———. "The Trials of Alice Mitchell: Sex, Science, and Sensationalism in Turn of the Century America." Ph.D. diss., University of Pennsylvania, 1992.

Dunn, Thomas R. *Queerly Remembered: Rhetorics for Representing the GLBTQ Past*. Columbia: University of South Carolina Press, 2016.

Dynes, Wayne R. "Legg, W. Dorr (1904–94)." In *Who's Who in Contemporary Gay and Lesbian History: From World War II to the Present Day*, edited by Robert Aldrich and Garry Wotherspoon, 244–45. London: Routledge, 2001.

Ellis, Havelock. *Studies in the Psychology of Sex*, 6 vols. Philadelphia: F. A. Davis, 1900–1905.

Epstein, Rob, dir. *The Times of Harvey Milk*. Black Sand Productions, 1984.

Ermayne, LauraJean. "The Sapphic Cinema." *Ladder* 4, no. 7 (April 1960): 5–9.

Escoffier, Jeffrey. *American Homo: Community and Perversity*. Berkeley: University of California Press, 1998.

———. *Bigger than Life: The History of Gay Porn Cinema from Beefcake to Hardcore*. Philadelphia: Running Press, 2009.

Feinberg, Leslie. *Transgender Warriors: Making History from Joan of Arc to RuPaul*. Boston: Beacon Press, 1996.

Ferentinos, Susan. *Interpreting LGBT History at Museums and Historic Sites*. Lanham, MD: Rowman & Littlefield, 2015.

Fingal, Mack. "Hadrian and Antinous: The Love-Life of an Emperor." *Mattachine Review* 1, no. 6 (November–December 1956): 21–22.

Foster, Jeannette H. *Sex Variant Women in Literature: A Historical and Quantitative Study*. New York: Vantage Press, 1956.

Frantz, David, and Mia Locks, eds. *Cruising the Archive: Queer Art and Culture in Los Angeles, 1945–1980*. Los Angeles: One National Gay and Lesbian Archives at USC, 2012.

Freedman, Estelle B. "Curriculum Vitae: Estelle B. Freedman." Stanford University. http://ebf.stanford.edu/cv.html.

Gallo, Marcia M. *Different Daughters: A History of the Daughters of Bilitis and the Rise of the Lesbian Rights Movement*. New York: Carroll & Graf, 2006.

Garber, Eric, and Lynn Paleo. *Uranian Worlds: A Guide to Alternative Sexuality in Science Fiction, Fantasy, and Horror*. Boston: G. K. Hall, 1990.

Garber, Marjorie. *Vice Versa: Bisexuality and the Eroticism of Everyday Life*. New York: Simon & Schuster, 1995.

Garde, Noel I. [pseudonym of Edgar Leoni]. *The Homosexual in Literature: A Chronological Bibliography, circa 700 BC–1958*. New York: Village Books, 1959.

———. "The Mysterious Father of American Homophile Literature: A Historical Study." *One Institute Quarterly: Homophile Studies* 1, no. 3 (Fall 1958): 94–98.

Gifford, James. "What Became of *The Intersexes*?" *The Gay & Lesbian Review Worldwide* 18, no. 5 (September–October 2011). http://www.glreview.org/article/what-became-of-the-intersexes.

Gilbert, O. P. *Men in Women's Guise: Some Historical Instances of Female Impersonation*, trans. Robert B. Douglas. New York: Brentano's, 1926.

Glendale Directory Co. *Glendale City Directory 1928*. Glendale, CA: Glendale Directory Co., 1928.

GPA Consulting, Carson Anderson, and Wes Joe. *SurveyLA: LGBT Historic Context Statement*. Los Angeles: Office of Historic Resources, Department of City Planning, City of Los Angeles, 2014.

Guido, Bruno. *Adventures in American Bookshops, Antique Stores, and Auction Rooms*. Detroit: The Douglas Book Shop, 1922.

Gutiérrez, Ramón A. "Marriage, Sex, and the Family: Social Change in Colonial New Mexico, 1690–1846." Ph.D. diss., University of Wisconsin, Madison, 1980.

———. "Must We Deracinate Indians to Find Gay Roots?" *OUT/LOOK* 1, no. 4 (Winter 1989): 61–67.

———. "Ramón Gutiérrez: Preston & Sterling Morton Distinguished Service Professor." Faculty Homepage, University of Chicago. https://history.uchicago.edu/directory/ramón-gutiérrez.

———. *When Jesus Came, the Corn Mothers Went Away: Marriage, Sexuality, and Power in New Mexico, 1500–1846*. Stanford, CA: Stanford University Press, 1991.

Halperin, David M. *How to Be Gay*. Cambridge, MA: Harvard University Press, 2012.

Hamblen, David. "Lesbianism and the Law." *Ladder* 5, no. 2 (November 1960): 6–9.

Hay, Harry. "The Homosexual and History: An Invitation to Further Study." In *Radically Gay: Gay Liberation in the Words of Its Founder*, edited by Will Roscoe, 94–119. Boston: Beacon Press, 1996.

Henry, Sean. "Mayne, Xavier." In *Who's Who in Gay and Lesbian History from Antiquity to World War II*, edited by Robert Aldrich and Gary Wotherspoon, 302–4. London: Routledge, 2001.

Herring, Scott. "Introduction." In Ralph Werther, *Autobiography of an Androgyne*. New Brunswick, NJ: Rutgers University Press, 2008.

Highleyman, Liz. "History of the Bi Movement: How We Got Here and Where We're Going." *Anything That Moves* 8 (Summer 1994): 24–25.

Hirschfeld, Magnus. *Die Homosexualität des Mannes und des Weibes*. Berlin: Louis Marcus Verlag, 1914.

——. *The Homosexuality of Men and Women*, trans. Michael Lombardi-Nash. Amherst, NY: Prometheus Books, 2000.

History UnErased. "History UnErased." https://historyunerased.com.

Hollibaugh, Amber. *My Dangerous Desires: A Queer Girl Dreaming Her Way Home*. Durham, NC: Duke University Press, 2000.

Hutchins, Loraine. "Making Bisexuals Visible." In *Identities and Place: Changing Labels and Intersectional Communities of LGBTQ and Two-Spirit People in the United States*, edited by Katherine Crawford-Lackey and Megan E. Springate. New York: Berghahn Books, 2019.

J.A.F. [Jacques d'Adelswärd-Fersen]. "P.S. Je tiens à signaler . . . ," *Akademos: Revue Mensuelle d'Art Libre et de Critique* 12 (1909): 974.

Johnson, David K. *The Lavender Scare: The Cold War Persecution of Gays and Lesbians in the Federal Government*. Chicago: University of Chicago Press, 2004.

Jones, Diana Novak. "Old Town Site of Nation's First Gay Rights Group Designated National Landmark." *Chicago Sun-Times*, 19 June 2015. http://chicago.suntimes.com/news/7/71/705597/old-town-site-nations-first-gay-rights-group-designated-national-landmark.

Kaczynski, Richard. *Perdurabo: The Life of Aleister Crowley*. Berkeley: North Atlantic Books, 2012.

Katz, Jonathan Ned. *Coming Out! A Documentary Play about Gay Life and Liberation in the USA*. New York: Arno Press, 1975.

——. *Gay American History: Lesbians and Gay Men in the USA—A Documentary*. New York: Thomas Y. Crowell Company, 1976.

——. "Introduction. Mary Casal, Pseudonym of Ruth Fuller Field: The Autobiography of an American Lesbian." http://www.outhistory.org/exhibits/show/casal/intro.

——. "Recalling My Play 'Coming Out!' June 1972." OutHistory.org, 3 September 2013. http://outhistory.org/oldwiki/Jonathan_Ned_Katz,_Recalling_My_Play_"Coming_Out!"_June_1972.

Keim, Adam G. *History of the Quatrefoil Library*. Golden Valley, MN: Friends of the Bill of Rights Foundation, 2009. http://www.qlibrary.org/wordpress/wp-content/uploads/2014/04/QUATRE_FINAL_E-BOOK.pdf.

Kennedy, Elizabeth Lapovsky, and Madeline D. Davis. *Boots of Leather, Slippers of Gold: The History of a Lesbian Community*. New York: Routledge, 1993.

Kennedy-Ajax, Susan G. "My Genealogy Home Page: Information about Joseph Richardson Parke." http://www.genealogy.com/ftm/k/e/n/Susan-G-Kennedy-Ajax/WEBSITE-0001/UHP-0109.html.

Kepner, Jim. "An Accidental Institution: How and Why a Gay and Lesbian Archives?" In *Daring to Find Our Names: The Search for Lesbigay Library History*, edited by James V. Carmichael, 175–82. Westport, CT: Greenwood Press, 1998.

———. "Editorial." *One Institute Quarterly: Homophile Studies* 1, no. 1 (Spring 1958): 3.

Kinsey Institute. "The Kinsey Institute: Chronology of Events and Landmark Publications." Archived at https://web.archive.org/web/20160304161639/http://www.kinseyinstitute.org/about/chronology.html.

———. *Kinsey Institute for Research in Sex, Gender and Reproduction*. Bloomington, IN: Kinsey Institute, 1984.

Koskovich, Gerard. "Displaying the Queer Past: Purposes, Publics, and Possibilities at the GLBT History Museum." *QED: A Journal in GLBTQ Worldmaking* 1, no. 2 (2014): 61–78.

———. "Libraries and Archives." In *LGBTQ America Today: An Encyclopedia*, vol. 2, edited by John C. Hawley, 684–92. Westport, CT: Greenwood Press, 2009.

Ladder. "Lesbiana." *Ladder* 1, no. 6 (March 1957): 12.

———. Masthead. *Ladder* 1, no. 5 (February 1957): 1.

———. "Mattachine Breaks through the Conspiracy of Silence." *Ladder* 4, no. 1 (October 1959): 18.

Latino GLBT History Project. "About Us: Our History." http://www.latinoglbthistory.org/our-history.

———. "Historical Archive." http://www.latinoglbthistory.org/about-the-archive.

Lauritsen, John. "Edward Irenaeus Prime-Stevenson (Xavier Mayne) (1868–1942)." In *Before Stonewall: Activists for Gay and Lesbian Rights in Historical Context*, edited by Vern L. Bullough, 35–39. Binghamton, NY: Harrington Park Press, 2002.

Legg, W. Dorr. *Homophile Studies in Theory and Practice*. Los Angeles: One Institute Press and San Francisco: GLB Publishers, 1994.

Lesbian and Gay Archives Roundtable. "Lavender Legacies Guide," 2012. Society for American Archivists. http://www2.archivists.org/groups/lesbian-and-gay-archives-roundtable-lagar/lavender-legacies-guide-introduction.

Lesbian Herstory Archives. "Lesbian Herstory Archives: History and Mission." http://www.lesbianherstoryarchives.org/history.html.

Licata, Salvatore John. "Gay Power: A History of the American Gay Movement, 1908–1974." Ph.D. diss., University of Southern California, 1978.

Lind, Earl [Ralph Werther, Jennie June]. *Autobiography of an Androgyne.* New York: Medico-Legal Journal, 1918.

Lindquist, Lisa J. "Images of Alice: Gender, Deviancy, and a Love Murder in Memphis." *Journal of the History of Sexuality* 6, no. 1 (July 1995): 30–61.

Locke, Alain, ed. *The New Negro: An Interpretation.* New York: Albert and Charles Boni, 1925.

Lombardi, Michael. "The Translation of the Works by Karl Heinrich Ulrichs with Special Emphasis on Research on *The Riddle of Man-Manly Love.*" Ph.D. diss., One Institute for Homophile Studies, 1984.

Los Angeles Times. "Salvatore J. Licata: Helped Found Gay Academic Union." *Los Angeles Times,* 12 January 1990, A30.

Luckenbill, Dan. *With Equal Pride: Gay and Lesbian Studies at UCLA—Catalog of an Exhibit at the University Research Library, January–March 1993.* Los Angeles: Department of Special Collections, University Research Library, University of California, 1993.

Malone, Scott. "History Unerased Aims to Cast Light on Gay Americans in School." *Reuters,* 2 June 2017. http://www.reuters.com/article/us-usa-lgbt-education-idUSKBN18T1AP.

Marston, Brenda. "Archivists, Activists, and Scholars: Creating a Queer History." In *Daring to Find Our Names: The Search for Lesbigay Library History,* edited by James V. Carmichael, 135–52. Westport, CT: Greenwood Press, 1998.

Martin, Del. "We've Moved." *Ladder* 2, no. 6 (March 1958): 4–5.

Martinac, Paula. *The Queerest Places: A National Guide to Gay and Lesbian Historic Sites.* New York: Henry Holt & Co., 1997.

Mattachine Review. "Bibliography of Books on the Homosexual (and Related) Subjects." *Mattachine Review* 3, no. 8 (August 1957): 24–29.

———. "Books: *Sex in History* by G. Rattray Taylor." *Mattachine Review* 3, no. 3 (March 1957): 8–10.

———. "Mattachine Review: Where to Buy It." *Mattachine Review* 1, no. 5 (September–October 1955): 35.

———. "Mattachine Society Inc.: First Decade, 1950–1960." *Mattachine Review* 6, no. 4 (April 1960): 2, 26–30.

———. "Organizational Directory." *Mattachine Review* 11, no. 1 (July 1966): 14–15.

Mayne, Xavier [pseudonym of Edward Iranaeus Prime-Stevenson]. *Imre: A Memorandum,* edited by James J. Gifford. Peterborough, Canada: Broadview Literary Texts, 2003.

———. *The Intersexes: A History of Similisexualism as a Problem in Social Life.* Privately printed, n.d.

McCaslin, Michael. "A Brief History of Gerber/Hart Library." *Illinois Libraries* 81, no. 4 (Fall 1999): 228–31. http://www.lib.niu.edu/1999/il9904228.html.

McGarry, Molly, and Fred Wasserman. *Becoming Visible: An Illustrated History of Lesbian and Gay Life in Twentieth Century America.* New York: New York Public Library/Penguin Group, 1998.

McKinney, Cait. "'Finding the Lines to My People': Media History and the Queer Bibliographic Encounter." *GLQ* 24, no. 1 (January 2018): 55–83.

Meeker, Martin. *Contacts Desired: Gay and Lesbian Communications and Community, 1940s–1970s*. Chicago: University of Chicago Press, 2006.

Michelson, Avra. "Description and Reference in the Age of Automation." *American Archivist* 50 (Spring 1987): 192–208.

Miller, Allison. "Historians on the Edge: The LGBTQ Historians Task Force Report and the AHA." *Perspectives on History*, February 2016, http://historians .org/publications-and-directories/perspectives-on-history/february-2016/ scholars-on-the-edge-the-lgbtq-historians-task-force-report-and-the-aha.

Mirande, Lucien. *Inversions 1924–1925, L'Amitié 1925: Deux revues homosexuelles françaises*. Lille, France: GayKitschCamp, 2006.

Moore, Lisa Jean. "The Native American Berdache." *Anything That Moves* 1 (Winter 1991): 27–30.

Morris, Charles E., III, ed. *Queering Public Address: Sexualities in American Historical Discourse*. Columbia: University of South Carolina Press, 2007.

Murray, James A. *The Oxford English Dictionary: Supplement and Bibliography*. Oxford: Clarendon Press, 1933.

National Museum of American History. "National Museum of American History Collects History Related to Lesbian, Gay, Bisexual, and Transgender History," media release, 19 August 2014. http://americanhistory.si.edu/press/releases/ museum-collects-lesbian-gay-bisexual-transgender-history.

Nestle, Joan. *A Fragile Union: New and Collected Writings*. San Francisco: Cleis Press, 1998.

——. "I Lift My Eyes to the Hill: The Life of Mabel Hampton." *Don't Stop Talking* 2, 27 October 2011. http://joannestle2.blogspot.com/2011/10/in-memory- on-october-26-i-lift-my-eyes.html.

——. "Introduction." JoanNestle.com, July 1998. http://www.joannestle.com/ fragileu.html.

New York Times. "Books Wanted." *New York Times*, 20 November 1921, 55.

——. "Salvatore J. Licata, 50, an Educator on AIDS." *New York Times*, 4 January 1990. http://www.nytimes.com/1990/01/04/obituaries/salvatore-j-lica ta-50-an-educator-on-aids.html.

Niles, Blair. *Strange Brother*. New York: Liveright, 1931.

Norton, Rictor. "Bibliography of Gay and Lesbian History: Theory." Gay History & Literature: Essays by Rictor Norton, 13 July 2008. http://rictornorton.co.uk/ bibliog/bibtheor.htm.

——. "Gay History and Literature: Essays by Rictor Norton." August 22, 2015. http://rictornorton.co.uk.

——. "The Homosexual Literary Tradition: An Interpretation." Ph.D. diss., Florida State University, Tallahassee, 1972.

——. *The Homosexual Literary Tradition: An Interpretation*. New York: Revisionist Press, 1974.

One Archives at the USC Libraries. "History." http://one.usc.edu/about/history.

One Institute Quarterly: Homophile Studies. "One Institute of Homophile Studies." *One Institute Quarterly: Homophile Studies* 1, no. 1 (Spring 1958): inside front cover.

One National Gay and Lesbian Archives. "Finding Aid of the Jim Kepner Papers, Coll. 2011.002." http://www.oac.cdlib.org/findaid/ark:/13030/kt8d5nf4c6/admin/.

Our Family Coalition. FAIR Education Act: Resources for Educators and Families. http://www.faireducationact.com/.

Parke, J. Richardson. *Human Sexuality: A Medico-Literary Treatise on the History and Pathology of the Sex Instinct for the Use of Physicians and Jurists.* Philadelphia: Professional Publishing Co., 1912.

Passat, Joanne Ellen. *Sex Variant Women: The Life of Jeannette Howard Foster.* New York: Da Capo Press, 2008.

Potter, LaForest. *Strange Loves: A Study in Sexual Abnormalities.* New York: Robert Dodsley, 1933.

Prager, Sarah. "Every LGBTQ+ Person Should Read This." *Huffington Post*, 2 February 2016. http://www.huffingtonpost.com/sarah-prager/every-lgbtq-person-should_b_8232316.html.

——. *Queer, There, and Everywhere: 23 People Who Changed the World.* New York: Harper, 2017.

Publisher's Weekly. "Books Wanted." *Publisher's Weekly*, 21 April 1917, 1284.

——. "Business Notes." *Publishers Weekly*, 29 July 1922, 419.

Quinlan, Casey. "The History of LGBTQ People Isn't Being Taught in Our Schools." *ThinkProgress*, 1 September 2017. https://thinkprogress.org/understanding-lgbtq-history-931fe0779aad/.

Retzloff, Tim. "Edward Weber, Retired Labadie Collection Curator at U of M, Dies at 83." *Pride Source*, 20 April 2006. http://www.pridesource.com/article.html?article=18419.

Romesburg, Don. "Presenting the Queer Past: A Case for the GLBT History Museum." *Radical History Review* 120 (2014): 131–44.

Romesburg, Don, and Amy Sueyoshi, eds. "Passionate Struggle: Dynamics of San Francisco's GLBT History." *Fabulas: The Journal of the Gay, Lesbian, Bisexual, Transgender Historical Society* (Winter 2008): 1–17.

Rubin, Gayle S., ed. *Deviations: A Gayle Rubin Reader.* Durham, NC: Duke University Press, 2011.

Ryan, Hugh. "What It Took to Create the World's First Gay Art Museum," *Smithsonian*, 7 July 2015. https://www.smithsonianmag.com/arts-culture/what-it-took-create-worlds-first-gay-art-museum-1-180955840.

Salak, Joseph Charles. "Civil War Heroine." *Mattachine Review* 6, no. 11 (November 1960): 5–6.

Sanborn-Perris Map Company. *Insurance Maps of the City of New York.* New York: Sanborn-Perris Map Co., 1892. http://digitalcollections.nypl.org/items/94a1adcb-e63b-7f2b-e040-e00a18060d94.

Schaff, Morris. *The Spirit of Old West Point, 1858–1862.* Boston: Houghton Mifflin, 1907.

Schroeder, Theodore. *"Obscene" Literature and Constitutional Law: A Forensic Defense of Freedom of the Press.* New York: privately printed, 1911.

Schulman, Sarah. "ACT UP Oral History Project: Interview of Amy Bauer." New York: New York Lesbian & Gay Experimental Film Festival, 7 March 2004. http://www.actuporalhistory.org/interviews/images/bauer.pdf.

Sears, James T. *Behind the Mask of Mattachine: The Hal Call Chronicles and the Early Movement for Homosexual Emancipation.* Binghamton, NY: Harrington Park Press, 2006.

Serlin, David. "Built for Living: Imagining the American Body through Medical Science, 1945–65." Ph.D. diss., New York University, 1999.

Snyder, Stephanie, ed. *Out at the Library: Celebrating the James C. Hormel Gay and Lesbian Center.* San Francisco: San Francisco Public Library, 2005.

Springate, Megan E., ed. *LGBTQ America: A Theme Study of Lesbian, Gay, Bisexual, and Transgender History.* Washington, DC: National Park Foundation and National Park Service, 2016. https://www.nps.gov/subjects/tellingallamericansstories/lgbtqthemestudy.htm.

Stein, Marc. "Committee on Lesbian and Gay History Survey on LGBTQ History Careers." Committee on Lesbian, Gay, Bisexual, and Transgender History website, June 2001. http://clgbthistory.org/resources/reports/lgbtq-history-careers.

———. *Rethinking the Gay and Lesbian Movement.* New York: Routledge, 2012.

———. "Theoretical Politics, Local Communities: The Making of U.S. LGBT Historiography." *GLQ: A Journal of Gay and Lesbian Studies* 11, no. 4 (2005): 605–25.

Stewart, Omer C. "Homosexuality among American Indians and Other Native Peoples of the World." *Mattachine Review* 6, no. 1 (January 1960): 9–15.

———. "Homosexuality among American Indians and Other Native Peoples of the World." *Mattachine Review* 6, no. 2 (February 1960): 13–18.

Stone, Amy L., and Jamie Cantrell, eds. *Out of the Closet, Into the Archives: Researching Sexual Histories.* Albany: State University of New York Press, 2015.

Stonewall National Museum and Archives. "About Us: History." http://www.stonewall-museum.org/about-us/history.

Sullivan, Gerard. "Cory, Donald Webster." In *Who's Who in Contemporary Gay and Lesbian History from World War II to Today*, edited by Robert Aldrich and Gary Wotherspoon, 92–93. London: Routledge, 2001.

Thistlethwaite, Polly J. "Building 'A Home of Our Own': The Construction of the Lesbian Herstory Archives." In *Daring to Find Our Names: The Search for Lesbigay Library History*, edited by James V. Carmichael Jr., 153–73. Westport, CT: Greenwood Press, 1998.

Tilchen, Maida. "The Legendary Lesbian Treasure Map." In *The Lesbian in Literature*, edited by Barbara Grier, xi–xii. Tallahassee, FL: Naiad Press, 1981.

Timmons, Stuart. *Out West: L.A.'s Influence on the Lesbian and Gay Movement*. Los Angeles: Doheny Memorial Library, University of Southern California, 2003.

Tyburczy, Jennifer. *Sex Museums: The Politics and Performance of Display*. Chicago: University of Chicago Press, 2016.

Ulrichs, Karl-Heinrich, *The Riddle of Man-Manly Love: The Pioneering Work on Male Homosexuality*, trans. Michael Lombardi-Nash. Buffalo: Prometheus Books, 1994.

University of Southern California. "Schedule of Classes and Registration Instructions, Spring Semester 1976." *Bulletin of the University of Southern California* 71, no. 9 (15 November 1975).

Wakimoto, Diana Kiyo. "Queer Community Archives in California since 1950." Ph.D. diss., Queensland University of Technology, Brisbane, Australia, 2012.

Weber, Bruce. "Leslie Feinberg, Writer and Transgender Activist Dies at 65." *New York Times*, 24 November 2014. http://www.nytimes.com/2014/11/25/nyregion/leslie-feinberg-writer-and-transgender-activist-dies-at-65.html.

Werther, Ralph–Jennie June [Earl Lind]. *Autobiography of an Androgyne*, edited and with an introduction by Scott Herring. New Brunswick, NJ: Rutgers University Press, 2008.

——. *The Female-Impersonators*. New York: Medico-Legal Journal, 1922.

White, C. Todd. *Pre-Gay L.A.: A Social History of the Movement for Homosexual Rights*. Urbana: University of Illinois Press, 2009.

Williams, Nancy. "Estelle Freedman Wins Long Battle for Tenure." *Stanford Daily* 184, no. 1 (26 September 1983): 1, 15. http://stanforddailyarchive.com/cgi-bin/stanford?a=d&d=stanford19830926-01.2.3.

CHAPTER 3

Taking Action

An Overview of LGBTQ Preservation Initiatives

Gail Dubrow

Introduction

Those who have sought to make places associated with LGBTQ history publicly visible have employed a wide array of strategies, including and extending beyond the core tools of cultural resource management. Landmark designations and historic markers have proven useful for recognizing, within the guidelines of particular programs, the significance of historic properties, while public art projects have taken more creative liberties with the forms in which queer histories are represented. Market forces are not only affecting the survival of queer landmarks, but are also reshaping urban tourism in some places, raising new questions about which aspects of queer heritage will be foregrounded or rendered invisible as subjects for public consumption in tourism-based urban revitalization schemes. Within an expansive range of scholarly and professional organizations, LGBTQ professionals and their allies have organized to advance a more inclusive agenda. Together these factors have contributed to a new ethos within the historic preservation movement more accepting of queer history as American history, a development more than thirty years in the making.

Strategies for Increasing LGBTQ Visibility in American Cities

A variety of strategies have been adopted to make LGBTQ luminaries, communities, and history visible on public streets, even when there is no direct connection to preserving historic resources. Chicago's Boystown was the object of a 1998 neighborhood streetscape investment by Mayor Richard M. Daley intended to recognize and make visible its significance as an LGBTQ neighborhood. The resulting urban design project erected ten pairs of rainbow pylons, with memorial plaques honoring icons of LGBTQ history, which together define a Legacy Walk along the North Halsted Street corridor.[1] Street naming initiatives have commemorated major figures in the LGBTQ rights movement, including Frank Kameny (Washington, DC, 2010), Barbara Gittings (Philadelphia, Pennsylvania, 2012), José Sarria (San Francisco, California, 2006), Sylvia Rivera (New York City, New York, 2005), Harvey Milk (San Diego, California, 2012; Salt Lake City, Utah, 2016), and Bettie Naylor (Austin, Texas, 2012). In 2015, Staten Island renamed a street to honor Jimmy Zappalorti, a gay military veteran who was brutally murdered in a gay bashing in 1990. In 2011, Los Angeles's Silver Lake Neighborhood Council voted to rename the Cove Avenue Stairway in honor of gay rights activist Harry Hay.

Historical marker programs, such as the one run by the Pennsylvania Historical and Museum Commission, have begun to commemorate sites associated with LGBTQ heritage. In 2005, they erected a state historical marker across from Independence Hall in Philadelphia to honor the LGBTQ activists who held annual Fourth of July Reminder Day demonstrations there from 1965 to 1969 calling for equality (figure 3.1).[2] In 2016, the state erected a state historical marker commemorating the life and work of Barbara Gittings.[3] A state historic marker recognizes the birthplace of lesbian poet Natalie Clifford Barney in Dayton, Ohio, and in Hidalgo County, Texas, a state marker was placed in 2015 at the grave of Gloria Anzaldúa, an influential cultural theorist who had relationships with both men and women. The block of Taylor Street in San Francisco where Compton's Cafeteria was located was renamed Gene Compton's Cafeteria Way in June 2016, in recognition of patrons' 1966 protest against homophobic police harassment.

Artists have also played a role in making LGBTQ history more visible at historic sites and buildings, independent of their official status in designation and preservation programs. In a 1994 temporary street sign installation project called Queer Spaces, the artists' collective REPOHistory boldly called attention to nine New York City landmarks of LGBTQ history with text screened onto pink triangles made of chipboard, queering the narrative usually found on historical markers.[4] Similar to other REPOHistory projects, the signs were intended as counter-monuments to provoke public reflection on why some histories are visible, while others remain obscured in public memory. Since 1989, the Visual AIDS

Figure 3.1. Independence Hall seen from inside the Liberty Bell pavilion, Philadelphia, 2017. Photo by Megan E. Springate, National Park Service.

organization has used art projects to increase AIDS awareness and pre-vention, document the work of artists with HIV/AIDS, and promote the artistic contribution of the AIDS movement. It offers a reminder of the impact of the epidemic on an entire generation, including its artists, and points to the enormous shadow it casts over LGBTQ preservation efforts.[5] While none of these strategic interventions in urban design, public art, or streetscape projects has led directly to the preservation of historic resources, together they have helped to gain traction for emerg-ing heritage preservation initiatives.

Leveraging the Tourist Industry to Promote LGBTQ Heritage Preservation

A complementary force informing all of these initiatives is a growing segment of the tourist industry that markets its services to LGBTQ peo-ple, contributing in direct and indirect ways to creating a market for LGBTQ heritage tourism. Some travel agents, resorts, cruise ships, and lodging owners have built their reputation on being LGBTQ-friendly, advertising places of respite in a heteronormative and homophobic world.[6] Many of these enterprises operate under the banner of the In-ternational Gay and Lesbian Travel Association, founded in 1983, whose reach now extends to eighty countries on six continents.[7] Tourist itiner-aries that highlight places significant in LGBTQ heritage have been bol-stered by this industry, for example in world cities that have hosted the Gay Games, which feature a robust slate of athletic and cultural events.[8] In 1998, when Amsterdam became the first city outside of North Amer-ica to serve in that role, the usual canal cruises were augmented with tours of local queer heritage.

Over time, some cities have intentionally promoted their reputation as being LGBTQ-friendly in a bid for tourist revenue. Some places that took the lead in legalizing same-sex marriage or civil unions launched campaigns to become destinations of choice for couples unable to tie the knot in their home state. These segmented marketing campaigns have highlighted local history, cultural resources, and commercial es-tablishments of particular interest to queer visitors. Beginning in 2002, for example, the Philadelphia Gay Tourism Caucus began marketing its attractions with a website provocatively titled, "Get Your History Straight and Your Nightlife Gay."[9] This advertising tends to feature current busi-nesses, but sometimes is linked to LGBTQ heritage tours. In Philadel-phia, Bob Skiba bridged the marketing of Philadelphia as a gay-friendly tourist destination and related heritage tourism: while president of the Philadelphia Association of Tour Guides in 2008, he prepared a series of maps that documented LGBTQ businesses in Center City. Later, as curator at the William Way LGBT Community Center's John J. Wilcox Jr. Archives, Skiba created a blog called *The Philadelphia Gayborhood Guru*, which translates the city's queer history into site-specific histori-cal information, occasionally leading walking tours of these places un-der the Way Center's auspices.[10]

Small-scale heritage tours were established early on in the most queer-friendly cities, notably Trevor Hailey's walking tour, "Cruisin' the Castro," which started in 1989.[11] While much of the mapping of LGBTQ historic places—and occasional tours—have been advanced by non-profit organizations such as DC's Rainbow History Project or the North-west Lesbian and Gay History Museum Project in Seattle, tours that high-light places of contemporary and historical significance have emerged as more elaborate profit-making enterprises in recent years. Paid walk-ing tours can be found in New Orleans and Chicago, while bus tours are available in Manhattan and Los Angeles.[12] The combined forces of LGBTQ pride, queer entrepreneurship, and urban boosterism has en-hanced the commercial viability of heritage-oriented LGBTQ enter-prises from the 1990s onward. It was in this broader context, and amid growing interest in LGBTQ history generally, that Paula Martinac found a welcoming audience for the 1997 publication of her national guide to historic sites, *The Queerest Places*.[13]

The Rise of LGBTQ Advocacy in Fields Associated with Preservation

Developments within scholarly and professional associations have buoyed LGBTQ preservation efforts both directly and indirectly. In all cases, LGBTQ heritage and cultural resources professionals have built networks of mutual support, organized to advocate for their interests, and promoted visibility for emerging scholarship in their fields, includ-ing in flagship journals and on the programs of annual meetings. The Committee on LGBT History, founded in 1979 as the Committee on Les-bian and Gay History, has played an important advocacy role within the American Historical Association (AHA), with which it has been affiliated since 1982.[14] As public memory and the power of place increasingly have become analytical categories within historical scholarship, AHA sessions sponsored by the committee, such as one at the 2013 annual conference in New Orleans on "Locating LGBT History in Urban Spaces," have become increasingly relevant to the project of queer heritage preservation.[15] The Committee on the Status of LGBTQ Historians and Histories, established in 2013, has played a similar role within the Organization of American Historians (OAH). Links between scholarship and tangible heritage are illustrated by the committee's offerings at the 2015 OAH meeting, which included a walking tour of the queer history of St. Louis's Central West End, as well as selections from the exhibit *Gateway to History*, featuring the city's LGBTQ history.[16] The National Council on Public History also has been a welcoming home for LGBTQ content at its annual meetings.

Founded in 1989, the Lesbian and Gay Archives Roundtable (LAGAR), an interest group within the Society of American Archivists, formed to advance queer history and the status of LGBTQ people in the archival profession. In addition to basic advocacy work, LAGAR has created a guide to collections of interest to the LGBTQ community and a manual outlining best practices for community archives.[17]

Within the museum world, the LGBTQ Alliance, a professional network within the American Alliance of Museums (AAM), is committed to advancing a more inclusive agenda. While its concerns include issues of representation and visibility at large institutions, its membership includes managers of historic sites and independent museum professionals who are grappling with how issues of sex and sexuality—as well as race, class, and gender—can be integrated into interpretive programs.[18] A useful tool, two years in the making by Alliance members and released at the May 2016 AAM meeting, articulates "Welcoming Guidelines" that set standards for LGBTQ inclusion in museums.[19] The volume of scholarship related to the interpretation of LGBTQ history at museums and historic sites is growing, from focused case studies of particular sites, for example Michael Lesperance's study of Virginia's Glen Burnie, to a comprehensive treatment in Susan Ferentinos's award-winning book.[20] In a related field with implications for museums, the Queer Caucus for Art, initiated in 1989 as a society of the College Art Association (CAA), has been instrumental in advancing art history, theory, criticism, and art practice related to LGBTQ themes, issuing its first newsletter in 1995 and holding sessions, exhibitions, and related activities at annual meetings of the CAA.[21]

The emergence of LGBTQ advocacy groups within the architecture and design professions has had direct consequences for historic preservation.[22] As well as OLGAD's work in New York City,[23] Boston Gay and Lesbian Architects and Designers (BGLAD), formed in 1991 as a committee of the Boston Society of Architects, worked with the Boston Area Gay and Lesbian History Project to produce a map of known lesbian and gay historic places in 1995.[24] *Progressive Architecture* reported on OLGAD's inaugural Design Pride Conference in New York City, held in 1994, which provided a forum for discussing concerns about the status of lesbians and gays in architectural firms and helped to build an audience for an array of new publications about the relationship between (homo)sexuality and space.[25] The Arcus Endowment and Foundation Chair, established at University of California, Berkeley, in 2000, is the rare university-based resource supporting emerging experts and projects at the intersection of LGBTQ issues and the professions of architecture, landscape architecture, and planning.[26]

At the American Planning Association (APA) national conference in Boston in 1998, Gays and Lesbians in Planning (GALIP) became a new division of the APA, having functioned as an informal network since they met for the first time in 1992 at the national conference in Washington, DC.[27] Similar to the other scholarly societies and professional organizations previously mentioned, GALIP provides a venue for information exchange, mutual support, and promoting scholarship in city and regional planning. The field of planning has produced several articles and two volumes on LGBTQ themes that incorporate historic preservation into the queer planning agenda.[28] Beyond professional associations, citizen planners began to organize in the mid-1990s to protect queer interests in gay neighborhoods facing runaway development pressures, for example the Bay Area group Castro Area Planning + Action.[29]

The intellectual foundations for efforts to map queer space have been reinforced by academic work at the intersection of geography and urban and regional planning, as spatially oriented social scientists began in the 1990s to engage with sexuality as a category of analysis in addition to race, class, and gender.[30] While early architectural publications tilted toward the experiences of white gay men, geography proved to be more inclusive of the spatial dimensions of lesbian lives.[31] Within the Association of American Geographers (AAG), the specialty group Sexuality and Space formed in 1996, arising out of serious concern about the "unquestioned heterosexuality of the geographic enterprise."[32] Over time, the specialty group has become an intellectually vital force in mapping out a new subfield of geographic study by holding preconferences in conjunction with annual AAG meetings and bringing recognition to outstanding scholarship. Two of its members, Larry Knopp and Michael Brown, have been central to a project that mapped Seattle's LGBTQ landmarks.

Established in 2014 after more than a decade of effort, the Queer Archaeology Interest Group is one of more than a dozen affiliates of the Society for American Archaeology, providing a network for LGBTQ archaeologists and an engine for advancing research and pedagogy.[33] Beyond providing a gathering place for scholars working in this area, the formation of the interest group is a landmark achievement in its own right by overcoming "the difficulties often associated with being LGBTQI and stigmatization within [the] discipline and society at large."[34] While the theoretical and methodological implications of this field are emerging, it is not yet clear what will be required to integrate insights from queer archaeology into the public interpretation of archaeological sites.[35] Past struggles to incorporate LGBTQ history into the interpretive programs at historic properties points to the likelihood of a significant lag between the state of knowledge in the field and successful implementation in public archaeology practice.

The Rise of a LGBTQ-Inclusive Preservation Movement

Advocacy for LGBTQ issues directly within the preservation movement began to coalesce at the end of the 1980s and firmly took hold in the 1990s, powered by the combined forces of local and national initiatives. Grassroots activities in San Francisco drew the Western Regional Office of the National Trust for Historic Preservation (NTHP) into issues of preservation that involved LGBTQ communities, a position that put it out in front of the parent organization in many respects. At a time when the preservation movement was still resistant to addressing LGBTQ issues and the community had not yet explicitly embraced preservation within its broader agenda for political equality and cultural equity, the advocacy group Friends of 1800 formed in San Francisco to articulate the connections.

Friends of 1800 organized in 1987 as advocates for the preservation of San Francisco's nearly century-old Carmel Fallon building, whose future was threatened by demolition plans intended to make way for a LGBTQ community center.[36] Thus, the Friends' initial cause required work to build awareness of and appreciation for the value of historic preservation *within* the LGBTQ community, though it also raised awareness of LGBTQ issues among many preservation professionals. These goals ultimately shaped the organization's mission to preserve "significant historical buildings, landmarks and the architectural heritage of

San Francisco with a special interest in the identification and recognition of issues and sites important to GLBT history and culture."[37]

For a time, the Friends of 1800's website was *the* place to go for information on LGBTQ preservation. Following the organization's success
in preserving the Fallon Building,[38] the Friends organized a 2001 conference in San Francisco focused on preserving LGBTQ heritage, Looking
Back and Forward, in collaboration with the GLBT Northern California
Historical Society and the James C. Hormel LGBTQIA Center at the San
Francisco Public Library. As organizer Gerry Takano recalled, the conference broke new ground:

> Back then only a few bona fide preservations sanctioned the legiti-
> macy of the glbt community's minority status. The basis of a cultural
> resource's recognition and significance, instead, was commonly de-
> fined by race and ethnic origin, not sexual orientation. Furthermore,
> the high proportion of gay men and lesbians involved in some form of
> preservation activity was trivialized as inconsequential and negligible.

For that reason, the conference highlighted a wide array of places significant for their connection with LGBTQ communities, and helped to
coalesce advocacy for LGBTQ cultural resources among preservationists.[39] The vocal contingent of LGBTQ preservationists who organized to
save the Carmel Fallon Building served as a bridge between the LGBTQ
and preservation communities, raising questions of where their concerns fit on each other's agendas. Friends of 1800 also directly advanced
the cause of identifying places of significance in LGBTQ heritage by
producing the first historic context statement in the United States on
LGBTQ properties.[40]

Institutional Transformation: Gaining Traction
for LGBTQ Issues within the National Trust for
Historic Preservation and the National Park Service

These early initiatives helped to seed a network of concerned LGBTQ
preservationists and their allies, who in turn leveraged momentum to
press for a more visible place on the program of annual meetings of the
NTHP with the goals of embedding issues of sexual orientation within
the organization and institutionalizing change. Behind the scenes, there
were wrenching struggles over the prominence of LGBTQ topics on the
program of NTHP annual conferences, as the organization's leadership

was concerned about antagonizing and alienating conservative elements of the membership at a time when the culture wars were raging.

Progress in advancing organizational change advanced incrementally. The first sign of progress was the NTHP's commitment to hosting an October 1996 social gathering for LGBTQ preservationists at its fiftieth annual conference in Chicago. It foreshadowed a more significant commitment the following year to a full educational session, "Hidden History: Identifying and Interpreting Gay and Lesbian Places," at its National Preservation Conference in Santa Fe, New Mexico.[41] The resounding success of that session paved the way for LGBTQ receptions and heritage tours at the National Trust's annual conferences. These steps cumulatively laid the foundation for addressing LGBTQ issues within the NTHP's publications: *Preservation Magazine*, which is a perk of general membership; and *Forum*, which is followed mainly by preservation practitioners and educators.

Coverage of the San Francisco walking tour "Cruisin' the Castro" broke the silence about LGBTQ heritage within *Preservation* in 1997.[42] It was followed in 1998 by the publication of my essay, "Blazing Trails with Pink Triangles and Rainbow Flags," in *Forum*.[43] Drawn from my presentation at the New Mexico session, the article outlined an agenda for action, including (1) writing gays and lesbians into the history of the preservation movement; (2) improving the interpretation of LGBT history at existing landmarks; (3) identifying and listing overlooked historic resources; (4) increasing public education and awareness of LGBT heritage; (5) building advocacy for the protection of historic resources; and (6) building institutional capacity within preservation advocacy organizations and cultural resource management agencies to address these issues effectively.

Still, it was unclear to what extent the NTHP was prepared to address LGBTQ themes at historic properties in its own portfolio, as evidenced by pressure from *Forum* editors to drop references in my "Blazing Trails" article to the Trust's planned acquisition of Philip Johnson's Glass House in New Canaan, Connecticut, and negotiations in process over Georgia O'Keeffe's Ghost Ranch in Abiquiu, New Mexico.[44] My point in the article was that the acquisition of these historic properties would provide the NTHP with the opportunity to demonstrate its commitment to LGBTQ inclusive policies and practices, since same-sex relationships were essential to their creation; however, the editorial conflict captured the leadership at a moment of deep ambivalence, caught between the demands of LGBTQ preservationists in its own ranks, who were frustrated by chronic silences that devalued their contributions to the movement and obscured important elements of their history, and a conservative faction within the membership still struggling with unvarnished presentations about the horrors of slavery at NTHP properties, much less shame-free narratives about gay, lesbian, bisexual, and transgender people.

Ultimately, Ghost Ranch remained in the hands of the Presbyterian Church, which runs it as an education and retreat center. To date, the contributions of Maria Chabot to building the house, and her intimate relationship with O'Keeffe, have little purchase. In contrast, the Glass House, which Johnson ultimately bequeathed to the NTHP, has become a model of candor since opening to the public in 1987. Both the website and site-based programs directly address its gay content as a landmark of modern architecture designed by a gay architect, Philip Johnson, whose partner of forty-five years, David Whitney, was instrumental in shaping their private art collection. The fact that Johnson stepped out of the closet late in life helped make it possible to address his sexual orientation and same-sex partnership without the shadow of outing someone against their wishes.[45] It has become one of the rare historic houses that explicitly acknowledges a same-sex life partnership on its website as well as in creative site-based programming.[46] In May 2016, for example, Glass House hosted a performance of "Modern Living" by Brennan Gerard and Ryan Kelly, whose work is a meditation on "how the house sheltered and protected a queer subculture."[47] The property is a bellwether of the NTHP's growing embrace of LGBTQ issues. Today the preservation advocacy organization broadcasts its commitment to inclusion in multiple ways, sponsoring a listserv for those interested in LGBTQ issues, publicizing examples of historic places, and bringing advocates into broader conversations about diversity and inclusion in the preservation movement.[48]

By the end of the 1990s, the foundation for an LGBTQ-inclusive preservation movement had been established through grassroots initiatives, the formation of new interest groups focused on LGBTQ heritage within professional associations, and an increasingly vocal contingent of out lesbians and gay men working within the field of preservation. Preservation professionals, some of whom had been active in grassroots initiatives, mobilized to make the major preservation organizations and agencies more responsive to their concerns. These efforts were complemented by progressive developments in a wide range of scholarly and professional organizations in the fields of history, archival and museum administration, architecture, art, planning, and geography, which lent support to changes in the preservation movement's approach to LGBTQ issues.

The National Park Service exhibited similar concerns in the 1990s about the prospect of political fallout in response to any effort to designate historic places tied to LGBTQ people and events. At a time when the culture wars were raging, matters of historical interpretation became highly politicized at the federal level. Intense controversy in 1989 over the National Endowment for the Arts' support for Andres Serrano's provocative photograph, *Piss Christ*, and the Smithsonian's National Air and Space Museum's planned 1994 exhibit of the Enola Gay—the plane used to drop atomic weapons on Japan—put federal agencies on notice that a coalition of conservative politicians and their constituents, particularly religious organizations, would use the threat of budget cuts to enforce their views.

In this climate, some NHL nominations prepared for the congressionally-funded Women's History Landmark Study that touched on controversial contemporary issues such as birth control, abortion, sexuality, and radical politics—for example, Margaret Sanger's Birth Control Clinic and Emma Goldman's apartment, where her ideology of free love was practiced and the *Mother Earth News* was published—were sidelined. Conservative hostility toward critiques of American history, feminism, and LGBTQ rights reached into the next decade and occasionally derailed unrelated NHL nominations, such as Seattle's Panama Hotel, which is significant in Japanese American history for many reasons, including the circa 1915 traditional Japanese bathhouse, Hashidate-Yu, in the basement.[49] In the nomination review process, the bathhouse—a model of propriety—was erroneously conflated with gay bathhouses, where public sex has been a feature of male sociality and a celebration of same-sex attraction. The 2002 nomination stalled for four years before finally securing NHL status.

But its eventual success begs the question: what if actual gay bathhouses were proposed for landmark designation, such as the Everard, Lafayette, Continental, and New St. Marks in New York City; or their San Francisco equivalents: the Palace, Jack's, Ritch Street, Barracks, and Liberty Baths, among many others?[50] These types of sites, far more provocative than domestic idylls, are just beginning to be considered for recognition, for example San Francisco's Ringold Alley in the South of Market neighborhood. Once a cruising spot for gay men seeking quick pickups and sex, it is now a commemorative plaza, including bronze footprints in the pavement and the reproduction of an iconic mural from the Tool Box leather bar, harkening back to its heyday from 1962 to the mid-1960s.[51] The volatile relationship between politics and culture that settled into American public life in the 1990s (which has morphed into new debates over the impact of LGBTQ rights on those who object on moral or religious grounds) provides a context for appreciating the cultural victory that Stonewall's listing as a National Historic Landmark represented in 2000.

The contentious political climate in this period also explains why much of the forward momentum to recognize places of significance in LGBTQ history can be traced to grassroots initiatives. The Victorian-era building that housed Harvey Milk's Castro Camera shop and residence, which also served as headquarters for his four campaigns for public office, was designated San Francisco Landmark #227 in July 2000. The iconic Stonewall Inn, part of the Greenwich Village Historic District, was entered into the National Register of Historic Places in 1999 and designated a National Historic Landmark in 2000. It would take fifteen more years, however, before the property would be approved as a New York City landmark.[52]

In DC, the group Rainbow History Project was the driving force behind the addition of gay rights activist Frank Kameny's home and offices to the roster of local landmarks, with support from the DC Preservation League. The research and writing process began in 2003 and resulted in a completed National Register nomination in 2006, with the property becoming a DC landmark in 2009 and listing on the NRHP in 2011.[53] A contributor to the delay was the standard practice of limiting NRHP designations to those no longer living. While Kameny had the satisfaction of living to see his home and office listed as a DC landmark, the property was added to the NRHP only after his death, becoming the first property to honor a major figure in the LGBTQ rights movement.

Support within the Department of Interior for listing these overlooked properties on the NRHP and recognizing the most outstanding examples as NHLs came from members of the federal employee organization, GLOBE (Gay, Lesbian, or Bisexual Employees). Interior GLOBE, a mutual support and advocacy group founded in 1994 and run by and for employees of the Department of the Interior, played a key role in advancing Stonewall for listing on the NRHP as a first step toward NHL designation.[54] This level of designation is restricted to properties with the highest levels of significance and integrity. According to Stephen A. Morris, a founding member of Interior GLOBE, it was at one of its monthly meetings in the summer of 1998 that the idea of honoring Stonewall as an official historic site was first discussed—the members hit on this as a bit of a legacy project for the Clinton Administration, which had brought so many openly gay political appointees into the Department of the Interior.[55]

Their partnership with the GVSHP, OLGAD, and Andrew Dolkart and colleagues, who authored the nomination, moved the project beyond the roadblocks encountered in an attempt several years earlier. Interior GLOBE also lent support to the inclusion of Frank Kameny's house on the NRHP.[56]

Connecting Grassroots Initiatives with Landmark Designation Programs

One of the major limitations of the many local, community-based mapping projects, from the perspective of historic preservation, is that they did not directly advance the protection of resources significant in LGBTQ heritage or integrate them into programs to designate landmarks. Nevertheless, as momentum grew within the preservation movement, grassroots mapping projects became a source of actual nominations. Virginia-based Rainbow Heritage Network has proven to be a particularly fruitful generator of nominations, widening the coverage of places associated with women and people of color. Rainbow Heritage Network cofounder Mark Meinke, along with homeowner Robert Pohl, led efforts to nominate the Capitol Hill row house that was the main home and operational center for the Furies as a DC landmark and to the NRHP. The Furies was a small lesbian-feminist collective founded in 1971 that played a key role in the rise of second-wave feminism, lesbian separatism, and the LGBTQ movement. The building's large basement hosted meetings of the collective and was the headquarters for publishing its newspaper, *The Furies: Lesbian/Feminist Monthly*. The property was listed on the National Register of Historic Places on 2 May 2016 and has also been documented by the Historic American Buildings Survey (figure 3.2).[57]

The DC home of the Furies' Collective is not the only site with significant connections to the rise of lesbian feminism. There are others that also have the potential to become landmarks. The homes of some of the movement's most articulate proponents—for example, Black lesbian feminist writer and activist Audre Lorde, which stands in Staten Island, or preeminent American poet Adrienne Rich, who established long-term residences with her partner, the writer and editor Michelle Cliff, in Montague, Massachusetts, and later in Santa Cruz, California—could become the late twentieth century's equivalents of a prior generation's drive to save Willa Cather's and Walt Whitman's houses.[58] Moreover, collective spaces such as the offices of Olivia Records, founded in 1973 to record and distribute women's music (based in Los Angeles and subse-

Figure 3.2. The Historic American Buildings Survey poster of the Furies House. The caption reads, "HABS/HAER/HALS documentation of the Furies Collective House, DC. The National Park Service pays tribute to LGBTQ communities by recording sites and structures that help to illustrate their contributions to American history and achievement." Photo by Todd Croteau, National Park Service.

quently located in Oakland), along with critical sites of political action by groups such as ACT UP and the Lesbian Avengers, both of which shunned conventional forms of protest in favor of bolder tactics, await recognition for their distinctive roles in LGBTQ history.[59]

Fortunately, work to identify and designate places associated with some of the most compelling LGBTQ figures in American history has begun to move beyond the lives of white gay men to include women and people of color. Trailblazing civil rights activist Bayard Rustin's (1912–1987) residence at the Penn South Complex in Manhattan was recognized as a landmark by the New York State Board for Historic Preservation in 2015 and added to the NRHP in 2016.[60] An African American gay man, Rustin was active in American movements for civil rights, socialism, nonviolence, and gay rights, earning a reputation as the best organizer in America. He purchased the apartment in 1962, joined by his life partner Walter Naegle in 1977. Rustin lived there until his death in 1987, after which Naegle preserved it almost exactly as it had been during Rustin's time. Rustin was posthumously awarded the Presidential Medal of Freedom, the highest civilian honor, by President Barack Obama in 2013.[61] The childhood home of Pauli Murray, an influential African American civil rights leader who struggled with her sexuality and gender identity, was designated an NHL on 11 January 2017.[62]

One little-recognized source of information feeding LGBTQ preservation projects are theses and dissertations by students pursuing graduate degrees in historic preservation and related fields (particularly architecture, urban planning, museum studies, and public history) who are eager to connect their political concerns and identity to their chosen profession.[63] Ken Lustbader's 1993 Columbia University thesis on Greenwich Village laid a foundation for two decades of initiatives addressing LGBTQ history within the historic district and pointed the way for broader initiatives to recover NYC's queer cultural resources.[64] Bill Adair's graduate thesis and Moira Kenney's dissertation, both completed in UCLA's Urban Planning program, fed into a grassroots project to map the city's gay and lesbian landmarks, an initiative that was supported by the Western Regional Office of the National Trust for Historic Preservation.[65] Similarly, Shayne Watson's 2009 University of Southern California thesis, which identified the tangible remains of San Francisco's lesbian community in North Beach in the period from 1933 to 1960, provided both methodological insights and a stream of information for a recent citywide context document.[66] Many of these projects created experts and leaders in the area of LGBTQ heritage. It points to the possibilities for cultivating a next generation of leadership by supporting the work of graduate students with an interest in and aptitude for preserving queer heritage.

Because much of the foundational work to preserve LGBTQ historic places was not commissioned or sponsored by formal preservation advocacy groups or agencies, the mapping projects and growing number of individual landmark designations were done without some of the most useful tools for preservation planning, namely, (1) detailed historic context documents that identify the range of themes and property types significant in LGBTQ heritage within a particular locale and which provide a comparative context for assessing the relative significance and integrity of places associated with those themes, and (2) systematic surveys that document the history and condition of extant resources. These kinds of projects require substantial resources to produce high-quality products and go well beyond the capacity of purely voluntary efforts. Fortunately, there are now several model projects to guide further work of this type, and new projects in the pipeline.

Employing the Tools of Preservation Planning: LGBTQ Context Documents, Field Surveys, and Nominations

The first known example of an LGBTQ context document, prepared by Damien Scott in 2004, grew out of the foundational work done by Friends of 1800 in San Francisco and was carried out with very limited funding. Faced with financial constraints, project organizers are rarely able to engage the full range of constituencies nominally organized under the banner of LGBTQ. More than a decade later, the City and County of San Francisco deepened its commitment to planning for the protection of its queer heritage by commissioning a new context document that built upon and reached beyond the pioneering 2004 project. San Francisco's leadership points to the level of political mobilization, advocacy, organization, and volunteer effort required to bring LGBTQ heritage to the fore, and explains why it remains obscured elsewhere in the American landscape, despite the fact that LGBTQ people have resided everywhere. Fortunately, this picture is beginning to change as groups outside the metropoles of San Francisco, Los Angeles, Chicago, and New York City are organizing to preserve their cultural queer resources.

The ability to carry out systematic surveys of LGBTQ places has hinged on the willingness of preservation agencies to allocate funding, which in turn depends on the political clout of the local LGBTQ communities. For that reason, the cities of Los Angeles and San Francisco have been at the forefront of supporting the development of historic context documents. Nestled within the larger project "Survey LA," the City of Los Angeles completed an LGBT Historic Context Statement in 2014 with support from the NPS and the California Office of Historic Preservation.[67] It focused on resources dating from the 1930s through the 1970s, principally located in neighborhoods between Downtown and Hollywood such as Westlake, Angelino Heights, Echo Park, and Silver Lake. The project used an online forum to gather information from members of the community and concerned groups, a strategy that augmented information exchange at a public meeting. The final report highlighted several themes, including (1) the Gay Liberation Movement; (2) LGBT persons and their impact on the entertainment industry; (3) the reconciliation of homosexuality and religion; (4) gay bars as social institutions; (5) the misguided labeling of homosexuality as a mental illness; (6) the LGBT community and the media; (7) gays and lesbians on the Los Angeles literary scene; and (8) queer art. Each theme generated information about multiple properties.

The most comprehensive citywide historic context statement on LGBTQ history completed to date began in 2013 and was completed in 2015 by Donna Graves and Shayne Watson for San Francisco, funded by a grant from the City and County's Historic Preservation Fund.[68] This context statement covered a longer timeline and wider range of themes than its Los Angeles counterpart, including (1) early influences on LGBTQ identities and communities; (2) the development and building of local LGBTQ communities; (3) police harassment; (4) homophile movements; (5) the evolution of LGBTQ enclaves and development of new neighborhoods; (6) gay liberation, pride, and politics; (7) LGBTQ medicine; and (8) the city's experience of the AIDS epidemic.

The San Francisco project has clarified the value of engaging in an intensive process of grassroots consultation to generate information about properties meaningful to various segments of the LGBTQ community, a process that requires more funding than typically is needed for well-documented aspects of history. So, too, it has highlighted the problems that arise when urgently trying to protect historic places whose significance was overlooked for decades and whose survival is threatened by rising land rents and the rapid pace of development in a superheated regional economy, in this case fueled by the tech boom.[69]

NPS funding, directed toward local projects to advance preservation in underrepresented communities, is supporting systematic surveys of LGBTQ heritage in New York City; the development of an LGBTQ context document and amendment of several NRHP nominations in Louisville,

Kentucky; a Historic American Buildings Survey of places associated with LGBTQ nightlife in Washington, DC; and the nomination of civil rights properties (including LGBTQ) to the NRHP in San Francisco.[70] Funding for the NPS Underrepresented Communities Grants was approved for 2017.[71] These sorts of investments will begin the hard work of filling gaps in our shared understanding of the lives of lesbian, gay, bisexual, and transgender Americans, and increase the possibilities for preserving the tangible resources associated with their heritage in the future.

Once more work has been done to identify the landmarks of LGBTQ history across the American landscape and to understand their comparative significance and integrity, it will be possible to develop a more comprehensive agenda for preservation and interpretation. The case of NHL designations for Frances Perkins, Molly Dewson, or others in the Roosevelts's political and social circle (see chapter 2) points to the value of considering all of the possible sites before narrowing the focus of preservation efforts to one or more properties. The same is true for some of the highest-profile LGBTQ designations.

Prepared as an individual nomination rather than as part of a comprehensive study, Stonewall was designated without necessarily considering the comparative significance and integrity of other contemporary sites of rebellion. Well-documented clashes occurred years earlier, in August 1966 at Compton's Cafeteria in San Francisco, sparked by resistance to police harassment.[72] Two parallel riots occurred in Los Angeles: the first at the popular downtown location, Cooper's Donut shop, in May 1959, which was a hangout for drag queens and hustlers because they were barred from entering either of the gay bars that flanked it; and the second at the Black Cat Tavern in Los Angeles, which occurred on 1 January 1967.[73] It inspired demonstration the following month that drew hundreds of people to protest police raids, harassment, and violence. The Black Cat was designated as a Los Angeles Cultural-Historic Landmark in 2008.

There's no debate about Stonewall's significance or its merit for NHL designation. However, it would hew closer to historical reality to recognize that most national social movements emerge as multinodal phenomena over an extended time period and, accordingly, to designate a cluster of associated tangible resources as a thematic group, rather than searching for one iconic property. While local studies are currently the path along which progress is advancing, thematic studies that cross geographic boundaries—for example, of the homophile movement, resistance to discrimination in the military, or the emergence of same-sex marriage in America—would benefit from a careful examination of extant historic properties nationally, rather than on a case-by-case basis. The themes explored in the theme study *LGBTQ America* provide the foundation for a more comprehensive approach to planning for the protection of LGBTQ resources, but additional progress depends on moving to the next stage by commissioning field surveys of the extant tangible resources.[74]

The Queer Future of Preservation Action

Much of the work in LGBTQ preservation undertaken to date has focused on identifying landmarks, increasing public awareness of their significance, and securing their presence on local, state, and federal registers of historic places. Realizing the goals of preserving LGBTQ heritage, however, will require concerted action to protect places of significance from demolition or damaging alterations. Development pressures, especially in cities with runaway growth, make it difficult to preserve historic landmarks under any circumstances. But the long neglect of LGBTQ heritage, uneven knowledge base, and limited mobilization of advocates complicate the process of trying to save threatened cultural resources. San Francisco routinely reports the planned demolition and redevelopment of properties that were identified in its recent theme study. Entry of information about the LGBTQ historic places into the city's Property Information Map makes it possible to flag them when applications for demolition permits are filed and to include them in broader planning studies, but it doesn't guarantee protection.[75]

Where the LGBTQ community exercises considerable political influence, including within local advocacy organizations, negotiations have begun over the fate of threatened landmarks. One property identified as significant within the Survey L.A. LGBT Historic Context Statement is the Circus Disco, a prominent gay and lesbian bar founded in 1975 that had a large Latinx following.[76] In addition to being a place to socialize, it also played an important role in political organizing and coalition building: "In 1983, civil rights and labor leader Cesar Chavez addressed roughly one hundred members of the Project Just Business gay and lesbian coalition at the bar, where he offered strategies for organizing boycotts and coalition fundraising."[77]

Circus Disco was recommended by city staff for consideration as a Los Angeles landmark. It was not, however, deemed significant or worthy of designation in the Environmental Impact Report prepared for the Lexington Project, the development scheduled to replace it. Early in 2016, Hollywood Heritage struck a deal with the developer to save key artifacts from the property. While it wasn't a total victory from the perspective of preservation, it signaled a new level of activism to protect the tangible remains of LGBTQ heritage.[78] Most news is bleaker because of the shuttering of legacy businesses. Redevelopment threatens these historic properties through soaring rents and demolition.[79] Clearly much work remains to be done to translate a growing knowledge base about LGBTQ cultural resources into effective preservation action.

Recent Progress in Reinterpreting LGBTQ Historic Properties

Beyond the designation and protection of places previously overlooked in preservation planning, the work of reinterpreting designated historic properties is advancing on many fronts. At the Hull-House Museum, where the nature of Mary Rozet Smith's relationship with founder Jane Addams has long been a point of contention, new leadership in 2006 opened the door to engaging with the interpretive issue directly.[80] Under Lisa Yun Lee's direction, museum staff invited visitor responses to alternative descriptions of the bonds between these women:

> After consulting with historians and descendants, museum staff crafted three different labels and displayed them next to the painting, . . . inviting visitors to indicate which label they found most meaningful by posting their comments on a nearby large public response board. Staff hoped the project would inspire visitors to think more critically about the history presented at the museum and to reflect on what was at stake—the determining of the meaning of history and who gets to decide. Thousands of people responded to the project, both at the museum and online, and these responses ultimately informed the treatment of the painting in . . . the museum's new permanent exhibit. The exhibit now includes additional artifacts and photographs illustrating the deep emotional intimacy the two women shared.[81]

"Gender and Sexuality" is a relatively recent addition to the tour options for Hull-House Museum visitors.[82] Other historic places with submerged LGBTQ histories have contended with greater degrees of resistance, conflict, and controversy before site administrators accepted the need for making adjustments. A case in point is Clear Comfort, the home of pioneering photographer Alice Austen located on the north shore of Staten Island.[83] The NHL nomination, which was generated in the context of a congressionally mandated study of women's history landmarks, like many others of their day, comes close to addressing LGBTQ issues while ultimately skirting the subject:

> Many of Austen's pictures explored not only conventional Victorian morals but also gender roles. Often, she and her friends are shown in intimate poses, revealing glimpses of underwear or sharing a bed, private things that no man would have dared to photograph. Other pictures show cigarettes dangling from their lips (at a time when women could be arrested for smoking in public). To further test gender boundaries Austen would dress her friends in male clothing and encourage them to parody what they viewed as typical male poses. Perhaps her rebellion against conventional Victorian standards explains the fact that Austen never married. Her friends said, "she was too good for men, that is she could do everything better." Instead, she and friend Gertrude Tate formed a fifty-year partnership in which each complemented the other. Austen and Gertrude Tate traveled extensively. In her lifetime Austen made over twenty trips abroad and travelled through much of the United States.[84]

The Friends of Alice Austen, which manages the property on behalf of New York City's Department of Parks and Recreation, resisted pressure to deal directly with the issue, a controversy that has been documented by heritage planner Tatum Taylor, who wrote her 2012 graduate thesis in Columbia University's Historic Preservation Program on the dilemmas of interpreting marginalized aspects of heritage.[85] In fact, the museum's board threatened to close the house as a debate swelled over whether Alice's supposed lesbianism was being intentionally suppressed, or whether it was a fact irrelevant to the interpretation of Clear Comfort's historic significance. The debate was marked by a 1994 protest at the house held by the Lesbian Avengers.[86]

In recent years, visitors have benefited from a slightly more candid interpretation of Austen's relationship with Gertrude Tate, who lived with her at Clear Comfort from 1917 to 1935. Addressing their relationship is not only an important biographical fact, but also a key context for understanding some of the subjects of Austen's photographs. As the Alice Austen House website explains it,

> On one such summer excursion in 1899, visiting a Catskill hotel known as "Twilight Rest," Alice met Gertrude Tate, who was recuperating there from a bad case of typhoid fever. Gertrude was twenty-eight, a kindergarten teacher and professional dancing instructor, who worked to support her younger sister and widowed mother in Brooklyn. Judging from the small personal photo album that commemorates that summer, Gertrude's spontaneous gaiety and warm humor enchanted Alice,

who was then thirty-three. Gertrude began regularly to visit the Austen House, then to spend long summer holidays in Europe with Alice. But not until 1917, when her younger sister and mother gave up their Brooklyn home, did Gertrude, overriding her family's appalled objections over her "wrong devotion" to Alice, finally move into Clear Comfort.[87]

Because the website and interpretation of the historic house made limited direct references to Austen and Tate's relationship when Taylor examined them in 2012, she was critical of the omissions in the museum's displays, its orientation film, and related aspects of public interpretation.[88] On 23 March 2017, an amended nomination for Clear Comfort was listed on the NRHP. This amended nomination specifically addresses the LGBTQ history at the site. The NHL nomination for Clear Comfort remains unamended. Landmark nominations for this property and others like it that have not been amended to address LGBTQ themes run the risk of overlooking—and potentially threatening—aspects of the physical fabric that merit inclusion in historic properties' preservation, interpretation, collections management, and restoration plans.

But even in cases where historic site administrators remain reluctant to embrace LGBTQ history, it is possible to convey that history to the public through independent projects presented on the internet or in public spaces adjacent to the property. The New York City Landmarks Preservation Commission, for example, has prepared a presentation that explains the LGBTQ connections to many listed properties, including the Austen House, and there are many models for site-specific art projects that mark placed-based histories in public space.[89] Independent initiatives that do not require obtaining the consent of property owners or nonprofit boards offer paths to interpretive freedom. Buy-in is critical for institutionalizing and embedding reforms on site, but direct action has the virtue of disengaging from intractable resistance to make claims to LGBTQ heritage at historic properties that lie beyond current grasp.

At many historic properties, decisions about how much to reveal remain in the hands of individual docents, who often calibrate presentations based on their own perceptions of each visitor's receptivity. Such is the case at the Gibson House Museum in Boston's Back Bay, another example of an NHL where little is officially recognized about the place's connections to LGBTQ history, but where individual guides with an interest in the subject have begun to address visitors' questions about the sexuality of key interpretive figures. In this case, the figure is Charles Hammond Gibson Jr. (1874–1954), who was the leading force in preserving the family home as a museum.[90] Gibson House guide Jonathan Vantassel is, according to a *Boston Globe* article, circumspect about the love life of Charles Hammond Gibson Jr., who preserved his family's Victorian home for the public, but forthcoming when asked directly about Gibson's sexuality—often by LGBT visitors. "It's very clear that he was very open and proud about who he was," Vantassel says. "I think that absolutely we have to . . . give that to our visitors. Otherwise, we're not telling the whole story."[91]

This revised interpretation complicates Gibson's self-representation as an exceedingly formal and patrician man, who was viewed by others as aloof and lonely.[92]

Deepening research about the LGBTQ dimensions of historic places, such as Beauport, located in Massachusetts, is transforming their presentation to the public.[93] Located atop a rocky ledge overlooking Gloucester Harbor, Beauport was the creation of and home to self-taught designer Henry Davis Sleeper (1878–1934), a gay man who was a nationally recognized antiquarian, collector, and interior decorator. The property, designated an NHL in 2003 and operated as an historic house museum, marks Sleeper's contributions to American decorative arts, and is one of only two places illustrating his career as a designer that survive with a high degree of integrity. Sleeper is described in most accounts as a life-long bachelor, and tour guides originally responded to questions about Sleeper's sexuality by stating he never married. Close examination of his passionate letters to A. Piatt Andrew Jr. offered new insight into his same-sex relations, providing an evidentiary base for addressing his homosexuality on guided tours of the property.[94] Since 2008, tour guides at Beauport have acknowledged that Sleeper was gay, making it a positive example of the ways LGBTQ heritage can be incorporated into the interpretation of historic places that in the past have principally been recognized for their architectural significance.[95]

Appropriating New Technologies to Improve the Protection of LGBTQ Heritage

Projects to map LGBTQ sites are becoming more technologically sophisticated, drawing on geographic information systems that marry databases to geolocation programs. Where a community is willing and able to contribute its memories and knowledge of historic places to online venues, the interactive capability of these types of projects allows for crowd-sourced information exchange. Several major projects of this type are directly lodged in the preservation community. Founded in 2012 by Gerard Koskovich, Shayne Watson, and Donna Graves, "Preserving LGBT Historic Sites in California" is a Facebook page that welcomes posts and comments. California Pride: Mapping LGBTQ Histories is an intensive online archive dedicated to the identification, interpretation, and commemoration of queer historic places. It was launched in 2014 with seed funding from the NTHP. Rainbow Heritage Network, organized in 2015 by Megan Springate and Mark Meinke, has also established a web-based approach to connecting those interested in LGBTQ preservation, sharing information about relevant issues on Facebook, and feeding information into a map locating LGBTQ historic properties.[96] The issue with web-based interactive projects, however, is that they require consistent funding to maintain and to support ongoing engagement with members of relevant communities. For these reasons, the long-term success of what started as independent projects will require ongoing institutional commitments, hosts, and homes that stabilize the infrastructure for information collection, dissemination, and mobilization to advance the preservation of LGBTQ heritage.

Conclusion: Strategies for Realizing an Inclusive Preservation Agenda

This overview of the history of LGBTQ preservation points to the many independent initiatives, collective efforts, and organized struggles for institutional change that have moved the needle over the past three decades. Future progress depends not only on coalescing LGBTQ activism, but also on integrating issues of sexuality and gender identity into the larger movement to transform preservation from its elite origins to become more democratic and inclusive. The same identity politics that have energized campaigns to preserve overlooked aspects of women's history, ethnic history, and LGBTQ history run the risk of missing the intersections among and between them.[97] As new investment is directed toward preparing nominations of LGBTQ properties, it makes sense to prioritize places that have the potential to illuminate the overlapping areas.

A nomination in progress for the San Francisco Women's Building captures multiple layers of historical significance and intersectional themes.[98] A four-story building in San Francisco's Mission District, it was built in 1910 as a Turn Hall, which housed German social and athletic clubs, and subsequently purchased in 1939 by the Sons and Daughters of Norway. In 1978 a group of women who founded San Francisco Women's Centers initiated the purchase of this building to provide an incubator and hub for a wide array of projects dedicated to improving the lives of women. Known as the Women's Building, it became the first women-owned and operated community center in the United States.[99] Renovations and seismic retrofits in 2000 retained elements from former uses while addressing contemporary functional needs. Over time, the Women's Building has housed more than 170 independent organizations, such as San Francisco Women Against Rape, Lilith Lesbian Theater Collective, Lesbian Youth Recreation and Information Center, and Somos Hermanas, a Central American solidarity group led by lesbians of color. A National Register of Historic Places nomination for the Women's Building currently is being prepared by Donna Graves that highlights its important roles in second-wave feminism and the LGBTQ movement, addressing the connections among and between the politics of gender, race, class, and sexuality as second-wave feminism unfolded from the 1970s to the present.

Another priority for advancing an LGBTQ preservation agenda is identifying sites that illuminate the complexity of political alliances and differences among and between lesbians, gay men, bisexuals, and transgender people. The spatial implications of racism are etched deeply into the landscape of community, resulting in a pattern of bars and other institutions having been more or less welcoming to people of color. Before Stonewall, some gay bars and their patrons kept a distance from drag queens and others who crossed customary gender boundaries because the criminalization of public cross-dressing provided ready opportunities for police harassment. Some of the alliances that produced a political movement inclusive of LGBTQ people under one banner actually fray upon closer inspection—for example, ideological divisions between lesbian feminists who limited entry to the Michigan Womyn's Music Festival to "womyn-born-womyn" and those who denounced the policy as transphobic. An annual event held on land in Oceana County, Michigan, for forty years from 1976 to 2015, the festival's popularity waned with the decline of women's record labels such as Olivia, the mainstreaming of female recording artists, and a new generation of feminists disinclined toward binary conceptions of sex and gender, and therefore with a different attitude toward women-only events. The festival ended permanently in 2016 over irreconcilable political differences between the separatist ethos that shaped its origins and the rise of greater activism related to the rights of transgender people.

When previously suppressed aspects of history are finally brought to light, the temptation is often to critique societal forces of oppression and valorize the oppressed. An accurate and complete representation of history, however, demands a critical perspective on the complex dynamics of gender, race, and class, among other categories of social analysis, that have shaped the circumstances, standpoint, status, and political consciousness of particular LGBTQ people. Finally, there is a need to move beyond marking places associated with LGBTQ history per se to identify places that have been essential to producing and policing heteronormativity. Marking gay bars that were sites of rebellion is a powerful act; however, as a matter of social justice, police stations and liquor licensing offices that once led the charge in harassing LGBTQ people are also critical sites for telling the story. Similarly, historic places such as psychiatric hospitals where queer people were incarcerated and "treated" under the mistaken medical belief that they possessed disorders should address the dark and difficult aspects of their history as part of site interpretation. It is necessary, but far from sufficient, to mark this history at the few sites LGBTQ people historically claimed. Justice demands a critical perspective and more LGBTQ-positive message at places that played an instrumental role in enforcing heterosexuality as normative: churches, hospitals, military facilities, and more. As an instrument of social justice, cultural work on behalf of oppressed groups requires telling difficult truths about the past, honoring their struggles to achieve equity, and reclaiming the wider world from which they were so often excluded as a welcoming place for all American people. Historic places and their interpretation cannot in themselves bring about justice for historic inequities in the treatment of indigenous people, women, people of color, or those whose sexuality and gender expression defied social norms. But these forms of cultural work can disrupt the oppressive logic of settler colonialism, sexism, racism, and homophobia; signal a public ethos of equality; and promote civic dialogue about the gaps that remain between our actual practices and our aspirations for a democratic and inclusive society.

While preservation advocacy built around the politics of identity thus far has marginally improved representations of women, ethnic communities of color, and LGBTQ people at historic places, in the long run it risks diluting the collective power of previously underrepresented groups to change discriminatory policies and practices that pose structural and institutional barriers to equity.[100] The standards of significance and integrity that guided the designation of NHLs were set at a time when the activities and accomplishments of elite white men of a propertied class were at the center of historical scholarship. Now that history includes not only those who were significantly disadvantaged but also dispossessed, or considered property themselves, notions about the integrity of the places associated with them merit re-examination. In this sense, many underrepresented groups share a common cause for reform of standard preservation policies and practices that a focus on a particular identity may obscure. For that reason, building alliances among groups whose histories have been marginalized, and supporting the development of emerging leaders inclined to build bridges between them, is critical to realizing a progressive vision for historic preservation.

Dr. Gail Dubrow is a professor of architecture, landscape architecture, public affairs and planning, and history at the University of Minnesota.

Notes

1. "The Legacy Walk . . . ," Legacy Project website, http://www.legacyproject chicago.org/About.html.
2. Independence Hall is located at 520 Chestnut Street, Philadelphia, Pennsylvania. It is part of Independence National Historical Park, established 28 June 1948 and designated an NHL district on 15 October 1966.
3. "Barbara Gittings," National LGBT 50th Anniversary website, http://lgbt50 .org/barbara-gittings.
4. "History That Disturbs the Present: An Interview with REPOHistory Artist Greg Sholette," interview by Dipti Desai, 26 April 2007, http://www .gregorysholette.com/wp-content/uploads/2011/04/History-that-disturbs-the-Present1.pdf.
5. For more information on LGBTQ art and artists, see Tara Burk, "LGBTQ Art and Artists," in *Communities and Place: A Thematic Approach to the Histories of LGBTQ Communities in the United States*, edited by Katherine Crawford-Lackey and Megan E. Springate (New York: Berghahn Books, forthcoming).
6. A typical feature reads: "Great Inns for Gay Girls: Ten Lesbian-Owned Bed-and-Breakfasts from Florida to New England," *Curve* 19, no. 3 (April 2009): 50. There is also a body of scholarship on LGBTQ tourism; see, for example, Yaniv Poria, "Assessing Gay Men and Lesbian Women's Hotel Experiences," *Journal of Travel Research* 44, no. 3 (2006): 327–34. See also Katherine Schweighofer, "LGBTQ Sport and Leisure," in *LGBTQ America: A Theme Study of Lesbian, Gay, Bisexual, Transgender, and Queer History*, edited by Megan E. Springate (Washington, DC: National Park Foundation and National Park Service, 2016), https://www.nps.gov/articles/lgbtqtheme-sport.htm.
7. IGLTA holds an annual convention and sponsors a foundation. One of their heritage tourism-focused members, for example, is Oscar Wilde Tours, whose offerings range from walking tours of Greenwich Village to multiday European itineraries. See the IGLTA website at https://www.iglta.org.

8. The Federation of Gay Games has had a Culture Committee since 1993, whose mission is to identify "the censorship and oppression that block artistic and cultural expression, [examine] the production of successful arts/cultural events, [identify] guidelines to guarantee inclusion, and [explore] nontraditional ways to present art and culture." Heritage tours have been featured by some of the commercial enterprises attached to the Gay Games; see the Federation of Gay Games website at https://gaygames.org/wp.

9. This was noted by Sarah Nusser in "What Would a Non-Heterosexist City Look Like? A Theory on Queer Space and the Role of Planners in Creating the Inclusive City," master's thesis, Urban Studies and Planning, Massachusetts Institute of Technology, 2010. She cited the Visit Philadelphia website, which features a map of Philadelphia's Center City "gayborhood," see http://gophila.com/pub/campaign/gay.

10. See "The Philadelphia Gayborhood Guru: About the Author," *Philadelphia Gayborhood Guru* blog, https://thegayborhoodguru.wordpress.com/about-the-author.

11. Upon Hailey's retirement in 2005, Cruisin' the Castro Walking Tours was sold to professional tour guide Kathy Amendola, a sign of the growing commercial viability of LGBTQ heritage enterprises; see the company's website at http://www.cruisinthecastro.com/tours.html.

12. Sarah Prager, "LGBT History Walking Tours for Every City," Quist website, 13 September 2015, http://www.quistapp.com/lgbt-history-walking-tours-for-every-city.

13. Paula Martinac, *The Queerest Places: A Guide to Gay and Lesbian Historic Sites* (New York: Henry Holt and Company, 1997).

14. For information on the Committee on Lesbian, Gay, Bisexual, and Transgender History, see their website at http://clgbthistory.org.

15. See "Committee on LGBT History at the 2013 AHA [Convention] in New Orleans, LA," Committee on LGBT History website, http://clgbthistory.org/aha-convention-2013.

16. See "2015 OAH Annual Meeting. Sessions by Special Interest: LGBTQ," Organization of American Historians website, http://www.oah.org/meetings-events/2015/highlights/lgbtq.

17. See "Lesbian and Gay Archives Roundtable," Society of American Archivists website, http://www2.archivists.org/groups/lesbian-and-gay-archives-roundtable-lagar#.VwQaOjYrI1I.

18. See also Susan Ferentinos, "Interpreting LGBTQ Historic Sites," this volume.

19. Renae Youngs, Christopher Leitch, and Michael Lesperance, "Setting the Standard for LGBTQ Inclusion," *Museum*, January/February 2016, 33–35; American Alliance of Museums, *LGBTQ Alliance: Welcoming Guidelines for Museums*, American Alliance of Museums, 2016, http://aam-us.org/docs/default-source/professional-networks/lgbtq_welcome_guide.pdf. For an application of these welcoming guidelines from the perspective of a chil-

dren's museum, see Katie Slivovsky, "10 Easy Ways Museums Can Be More LGBTQ-friendly," *Alliance Labs*, 30 October 2017, http://labs.aam-us.org/blog/10-easy-ways-museums-can-be-more-lgbtq-friendly/.

20. The Glen Burnie House is located at 901 Amherst Street, Winchester, Virginia. It was listed on the NRHP on 10 September 1979. For a single-site case study, see Michael Lesperance, "Rearranging the Closet: Decoding the LGBT Exhibit Space," *InPark Magazine*, 15 April 2014, https://www.themsv.org/sites/default/files/InPark%20Magazine%20%E2%80%93%20Rearranging%20the%20Closet_%20Decoding%20the%20LGBT%20Exhibit%20Space.pdf. For comprehensive treatment, see Susan Ferentinos, ed., *Interpreting LGBT History at Museums and Historic Sites* (Lanham, MD: Rowman and Littlefield, 2015).

21. Archived newsletters produced by the Queer Caucus for Art can be found online at http://artcataloging.net/glc/glcn.html. A summary chronology of its activities is located at http://artcataloging.net/glc/chronology.html.

22. See, for example, Kathryn H. Anthony, *Designing for Diversity: Gender, Race, and Ethnicity in the Architectural Profession* (Champaign: University of Illinois Press, 2007).

23. See Organization of Lesbian and Gay Architects and Designers (OLGAD), *A Guide to Lesbian & Gay New York Historical Landmarks*.

24. See *Location: A Historical Map of Lesbian and Gay Boston* (Boston: Boston Area Gay and Lesbian History Project and Boston Gay and Lesbian Architects and Designers, 1995).

25. Philip Arcidi, "Defining Gay Design," *Progressive Architecture* 75, no. 8 (August 1994): 36. An earlier symposium on "Sexuality and Space," organized by Beatriz Colomina in March 1990, pioneered the topic, though it was not entirely focused on LGBTQ issues. It was the basis for a published volume: Beatriz Colomina, ed., *Sexuality and Space* (Princeton, NJ: Princeton Architectural Press, 1996). Related articles about architecture and same-sex desire, published around the time of the first OLGAD conference, included Henry Urbach, "Spatial Rubbing: The Zone," *Sites* 25 (1993): 90–95; Aaron Betsky, "Closet Conundrum: How 'Out' Can the Design Professions Be?" *Architectural Record* 182, no. 6 (June 1994): 36; John Paul Ricco, "Coming Together," *A/R/C Architecture, Research, Criticism* 1, no. 5 (1994–1995): 26–31; and Henry Urbach, "Closets, Clothes, Disclosure," *Assemblage* 30 (August 1996): 62–73. The edited volume *Stud: Architectures of Masculinity*, ed. Joel Sanders (Princeton, NJ: Princeton University Press, 1996), also addressed gay male experience and drew on queer theory for analyses of the social construction of masculinity in urban and architectural space. Also see Aaron Betsky, *Building Sex: Men, Women, Architecture, and the Construction of Sexuality* (New York: William Morrow, 1995); Gordon Brent Ingram, Anne-Marie Bouthillette, and Yolanda Retter, eds., *Queers in Space: Communities, Public Spaces, Sites of Resistance* (Seattle: Bay Press, 1997).

26. See College of Environmental Design, "Arcus Endowment and Arcus Foundation Chair," College of Environmental Design, University of California, Berkeley, website, http://ced.berkeley.edu/give-to-ced/faculty-support/arcus-endowment-and-arcus-foundation-chair.

27. See American Planning Association, "Gays and Lesbians in Planning," American Planning Association website, https://www.planning.org/divisions/galip.

28. Early and influential articles explaining the import of LGBTQ populations for planning practice included Ann Forsyth, "Sexuality and Space: Nonconformist Populations and Planning Practice," *Journal of Planning Literature* 15, no. 3 (2001): 339–58; and Michael Frisch, "Planning as a Heterosexist Project," *Journal of Planning Education and Research* 21, no. 3 (March 2002): 254–66. The edited volumes by Petra L. Doan include *Queerying Planning: Challenging Heteronormative Assumptions and Reframing Planning Practice* (New York: Routledge, 2011); and *Planning and LGBTQ Communities: The Need for Inclusive Queer Spaces* (New York: Routledge, 2015).

29. Anthony, *Designing for Diversity*, 105.

30. Influential early work on the geography of LGBTQ communities included Sy Adler and Johanna Brenner, "Gender and Space: Lesbians and Gay Men in the City," *International Journal of Urban and Regional Research* 16, no. 1 (March 1992): 24–34; David Bell and Gill Valentine, *Mapping Desire* (New York: Routledge, 1995); Gill Valentine, "Out and About: Geographies of Lesbian Landscapes," also published in the *International Journal of Urban and Regional Research* 19, no. 1 (1995): 96–111; and Ruth Fincher and Jane M. Jacobs, eds., *Cities of Difference* (New York: The Guilford Press, 1998).

31. Examples of scholarship in the geography of LGBTQ communities include Adler and Brenner, "Gender and Space: Lesbians and Gay Men in the City"; Bell and Valentine, *Mapping Desire*; Valentine, "Out and About: Geographies of Lesbian Landscapes"; Fincher and Jacobs, *Cities of Difference*; James T. Sears, *Rebels, Rubyfruit, and Rhinestones: Queering Space in the Post Stonewall South* (New Brunswick, NJ: Rutgers University Press, 2001); Michael Brown and Larry Knopp, "Queer Cultural Geographies: We're Here! We're Queer! We're Over There Too!" in *The Handbook of Cultural Geography*, ed. Kay Anderson et al. (London: Sage, 2002), 460–81; Charles I. Nero, "Why Are the Gay Ghettos White?" in *Black Queer Studies: A Critical Anthology*, ed. E. Patrick Johnson and Mae G. Henderson (Durham, NC: Duke University Press, 2005), 228–45; Michael Brown and Larry Knopp, "Queering the Map: The Productive Tensions of Colliding Epistemologies," *Annals of the Association of American Geographers* 98, no. 1 (March 2008): 40–58; Michael Brown, Sean Wang, and Larry Knopp, "Queering Gay Space," in *Seattle Geographies*, ed. Michael Brown and Richard Morrill (Seattle: University of Washington Press, 2011), 155–62; J. Gieseking, "Crossing Over into Territories of the Body: Urban Territories, Borders, and Lesbian-Queer Bodies in New York City," *Area* 48, no. 3 (2015): 262–70, doi: 10.1111/area.12147.

32. A reliable account of the formation of the AAG's Sexuality and Space specialty group is contained in Glen Elder, Lawrence Knopp, and Heidi Nast, "Sexuality and Space," in *Geography in America at the Dawn of the 21st Century*, ed. Gary L. Gaile and Cort J. Willmott (New York: Oxford University Press, 2004), 200–8.

33. The Society of American Archaeology published a special section edited by Dawn Ruteki and Chelsea Blackmore, "Toward an Inclusive Queer Archaeology," in its journal, *Archaeological Record* 16, no. 1 (January 2016), that provides the best overview of the current state of the field. For an introduction to the scholarly literature, see Tom Boellstorff, "Queer Studies in the House of Anthropology," *Annual Review of Anthropology* 36 (October 2007): 17–35; Barbara Voss, "Sexuality Studies in Archaeology," *Annual Review of Anthropology* 37 (2008): 317–36; Thomas A. Dowson, ed., "Queer Archaeologies," a special issue of *World Archaeologies* 32, no. 2 (2000); Robert A. Schmidt, "The Iceman Cometh: Queering the Archaeological Past," in *Out in Theory: The Emergence of Lesbian and Gay Anthropology*, ed. Ellen Lewin and William L. Leap (Chicago: University of Illinois Press, 2002), 155–85; Susan Terendy, Natasha Lyons, Michelle Janse-Smekal, eds., *Que(e)rying Archaeology: Proceedings of the Thirty-Seventh Annual Chacmool Conference, University of Calgary* (Calgary: Archaeological Association, University of Calgary, 2009).

34. Chelsea Blackmore and Dawn M. Ruteki, "Introducing the Queer Archaeology Interest Group: Who We Are and Why We Need Your Support," *The SAA Archaeological Record* 14, no. 5 (November 2014): 18–19.

35. For a discussion of how LGBTQ archaeology can be incorporated into larger questions of interpretation, see Megan E. Springate, "LGBTQ Archeological Context," this volume.

36. The Carmel Fallon Building is located at 1800–1806 Market Street, San Francisco, California. See "About Friends of 1800," The Friends of 1800 website, http://www.friendsof1800.org/friendsof1800.html.

37. "About the Friends of 1800."

38. The Carmel Fallon Building is San Francisco Landmark #223 (1998).

39. Gerry Takano, "Tiptoeing through the GLBT Preservation Movement," 28 April 2011, http://www.friendsof1800.org/EVENTS/Tiptoeing-through-GLBT-Preservation.pdf.

40. Damon Scott for the Friends of 1800, "Sexing the City: The Development of Sexual Identity Based Subcultures in San Francisco, 1933–1979," Final Draft Historic Context Statement, July 2004.

41. For an account of this struggle within the NTHP, see Gail Dubrow, "Blazing Trails with Pink Triangles and Rainbow Trails," *Restoring Women's History through Historic Preservation*, ed. Gail Dubrow and Jennifer Goodman (Baltimore: Johns Hopkins University Press, 2003), 281–99.

42. Dennis Drabelle, "Out and About in the City," *Preservation* 49, no. 1 (January–February 1997): 76–78.

43. Gail Dubrow, "Blazing Trails with Pink Triangles and Rainbow Flags: New Directions in the Preservation and Interpretation of Gay and Lesbian Heritage," *Preservation Forum* 12, no. 3 (Spring 1998): 31–44.

44. Philip Johnson's Glass House is located at 798–856 Ponus Ridge Road, New Canaan, Connecticut. It was added to the NRHP and designated an NHL on 18 February 1997. Ghost Ranch Education and Retreat Center is located at 280 Private Drive 1708, Abiquiu, New Mexico. It was designated a National Natural Landmark in 1975.

45. The couple became more open about the significance of their relationship in the 1990s. Johnson boldly appeared on the cover of *Out Magazine* in 1996. Other open treatment of their relationship includes Martin Fuller, "Art: The Architect of a Master Builder's Art," *New York Times*, 2 June 1996. For a description of the couple's routine at the Glass House, see Alexandra Lange, "Philip Johnson's Not Glass Houses," *New York Times Magazine*, 13 February 2015.

46. See, for example, ubiquitous references to Whitney on the Glass House website at http://theglasshouse.org/learn/new-canaan-with-philip-johnson.

47. Julie Baumgardner, "A Performance Project That Brings Some Mystery to the Glass House," *New York Times*, 10 May 2016.

48. See, for example, "LGBT Heritage Stories," National Trust for Historic Preservation website, https://savingplaces.org/story-categories/lgbt-heritage-stories; or its affinity-group listserv for those interested in LGBT preservation issues, subscribe-lgbtpreservation-l@lists.nationaltrust.org.

49. Gail Dubrow and Connie Walker, "Panama Hotel [and Hashidate-Yu]," 605 South Main Street and 302 Sixth Avenue South, Seattle, Washington, NRHP Registration Form, 18 July 2002. The Panama Hotel was added to the NRHP and designated an NHL on 20 March 2006.

50. For example, for a history of San Francisco's gay bathhouses, see Allan Bérubé, "The History of Gay Bathhouses," *Journal of Homosexuality* 44, no. 3 (2003): 33–53. The Everard Baths were located at 28 West 28th Street, New York City; they were open from 1888 through 1986. The Lafayette Baths were located at 403–405 Lafayette Street, New York City (now demolished). The Continental Baths were located in the basement of the Ansonia Hotel, 2101–2119 Broadway, New York City, from 1968 to 1975; the Ansonia Hotel was listed on the NRHP on 10 January 1980. The New St. Marks Baths were located at 6 St. Marks Place, New York City, New York, from 1979 until closed by the city in response to the AIDS epidemic in 1985. The New St. Marks Baths opened in the former location of the Saint Marks Baths, a Turkish bath that served the area's immigrant population beginning in 1913. In the 1950s, a gay clientele began to visit the baths in the evenings; by the 1960s, it became exclusively gay. Jack's Baths was located at 1052 Geary, San Francisco, California, from circa 1936 through 1941, when they moved to 1143 Post Street, San Francisco, California. They closed in the 1980s. The Ritch Street Health Club, 330 Ritch Street, San Francisco, Califor-

nia, was popular in the 1960s and 1970s. The Barracks at 72 Hallam Street, San Francisco, California, opened in 1972, and burned in 1981. The Liberty Baths were open at 1157 Post Street in the Polk Gulch neighborhood of San Francisco, California, in the 1970s. They closed in the 1980s during the early years of the AIDS epidemic.

51. Brock Keeling, "SOMA to Get Another LGBT-Themed Public Space," | *Curbed San Francisco*, 2 June 2016, http://sf.curbed.com/2016/6/2/1184 1692/soma-leather-kink-public-space. Cindy, "Ringold Alley's Leather Memoir," *Public Art and Architecture from Around the World*, 17 July 2017, http://www.artandarchitecture-sf.com/ringold-alleys-leather-mem oir.html. The Tool Box, located on the corner of Fourth Street and Harrison in the South of Market neighborhood of San Francisco, California, opened in 1962 and closed in 1971, when the building was demolished for redevelopment. Gayle Rubin, "Folsom Street: The Miracle Mile, Part One," *Found SF*, http://www.foundsf.org/index.php?title=Folsom_Street:_The_Miracle_ Mile.

52. The principal authors of and advocates for the Stonewall nominations were former members of OLGAD, such as Andrew Dolkart, Ken Lustbader, and Jay Shockley, who first worked on raising the visibility of these types of sites in their 1994 guide to lesbian and gay sites in New York City. Their dedication, persistence, and the platform of their professional positions have been critical to changing the climate for LGBTQ heritage preservation. Stonewall, which encompasses the bar at 51–53 Christopher Street, New York City, and surrounding areas, was listed on the NRHP on 28 June 1999 and designated an NHL on 16 February 2000. It was designated as Stonewall National Monument on 24 June 2016.

53. Mark Meinke, "Dr. Franklin E. Kameny Residence," National Register of Historic Places Registration Form, 22 July 2006. The Dr. Franklin E. Kameny Residence in northwestern Washington, DC, was added to the NRHP on 2 November 2011, approximately three weeks after his death on 11 October 2011.

54. DOI GLOBE. "Envision a workplace . . . ," https://m.facebook.com/story.php ?story_fbid=1315450811803919&id=281723751843302.

55. Stephen A. Morris, "Interior Globe Sparked and Guided the Collaborative Effort to Recognize Stonewall Inn," *Interior Globe News* 1 (Spring 2000).

56. Stephen A. Morris, email to author, 13 April 2016.

57. Jenna Sauber, "Saving the House of the Furies," National Trust for Historic Preservation website, 9 December 2015, https://savingplaces.org/stories/ the-house-of-the-furies#.Vw6T1DYrI1I; and Lou Chibbaro Jr., "Honoring Home of D.C.'s Furies," *Washington Blade*, 20 January 2016, http://www .washingtonblade.com/2016/01/20/honoring-home-of-d-c-s-furies. For a history of the Furies, see Julie N. Enszner, "Have Fun So We Do Not Go Mad in "Male Supremacist Heterosexual Amerika: Lesbian-Feminist Poetry in The Furies," *Beltway Poetry Quarterly* 11, no. 2 (Spring 2010), http://wash ingtonart.com/beltway/furies.html. The Furies Collective house in the Capi-

tol Hill neighborhood of Washington, DC, was listed on the NRHP on 2 May 2016.

58. "Audre Lorde Residence, Staten Island, New York, St. Paul's Avenue/Stapleton Heights Historic District," in Christopher D. Brazee, Gale Harris, and Jay Shockley, *150 Years of LGBT History*, PowerPoint presentation prepared for LGBT Pride 2014, New York: New York City Landmarks Preservation Commission, 2014, http://www.nyc.gov/html/lpc/downloads/pdf/LGBT-PRI DE_2014.pdf.

59. See, for example, Laraine Sommella's interview with Maxine Wolfe, "This Is about People Dying: The Tactics of Early ACT UP and Lesbian Avengers in New York City," *Queers in Space*, ed. Ingram, Bouthillette, and Retter, 407–38; and The Lesbian Avengers' website at http://lesbianavengers.com.

60. For an excellent treatment of Rustin's life, see John D'Emilio, *Lost Prophet: The Life and Times of Bayard Rustin* (Chicago: University of Chicago Press, 2004). For a brief overview, see Steven Thrasher, "Bayard Rustin: The Man Homophobia Almost Erased from History," *BuzzFeed LGBT*, 27 August 2013, http://www.buzzfeed.com/steventhrasher/walter-naegle-partner-of-the-late-bayard-rustin-talks-about. Also see "Bayard Rustin Residence," National Park Service website, https://www.nps.gov/places/bayard-rustin-residence .htm. The Bayard Rustin Home, located in the Chelsea neighborhood of New York City, was added to the NRHP on 8 March 2016.

61. Justin Snow, "Obama Honors Bayard Rustin and Sally Ride with Medal of Freedom," *Metro Weekly*, 20 November 1913, http://www.metroweekly.com/2013/11/obama-honors-bayard-rustin-and.

62. The Pauli Murray Family Home is located at 906 Carroll St., Durham, North Carolina.

63. Some relevant student projects include Meaghan K. Nappo, "Not a Quiet Riot: Stonewall and the Creation of Lesbian, Gay, and Transgender Community and Identity through Public History Techniques," master's thesis, Department of History, University of North Carolina at Wilmington, 2010, http://dl.uncw.edu/etd/2010-3/nappom/meaghannappo.pdf; Tatum Taylor, "Undeniable Conjecture: Placing LGBT Heritage," 2011 Cleo and James Marston Fitch Prize, Preservation Alumni, Columbia University, http://pres ervationalumni.org/Resources/Documents/Fitch%20Prize%202011%20Tay lor.pdf; Elizabeth Rose Hessmiller, "Saving Each Other: Using Historic Preservation as a Tool for Therapeutic City Planning," master's thesis, University of Pennsylvania, 2013; Catherine Aust, "Be Proud: The Recognition and Preservation of Lesbian, Gay, Bisexual, Transgender, and Queer Heritage in the United States," master's thesis, Graduate Program in Art History, Rutgers University, 2014; Kasey Jaren Fulwood, "The National Register of Historic Places and Lesbian, Gay, Bisexual, and Transgender Heritage," master's thesis, University of Georgia, 2014, https://getd.libs.uga.edu/pdfs/fulwood_kasey_ j_201405_mhp.pdf; Vigdís María Hermannsdóttir, "Here I Am and Here I'm Not: Queer Women's Use of Temporary Urban Spaces in Post-Katrina New Orleans," master's thesis, University of New Orleans, 2015, http://scholar

works.uno.edu/cgi/viewcontent.cgi?article=3060&context=td; Grey Pierce, "Throwing Open the Door: Preserving Philadelphia's Gay Bathhouses," master's thesis, Historic Preservation, University of Pennsylvania, 2015, http://repository.upenn.edu/cgi/viewcontent.cgi?article=1586&context=hp_theses; and Richard Freitas, "'The Land at Our Feet': Preserving Pioneer Square's Queer Landscape" [Seattle, WA], master's thesis, University of Washington, 2017.

64. Ken Lustbader, "Landscape of Liberation: Preserving Gay and Lesbian History in Greenwich Village," master's thesis, Historic Preservation Program, Columbia University, 1993.

65. Moira Rachel Kenney, "Strategic Invisibility: Gay and Lesbian Place-Claiming in Los Angeles, 1970–1994," PhD diss., Urban Planning, University of California Los Angeles, 1994; and Bill Adair, "Celebrating a Hidden History: Gay and Lesbian Historic Places in Los Angeles," master's thesis, Urban Planning, University of California Los Angeles, 1997. Coverage of the "Gay and Lesbian LA History Map" produced by Jeff Samudio, Rachel Kenney, and Bill Adair can be found in Larry Gordon, "A Guide to Where L.A.'s Gays Came of Age," *Los Angeles Times*, 8 July 2001.

66. Shayne Elizabeth Watson, "Preserving the Tangible Remains of San Francisco's Lesbian Community in North Beach, 1933 to 1960," master's thesis, Master of Historic Preservation, University of Southern California, 2009.

67. Office of Historic Resources, Department of City Planning, City of Los Angeles, "Survey LA: LGBT Historic Context Statement," prepared by GPA Consulting with contributions from Carson Anderson, Senior Architectural Historian, ICF/Jones & Stokes, and Wes Joe, Community Activist (September 2014), http://www.preservation.lacity.org/files/LGBT%20Historic%20Context%209-14.pdf#page=66&zoom=auto,-73,373.

68. Donna J. Graves and Shayne E. Watson, "Citywide Historic Context Statement for LGBTQ History in San Francisco" (San Francisco, CA: City and County of San Francisco, October 2015), http://208.121.200.84/ftp/files/Preservation/lgbt_HCS/LGBTQ_HCS_October2015.pdf. San Diego has also completed a citywide historic context statement: GPA Consulting, "San Diego Citywide LGBTQ Historic Context Statement" (San Diego: City of San Diego, Department of City Planning, September 2016), https://www.sandiego.gov/sites/default/files/san_diego_lgbtq_historic_context_final.pdf.

69. These observations were developed in conversation with Donna Graves, who with Shayne Watson authored the San Francisco study.

70. United States Department of the Interior, "Secretary Jewell, Director Jarvis Announce $500,000 in Matching Grants to Support Diversity in National Register of Historic Places," U.S. Department of the Interior press release, 2 October 2014; and "Interior Department Announces Grants for Underrepresented Communities through Historic Preservation Fund," U.S. Department of the Interior press release, 6 November 2015, https://www.doi.gov/pressreleases/interior-department-announces-grants-underrep

resented-communities-through-historic. Catherine Fosl, Daniel J. Vivian, and Jonathan Coleman, *Kentucky LGBTQ Historic Context Narrative*, Anne Braden Institute for Social Justice Research, Kentucky, 2016, https://www .nps.gov/articles/kentucky-statewide-lgbtq-historic-context-narrative.htm. Other projects within the NPS include regional studies of LGBTQ properties in the Northeast and National Capital Regions, as well as a Historic American Buildings Survey consisting of a historic context statement and a survey of five properties associated with Washington, DC's LGBTQ nightlife. Amber Bailey, "LGBTQ Nightlife in Washington, DC" (Washington, DC: Historic American Buildings Survey, National Park Service, 2016), https://www. nps.gov/articles/lgbtq-nightlife-in-washington-dc.htm.

71. National Park Service, "Underrepresented Community Grants," National Park Service website, https://www.nps.gov/preservation-grants/communi ty-grants.html.

72. Compton's Cafeteria was located at 101 Taylor Street, San Francisco, California. This building is a contributing element to the Uptown Tenderloin Historic District, listed on the NRHP on 5 February 2009.

73. Cooper's Donuts was located between 527 and 555 South Main Street, Los Angeles, California. This "seedy stretch" of Main Street was located between the Waldorf and Harold's bars, according to Lillian Faderman, *Gay L.A.: A History of Sexual Outlaws, Power Politics, and Lipstick Lesbians* (New York: Basic Books, 2006), 1. The Black Cat was located at 3909 West Sunset Boulevard, Los Angeles, California.

74. Megan E. Springate, *LGBTQ America: A Theme Study of Lesbian, Gay, Bisexual, Transgender, and Queer History*, Washington, DC: National Park Foundation and National Park Service, 2016.

75. To access the San Francisco Planning Department's Property Information Map, see http://propertymap.sfplanning.org.

76. The Circus Disco was located at 6655 Santa Monica Boulevard, Los Angeles, California. It closed in January 2016; see Lina Lecaro, "Say Goodbye to Circus Disco with One Last Night of Disco Music," *LA Weekly*, 4 December 2015, http://www.laweekly.com/music/say-goodbye-to-circus-disco-with-one-last-night-of-disco-music-6347338.

77. See "Circus Disco," Los Angeles Conservancy website, last updated 25 January 2016, https://www.laconservancy.org/issues/circus-disco.

78. "Historic Preservation; A Place in Gay History," *Los Angeles Times*, 22 January 2016, B2.

79. Seth Hemmelgarn, "Tea Room Theater Closing," *Bay Area Reporter*, 12 May 2016.

80. Hull House, located at 800 South Halsted, Chicago, Illinois, was listed on the NRHP on 15 October 1966 and designated an NHL on 23 June 1965.

81. "Jane Addams Hull-House Museum, Chicago, Illinois," in *Revealing Women's History: Best Practices at Historic Sites*, ed. Heather A. Huyck and Peg Strobel (Ukiah, CA: National Collaborative for Women's History Sites, 2011),

48. For an extended discussion of the reinterpretation of Hull-House, see Lisa Yun Lee, "Peering into the Bedroom: Restorative Justice at the Jane Addams's Hull House Museum," in *The Routledge Companion to Museum Ethics: Redefining Ethics for the Twenty-First Century Museum*, ed. Janet Marstine (Abington, Oxon: Routledge, 2011), 174–87.

82. Jennifer Brandel, "Should We Use the 'L Word' for Jane Addams?" Curious City, *WBEZ Online*, 5 September 2013, https://www.wbez.org/shows/wbez-news/should-we-use-the-l-word-for-jane-addams/2157704a-3738-4b8f-a879-b5aed91bb8f8. See also Victoria Bissell Brown, "Queer or Not: What Jane Addams Teaches Us about Not Knowing," in *Out in Chicago: LGBT History at the Crossroads*, ed. Jill Austin and Jennifer Brier (Chicago: Chicago History Museum, 2011), 63–76.

83. Clear Comfort, the Alice Austen House, is located at 2 Hylan Boulevard, Staten Island, New York. It was listed on the NRHP on 28 July 1970 and designated an NHL on 19 April 1993.

84. Jill Messirow and Page Putnam Miller, "Alice Austen House a.k.a. Clear Comfort: NHL Nomination," 23 June 1992.

85. Tatum Taylor, "Concealed Certainty and Undeniable Conjecture: Interpreting Marginalized Heritage," master's thesis, Graduate School of Architecture, Planning and Preservation, Columbia University, 2012.

86. Taylor, "Undeniable Conjecture: Placing LGBT Heritage."

87. See "Her Life," Alice Austen House website, http://aliceausten.org/her-life.

88. Friends of Alice Austen House recently received an NEH planning grant to reinterpret Austen through "new eyes." Of the nearly fifty projects funded under this category from 2012 through 2015, this is the only one with obvious potential to advance the interpretation of LGBTQ history. However as of the May 2016 project end date, there was little evidence of improved coverage on the Austen House's official website. On 23 March 2017, an amended nomination for Clear Comfort was listed on the NRHP. This amended nomination specifically addresses the LGBTQ history at the site.

89. LPC, *150 Years of LGBT History*.

90. The Gibson house is featured in a critique of the silencing of gay history in Joshua G. Adair, "House Museums or Walk-In Closets? The (Non)representation of Gay Men in the Museums They Called Home," in *Gender, Sexuality, and Museums*, ed. Amy Levin (Abingdon, Oxon: Routledge, 2010), 264–78. The Gibson House Museum is located at 137 Beacon Street, Boston, Massachusetts. It was listed on the NRHP and designated an NHL on 7 August 2001. It is also within the Back Bay Historic District, listed on the NRHP on 14 August 1973.

91. Jeremy C. Fox, "A Gloucester Mansion Leads the Way for LGBT Figures," *Boston Globe*, 21 June 2014, https://www.bostonglobe.com/business/2014/06/21/gloucester-mansion-leads-way-for-gay-inclusion-history/unMQkBY4nAzgbv6q9SabCI/story.html.

92. See Gibson House Museum, "The Gibson Family," Gibson House Museum website, http://www.thegibsonhouse.org/the-family.html.

93. Beauport, the Sleeper-McCann House, is located at 75 Eastern Point Boulevard, Gloucester, Massachusetts. It was added to the NRHP and designated an NHL on 27 May 2003.

94. History Project, *Improper Bostonians*, 92; see Henry Davis Sleeper, *Beauport Chronicle: The Intimate Letters of Henry Davis Sleeper to Abram Piatt Andrew, Jr., 1906–1915*, ed. E. Parker Hayden Jr. and Andrew L. Gray (Boston: Society for the Preservation of New England Antiquities, 1991).

95. Fox, "A Gloucester Mansion Leads the Way for LGBT Figures." Beauport's potential for interpretation as a LGBT-related historic property is explored by Kenneth C. Turino, "Case Study: The Varied Telling of Queer History at Historic New England," in *Interpreting LGBT History at Museums and Historic Sites*, ed. Susan Ferentinos (Lanham, MD: Rowman and Littlefield, 2015), 132–33.

96. See "Preserving LGBT Historic Sites in California," Facebook, https://www.facebook.com/PreservingLGBTHistory; "California Pride: Mapping Lesbian, Gay, Bisexual, Transgender, and Queer Histories," Historypin website, https://www.historypin.org/project/469-california-pride/#!map/index/#!/geo:37.271875,-119.270415/zoom:6; and Rainbow Heritage Network, http://rainbowheritagenetwork.org, and on Facebook at https://www.facebook.com/groups/439557382858786. LGBTQ America, a Historypin project begun by the National Park Service, Rainbow Heritage Network, and Quist, is one place where members of the public can pin historic LGBTQ places across the United States as part of a larger project; see https://www.historypin.org/en/lgbtq-america/.

97. Megan E. Springate, "A Note about Intersectionality, LGBTQ Communities, History, and Place," in *Communities and Place.*

98. The San Francisco Women's Building is located at 3543 Eighteenth Street, San Francisco, California.

99. See Women's Building, "History and Mission," The Women's Building website, http://womensbuilding.org/about/mission-history.

100. For an extended argument about the need to forge alliances among interest groups organized around specific identities, see Gail Dubrow, "From Minority to Majority: Building on and Moving beyond the Politics of Identity in Historic Preservation," in *Bending the Future: Fifty Ideas for the Next Fifty Years of Historic Preservation in the United States*, ed. Max Page and Marla Miller (Amherst: University of Massachusetts Press, 2016), 72–75.

Bibliography

Adair, Bill. "Celebrating a Hidden History: Gay and Lesbian Historic Place in Los Angeles." Master's thesis, University of California Los Angeles, 1997.

Adair, Joshua G. "House Museums or Walk-In Closets? The (Non)representation of Gay Men in the Museums They Called Home." In *Gender, Sexuality, and Museums*, edited by Amy Levin, 264–78. Abingdon, Oxon: Routledge, 2010.

Adler, Sy, and Johanna Brenner. "Gender and Space: Lesbians and Gay Men in the City." *International Journal of Urban and Regional Research* 16, no. 1 (March 1992): 24–34.

Alice Austen House. "Her Life." Alice Austen House website. http://aliceausten .org/her-life.

American Alliance of Museums. *LGBTQ Alliance: Welcoming Guidelines for Museums*. American Alliance of Museums, 2016. http://aam-us.org/docs/de fault-source/professional-networks/lgbtq_welcome_guide.pdf.

American Planning Association. "Gays and Lesbians in Planning." American Planning Association website. https://www.planning.org/divisions/galip.

Anthony, Kathryn H. *Designing for Diversity: Gender, Race, and Ethnicity in the Architectural Profession*. Champaign: University of Illinois Press, 2007.

Arcidi, Philip. "Defining Gay Design." *Progressive Architecture* 75, no. 8 (August 1994): 36.

Aust, Catherine. "Be Proud: The Recognition and Preservation of Lesbian, Gay, Bisexual, Transgender, and Queer Heritage in the United States." Master's thesis, Rutgers University, 2014.

Bailey, Amber. "LGBTQ Nightlife in Washington, DC." Washington, DC: Historic American Buildings Survey, National Park Service, 2016. https://www.nps .gov/articles/lgbtq-nightlife-in-washington-dc.htm.

Baumgardner, Julie. "A Performance Project That Brings Some Mystery to the Glass House." *New York Times*, 10 May 2016.

Bell, David, and Gill Valentine. *Mapping Desire*. New York: Routledge, 1995.

Berube, Allan. "The History of Gay Bathhouses." *Journal of Homosexuality* 44, no. 3 (2003): 33–53.

Betsky, Aaron. *Building Sex: Men, Women, Architecture, and the Construction of Sexuality*. New York: William Morrow, 1995.

———. "Closet Conundrum: How 'Out' Can the Design Professions Be?" *Architectural Record* 182, no. 6 (June 1994): 36.

Blackmore, Chelsea, and Dawn M. Rutecki. "Introducing the Queer Archaeology Interest Group: Who We Are and Why We Need Your Support." *The SAA Archaeological Record* 14, no. 5 (November 2014): 18–19.

Boellstorff, Tom. "Queer Studies in the House of Anthropology." *Annual Review of Anthropology* 36 (October 2007): 17–35.

Boston Area Gay and Lesbian History Project and Boston Gay and Lesbian Architects and Designers (BGLAD). *Location: A Historical Map of Lesbian and Gay Boston*. Boston: Boston Area Gay and Lesbian History Project and BGLAD, 1995.

Brandel, Jennifer. "Should We Use the 'L Word' for Jane Addams?" Curious City, *WBEZ Online*, 5 September 2013. https://www.wbez.org/shows/wbez-news/should-we-use-the-l-word-for-jane-addams/2157704a-3738-4b8f-a879-b5aed91bb8f8.

Brazee, Christopher D., Gale Harris, and Jay Shockley. *150 Years of LGBT History*. PowerPoint presentation prepared for LGBT Pride 2014. New York:

Landmarks Preservation Commission, 2014. http://www.nyc.gov/html/lpc/downloads/pdf/LGBT-PRIDE_2014.pdf.

Brown, Michael, and Larry Knopp. "Queer Cultural Geographies: We're Here! We're Queer! We're Over There Too!" In *The Handbook of Cultural Geography*, edited by Kay Anderson, Mona Domosh, Steve Pile, and Nigel Thrift, 460–81. London: Sage, 2002.

———. "Queering the Map: The Productive Tensions of Colliding Epistemologies." *Annals of the Association of American Geographers* 98, no. 1 (March 2008): 40–58.

Brown, Michael, Sean Wang, and Larry Knopp. "Queering Gay Space." In *Seattle Geographies*, edited by Michael Brown and Richard Morrill, 155–62. Seattle: University of Washington Press, 2011.

Brown, Victoria Bissell. "Queer or Not: What Jane Addams Teaches Us about Not Knowing." In *Out in Chicago: LGBT History at the Crossroads*, edited by Jill Austen and Jennifer Brier, 63–76. Chicago: Chicago History Museum, 2011.

Burk, Tara. "LGBTQ Art and Artists." In *Communities and Place: A Thematic Approach to the Histories of LGBTQ Communities in the United States*, edited by Katherine Crawford-Lackey and Megan E. Springate. New York: Berghahn Books, forthcoming.

Chibbaro, Lou, Jr. "Honoring Home of DC's Furies." *Washington Blade*, 20 January 2016. http://www.washingtonblade.com/2016/01/20/honoring-home-of-d-c-s-furies.

Cindy. "Ringold Ally's Leather Memoir." *Public Art and Architecture from Around the World*, 17 July 2017. http://www.artandarchitecture-sf.com/ringold-alleys-leather-memoir.html.

College of Environmental Design. "Arcus Endowment and Arcus Foundation Chair." College of Environmental Design, University of California, Berkeley. http://ced.berkeley.edu/give-to-ced/faculty-support/arcus-endowment-and-arcus-foundation-chair.

Colomina, Beatriz. *Sexuality and Space*. Princeton, NJ: Princeton Architectural Press, 1996.

Committee on LGBT History. "Committee on LGBT History at the 2013 AHA [Convention] in New Orleans, LA." Committee on LGBT History website. http://clgbthistory.org/aha-convention-2013.

Curve. "Great Inns for Gay Girls: Ten Lesbian-Owned Bed-and-Breakfasts from Florida to New England." *Curve* 19, no 3 (April 2009): 50.

D'Emilio, John. *Lost Prophet: The Life and Times of Bayard Rustin*. Chicago: University of Chicago Press, 2004.

Desai, Dipti, and Greg Sholette. "History That Disturbs the Present: An Interview with REPOHistory Artist Greg Sholette." Gregory Sholette, 26 April 2007. http://www.gregorysholette.com/wp-content/uploads/2011/04/History-that-disturbs-the-Present1.pdf.

Doan, Petra L., *Planning and LGBTQ Communities: The Need for Inclusive Queer Spaces*. New York: Routledge, 2015.

——, ed. *Queerying Planning: Challenging Heteronormative Assumptions and Reframing Planning Practice*. New York: Routledge, 2011.

Dowson, Thomas A., ed. "Queer Archaeologies." Special issue, *World Archaeologies* 32, no. 2 (2000).

Drabelle, Dennis. "Out and About in the City." *Preservation* 49, no. 1 (January–February 1997): 76–78.

Dubrow, Gail. "Blazing Trails with Pink Triangles and Rainbow Flags: New Directions in the Preservation and Interpretation of Gay and Lesbian Heritage." *Preservation Forum* 12, no. 3 (Spring 1998): 31–44.

——. "Blazing Trails with Pink Triangles and Rainbow Trails." In *Restoring Women's History through Historic Preservation*, edited by Gail Dubrow and Jennifer Goodman, 281–99. Baltimore: Johns Hopkins University Press, 2003.

——. "From Minority to Majority: Building on and Moving beyond the Politics of Identity in Historic Preservation." In *Bending the Future: Fifty Ideas for the Next Fifty Years of Historic Preservation in the United States*, edited by Max Page and Marla Miller, 72–75. Amherst: University of Massachusetts Press, 2016.

Dubrow, Gail, and Connie Walker. "National Register of Historic Places Nomination: Panama Hotel [and Hashidate-Yu]." National Register of Historic Places, National Park Service, Washington, DC, 2002.

Elder, Glen, Lawrence Knopp, and Heidi Nast. "Sexuality and Space." In *Geography in America at the Dawn of the 21st Century*, edited by Gary L. Gaile and Cort J. Willmott, 200–8. New York: Oxford University Press, 2004.

Enszer, Julie. "Have Fun So We Do Not Go Mad in Male Supremacist Heterosexual Amerika: Lesbian-Feminist Poetry in *The Furies*." *Beltway Poetry Quarterly* 11, no. 2 (Spring 2010). http://washingtonart.com/beltway/furies.html.

Faderman, Lillian. *Gay L.A.: A History of Sexual Outlaws, Power Politics, and Lipstick Lesbians*. New York: Basic Books, 2006.

Ferentinos, Susan. *Interpreting LGBT History at Museums and Historic Sites*. Lanham, MD: Rowman and Littlefield, 2015.

——. "Interpreting LGBTQ Historic Sites." In *Preservation and Place: Historic Preservation by and of LGBTQ Communities in the United States*, edited by Katherine Crawford-Lackey and Megan E. Springate. New York: Berghahn Books, 2019.

Fincher, Ruth, and Jane M. Jacobs, eds. *Cities of Difference*. New York: The Guilford Press, 1998.

Forsyth, Ann. "Sexuality and Space: Nonconformist Populations and Planning Practice." *Journal of Planning Literature* 15, no. 3 (March 2002): 264–66.

Fosl, Catherine, Daniel J. Vivian, and Jonathan Coleman. *Kentucky LGBTQ Historic Context Narrative*. Kentucky: Anne Braden Institute for Social Justice Research, 2016. https://www.nps.gov/articles/kentucky-statewide-lgbtq-historic-context-narrative.htm.

Fox, Jeremy C. "A Gloucester Mansion Leads the Way for LGBT Figures." *Boston Globe*, 21 June 2014. https://www.bostonglobe.com/business/2014/06/21/

gloucester-mansion-leads-way-for-gay-inclusion-history/unMQkBY4n
Azgbv6q9SabCI/story.html.

Freitas, Richard. "The Land at Our Feet: Preserving Pioneer Square's Queer Landscape." Master's thesis, University of Washington, 2017.

Friends of 1800. "About Friends of 1800." Friends of 1800 website. http://www
.friendsof1800.org/friendsof1800.html.

Frisch, Michael. "Planning as a Heterosexist Project." *Journal of Planning Education and Research* 21, no. 3 (March 2002): 254–66.

Fuller, Martin. "Art: The Architect of a Master Builder's Art." *New York Times*, 2
June 1996.

Fulwood, Kasey Jaren. "The National Register of Historic Places and Lesbian, Gay,
Bisexual, and Transgender Heritage." Master's thesis, University of Georgia,
2014. https://getd.libs.uga.edu/pdfs/fulwood_kasey_j_201405_mhp.pdf.

Gibson House Museum. "The Gibson Family." Gibson House Museum, http://
www.thegibsonhouse.org/the-family.html.

Gieseking, J. "Crossing Over into Territories of the Body: Urban Territories, Borders, and Lesbian-Queer Bodies in New York City." *Area* 48, no. 3 (2015):
262–70, doi: 10.1111/area.12147.

Gordon, Larry. "A Guide to Where L.A.'s Gays Came of Age." *Los Angeles Times*,
8 July 2001.

GPA Consulting. "Survey LA: LGBT Historic Context Statement" with contributions from Carson Anderson, Senior Architectural Historian, ICF/Jones &
Stokes, and Wes Joe, community activist. Los Angeles: Office of Historic Resources, Department of City Planning, City of Los Angeles, September 2014.
http://www.preservation.lacity.org/files/LGBT%20Historic%20Context%20
9-14.pdf#page=66&zoom=auto,-73,373.

———. "San Diego Citywide LGBTQ Historic Context Statement." San Diego: City
of San Diego, Department of City Planning, September 2016. https://www
.sandiego.gov/sites/default/files/san_diego_lgbtq_historic_context_final.pdf

Graves, Donna J. and Shayne E. Watson. *Citywide Historic Context Statement
for LGBTQ History in San Francisco*. San Francisco: City and County of San
Francisco, October 2015. http://208.121.200.84/ftp/files/Preservation/lgbt_
HCS/LGBTQ_HCS_October2015.pdf.

Hemmelgarn, Seth. "Tea Room Theater Closing." *Bay Area Reporter*, 12 May
2016.

Hermannsdóttir, Vigdís María. "Here I Am and Here I'm Not: Queer Women's Use
of Temporary Urban Spaces in Post-Katrina New Orleans." Master's thesis,
University of New Orleans, 2015. http://scholarworks.uno.edu/cgi/viewcon
tent.cgi?article=3060&context=td.

Hessmiller, Elizabeth Rose. "Saving Each Other: Using Historic Preservation as a
Tool for Therapeutic City Planning." Master's thesis, University of Pennsylvania, 2013.

History Project. *Improper Bostonians: Lesbian and Gay History from the Puritans
to Playland*. Boston: Beacon Press, 1998.

Ingram, Gordon Brent, Anne-Marie Bouthillette, and Yolanda Retter, eds. *Queers in Space: Communities, Public Spaces, Sites of Resistance.* Seattle: Bay Press, 1997.

"Jane Addams Hull-House Museum, Chicago, Illinois." In *Revealing Women's History: Best Practices at Historic Sites,* edited by Heather A. Huyck and Peg Strobel, 48. Ukiah, CA: National Collaborative for Women's History Sites, 2011.

Keeling, Brock. "SOMA to Get Another LGBT-Themed Public Space." *Curbed San Francisco,* 2 June 2016. http://sf.curbed.com/2016/6/2/11841692/soma-leather-kink-public-space.

Kenney, Moira Rachel. *Strategic Invisibility: Gay and Lesbian Place-Claiming in Los Angeles, 1970–1994.* Ph.D. diss., University of California Los Angeles, 1994.

Lange, Alexandra. "Philip Johnson's Not Glass Houses." *New York Times Magazine,* 13 February 2015.

Lecaro, Lina. "Say Goodbye to Circus Disco with One Last Night of Disco Music." *LA Weekly,* 4 December 2015. http://www.laweekly.com/music/say-good-bye-to-circus-disco-with-one-last-night-of-disco-music-6347338.

Lee, Lisa Yun. "Peering into the Bedroom: Restorative Justice at the Jane Addam's Hull House Museum." In *The Routledge Companion to Museum Ethics: Redefining Ethics for the Twenty-First Century Museum,* edited by Janet Marstine, 174–87. Abington, Oxon: Routledge, 2011.

Legacy Project. "The Legacy Walk . . . ." Legacy Project website. http://www.legacyprojectchicago.org/About.html.

Lesperance, Michael. "Rearranging the Closet: Decoding the LGBT Exhibit Space." *InPark Magazine,* 15 April 2014. https://www.themsv.org/sites/default/files/InPark%20Magazine%20E2%80%93%20Rearranging%20the%20Closet_%20Decoding%20the%20LGBT%20Exhibit%20Space.pdf.

LGBT 50th. "LGBT Civil Rights Movement: Barbara Gittings." LGBT 50th website. http://lgbt50.org/barbara-gittings.

Los Angeles Conservancy. "Circus Disco." Los Angeles Conservancy, last updated 22 January 2016. https://www.laconservancy.org/issues/circus-disco.

Los Angeles Times. "Historic Preservation: A Place in Gay History." 22 January 2016.

Lustbader, Ken. "Landscape of Liberation: Preserving Gay and Lesbian History in Greenwich Village." Master's thesis, Columbia University, 1993.

Martinac, Paula. *The Queerest Places: A Guide to Gay and Lesbian Historic Sites.* New York: Henry Holt & Co., 1997.

Meinke, Mark. "National Register of Historic Places Nomination: Dr. Franklin E. Kameny Residence." National Register of Historic Places, National Park Service, Washington, DC, 2006.

Messirow, Jill, and Page Putnam Miller. "National Historic Landmark Nomination: Alice Austen House a.k.a. Clear Comfort." National Historic Landmarks Program, National Park Service, Washington, DC, 1992.

Morris, Stephen A. "Interior GLOBE Sparked and Guided the Collaborative Effort to Recognize the Stonewall Inn." *Interior GLOBE News* 1 (Spring 2000).

Nappo, Meaghan K. "Not a Quiet Riot: Stonewall and the Creation of Lesbian, Gay, and Transgender Community and Identity through Public History Techniques." Master's thesis, University of North Carolina at Wilmington, 2010. http://dl.uncw.edu/etd/2010-3/nappom/meaghannappo.pdf.

National Park Service. "Bayard Rustin Residence." National Park Service website. https://www.nps.gov/places/bayard-rustin-residence.htm.

——. "Underrepresented Community Grants." National Park Service website. https://www.nps.gov/preservation-grants/community-grants.html.

National Trust for Historic Preservation. "LGBT Heritage Stories." National Trust for Historic Preservation. https://savingplaces.org/story-categories/lgbt-heritage-stories.

Nero, Charles I. "Why Are the Gay Ghettos White?" In *Black Queer Studies: A Critical Anthology*, edited by E. Patrick Johnson and Mae G. Henderson, 228–45. Durham, NC: Duke University Press, 2005.

Nusser, Sarah. "What Would A Non-Heterosexist City Look Like? A Theory on Queer Space and the Role of Planners in Creating the Inclusive City." Master's thesis, Massachusetts Institute of Technology, 2010.

Organization of American Historians. "2015 OAH Annual Meeting. Sessions by Special Interest: LGBTQ." Organization of American Historians. http://www.oah.org/meetings-events/2015/highlights/lgbtq.

Organization of Lesbian and Gay Architects and Designers. *A Guide to Lesbian & Gay New York Historical Landmarks*. New York: Organization of Lesbian and Gay Architects and Designers, 1994. http://www.gvshp.org/LGBTguide.htm.

Philadelphia Gayborhood Guru [Bob Skiba]. "The Philadelphia Gayborhood Guru: About the Author." *Philadelphia Gayborhood Guru* blog. https://thegayborhoodguru.wordpress.com/about-the-author.

Pierce, Grey. "Throwing Open the Door: Preserving Philadelphia's Gay Bathhouses." Master's thesis, University of Pennsylvania, 2015. http://repository.upenn.edu/cgi/viewcontent.cgi?article=1586&context=hp_theses.

Poria, Yaniv. "Assessing Gay Men and Lesbian Women's Hotel Experiences." *Journal of Travel Research* 44, no. 3 (2006): 327–34.

Prager, Sarah. "LGBT History Walking Tours for Every City." Quist, 13 September 2015. http://www.quistapp.com/lgbt-history-walking-tours-for-every-city.

Ricco, John Paul. "Coming Together." *A/R/C Architecture, Research, Criticism* 1, no. 5 (1994–1995): 26–31.

Rubin, Gayle. "Folsom Street: The Miracle Mile, Part One." *Found SF*, http://www.foundsf.org/index.php?title=Folsom_Street:_The_Miracle_Mile.

Rutecki, Dawn R., and Chelsea Blackmore, eds. "Towards an Inclusive Queer Archaeology." Special issue, *Archaeological Record* 16, no. 1 (January 2016).

Sanders, Joel, ed. *Stud: Architectures of Masculinity*. Princeton, NJ: Princeton University Press, 1996.

Sauber, Jenna. "Saving the House of the Furies." *National Trust for Historic Preservation*, 9 December 2015. https://savingplaces.org/stories/the-house-of-the-furies.

Schmidt, Robert A. "The Iceman Cometh: Queering the Archaeological Past." In *Out in Theory: The Emergence of Lesbian and Gay Anthropology*, edited by Ellen Lewin and William L. Leap, 155–85. Chicago: University of Illinois Press, 2002.

Schweighofer, Katherine. "LGBTQ Sport and Leisure." In *LGBTQ America: A Theme Study of Lesbian, Gay, Bisexual, Transgender, and Queer History*, edited by Megan E. Springate. Washington, DC: National Park Foundation and National Park Service, 2016. https://www.nps.gov/articles/lgbtqtheme-sport.htm.

Scott, Damon. "Sexing the City: The Development of Sexual Identity Based Sub-cultures in San Francisco, 1933–1979." Final Draft Historic Context Statement. San Francisco: Friends of 1800, July 2004.

Sears, James T. *Rebels, Rubyfruit, and Rhinestones: Queering Space in the Post Stonewall South*. New Brunswick, NJ: Rutgers University Press, 2001.

Sleeper, Henry Davis. *Beauport Chronicle: The Intimate Letters of Henry Davis Sleeper to Abram Piatt Andrew, Jr., 1906–1915*, edited by E. Parker Hayden Jr. and Andrew L. Gray. Boston: Society for the Preservation of New England Antiquities, 1991.

Slivovsky, Katie. "10 Easy Ways Museums Can Be More LGBTQ-friendly." *Alliance Labs*, 30 October 2017. http://labs.aam-us.org/blog/10-easy-ways-museums-can-be-more-lgbtq-friendly/.

Snow, Justin. "Obama Honors Bayard Rustin and Sally Ride with Medal of Freedom." *Metro Weekly*, 20 November 1913. http://www.metroweekly.com/2013/11/obama-honors-bayard-rustin-and.

Society of American Archivists. "Lesbian and Gay Archives Section" [also known as Lesbian and Gay Archives Roundtable]. Society of American Archivists website. http://www2.archivists.org/groups/lesbian-and-gay-archives-roundtable-lagar.

Sommella, Laraine, and Maxine Wolfe. "This is about People Dying: The Tactics of Early ACT UP and Lesbian Avengers in New York City." In *Queers in Space: Communities, Public Spaces, Sites of Resistance*, edited by Gordon Brent Ingram, Anne-Marie Bouthillette, and Yolanda Retter, 407–38. Seattle: Bay Press, 1997.

Springate, Megan E. "Beyond Identity: An LGBTQ Archaeological Context." In *Preservation and Place: Historic Preservation by and of LGBTQ Communities in the United States*, edited by Katherine Crawford-Lackey and Megan E. Springate. New York: Berghahn Books, 2019.

——. "A Note about Intersectionality, LGBTQ Communities, History, and Place." In *Communities and Place: A Thematic Approach to the Histories of LGBTQ Communities in the United States*, edited by Katherine-Crawford-Lackey and Megan E. Springate. New York: Berghahn Books, forthcoming.

Takano, Gerry. "Tiptoeing through the GLBT Preservation Movement." Friends of 1800, 28 April 2011. http://www.friendsof1800.org/EVENTS/Tiptoeing-through-GLBT-Preservation.pdf.

Taylor, Tatum. "Concealed Certainty and Undeniable Conjecture: Interpreting Marginalized Heritage." Master's thesis, Columbia University, 2012.

———. "Undeniable Conjecture: Placing LGBT Heritage." 2011 Cleo and James Marston Fitch Prize, Preservation Alumni, Columbia University. http://pres ervationalumni.org/Resources/Documents/Fitch%20Prize%202011%20Tay lor.pdf.

Terendy, Susan, Natasha Lyons, Michelle Janse-Smekal, eds. *Que(e)rying Archaeology: Proceedings of the Thirty-Seventh Annual Chacmool Conference, University of Calgary*. Calgary: Archaeological Association, University of Calgary, 2009.

Thrasher, Steven. "Bayard Rustin: The Man Homophobia Almost Erased from History." *BuzzFeed LGBT*, 27 August 2013. http://www.buzzfeed.com/stev enthrasher/walter-naegle-partner-of-the-late-bayard-rustin-talks-about#.tgK KoNZav.

Turino, Kenneth C. "Case Study: The Varied Telling of Queer History at Historic New England." In *Interpreting LGBT History at Museums and Historic Sites*, edited by Susan Ferentinos, 131–40. Lanham, MD: Rowman & Littlefield, 2015.

United States Department of the Interior. "Interior Department Announces Grants for Underrepresented Communities through Historic Preservation Fund." Press release, 6 November 2015. Washington, DC: United States Department of the Interior. https://www.doi.gov/pressreleases/interior-department-an nounces-grants-underrepresented-communities-through-historic.

———. "Secretary Jewell, Director Jarvis Announce $500,000 in Matching Grants to Support Diversity in National Register of Historic Places." Press release, 2 October 2014. Washington, DC: United States Department of the Interior.

Urbach, Henry. "Closets, Clothes, Disclosure." *Assemblage* 30 (August 1996): 62–73.

———. "Spatial Rubbing: The Zone." *Sites* 25 (1993): 90–95.

Valentine, Gill. "Out and About: Geographies of Lesbian Landscapes." *International Journal of Urban and Regional Research* 19, no. 1 (1995): 96–111.

Visit Philadelphia. "LGBT Philadelphia Maps and Downloads." Visit Philadelphia website. http://www.visitphilly.com/gay-downloads/.

Voss, Barbara. "Sexuality Studies in Archaeology." *Annual Review of Anthropology* 37 (2008): 317–36.

Watson, Shayne E. "Preserving the Tangible Remains of San Francisco's Lesbian Community in North Beach, 1933 to 1960." Master's thesis, University of Southern California, 2009.

Women's Building. "History and Mission." The Women's Building website. http://womensbuilding.org/about/mission-history.

Youngs, Renae, Christopher Leitch, and Michael Lesperance. "Setting the Standard for LGBTQ Inclusion." *Museum* (January/February 2016): 33–35.

CHAPTER 4

Beyond Identity
An LGBTQ Archaeological Context

Megan E. Springate

Introduction

This chapter was originally written for the theme study *LGBTQ America: A Theme Study of Lesbian, Gay, Bisexual, Transgender, and Queer History*.[1] The goal of the study was to provide a context for increasing the number of LGBTQ places represented on the National Register of Historic Places (NRHP) and designated as National Historic Landmarks (NHLs). Both of these programs are administered by the National Park Service (NPS). While this chapter retains its focus on the criteria for the NRHP and NHL programs, I hope that readers from other areas and with different goals in LGBTQ archaeology will also find it useful and thought provoking.

While there are many ways of commemorating and recognizing historic events, including historical markers, online exhibits, and walking tours, both the NRHP and the NHL program are place-based recognition programs. In order to be considered for inclusion, the places (buildings, structures, landscapes, and archaeological sites) must still exist. This is a challenge when looking at the history and heritage of historically marginalized populations, including sexual and gender minorities. These populations are often located at the edges of society—both figuratively and literally. These are places that become targets of demolition, redevelopment, urban renewal, and gentrification—all of which impact the physical places and force their inhabitants and businesses elsewhere. The further back in time, the more likely the buildings and structures that we often associate with historic places are no longer standing, and the more likely that landscapes have changed (forests grown or cut down, land tilled or left fallow, streets and railroads torn up or built, rivers channelized, and mountains razed). Archaeology—the study of past peoples and societies through the physical remains they left behind—is one way of studying the marginalized who are often neglected (or are otherwise under- or mis-represented) in the historical record, of learning about the past from physical remains when aboveground structures or landscapes are gone or changed, and of learning about the history of the people who inhabited what we now know as the United States long before Europeans arrived.[2] Archaeology is especially well-suited to revealing the everyday lives of people reflected in the ordinary objects of day-to-day life. While documentary records often identify specific individuals, archaeology focuses on the aggregate study of people in a place—household members (kin, chosen family, boarders, servants, slaves, etc.), workers in factories and other workplaces, and people in communities.

Many identities and practices encompassed under the umbrella of sexual and gender minorities include those that modern Western society has considered different from, and often inferior to, mainstream social norms. Other cultures, including many Native American groups, do not consider these identities as different or inferior, just less common. For consistency, LGBTQ and queer are used here broadly to refer to gender and sexual minorities. I use lesbian, gay, bisexual, transgender, two-spirit, and other specific terms when referring to specific identities.

This chapter introduces an archaeological context for LGBTQ sites,[3] beginning with an overview of the National Register and National Historic Landmark criteria and existing archaeological research of sexual and gender minorities. I then broaden the interpretive lens, examining how archaeology of LGBTQ places can inform some of the larger questions in archaeology. These include issues of identity, oppression and resistance, community creation and dissolution, intersectionality, and effects of a person's life course on the archaeological record.

National Register and National Historic Landmark Criteria

Both the NRHP and the NHL programs in the United States have criteria by which to evaluate archaeological sites for inclusion. These include places where only the belowground material survives, as well as places with extant aboveground buildings, structures, and landscapes. While archaeology is often considered solely in regard to NRHP Criterion D / NHL Criterion 6 (the potential to yield important new information), it can also inform other criteria, including Criterion A/1 (important events) and Criterion B/2 (important people).[4]

NRHP and NHL contexts include the types of places likely to be associated with significant history and events. These sites, features, properties, and landscapes are often limited by the theme of the context to only a few types of places. When considering LGBTQ history, however, the number of types of associated places is vast: homes, businesses, night clubs, health clinics and hospitals, prisons, religious buildings, community centers, places of protest and of celebration, cemeteries and memorials, schools, research facilities, government buildings, etc. Perhaps a more useful approach for sites in the context of LGBTQ and two-spirit archaeology is using four categories of places: those associated with LGBTQ and two-spirit community identity and formation; those associated with events, people, organizations, businesses, etc. that are important for other histories and are also in some way associated with LGBTQ and two-spirit identities or histories; those associated with LGBTQ and two-spirit art and aesthetics; and places where archaeological study can help understand sexual and gender minorities at the individual, household, and community levels.[5]

Archaeology at places associated with community and identity formation, including those of events, people, organizations, and businesses important to LGBTQ and two-spirit history, can reveal the use and organization of things and spaces that reflect these individuals' or groups' identities, strategies, and daily lives (NRHP Criteria A and/or B; NHL Criteria 1, 2, and/or 5). Examples of these types of places include the home of Dr. Franklin Kameny during the years he fought to help overturn the American Psychiatric Association's definition of homosexuality as a disease, and which served as the hub of gay rights organizing in Washington, DC, from 1962 when he bought the house; the Furies House, also in Washington, DC, which was the residence of the Furies Collective in 1971 and 1972 where they founded and published the *Furies*, a newspaper that spread and helped establish what we still understand as lesbian feminism and lesbian separatism; and the area in New York City where the Stonewall Uprising took place in June of 1969.[6]

Archaeology can also be done at places associated with events, people, organizations, businesses, etc. that are important to other histories (NRHP Criteria A and/or B; NHL Criteria 1, 2, and/or 5) and that are also in some way associated with LGBTQ and two-spirit identities or histories (figure 4.1). Archaeology at these locations can contribute information about the relationship between sexual and/or gender minority status and the other significant historical events. These types of places might include Hull House in Chicago, an early American settlement house that became the national standard for the settlement movement. It was co-

Figure 4.1. Gardens of Villa Vizcaya, Miami, Florida, ca. early 1940s. Agricultural tycoon James Deering lived here from 1916 through his death in 1925. He was commonly described as a "bachelor," often a euphemism for a homosexual man. From 1984 through 2010, Villa Vizcaya was the location for Miami's White Party, a fundraiser for local HIV/AIDS organizations. Postcard image courtesy of Megan E. Springate.

founded in 1889 by Jane Addams and her companion Ellen Gates Starr; after their relationship ended, Addams partnered with Mary Rozet Smith. In Durham, North Carolina, is the Reverend Dr. Pauli Murray's childhood home. Murray, who struggled with her sexual and gender identities, is best known for her civil rights work; her 1950 book, *States' Laws on Race and Color*, has been called the "bible" of the civil rights movement. She was also the first African American to receive a law degree from Yale Law School, and was the first African American woman ordained as an Episcopal priest. Another example is the site of the Battle of the Rosebud (also known as the Battle Where the Girl Saved Her Brother), which took place in what was then the Montana Territory, part of the Great Sioux War of 1876. This conflict pitted the Lakota Sioux and Northern Cheyenne people against the United States Army and its Crow and Shoshoni allies as American settlers and fortune hunters moved west. Among the Crow warriors during the Battle of the Rosebud was the *bote* Ohchiish, a person who we might today describe as two-spirit.[7]

Places associated with LGBTQ and two-spirit art and aesthetics (NRHP Criterion C; NHL Criterion 4) include gay architect Philip Johnson's Glass House in Connecticut; the landscape of remembrance, celebration, and mourning at the National AIDS Memorial Grove in San Francisco; and the Georgia O'Keeffe Home and Studio in New Mexico, which was designed and built by Maria Chabot, with whom O'Keeffe had a relationship.[8]

Archaeology can also help us better understand the history of sexual and gender minorities at the individual, household, and community levels (NRHP Criterion D; NHL Criterion 6). These types of sites include locations where buildings and structures associated with any of the above types of properties are no longer extant, but can also encompass those types of places that are still standing, and where archaeology can contribute to a more complete history and understanding of the place.

Introduction to the Archaeology of Gender and Sexual Minorities

Gender and sexuality are distinct, and yet deeply intertwined, aspects of human life. How these behaviors and identities are expressed, understood, and influence each other, however, are historically and culturally specific.[9] The study of gender and sexual minorities in archaeology developed out of gender, feminist, and queer archaeologies.[10] These, in turn, were informed by the work of anthropologists like Gayle Rubin, who disentangled sex, gender, and sexuality as areas of study, and of social theorists like Judith Butler, who showed us that gender is a context-specific and reflective performance that requires both actors and audience. Other influential theorists include Michel Foucault and Eve Sedgwick.[11]

I do not refer to queer archaeology here, as the term refers to a specific field of inquiry. While queer archaeology began by challenging heteronormative assumptions deeply ingrained in how archaeologists traditionally have thought about the past (i.e., that everyone in the past was in or interested only in opposite-sex relationships; that the nuclear family of a husband and wife and children living in a household was the norm; and that only two sexes or genders exist), it has broadened in scope to challenging other assumptions (like the clear demarcation between past and present) and different ways to interpret the past (like sensory archaeology).[12]

In the last twenty years, a handful of historical archaeologists, including Barbara Voss and Eleanor Casella, have been examining sexuality in archaeology. Under this umbrella, there have been a small handful of studies exploring same-sex relationships and an even smaller number of investigations of two-spirit identity in precontact and colonial periods. The lack of work that specifically addresses LGBTQ, two-spirit, and other sexual and gender minorities may reflect a documented hesitance by researchers to be associated with work considered controversial. They fear this may reduce their credibility (as through accusations of self-interest) or might otherwise hurt their careers.[13] Of the few studies done, even fewer come from the United States, with the majority emerging from work in different parts of the world and representing a wide range of times and cultures.[14]

Voss rightfully cautions us that studying only what we consider non-normative genders and sexualities reifies them as "other," and actually bolsters the patriarchal, heterosexist paradigm that we live within—even as we may be hoping to stretch our understanding of sexuality and gender in the past.[15] The solution she offers is to also problematize and investigate heterosexuality, monogamous family structure, and a focus on procreation as the main purpose of sexual and gender relations. In short, we should look at the effects of culturally sanctioned and nonsanctioned sexualities and gender relationships within particular societies.[16] Challenging ourselves in this way includes not applying our modern ideas about lesbian, gay, bisexual, transgender, and queer identities to people who might have chosen not to take those identities or could not, as these categories may not have existed or were not culturally relevant.[17] Two-spirit Native Americans, for example, fall outside the binary (male-female) sex and gender system dominant in Western culture. Despite this, they have been (and are) often described using terms like homosexual, transsexual, or transgender—terms that are rooted in a Western binary sex and gender system. In Native American cultures that have different ways of thinking about sexuality and gender, these descriptors lose their usefulness (figure 4.2).[18]

Early archaeological studies looked at evidence from burials, and identified individuals as two-spirit when their cultural gender (expressed by the artifacts they were buried with) differed from their physical sex (determined through skeletal analysis).[20] More recently, researchers have taken a more nuanced and holistic approach to understanding two-spirit identities in the past, including looking beyond burials. For example, Sandra Hollimon has re-examined Chumash burials in a broader context, including gender, sexuality, religion, and occupation.[21] She concluded that 'aqi identity in the Chumash culture is usually associated with those who are members of an undertaking guild and who do not engage in procreative sex. This includes several categories of identity that Western culture sees as distinct: biological men who live as women;

Figure 4.2. Mission San Antonio de Padua, near Jolon, California, 2006. The mission was founded on 14 July 1771. Natives who were not respectable, according to the missionaries, were punished or killed. Ethnographic descriptions of these punishments exist for Native Americans at Mission San Antonio de Padua, as well as many other California Missions.[19] Photo by Robert Stokstad (public domain: Wikimedia Commons).

men who have sex with other men; men without children; celibate people; and postmenopausal women. Similarly nuanced work has also been done by archaeologist Elizabeth Prine in her study of the *miati* of the Hidatsa and by Perry and Joyce in their examination of Zuni *lhamana* identities.[22]

Since the 1980s, there has been considerable work done, particularly in historical archaeology, looking at gender. Despite the explicitly sexual nature of some of these contexts, such as brothels, sexuality has been rarely addressed.[23] There are, however, some exceptions. For instance, in her work *The Archaeology of Ethnogenesis: Race and Sexuality in Colonial San Francisco*, Voss includes sexuality as part of a broad intersectional analysis of people becoming Californios. Same-sex sexuality, premarital sex, polygamy, and multiple genders, for example, were invoked as an example of the "savagery" of the indigenous people in the region, setting them apart from—and excluding them from becoming—Californio. This exclusion was not just in name, but included forcibly removing native peoples from their villages to Catholic missions for conversion.[24] In Australia, Eleanor Casella's work at the Ross

Female Factory, a mid-nineteenth-century women's prison, identified a currency of sexual relationships among women that could be variously and simultaneously predatory, strategic, economic, and affectionate.[25] Encompassing examples from colonial periods around the world, Voss and Casella's edited volume, *The Archaeology of Colonialism: Intimate Encounters and Sexual Effects*, foregrounds sexuality as fundamental to the colonial project: "a constellation of embodied and expressive human intimacies—that range from the seductive, pleasurable, and erotic through the familial, parental, nonnormative and homosocial, and into the involuntary, strategic, and exploitative."[26] This work expands the archaeology of sexualities—including same-sex sexualities—beyond the private, domestic spaces of bedroom and brothel, and into a broader scale of settlements, neighborhoods, and societies in general.

Beyond Identity: Avenues of Inquiry

Archaeology at LGBTQ sites and of LGBTQ identities and practices not only broadens our understanding of the queer past, but can also contribute to wider discussions in archaeology and anthropology. While one of the fundamental questions is whether and how LGBTQ material remains differ from those found associated with heterosexuality, important work can also be done examining the formation and negotiation of political and social communities and identities. Lacking a broad body of American LGBTQ and two-spirit work to draw from, this archaeological context poses questions, problems, and issues that can be addressed through excavation and interpretation at these kinds of sites. Many of these avenues of inquiry parallel research by archaeologists working in other contexts, including African American sites, those looking at gender, and those who study class. The work that has been done in these other areas provides precedence for methods and interpretive frameworks that can be applied to LGBTQ sites. The types of broader questions that archaeological investigation at LGBTQ and two-spirit sites can address are discussed below; where examples are known, they are included.

Classification and Identification

A key tension in archaeological investigations of identity is determining the scale of analysis: individuals versus communities versus populations. When studying gender and sexual minorities, are we looking at individuals who personally identify with particular social or political categories (i.e., lesbian, gay, queer, etc.), populations whose sexual preferences and activities or gender presentations are statistically in the minority, or communities that form around shared identities, activities, or politics?[27] Researchers also grapple with some very fundamental questions regarding how to "see" sexual and gender minorities in the archaeological record. How do we use artifacts and other things that survive physically to see variations in gender expression? Or to see heterosexuality compared with sexual minorities, including those who are lesbian, gay, bisexual, or queer? Considering these questions will influence the type and scope of research questions for a particular project, the methods used to collect data, and the analysis and interpretation of the results. While the questions can be considered on a broad, general level, they are also culturally, temporally, and site specific; interpretations from elsewhere can be useful in considering possibilities but should not be uncritically applied.[28] In thinking about such questions, we cannot assume that the people had only two genders, two sexes, or were necessarily heterosexual. This forces us to look closely at what the evidence tells us, rather than forcing the evidence into our own assumptions.

Just as archaeologists look at objects in the context of how they support and reinforce larger social structures like capitalism, class, and race, objects can also be interpreted in light of what they can tell us about the sexuality and gender systems in the past, including kinship, households, and the role of sexuality in conflict.[29] Researchers in other fields, including museum studies and English, have also grappled with material representations of past gender and sexual minorities.[30] In some cases, historical documents, oral histories, or ethnographic studies will be available. Those that have detailed information on how people organized themselves both interpersonally and spatially, and that have good descriptions of material culture and how it was used, will be particularly useful in considering what to look at, how to find it, and how to think about it in analysis and interpretation. We must, however, be cautious and critical when using the ethnographic record, particularly when considering indigenous cultures. These records are written from particular points of view, and these have historically been ones that ignore or demean these identities.[31]

Among the artifacts recovered from behind the landmark Halcyon House in the Georgetown neighborhood of Washington, DC, are an assortment of clothing-related artifacts, including corset clips, garters, and stockings. Generally interpreted as artifacts associated with women, documents reveal that the occupants of the home during the period represented by these objects were two men: Albert Clemons and a carpenter (whose name is unknown). Using this as a springboard, Jenn Porter-Lupu explores the assumptions of heterosexuality and gender conformity that underlies a lot of archaeological interpretation.[32]

Emergence and History of LGBTQ and Contemporary Two-Spirit Identities

A woman in the early twentieth century could not have identified herself as a lesbian (first used as a noun in 1925), just as someone before the late twentieth century could not have identified using the word transgender (first appearing in 1965 and gaining wider acceptance beginning in 1988). The word homosexual itself was not used until the turn of the twentieth century, introduced and defined by the psychological profession.[33] Examining the relationship between these changing categories of identity and material things and spaces is an important avenue of archaeological investigation. How have people used physical things and places to both stabilize and transform their identities? How have they responded when, as with psychologists "inventing" homosexuality at the turn of the twentieth century, they have had identities thrust upon them? Work done on LGBTQ and two-spirit sites can inform broader investigations into the materiality of identity by serving as case studies and in raising both issues and possible solutions to what is one of the key questions in archaeology. Previous work on the archaeology of identities and on emerging identities can serve as springboards for work at LGBTQ and two-spirit sites. In addition to Barb Voss's work looking at the ethnogenesis of Californios, Gerald Sider has looked at Native Americans both claiming and resisting identities that colonial powers thrust upon them; Laurie Wilkie has examined identities imposed on Africans in a slave context and how these identities were adapted, maintained, and contested; and archaeologist Alison Bell has explored the ethnogenesis of whiteness in the colonial Chesapeake.[34]

Shifting Personal Identities

This question looks at changing identities at a more personal, rather than cultural, level. Early work in identity, including LGBTQ and two-spirit identities, treated these aspects (including race, sexuality, and gender) as innate and unchanging individual characteristics. This is despite Kinsey's early-to-mid-1900s work showing that sexual orientation fell along a continuum that could shift depending on a person's changing social circumstances, and work by LGBTQ historians in the late 1900s that established homosexuality (and therefore sexuality in general) as a social construct.[35] This has been documented archaeologically in the diamond field settlements of South Africa, where male miners formed emotional and sexual bonds with each other while in the field, and returned to heterosexual relationships when their tenure was over.[36]

Archaeology is best suited to looking at broad patterns through time rather than associating individual artifacts with specific individuals and specific events, limiting its usefulness in examining shifting personal identities. Archaeology is, however, very good at revealing trends at the household level. While archaeologists cannot necessarily identify specific objects with specific people living in a household, it is possible to see changes both within and between households.[37] There are already archaeological studies looking at the life cycles of households and the changing material and physical environments of young singles versus households with children versus empty nesters versus the elderly.[38] These precedents can be used as jumping-off points for considering what the material signs of changing and shifting LGBTQ activities or identities of people within a household may be.

Intersectionality

Intersectionality is the recognition that various axes of identity (gender, sex, class, ethnicity, religion, sexuality, geographical location, etc.) influence and are influenced by each other. People with different sets of intersecting identities have often very different histories and lived experiences.[39] It is no accident that Black women were first to articulate the idea of intersectionality and interlocking oppressions as they described the impacts of being both Black and women.[40]

What can the study of intersectionality that includes LGBTQ and two-spirit identities contribute to the broader study of intersectionality in archaeological contexts? How can we explore intersectionality in the context of LGBTQ and two-spirit archaeological sites? Broadening the study of intersectional identities to include sexuality is an important intervention in research that has traditionally focused predominantly on gender, class, and ethnicity. It is only by looking at sexuality broadly that the role of LGBTQ gender and sexual identities can be understood in cultural context. Successful engagement with sexuality as part of an intersectional analysis include Barbara Voss and Eleanor Casella's collection of papers examining sexual effects and the colonial project, Whitney Battle-Baptiste's Black feminist archaeology, Barbara Voss's look at the ethnogenesis of Californios, Sandra Hollimon's analysis of two-spirit people in California, and Megan Springate's examination of respectability politics and capitalism in the context of summer vacations.[41]

Different Genders

Considerable work has been done since the 1980s in theorizing and looking at gender archaeologically. While much of the work has focused on women and female genders, some work on masculinities has recently begun to be published.[42] Other researchers are working to destabilize assumptions of a gender binary.[43] While two-spirit identities have often been used as "proof" that gender is socially constructed, they cannot be accurately interpreted using Western constructs.[44] Gender remains a broad area of archaeological study that can be influenced by work at LGBTQ sites.

Work done by theorists and anthropologists outside of archaeology can be used to help think about different genders and how they intersect with other axes of identity.[45] For example, while butch and femme gender expressions among women who have sex with women have traditionally been associated with the working classes, a recent study suggests that the perception of a masculine gender presentation by a woman can also vary by location.[46] Queer theorists like Jack Halberstam provide frameworks for understanding both how sexuality and gender interact to create multiple spectrums of identity and the possibility of (and ways of naming) more genders than male, female, and other.[47]

Recent work in gender archaeology, including investigations of masculinities, the gender spectrum, and how genders are formed communally (rather than individually), has begun to provide methodologies and ways of thinking about gender.[48] Within LGBTQ communities, however, are genders that have not previously been examined archaeologically. How do we recognize and analyze different gender identities and expressions within LGBTQ communities, including the different genders of women who have sex with women (butch, femme, lipstick lesbian, stud), genderqueer, drag kings and queens, people who identify along the transgender spectrum, "bears," and others?[49] Answering these questions and exploring these other gender expressions can expand the categories and understandings of gender in other areas of archaeology.

Marginalization, Oppression, and Resistance

In 1984, Gayle Rubin introduced the "Charmed Circle." At the center of the circle are culturally ideal sexual behaviors; in the United States at the time the article was published, these were monogamous, heterosexual, married, not kinky, done within the home. At the edges and outside the circle are those behaviors considered less acceptable or deviant—in this case, multiple partners, homosexual, unmarried, kinky, done in public. The circle, however, is not fixed. In addition to being culturally specific, behaviors once considered deviant can become increasingly acceptable, moving toward the center, and vice versa.[50] Despite this, archaeologists looking for difference have held heterosexuality as the norm or point of comparison, looking to identify queer sites based on their difference from nonqueer sites. Likewise, many analyses of the poor and working classes have held middle-classness as the norm, and ethnic analyses have held whiteness as the norm. These are powerful statements of what we, as researchers, consider normal and what we consider "other." These find their origins in structural privilege.[51] In order to truly understand the dynamics of power that mark some behaviors and people as deviant or other, we must interrogate and critically examine heterosexuality and other behaviors and identities held as "normal."[52]

The process through which groups come to be seen as socially and politically different—and come to understand themselves through these lenses—has been a central dynamic shaping LGBTQ history.[53] Using archaeology, we can look at the material reflections of these shifts as, for example, homosexuality has become more or less socially acceptable, and also how it (and other sexual and gender identities and practices) might have been used to regulate "normative" behavior and identification.[54]

Marginalization and oppression do not exist alone and are often accompanied by resistance. Examples of oppression include physical violence, being fired or denied housing, vilification, incarceration, harassment, and social exclusion leading, for example, to being closeted, and higher rates of suicide and homelessness. Examples of resistance include street protests and secret signs, like wearing a green carnation in one's lapel to indicate homosexuality or a double-headed axe (labrys) indicating identity as a lesbian.[55] How have LGBTQ and two-spirit individuals and communities responded to oppression, both by other individuals and by the state? For example, did LGBTQ households "hide" by maintaining a public facade of heterosexuality while internally organizing their homes to reflect the realities of same-sex interpersonal behavior? If so, what does this look like spatially and materially? How does this differ by ethnicity, class, gender, geographic location, and other intersectional axes?

In 1903, W. E. B. Du Bois described African Americans' experience of double consciousness or "two-ness": the tensions and struggles of living both within and outside two distinct worlds defined by color. In 1991, cultural theorist Chela Sandoval described differential consciousness as a way that people survive and operate within oppressive environments while simultaneously developing beliefs and tactics to resist domination and oppression.[56] Archaeologists studying African Americans, both free and enslaved, have done considerable work in exploring double consciousness and differential consciousness using archaeological data. This includes looking at oppression, resistance, and living lives that appear one way in private and another in public, as well as assimilationist versus oppositional responses to oppression.[57] Archaeologists studying labor, violence, and sabotage, as in the coal fields of Virginia, Pennsylvania, and Colorado, are also laying the groundwork for the investigation of oppression, resistance, and survival.[58]

Albert Clemons in Georgetown, DC, was noted in local newspapers as "reclusive" and "eccentric" but was wealthy enough that he was not harassed or incarcerated for it. One of the corset pieces in Clemons's household trash was branded "Nemo Triple Strip," a line of corsets designed to remold "stout women" into "graceful lines." We don't know if Clemons or the carpenter wore corsets in public, among friends, or only in private; the figure-altering nature of them may have made wearing them in public too obvious or risky (or perhaps they were part of what made Clemons "eccentric"). Porter-Lupu imagines that other items, like undergarment fasteners and clasps, could have been worn in public but known only to the wearer; a private expression of gender or sexuality. What we do know is that while trash collection was available while Clemons and the carpenter lived at Halcyon House, they chose to discard female-gendered clothing items (like corsets and stockings) and cosmetics jars (as for face powder) in their backyard—perhaps to keep them secret and private.[59]

Community

Moving to a broader lens, archaeology can be used to trace the development and decline of LGBTQ neighborhoods. Usually imagined as existing only in metropolitan areas like New York City and San Francisco, gay enclaves and neighborhoods are also found in less populous towns and cities, including Provincetown, Massachusetts; Fire Island Pines and Cherry Grove, New York; Saugatuck, Michigan; and Guerneville, California. These communities and the people who live there come together and dissipate for many reasons.[60] These include patterns of property ownership, gentrification, redevelopment, police harassment, and more recently, changes associated with an increase in the acceptance of LGBTQ people, particularly in urban areas.[61] Archaeology can be used to study these processes and effects at the levels of individual properties like households and businesses as well as communities as a whole. These communities are understood by looking at artifacts, buildings (standing and demolished), and landscapes.[62]

As well as studying communities in the past, archaeology can engage and serve current communities as a method of civic engagement, empowerment, and emancipation. Through engagement with living communities, archaeological research questions, methods, and interpretations can be used to address questions important to existing communities. Civically engaged and activist archaeologies recognize that the past and the present are inextricably intertwined. There is an extensive literature on civically engaged and community archaeology that includes methods, approaches, and case studies.[63] Examples of this type of work in LGBTQ archaeology includes Erin Rodriguez and Katrina Eichner's explicitly queer-informed and inclusive field school, Meghan Walley's work with members of the Inuit LGBTQ community, and Lylliam Posadas Vidales's work with LGBTQ youth.[64]

Conclusion

As a queer archaeologist, it is tempting to look for myself and other LGBTQ and two-spirit people, just as we are today, in the past—to legitimize our existence by "proving" that we have always been here. And yet, to paraphrase Barb Voss, we need to be wary of projects that essentialize sexual and gender identities by using archaeology to create a lineage of gay, lesbian, bisexual, and queer forefathers and foremothers and transgendered foreparents for present-day identities.[65] Archaeological projects that explore the full richness, diversity, and dynamism of gender and sexuality are ultimately much more useful (and interesting). The archaeology of LGBTQ and two-spirit places and landscapes can provide important information not only about past genders and sexualities, but also contribute to important dialogues in archaeology about the relationship between, and expressions of, sexuality and gender, community, cultural change, and identity.

Dr. Megan E. Springate is the National Coordinator for the National Park Service 19th Amendment Centennial Commemoration and editor of *LGBTQ America: A Theme Study of Lesbian, Gay, Bisexual, Transgender, and Queer History* (2016).

Notes

1. Megan E. Springate, ed. *LGBTQ America: A Theme Study of Lesbian, Gay, Bisexual, Transgender, and Queer History* (Washington, DC: National Park Foundation and National Park Service, 2016).
2. Historical documents exclude, misrepresent, or underrepresent many people: those who did not or could not own property, could not vote, could not serve in the military, were "others," and/or who did not make the news or end up in court. This includes many LGBTQ and two-spirit people, women, working classes, children, immigrants, and others. See, for example, Barbara J. Little, *Historical Archaeology: Why the Past Matters* (Walnut Creek, CA: Left Coast Press, 2007).
3. Also important, but not included here, are the experiences and discrimination of LGBTQ and two-spirit archaeologists in the field. See Dawn Rutecki and Chelsea Blackmore, eds, "Special Section: Towards an Inclusive Queer Archaeology," *Society for American Archaeology SAA Record* 16, no. 1 (2016): 9–39.
4. National Register Criteria for Evaluation: (A) "[places] are associated with events that have made a significant contribution to the broad patterns of our history"; (B) "[places] that are associated with the lives of significant persons in our past"; (D) "[places] that have yielded, or may be likely to yield, information important in prehistory or history"; Summary of the National Historic Landmarks Criteria for Evaluation: (1) "[places] that are associated with events that have made a significant contribution to, and are identified with, or that outstandingly represent, the broad national patterns of United States history and from which an understanding and appreciation of those patterns may be gained"; (2) "[places] that are associated importantly with the lives of persons nationally significant in the history of the United States"; (6) "[places] that have yielded or may be likely to yield information of major scientific importance by revealing new cultures, or by shedding light upon periods of occupation over large areas of the United States. Such sites are those which have yielded, or which may reasonably be expected to yield, data affecting theories, concepts, and ideas to a major degree." From U.S. Department of the Interior, National Park Service, *National Register Bulletin: How to Apply the National Register Criteria for Evaluation*, Sections II and IX, https://www.nps.gov/nr/publications/bulletins/nrb15/nrb15_2.htm and https://www.nps.gov/nr/publications/bulletins/nrb15/nrb15_9.htm. See also

Megan E. Springate and Caridad de la Vega, "Nominating LGBTQ Places to the National Register of Historic Places and as National Historic Landmarks: An Introduction," in *LGBTQ America: A Lesbian, Gay, Bisexual, Transgender, and Queer History* (Washington, DC: National Park Foundation and National Park Service, 2016).

5. With many thanks to Barb Voss, in personal communication with the author

6. The Dr. Franklin E. Kameny House in Washington, DC, was listed on the NRHP on 2 November 2011; the Furies Collective House in Washington, DC, was listed on the NRHP on 2 May 2016. Stonewall in New York City was listed on the NRHP on 28 June 1999, designated an NHL on 16 February 2000, and designated Stonewall National Monument (an NPS unit) on 24 June 2016.

7. Hull House in Chicago, Illinois, was listed on the NRHP on 15 October 1966 and designated an NHL on 23 June 1965; the Pauli Murray Childhood Home in Durham, North Carolina, was designated an NHL on 11 January 2017; the Rosebud Battlefield Site in Busby, Montana, was listed on the NRHP on 21 August 1972 and designated an NHL on 19 August 2008.

8. Philip Johnson's Glass House in New Canaan, Connecticut, was designated an NHL on 18 February 1997; the National AIDS Memorial Grove in San Francisco, California, was designated in 1996; the Georgia O'Keeffe Home and Studio in Abiquiú, New Mexico, was designated an NHL on 5 August 1998.

9. For examples, see Katherine Crawford-Lackey and Megan E. Springate, eds, *Queer Identities and Place: Place and the Histories of LGBTQ and Two-Spirit People in the United States* (New York: Berghahn Books, 2019); and Leisa Meyer and Helis Sikk, "Introduction to Lesbian, Gay, Bisexual, Transgender, and Queer (LGBTQ) History in the United States," in *LGBTQ America: A Theme Study of Lesbian, Gay, Bisexual, Transgender, and Queer History*, ed. Megan E. Springate (Washington, DC: National Park Foundation and National Park Service, 2016).

10. Queer archaeology is a specific field of inquiry that overlaps with the archaeology of gender and sexual minorities; see note 12. Some key works in gender and feminist archaeology include Margaret W. Conkey and Janet Spector, "Archaeology and the Study of Gender," in *Advances in Archaeological Method and Theory*, vol. 7, ed. M. B. Schiffer (New York: Academic Press, 1984), 1–38; Joan M. Gero, "Socio-Politics and the Woman-At-Home Ideology," *American Antiquity* 50, no. 2 (1985): 342–50; Janet Spector, *What This Awl Means: Feminist Archaeology at a Wahpeton Dakota Village* (St. Paul: Minnesota Historical Society Press, 1993); Margaret W. Conkey and Joan M. Gero, "Programme to Practice: Gender and Feminism in Archaeology," *Annual Review of Anthropology* 26 (1997): 411–37; Laurie A. Wilke, "The Other Gender: The Archaeology of an Early 20th Century Fraternity," *Proceedings of the Society for California Archaeology* 11 (1998): 7–11; Maria Franklin, "A Black Feminist-Inspired Archaeology?" *Journal of Social Ar-*

chaeology 1, no. 1 (2001): 108–25; Laurie A. Wilkie and Katherine H. Hayes, "Engendered and Feminist Archaeologies of the Recent and Documented Pasts," *Journal of Archaeological Research* 14, no. 3 (2006): 243–64; Rosemary A. Joyce, *Ancient Bodies, Ancient Lives: Sex, Gender, and Archaeology* (New York: Thames & Hudson, 2008); Pamela L. Geller, "Identity and Difference: Complicating Gender in Archaeology," *Annual Review of Anthropology* 38 (2009): 65–81; and Whitney Battle-Baptiste, *Black Feminist Archaeology* (Walnut Creek, CA: Left Coast Press, 2011).

11. Gayle Rubin, "The Traffic in Women: Notes on the 'Political Economy' of Sex," in *Toward an Anthropology of Women*, ed. Rayna Reiter (New York: Monthly Review Press, 1975); Judith Butler, *Gender Trouble: Feminism and the Subversion of Identity* (New York: Routledge, 1990); Michel Foucault, *Histoire de la sexualité*, vols. 1, 2, and 3, trans. Robert Hurley (France: Editions Gallimard, 1976, 1984, 1984); and Eve Sedgwick, *Epistemology of the Closet* (Berkeley: University of California Press, 1990).

12. See, for example, a theme volume of *World Archaeology* 32, no. 2 (2000); Susan Terendy, Natasha Lyons, and Michelle Janse-Smekal, eds, *Que(e)rying Archaeology: Proceedings of the Thirty-Seventh Annual Chacmool Conference* (Calgary: Archaeological Association of Calgary, 2009); Chelsea Blackmore, "How to Queer the Past without Sex: Queer Theory, Feminisms and Archaeology of Identity," *Archaeologies* 7, no. 1 (2011): 75–96; and James Aimers and Dawn M. Rutecki, "Brave New World: Interpreting Sex, Gender, and Sexuality in the Past," *SAA Archaeological Record* 16, no. 1 (2016): 12–17.

13. Thomas A. Dowson, "Why Queer Archaeology? An Introduction," *World Archaeology* 32, no. 2 (2000): 161–65; Gayle Rubin, "Sites, Settlements, and Urban Sex: Archaeology and the Study of Gay Leathermen in San Francisco 1955–1995," in *Archaeologies of Sexuality*, ed. Richard A. Schmidt and Barbara L. Voss (New York: Routledge, 2000), 65; and Cheryl Claassen, "Homophobia and Women Archaeologists," *World Archaeology* 32, no. 2 (2000): 173–79.

14. Keith Matthews, "An Archaeology of Homosexuality? Perspectives from the Classical World," in *TRAC 94: Proceedings of the Fourth Annual Theoretical Roman Archaeology Conference*, ed. S. Cottam et al. (Oxford: Oxbow Books, 1994), 118–32; Barbara L. Voss and Richard A. Schmidt, "Archaeologies of Sexuality: An Introduction," in *Archaeologies of Sexuality*, ed. Schmidt and Voss, 1–32; Barbara L. Voss, "Sexuality Studies in Archaeology," *Annual Review of Anthropology* 37 (2008): 317–36; Sandra E. Hollimon, "Archaeology of the "'Aqi: Gender and Sexuality in Prehistoric Chumash Society," in *Archaeologies of Sexuality*, ed. Schmidt and Voss, 176–96; Sandra E. Hollimon, "The Archaeology of Nonbinary Genders in Native North American Societies," in *Handbook of Gender in Archaeology*, ed. Sarah M. Nelson (Lanham, MD: AltaMira Press, 2006), 435–50; Eger, "Architectures of Desire"; Sandra E. Hollimon, "Examining Third and Fourth Genders in Mortuary Contexts," in

Que(e)rying Archaeology, ed. Terendy, Lyons, and Janse-Smekal (Calgary: Chacmool Archaeological Association, 2009), 171–75; Eleanor Casella, "Bull-daggers and Gentle Ladies: Archaeological Approaches to Female Homo-sexuality in Convict-Era Australia," in *Archaeologies of Sexuality*, ed. Schmidt and Voss, 143–59; Eleanor Casella, "Doing Trade: A Sexual Economy of Nineteenth-Century Australian Female Convict Prisons," *World Archaeology* 32, no. 2 (2000): 209–21; Lindsay Weiss, "The Currency of Intimacy: Transformations of the Domestic Sphere on the Late-Nineteenth-Century Diamond Fields," in *The Archaeology of Colonialism: Intimate Encounters and Sexual Effects*, ed. Barbara L. Voss and Eleanor Conlin Casella (New York: Cambridge University Press, 2012), 49–66.

15. Barbara L. Voss, "Looking for Gender, Finding Sexuality: A Queer Politic of Archaeology, Fifteen Years Later," in *Que(e)rying Archaeology*, ed. Terendy, Lyons, and Janse-Smekal (Calgary: Chacmool Archaeological Association, 2009), 29–39.

16. Voss, "Looking for Gender"; and Eleanor Conlin Casella and Barbara L. Voss, "Intimate Encounters: An Archaeology of Sexualities within Colonial Worlds," in *The Archaeology of Colonialism*, ed. Voss and Casella, 1–10.

17. These are themes that wind their way throughout discussions of LGBTQ history and place. Meyer and Sikk, "Introduction to Lesbian, Gay, Bisexual, Transgender, and Queer (LGBTQ) History"; Crawford-Lackey and Springate, *Queer Identities and Place*; and Barbara L. Voss, "Sexual Effects: Postcolonial and Queer Perspectives on the Archaeology of Sexuality and Empire," in *The Archaeology of Colonialism*, ed. Voss and Casella, 16–17.

18. The role of sexuality and gender as essential core characteristics of Western identity is described by Barbara Voss as being at the root of coming-out stories where confusing or puzzling feelings or actions are "explained" when the narrator realized they are "really" gay, lesbian, bisexual, and/or transgender. Barbara L. Voss, "Sexual Subjects: Identity and Taxonomy in Archaeological Research," in *Archaeology of Plural and Changing Identities: Beyond Identification*, ed. Eleanor C. Casella and Chris Fowler (New York: Kluwer/Plenum, 2005), 64, 66. The term "two-spirit" is used here as an um-brella term encompassing identities in both the past and the present. See Will Roscoe, "Sexual and Gender Diversity in Native America and the Pacific Islands," in *Queer Identities and Place*, ed. Crawford-Lackey and Springate.

19. Deborah A. Miranda, "Extermination of the *Joyas*: Gendercide in Spanish California." *GLQ: A Journal of Lesbian and Gay Studies* 16, no. 1–2 (2010): 161.

20. For a summary of early studies, see Voss, "Sexual Subjects," 64–65, and Hollimon, "Nonbinary Genders." Similar approaches have been used else-where in the world to identify gender diversity; for an overview see Bet-tina Arnold, "Gender and Archaeological Mortuary Analysis," in *Women in Antiquity: Theoretical Approaches to Gender and Archaeology*, ed. Sarah M. Nelson (Lanham, MD: AltaMira Press, 2007), 107–40; and Joanna Sofaer

and Marie Stig Sørensen, "Death and Gender," in *The Oxford Handbook of the Archaeology of Death and Burial*, ed. Sarah Tarlow and Liv Nilsson Stutz (Oxford: Oxford University Press, 2013), 527–42. For work that addresses the false dichotomy of biological sex, see Anne Fausto-Sterling, "The Five Sexes: Why Male and Female Are Not Enough," *The Sciences* 33, no. 2 (March/April 1993): 20–25; Anne Fausto-Sterling, "The Five Sexes, Revisited," *The Sciences* 40, no. 4 (July/August 2000): 18–23.

21. Hollimon, "'Aqi." The Chumash studied by Hollimon were located in the Santa Barbara Channel area of coastal southern California. The Chumash continue to live in and around this area.

22. Elizabeth Prine, "The Ethnography of Place: Landscape and Culture in Middle Missouri Archaeology," Ph.D. diss., University of California Berkeley, 1997; Elizabeth Prine, "Searching for Third Genders; Towards a Prehistory of Domestic Space in Middle Missouri Villages," in *Archaeologies of Sexuality*, ed. Schmidt and Voss, 197–219; Elizabeth M. Perry and Rosemary Joyce, "Providing a Past for 'Bodies that Matter': Judith Butler's Impact on the Archaeology of Gender," *International Journal of Gender and Sexuality Studies* 6, no. 1/2 (2001): 63–76. The Hidatsa studied by Prine lived in palisaded villages along the Missouri River in North Dakota from the fifteenth through the nineteenth centuries. The Hidatsa continue to live in and around this area. The Zuni studied by Perry and Joyce lived in New Mexico. The Zuni continue to live in and around this area.

23. Donna J. Seifert, "Within Sight of the White House: The Archaeology of Working Women," *Historical Archaeology* 24, no. 4 (1991): 82–108; Donna J. Seifert, Elizabeth Barthold O'Brien, and Joseph Balicki, "Mary Ann Hall's First-Class House: The Archaeology of a Capital Brothel," in *Archaeologies of Sexuality*, ed. Schmidt and Voss, 117–28; Julia G. Costello, "Red Light Voices: An Archaeological Drama of Late Nineteenth-Century Prostitution," in *Archaeologies of Sexuality*, ed. Schmidt and Voss, 160–75; Julia G. Costello, "A Night with Venus, a Moon with Mercury: The Archaeology of Prostitution in Historic Los Angeles," in *Restoring Women's History through Historic Preservation*, ed. Gail L. Dubrow and Jennifer B. Goodman (Baltimore, MD: Johns Hopkins Press, 2003), 177–96; Michael Foster, John M. Lindly, and Ronald F. Ryden, "The Soiled Doves of South Granite Street: The History and Archaeology of a Prescott Arizona Brothel," *KIVA* 70, no. 4 (2005): 349–74; a theme volume of *Historical Archaeology* 39, no. 1 (2005); Kristin Gensmer, "Of Painted Ladies and Patrons: An Analysis of Personal Items and Identity at a Victorian-Era Red Light District in Ouray, Colorado." Master's thesis, Colorado State University, Fort Collins (2012); Mary Van Buren and Kristin A. Gensmer, "Crib Girls and Clients in the Red-Light District of Ouray, Colorado: Class, Gender, and Dress." *Historical Archaeology* 51, no. 2 (2017): 218–39; Shannon Lee Dawdy and Richard Weyhing, "Beneath the Rising Sun: 'Frenchness' and the Archaeology of Desire, *International Journal of Historical Archaeology* 12: 370–87.

24. In *The Archaeology of Ethnogenesis*, same-sex sexuality is mentioned briefly as an example of the "savagery" of the indigenous people in the area, as described by missionaries and other early settlers. Barbara L. Voss, *The Archaeology of Ethnogenesis: Race and Sexuality in Colonial San Francisco* (Berkeley: University of California Press, 2008), 51. See also Barbara L. Voss, "Colonial Sex: Archaeology, Structured Space, and Sexuality in Alta California's Spanish Colonial Missions," in *Archaeologies of Sexuality*, ed. Schmidt and Voss, 35–61; and Barbara L. Voss and Eleanor Conlin Casella, eds. *The Archaeology of Colonialism: Intimate Encounters and Sexual Effects* (New York: Cambridge University Press, 2012).
25. Casella, "Doing Trade."
26. Casella and Voss, "Intimate Encounters," 1–2.
27. Barbara Voss, personal communication with the author.
28. See, for example, the discussion of personal artifacts and identity in Carolyn L. White and Mary C. Beaudry, "Artifacts and Personal Identity," in *The International Handbook of Historical Archaeology*, ed. Teresita Majewski and David Gaimster (New York: Springer, 2009), 209–25; and Meredith Reifschneider, "Towards a Queer Materialism in Archaeology: Materiality and the Sexed and Gendered Subject," paper presented at the Society for Historical Archaeology Conference, Quebec City, Canada, January 2014.
29. See Voss and Casella, *The Archaeology of Colonialism*, especially Casella and Voss, "Intimate Encounters," and Voss, "Sexual Effects," for elaboration on the idea of studying sexual effects; and Martin Hall, "Sexuality and Materiality: The Challenge of Method," in *The Archaeology of Colonialism*, 323–40, for a discussion about seeing sexual effects in the archaeological record.
30. See, for example, Matt Smith, "Queering the Museum," in *Contemporary Clay and Museum Culture: Ceramics in the Expanded Field*, ed. Christine Brown, Julian Stair, and Clare Twomey (New York: Routledge, 2016), 196–208; Orie Givens, "A Look at LGBT Artifacts from the National African-American Museum," *Advocate*, 30 September 2016, https://www.advocate.com/pride/2016/9/30/look-lgbt-artifacts-national-african-american-museum; and Abigail Katherine Joseph, "Queer Things: Victorian Objects and the Fashioning of Homosexuality," Ph.D. diss., English and Comparative Literature, Columbia University, 2012, https://doi.org/10.7916/D87P95GV.
31. For examples of this kind of approach, see Prine, "Third Genders," and Hollimon, "*Aqi*." For historical archaeology, the work done by art historian Kevin Murphy on gay and lesbian summer houses in New England could serve as a good jumping-off point for considering these types of issues. Kevin D. Murphy, "'Secure from All Intrusion': Heterotopia, Queer Space, and the Turn-of-the-Twentieth-Century American Resort," *Winterthur Portfolio* 43, no. 2/3 (2009): 185–228; Will Roscoe, "Sexual and Gender Diversity in Native America and the Pacific Islands"; and Deborah A. Miranda, "Extermination of the *Joyas*: Gendercide in Spanish California," *GLQ: A Journal of Lesbian and Gay Studies* 16, no. 1–2 (2010): 253–84.

32. Jennifer Porter-Lupu, "Performing a Queer Aesthetic in Early 20th Century Washington: Preliminary Findings from the Halcyon House Site." Paper presented at the Society for American Archaeology, Washington, DC, 2018.

33. For more detailed discussion, see Meyer and Sikk, "Introduction to Lesbian, Gay, Bisexual, Transgender, and Queer (LGBTQ) History in the United States."

34. See, for example, Voss, *Ethnogenesis*. For a discussion of personal artifacts and identity, see White and Beaudry, "Artifacts and Personal Identity." For a summary of current work in the archaeology of ethnogenesis, see Terrance M. Weik, "The Archaeology of Ethnogenesis." *Annual Review of Anthropology* 43 (2014): 291–305; Gerald Sider, "Identity as History: Ethnohistory, Ethnogenesis, and Ethnocide in the Southeastern United States," *Identities* 1, no. 1 (1994): 109–22; Laurie A. Wilkie, *Creating Freedom: Material Culture and African American Identity at Oakley Plantation* (Baton Rouge: Louisiana State University Press, 2000); Alison Bell, "White Ethnogenesis and Gradual Capitalism: Perspectives from Colonial Archaeological Sites in the Chesapeake," *American Anthropologist* 107, no. 3 (2005): 446–60. Other overviews of the archaeology of identities include Siân Jones, *The Archaeology of Ethnicity: Constructing Identities in the Past and Present* (New York: Routledge, 1997); Timothy Insoll, *The Archaeology of Identities* (New York: Routledge, 2007); Lynn Meskell, "The Intersections of Identity and Politics in Archaeology," *Annual Review of Anthropology* 31 (2002): 279–301.

35. Alfred C. Kinsey, Wardell B. Pomeroy, and Clyde E. Martin, *Sexual Behavior in the Human Male* (Philadelphia: Saunders, 1948); and Alfred C. Kinsey and the Institute for Sex Research, *Sexual Behavior in the Human Female* (Philadelphia: Saunders, 1953); Michel Foucault, *The History of Sexuality*, vol. 1: *An Introduction* (New York: Pantheon, 1978); Jeffrey Weeks, *Sex, Politics, and Society: The Regulation of Sexuality since 1800* (New York: Longman, 1981); and John D'Emilio, *Sexual Politics, Sexual Communities: The Making of the Homosexual Minority in the United States, 1940–1970* (Chicago: University of Chicago Press, 1983).

36. Weiss, "The Currency of Intimacy."

37. Examples of archaeology of households across several contexts include Kerri S. Barile and Jamie C. Brandon, eds, *Household Chores and Household Choices: Theorizing the Domestic Sphere in Historical Archaeology* (Tuscaloosa: University of Alabama Press, 2004); Thomas J. Pluckhahn, "Household Archaeology in the Southeastern United States: History, Trends, and Challenges," *Journal of Archaeological Research* 18, no. 4 (2010): 331–85; Kevin R. Fogle, James A. Nyman, and Mary C. Beaudry, eds, *Beyond the Walls: New Perspectives on the Archaeology of Historic Households* (Gainesville: University Press of Florida, 2015).

38. Mark D. Groover, "Linking Artifact Assemblages to Household Cycles: An Example from the Gibbs Site," *Historical Archaeology* 35, no. 4 (2001): 38–57; and Deborah L. Rotman, "Newlyweds, Young Families, and Spinsters:

A Consideration of Developmental Cycle in Historical Archaeologies of Gender," *International Journal of Historical Archaeology* 9, no. 1 (2005): 1–36. See also Aubrey Cannon, "Mortuary Expressions of Mother-Daughter Inheritance and Identity," in *Que(e)rying Archaeology*, ed. Terendy, Lyons, and Janse-Smekal (Calgary: Chacmool Archaeological Association, 2009), 67–76.

39. See Crawford-Lackey and Springate, *Queer Identities and Place*; John Jeffrey Auer IV, "Queerest Little City in the World: LGBTQ Reno," in *Communities and Place: A Thematic Approach to the Histories of LGBTQ Communities in the United States*, ed. Katherine Crawford-Lackey and Megan E. Springate (New York: Berghahn Books, forthcoming); Julio Capó, Jr., "Locating Miami's Queer History," in *Communities and Place*; Donna J. Graves and Shayne E. Watson, "San Francisco: Placing LGBTQ Histories in the City by the Bay" (this volume); Jessica Herczeg-Konecny, "Chicago: Queer Histories at the Crossroads of America," in *Communities and Place*; and Jay Shockley, "Preservation of LGBTQ Historic and Cultural Sites: A New York City Perspective" (this volume).

40. An understanding of intersectionality goes back at least to the nineteenth century (Sojourner Truth, "Ain't I a Woman" delivered December 1851 at the Women's Convention in Akron, Ohio), if not before. See also the Combahee River Collective, "A Black Feminist Statement [1977]," in *The Second Wave: A Reader in Feminist Theory*, ed. Linda Nicholson, 63–70; and Kimberlé Crenshaw, "Demarginalizing the Intersection of Race and Sex: A Black Feminist Critique of Antidiscrimination Doctrine, Feminist Theory and Antiracist Politics," *University of Chicago Legal Forum* 140 (1989): 139–67. See Megan E. Springate, "A Note about Intersectionality, LGBTQ Communities, History, and Place," in *Queer Identity and Place*, for a more in-depth discussion in the context of LGBTQ places.

41. Battle-Baptiste, *Black Feminist Archaeology*; Hollimon, "*Aqi*" and "Examining Third and Fourth Genders"; Megan E. Springate, "Respectable Holidays: The Archaeology of Capitalism and Identity at the Crosbyside Hotel (c. 1870–1902) and Wiawaka Holiday House (mid-1910s–1929), Lake George, New York," Ph.D. diss., University of Maryland College Park, 2017; Voss and Casella, *The Archaeology of Colonialism*.

42. Conkey and Gero, "Programme to Practice"; Perry and Joyce, "Bodies that Matter"; Rosemary A. Joyce, "Embodied Subjectivity: Gender, Femininity, Masculinity, Sexuality," in *A Companion to Social Archaeology*, ed. Lynn Meskell and Robert W. Preucel (Oxford: Blackwell, 2004), 82–95; Benjamin Alberti, "Archaeology, Men, and Masculinities," in *Handbook of Gender in Archaeology*, 401–34; Geller, "Identity and Difference"; Barbara L. Voss, "Engendered Archaeology: Men, Women, and Others," in *Historical Archaeology*, ed. Martin Hall and Stephen W. Silliman (Malden, MA: Blackwell, 2006), 107–27; Joyce, *Ancient Bodies*; and Voss, "Looking for Gender."

43. Blackmore, "How to Queer the Past."

44. Voss, "Sexual Subjects," 64. See above for a discussion of the archaeology of two-spirit identities.

45. Esther Newton, *Mother Camp: Female Impersonators in America* (Englewood Cliffs, NJ: Prentice-Hall, 1972); Esther Newton, "Beyond Freud, Ken, and Barbie," in *Margaret Mead Made Me Gay: Personal Essays, Public Ideas*, ed. Esther Newton (Durham, NC: Duke University Press, 2000), 189–94; Elizabeth L. Kennedy and Madeline D. Davis, *Boots of Leather, Slippers of Gold: The History of a Lesbian Community* (New York: Routledge, 1993); Esther Newton, "My Butch Career," in *Margaret Mead Made Me Gay*, 204–6; Ellen Lewin, "Who's Gay? What's Gay? Dilemmas of Identity among Gay Fathers," in *Out in Public: Reinventing Lesbian/Gay Anthropology in a Globalizing World*, ed. Ellen Lewin and William L. Leap (Malden, MA: Wiley-Blackwell, 2009), 86–103.

46. Emily Kazyak, "Midwest or Lesbian? Gender, Rurality, and Sexuality," *Gender & Society* 26, no. 6 (2012): 825–48.

47. J. Jack Halberstam, *Female Masculinity* (Durham, NC: Duke University Press, 1998).

48. Alberti, "Men and Masculinities"; S. Voutaski, "Agency and Personhood at the Onset of the Mycenaean Period," *Archaeological Dialogues* 17, no. 1 (2010): 65–92; Blackmore, "How to Queer the Past."

49. See Judith M. Bennett, "'Lesbian-Like' and the Social History of Lesbianisms," *Journal of the History of Sexuality* 9 (2000): 10–11, for a discussion of the instability of a lesbian identity (and therefore of other sexual/gender identities).

50. Rubin, "Thinking Sex."

51. For example, whiteness is not often actively engaged with as a racial or ethnic identity. An important and accessible exploration of how this kind of privilege plays out can be found in Peggy McIntosh, "White Privilege and Male Privilege: A Personal Account of Coming to See Correspondences through Work in Women's Studies," Working Paper No. 189 (Wellesley, MA: Massachusetts Center for Research on Women, Wellesley College, 1988), often cited in various versions as "White Privilege: Unpacking the Invisible Backpack." For an overview of the costs of these assumptions and a discussion of "deviance" in the archaeological record, see Aimers and Rutecki, "Brave New World."

52. See, for example, Voss, "Looking for Gender"; Voss and Casella, *The Archaeology of Colonialism*.

53. Barbara Voss, personal communication with the author.

54. Voss, "Sexual Subjects," 67; see also Voss and Casella, *The Archaeology of Colonialism*.

55. For examples of sexual oppression and resistance in several colonial contexts, see Voss and Casella, *The Archaeology of Colonialism*.

56. W. E. B. Du Bois, *The Souls of Black Folk* (Chicago: A. C. McClurg & Co., 1903), 3; and Chela Sandoval, "US Third World Feminism: The Theory and

Method of Oppositional Consciousness in the Postmodern World," *Genders* 10 (1991): 1–24.

57. For slave resistance and rebellion, see Charles E. Orser Jr. and Pedro P. A. Funari, "Archaeology and Slave Resistance and Rebellion," *World Archaeology* 33, no. 1 (2001): 61–72. For African and African American resistance and rebellion in the United States, see Terry Weik, "The Archaeology of Maroon Societies in the Americas: Resistance, Cultural Continuity, and Transformation in the African Diaspora," *Historical Archaeology* 31, no. 2 (1997): 81–92; and Christopher C. Fennell, "Early African America: Archaeological Studies of Significance and Diversity," *Journal of Archaeological Research* 19 (2011): 29–33. For work dealing with double consciousness, see Megan E. Springate, "Double Consciousness and the Intersection of Beliefs in an African American Home in Northern New Jersey," *Historical Archaeology* 48, no. 3 (2014): 125–43; Kathryn H. Deeley, "Double 'Double Consciousness': An Archaeology of African American Class and Identity in Annapolis, Maryland, 1850–1930," Ph.D. diss., University of Maryland, 2015. For a discussion of religion, see Lu Ann De Cunzo, *A Historical Archaeology of Delaware: People, Contexts, and the Cultures of Agriculture* (Knoxville: University of Tennessee Press, 2004); Fennell, "Early African America," 34–36; and Springate, "Double Consciousness." Important work on the archaeology of late-twentieth-century repression and resistance has also been done in a Latin American context and in the context of political (anti-war) protests; Pedro Funari, Andrés Zarankin, and Melisa Salerno, eds, *Memories from Darkness: Archaeology of Repression and Resistance in Latin America* (New York: Springer, 2009); and Yvonne Marshall, "Archaeologies of Resistance," in *Que(e)rying Archaeology*, ed. Terendy, Lyons, and Janse-Smekal (Calgary: The Archaeological Association of the University of Calgary, 2009), 12–20.

58. Randall H. McGuire and Paul Reckner, "Building a Working-Class Archaeology: The Colorado Coal Field War Project," *Industrial Archaeology Review* 25, no. 2 (2003): 83–95; Karin Larkin and Randall H. McGuire, *The Archaeology of Class War: The Colorado Coalfield Strike of 1913–1914* (Boulder: University Press of Colorado, 2009); Michael Roller, "Rewriting Narratives of Labor Violence: A Transnational Perspective of the Lattimer Massacre," *Historical Archaeology* 42, no. 2 (2013): 109–23; Michael Roller, *An Archaeology of Structural Violence: Life in a Twentieth-Century Coal Town* (Gainesville: University Press of Florida, 2018); Brandon Nida and Michael Jessee Adkins, "The Social and Environmental Upheaval of Blair Mountain: A Working Class Struggle for Unionisation and Historic Preservation," in *Heritage, Labour, and the Working Classes*, ed. Laurajane Smith, Paul A Shackel, and Gary Campbell (New York: Routledge, 2011), 52–68.

59. Porter-Lupu, "Performing a Queer Aesthetic."

60. See Katherine Crawford-Lackey and Megan E. Springate, eds, *Communities and Place*; Donna J. Graves and Shayne E. Watson, "San Francisco: Placing LGBTQ Histories in the City by the Bay" (this volume); Jay Shockley, "Pres-

ervation of LGBTQ Historic and Cultural Sites: A New York City Perspective" (this volume).

61. For San Francisco, see Rubin, "Urban Sex"; Christina B. Hanhardt, *Safe Space: Gay Neighborhood History and the Politics of Violence* (Durham, NC: Duke University Press, 2013); and Nan Alamilla Boyd, *Wide Open Town: A History of Queer San Francisco to 1965* (Oakland: University of California Press, 2005); for Washington, DC, see William Leap, "Professional Baseball, Urban Restructuring and (Changing) Gay Geographies in Washington, DC," in *Out in Public*, ed. Lewin and Leap, 202–21; for New York City, see Jen Jack Gieseking, *A Queer New York: Geographies of Lesbians, Dykes, and Queer Women 1983–2008* (New York: NYU Press, 2019); and Hanhardt, *Safe Space*; and for Atlanta, see Petra L. Doan and Harrison Higgins, "The Demise of Queer Space? Resurgent Gentrification and the Assimilation of LGBT Neighborhoods," *Journal of Planning Education and Research* 31, no. 1 (2011): 6–25. See also Amin Ghaziani, *There Goes the Gayborhood?* (Princeton, NJ: Princeton University Press, 2014).

62. For landscape archaeology, see overviews by Rebecca Yamin and Karen B. Metheny, eds, *Landscape Archaeology: Reading and Interpreting the American Historical Landscape* (Knoxville: University of Tennessee Press, 1996); Kurt F. Anschuetz, Richard H. Wilshusen, and Cherie L. Scheick, "An Archaeology of Landscapes: Perspectives and Directions," *Journal of Archaeological Research* 9, no. 2 (2001): 157–211; Julian Thomas and David Bruno, eds, *Handbook of Landscape Archaeology* (Walnut Creek, CA: Left Coast Press, 2008); Suzanne M. Spencer-Wood, "A Feminist Framework for Analyzing Powered Cultural Landscapes in Historical Archaeology," *International Journal of Historical Archaeology* 14, no. 4 (2010): 498–526. For archaeological work on communities, see overviews and examples by Lynda Carroll, "Communities and Other Social Actors: Rethinking Commodities and Consumption in Global Historical Archaeology," *International Journal of Historical Archaeology* 3, no. 3 (1999): 131–36; Marcello Canuto and Jason Yaeger, eds, *The Archaeology of Communities: A New World Perspective* (New York: Routledge, 2000); and Suzanne M. Spencer-Wood, "A Feminist Theoretical Approach to the Historical Archaeology of Utopian Communities," *Historical Archaeology* 40, no. 1 (2006): 152–85.

63. Yvonne Marshall, "What is Community Archaeology?" *World Archaeology* 34, no. 2 (2002): 211–19; Carol McDavid, "Archaeologies that Hurt; Descendants that Matter: A Pragmatic Approach to Collaboration in the Public Interpretation of African-American Archaeology," *World Archaeology* 34, no. 2 (2002): 303–14; Dean J. Saitta, "Ethics, Objectivity and Emancipatory Archaeology," in *Archaeology and Capitalism: From Ethics to Politics*, ed. Yannis Hamilakis and P. G. Duke (Walnut Creek, CA: Left Coast Press, 2007), 267–80; Barbara J. Little and Paul A. Shackel, eds, *Archaeology as a Tool of Civic Engagement* (Lanham, MD: AltaMira Press, 2007); M. Jay Stottman, ed., *Archaeologists as Activists: Can Archaeologists Change the World?* (Tus-

caloosa: University of Alabama Press, 2010); Gemma Tully, "Community
Archaeology: General Methods and Standards of Practice," *Public Archaeol-
ogy* 6, no. 3 (2007): 155–87; Sonya Atalay, *Community-Based Archaeology:
Research with, by, and for Indigenous and Local Communities* (Berkeley:
University of California Press, 2012); Barbara J. Little and Paul A. Shackel,
*Archaeology, Heritage, and Civic Engagement: Working toward the Public
Good* (Walnut Creek, CA: Left Coast Press, 2014).

64. Erin C. Rodriguez, "A Multiplicity of Voices: Towards a Queer Field School
Pedagogy," paper presented at the Society for Historical Archaeology, Seattle, 2015; Lylliam Posadas Vidales, "We Want In on This: Contemporary
Queer Archaeology and the Preservation of Queer Cultural History," poster
presented at the Society for American Archaeology, San Francisco, 2015;
Meghan Walley, "Queering the Inuit Past: Archaeology as LGBTQ Allyship,"
paper presented at the Society for American Archaeology, Vancouver, Canada, 2017.

65. Voss, "Looking for Gender," 34.

Bibliography

Aimers, James, and Dawn M. Rutecki. "Brave New World: Interpreting Sex, Gender, and Sexuality in the Past." *SAA Archaeological Record* 16 no. 1 (2016):
12–17.

Alberti, Benjamin. "Archaeology, Men, and Masculinities." In *Handbook of Gender in Archaeology*, edited by Sarah M. Nelson, 401–34. Lanham, MD: Alta-
Mira Press, 2006.

Anschuetz, Kurt F., Richard H. Wilshusen, and Cherie L. Scheick. "An Archaeology
of Landscapes: Perspectives and Directions." *Journal of Archaeological Research* 9, no. 2 (2001): 157–211.

Arnold, Bettina. "Gender and Archaeological Mortuary Analysis." In *Women in
Antiquity: Theoretical Approaches to Gender and Archaeology*, edited by
Sarah M. Nelson, 107–40. Lanham, MD: AltaMira Press, 2007.

Atalay, Sonya. *Community-Based Archaeology: Research with, by, and for Indigenous and Local Communities*. Berkeley: University of California Press,
2012.

Auer, John Jeffrey, IV. "Queerest Little City in the World: LGBTQ Reno." In *Communities and Place: A Thematic Approach to the Histories of LGBTQ Communities in the United States*, edited by Katherine Crawford-Lackey and
Megan E. Springate. New York: Berghahn Books, forthcoming.

Barile, Kerri S., and Jamie C. Brandon, eds. *Household Chores and Household
Choices: Theorizing the Domestic Sphere in Historical Archaeology*. Tuscaloosa: University of Alabama Press, 2004.

Battle-Baptiste, Whitney. *Black Feminist Archaeology*. Walnut Creek, CA: Left
Coast Press, 2011.

Bell, Alison. "White Ethnogenesis and Gradual Capitalism: Perspectives from

Colonial Archaeological Sites in the Chesapeake." *American Anthropologist* 107, no. 3 (2005): 446–60.

Bennett, Judith M. "'Lesbian-Like' and the Social History of Lesbianisms." *Journal of the History of Sexuality* 9 (2000): 1–24.

Blackmore, Chelsea. "How to Queer the Past without Sex: Queer Theory, Feminisms and the Archaeology of Identity." *Archaeologies* 7, no. 1 (2011): 75–96.

Boyd, Nan Alamilla. *Wide Open Town: A History of Queer San Francisco to 1965.* Oakland: University of California Press, 2013.

Butler, Judith. *Gender Trouble: Feminism and the Subversion of Identity.* New York: Routledge, 1990.

Cannon, Aubrey. "Mortuary Expressions of Mother-Daughter Inheritance and Identity." In *Que(e)rying Archaeology: Proceedings of the Thirty-Seventh Annual Chacmool Conference, University of Calgary,* edited by Susan Terendy, Natasha Lyons, and Michelle Janse-Smekal, 67–76. Calgary: Archaeological Association of the University of Calgary, 2009.

Canuto, Marcello, and Jason Yaeger, eds. *The Archaeology of Communities: A New World Perspective.* New York: Routledge, 2000.

Capo, Julio, Jr. "Locating Miami's Queer History." In *Communities and Place,* edited by Crawford-Lackey and Springate. New York: Berghahn Books, forthcoming.

Carroll, Lynda. "Communities and Other Social Actors: Rethinking Commodities and Consumption in Global Historical Archaeology." *International Journal of Historical Archaeology* 3, no. 3 (1999): 131–36.

Casella, Eleanor. "Bulldaggers and Gentle Ladies: Archaeological Approaches to Female Homosexuality in Convict-Era Australia." In *Archaeologies of Sexuality,* edited by Richard A. Schmidt and Barbara L. Voss, 143–59. New York: Routledge, 2000.

——. "Doing Trade: A Sexual Economy of Nineteenth-Century Australian Female Convict Prisons." *World Archaeology* 32, no. 2 (2000): 209–21.

Casella, Eleanor Conlin, and Barbara L. Voss. "Intimate Encounters: An Archaeology of Sexualities within Colonial Worlds." In *The Archaeology of Colonialism: Intimate Encounters and Sexual Effects,* edited by Barbara L. Voss and Eleanor Conlin Casella, 1–10. New York: Oxford University Press, 2012.

Claassen, Cheryl. "Homophobia and Woman Archaeologists." *World Archaeology* 32 (2000): 173–97.

Combahee River Collective. "A Black Feminist Statement [1977]." In *The Second Wave: A Reader in Feminist Theory,* edited by Linda Nicholson, 63–70. New York: Routledge, 1997.

Conkey, Margaret W., and Janet Spector. "Archaeology and the Study of Gender." In *Advances in Archaeological Method and Theory,* vol. 7, edited by Michael B. Schiffer, 1–38. New York: Academic Press, 1984.

Conkey, Margaret W., and Joan M. Gero. "Programme to Practice: Gender and Feminism in Archaeology." *Annual Review of Anthropology* 26 (1997): 411–37.

Costello, Julia G. "A Night with Venus, a Moon with Mercury: The Archaeology of Prostitution in Historic Los Angeles." In *Restoring Women's History through Historic Preservation*, edited by Gail L. Dubrow and Jennifer B. Goodman, 177–96. Baltimore, MD: Johns Hopkins Press, 2003.

———. "Red Light Voices: An Archaeological Drama of Late Nineteenth-Century Prostitution." In *Archaeologies of Sexuality*, edited by Schmidt and Voss, 160–75. New York: Routledge, 2000.

Crawford-Lackey, Katherine, and Megan E. Springate, eds. *Communities and Place: A Thematic Approach to the Histories of LGBTQ Communities in the United States*. New York: Berghahn Books, forthcoming.

———. *Queer Identities and Place: Place and the Histories of LGBTQ and Two-Spirit People in the United States*. New York: Berghahn Books, 2019.

Crenshaw, Kimberlé. "Demarginalizing the Intersection of Race and Sex: A Black Feminist Critique of Antidiscrimination Doctrine, Feminist Theory and Anti-racist Politics." *University of Chicago Legal Forum* 140 (1989): 139–67.

Dawdy, Shannon Lee, and Richard Weyhing. "Beneath the Rising Sun: "French-ness" and the Archaeology of Desire." *International Journal of Historical Archaeology* 12 (2008): 370–87.

De Cunzo, Lu Ann. *A Historical Archaeology of Delaware: People, Contexts, and the Culture of Agriculture*. Knoxville: University of Tennessee Press, 2004.

Deeley, Kathryn H. "Double 'Double Consciousness': An Archaeology of African American Class and Identity in Annapolis, Maryland, 1850–1930." Ph.D. diss., University of Maryland, 2015.

D'Emilio, John. *Sexual Politics, Sexual Communities: The Making of the Homosexual Minority in the United States, 1940–1970*. Chicago: University of Chicago Press, 1983.

Doan, Petra L., and Harrison Higgins. "The Demise of Queer Space? Resurgent Gentrification and the Assimilation of LGBT Neighborhoods." *Journal of Planning Education and Research* 31, no. 1 (2011): 6–25.

Dowson, Thomas A. "Why Queer Archaeology? An Introduction." *World Archaeology* 32, no. 2 (2000): 161–65.

Du Bois, W. E. B. *The Souls of Black Folk*. Chicago: A.C. McClurg & Co., 1903.

Eger, A. Asa. "Architectures of Desire and Queered Space in the Roman Bath-house." In *Que(e)rying Archaeology*, edited by Terendy, Lyons, and Janse-Smekal, 118–28. Calgary, Alberta, Canada: Chacmool Archaeological Association, 2009.

Fausto-Sterling, Anne. "The Five Sexes, Revisited." *The Sciences* 40, no. 4 (July/August 2000): 18–23.

———. "The Five Sexes: Why Male and Female Are Not Enough." *The Sciences* 33, no. 2 (March/April 1993): 20–25.

Fennell, Christopher C. "Early African America: Archaeological Studies of Significance and Diversity." *Journal of Archaeological Research* 19 (2011): 29–33.

Fogle, Kevin R., James A. Nyman, and Mary C. Beaudry, eds. *Beyond the Walls: New Perspectives on the Archaeology of Historic Households*. Gainesville: University Press of Florida, 2015.

Foster, Michael, John M. Lindly, and Ronald F. Ryden. "The Soiled Doves of South Granite Street: The History and Archaeology of a Prescott Arizona Brothel." *KIVA* 70, no. 4 (2005): 349–74.

Foucault, Michel. *Histoire de la sexualité*, vols. 1, 2, and 3. Translation by Robert Hurley. France: Editions Gallimard, 1976, 1984, 1984.

Franklin, Maria. "A Black Feminist-Inspired Archaeology?" *Journal of Social Archaeology* 1, no. 1 (2001): 108–25.

Funari, Pedro, Andrés Zarankin, and Melisa Salerno, eds. *Memories from Darkness: Archaeology of Repression and Resistance in Latin America*. New York: Springer, 2009.

Geller, Pamela L. "Identity and Difference: Complicating Gender in Archaeology." *Annual Review of Anthropology* 38 (2009): 65–81.

Gensmer, Kristin. "Of Painted Ladies and Patrons: An Analysis of Personal Items and Identity at a Victorian-Era Red Light District in Ouray, Colorado." Master's thesis, Colorado State University, Fort Collins, 2012.

Gero, Joan M. "Socio-Politics and the Woman-At-Home Ideology." *American Antiquity* 50, no. 2 (1985): 342–50.

Ghaziani, Amin. *There Goes the Gayborhood?* Princeton, NJ: Princeton University Press, 2014.

Gieseking, Jen Jack. *A Queer New York: Geographies of Lesbians, Dykes, and Queer Women 1983–2008*. New York: NYU Press, 2019.

Givens, Orie. "A Look at LGBT Artifacts from the National African-American Museum." *Advocate*, 30 September 2016. https://www.advocate.com/pride/2016/9/30/look-lgbt-artifacts-national-african-american-museum.

Groover, Mark D. "Linking Artifact Assemblages to Household Cycles: An Example from the Gibbs Site." *Historical Archaeology* 35, no. 4 (2001): 38–57.

Halberstam, J. Jack. *Female Masculinity*. Durham, NC: Duke University Press, 1998.

Hall, Martin. "Sexuality and Materiality: The Challenge of Method." In *The Archaeology of Colonialism*, edited by Voss and Casella, 323–40. New York: Cambridge University Press, 2012.

Hanhardt, Christina B. *Safe Space: Gay Neighborhood History and the Politics of Violence*. Durham, NC: Duke University Press, 2013.

Herczeg-Konecny, Jessica. "Chicago: Queer Histories at the Crossroads of America." In *Communities and Place*, edited by Crawford-Lackey and Springate. New York: Berghahn Books, forthcoming.

Hollimon, Sandra E. "Archaeology of the 'Aqi: Gender and Sexuality in Prehistoric Chumash Society. In *Archaeologies of Sexuality*, edited by Schmidt and Voss, 176–96. New York: Routledge, 2000.

——. "The Archaeology of Nonbinary Genders in Native North American Societies." In *Handbook of Gender in Archaeology*, edited by Sarah M. Nelson, 435–50. Lanham, MD: AltaMira Press, 2006.

——. "Examining Third and Fourth Genders in Mortuary Contexts." In *Que(e)rying Archaeology*, edited by Terendy, Lyons, and Janse-Smekal, 171–75. Calgary: The Archaeological Association of the University of Calgary, 2009.

Insoll, Timothy. *The Archaeology of Identities*. New York: Routledge, 2007.

Jones, Sian. *The Archaeology of Ethnicity: Constructing Identities in the Past and Present*. New York: Routledge, 1997.

Joseph, Abigail Katherine. "Queer Things: Victorian Objects and the Fashioning of Homosexuality." Ph.D. diss., English and Comparative Literature, Columbia University, 2012, https://doi.org/10.7916/D87P95GV.

Joyce, Rosemary A. *Ancient Bodies, Ancient Lives: Sex, Gender, and Archaeology*. New York: Thames & Hudson, 2008.

———. "Embodied Subjectivity: Gender, Femininity, Masculinity, Sexuality." In *A Companion to Social Archaeology*, edited by Lynn Meskell and Robert W. Preucel, 82–95. Oxford: Blackwell, 2004.

Kazyak, Emily. "Midwest or Lesbian? Gender, Rurality, and Sexuality." *Gender & Society* 26, no. 6 (2012): 825–48.

Kennedy, Elizabeth L., and Madeline D. Davis. *Boots of Leather, Slippers of Gold: The History of a Lesbian Community*. New York: Routledge, 1993.

Kinsey, Alfred C., and the Institute for Sex Research. *Sexual Behavior in the Human Female*. Philadelphia: W. B. Saunders, 1953.

Kinsey, Alfred C., Wardell B. Pomeroy, and Clyde E. Martin. *Sexual Behavior in the Human Male*. Philadelphia: W. B. Saunders, 1948.

Larkin, Karin, and Randall H. McGuire. *The Archaeology of Class War: The Colorado Coalfield Strike of 1913–1914*. Boulder: University Press of Colorado, 2009.

Leap, William. "Professional Baseball, Urban Restructuring and (Changing) Gay Geographies in Washington, DC." In *Out in Public: Reinventing Lesbian/Gay Anthropology in a Globalizing World*, edited by Ellen Lewin and William Leap, 202–21. Malden, MA: Wiley-Blackwell, 2009.

Lewin, Ellen. "Who's Gay? What's Gay? Dilemmas of Identity among Gay Fathers." In *Out in Public*, edited by Lewin and Leap, 86–103. Malden, MA: Wiley-Blackwell, 2009.

Little, Barbara J. *Historical Archaeology: Why the Past Matters*. Walnut Creek, CA: Left Coast Press, 2007.

Little, Barbara J., and Paul A. Shackel. *Archaeology, Heritage, and Civic Engagement: Working toward the Public Good*. Walnut Creek, CA: Left Coast Press, 2014.

Little, Barbara J., and Paul A. Shackel, eds. *Archaeology as a Tool of Civic Engagement*. Lanham, MD: AltaMira Press, 2007.

Marshall, Yvonne. "Archaeologies of Resistance." In *Que(e)rying Archaeology*, edited by Terendy, Lyons, and Janse-Smekal, 12–20. Calgary: The Archaeological Association of the University of Calgary, 2009.

———. "What is Community Archaeology?" *World Archaeology* 34, no. 2 (2002): 211–19.

Matthews, Keith. "An Archaeology of Homosexuality? Perspectives from the Classical World." In *TRAC 94: Proceedings of the Fourth Annual Theoretical Roman Archaeology Conference*, edited by S. Cottam, D. Dungworth, S. Scott, and J. Taylor, 118–32. Oxford: Oxbow Books, 1994.

McDavid, Carol. "Archaeologies that Hurt; Descendants that Matter: A Pragmatic Approach to Collaboration in the Public Interpretation of African-American Archaeology." *World Archaeology* 34, no. 2 (2002): 303–14.

McGuire, Randall H., and Paul Reckner. "Building a Working-Class Archaeology: The Colorado Coal Field War Project." *Industrial Archaeology Review* 25, no. 2 (2003): 83–95.

McIntosh, Peggy. "White Privilege and Male Privilege: A Personal Account of Coming to See Correspondences through Work in Women's Studies." Working Paper No. 189. Wellesley: Massachusetts Center for Research on Women, Wellesley College, 1988.

Meskell, Lynn. "The Intersections of Identity and Politics in Archaeology." *Annual Review of Anthropology* 31 (2002): 279–301.

Meyer, Leisa, and Helis Sikk. "Introduction to Lesbian, Gay, Bisexual, Transgender, and Queer (LGBTQ) History in the United States." In *LGBTQ America: A Theme Study of Lesbian, Gay, Bisexual, Transgender, and Queer History*, edited by Megan E. Springate. Washington, DC: National Park Foundation and National Park Service, 2016. https://www.nps.gov/articles/lgbtqtheme-history.htm.

Miranda, Deborah A. "Extermination of the *Joyas*: Gendercide in Spanish California." *GLQ: A Journal of Lesbian and Gay Studies* 16, no. 1–2 (2010): 253–84.

Murphy, Kevin D. "Secure from All Intrusion: Heterotopia, Queer Space, and the Turn-of-the-Twentieth-Century American Resort." *Winterthur Portfolio* 43, no. 2/3 (2009): 185–228.

Newton, Esther. "Beyond Freud, Ken, and Barbie." In *Margaret Mead Made Me Gay: Personal Essays, Public Ideas*, edited by Esther Newton, 189–94. Durham, NC: Duke University Press, 2000.

———. *Mother Camp: Female Impersonators in America*. Englewood Cliffs, NJ: Prentice-Hall, 1972.

———. "My Butch Career." In *Margaret Mead Made Me Gay*, edited by Newton, 204–6. Durham, NC: Duke University Press, 2000.

Nida, Brandon, and Michael Jessee Adkins. "The Social and Environmental Upheaval of Blair Mountain: A Working Class Struggle for Unionisation and Historic Preservation." In *Heritage, Labour, and the Working Classes*, edited by Laurajane Smith, Paul A Shackel, and Gary Campbell, 52–68. New York: Routledge, 2011.

Orser, Charles E., Jr., and Pedro P. A. Funari. "Archaeology and Slave Resistance and Rebellion." *World Archaeology* 33, no. 1 (2001): 61–72.

Perry, Elizabeth M., and Rosemary Joyce. "Providing a Past for 'Bodies that Matter': Judith Butler's Impact on the Archaeology of Gender." *International Journal of Gender and Sexuality Studies* 6, no. 1/2 (2001): 63–76.

Pluckhahn, Thomas J. "Household Archaeology in the Southeastern United States: History, Trends, and Challenges." *Journal of Archaeological Research* 18, no. 4 (2010): 331–85.

Porter-Lupu, Jennifer. "Performing a Queer Aesthetic in Early 20th Century Washington: Preliminary Findings from the Halcyon House Site." Paper presented at the Society for American Archaeology, Washington, DC, 2018.

Prine, Elizabeth. "The Ethnography of Place: Landscape and Culture in Middle Missouri Archaeology." Ph.D. diss., University of California Berkeley, 1997.

———. "Searching for Third Genders: Towards a Prehistory of Domestic Space in Middle Missouri Villages." In *Archaeologies of Sexuality*, edited by Schmidt and Voss, 197–219. New York: Routledge, 2000

Reifschneider, Meredith. "Towards a Queer Materialism in Archaeology; Materiality and the Sexed and Gendered Subject." Paper presented at the Society for Historical Archaeology Conference, Quebec City, Canada, 2014.

Rodriguez, Erin C. "A Multiplicity of Voices: Towards a Queer Field School Pedagogy." Paper presented at the annual meeting for the Society for Historical Archaeology, Seattle, 2015.

Roller, Michael. *An Archaeology of Structural Violence: Life in a Twentieth-Century Coal Town.* Gainesville: University of Florida, 2018.

———. "Rewriting Narratives of Labor Violence: A Transnational Perspective of the Lattimer Massacre." *Historical Archaeology* 42, no. 2 (2013): 109–23.

Roscoe, Will. "Sexual and Gender Diversity in Native America and the Pacific Islands." In *Queer Identities and Place: Place and the Histories of LGBTQ and Two-Spirit People in the United States*, edited by Katherine Crawford-Lackey and Megan E. Springate. New York: Berghahn Books, 2019.

Rotman, Deborah L. "Newlyweds, Young Families, and Spinsters: A Consideration of Developmental Cycle in Historical Archaeologies of Gender." *International Journal of Historical Archaeology* 9, no. 1 (2005): 1–36.

Rubin, Gayle. "The Traffic in Women: Notes on the 'Political Economy' of Sex." In *Toward an Anthropology of Women*, edited by Rayna Reiter. New York: Monthly Review Press, 1975.

———. "Thinking Sex: Notes for a Radical Theory of the Politics of Sexuality." In *Culture, Society and Sexuality: A Reader*, edited by Richard Parker and Peter Aggleton, 143–78. New York: Routledge, 1984.

———. "Sites, Settlements, and Urban Sex: Archaeology and the Study of Gay Leathermen in San Francisco 1955–1995." In *Archaeologies of Sexuality*, edited by Schmidt and Voss, 62–88. New York: Routledge, 2000.

Rutecki, Dawn, and Chelsea Blackmore, eds. "Special Section: Towards an Inclusive Queer Archaeology." *Society for American Archaeology SAA Record* 16, no. 1 (2016): 9–39.

Saitta, Dean J. "Ethics, Objectivity and Emancipatory Archaeology." In *Archaeology and Capitalism: From Ethics to Politics*, edited by Yannis Hamilakis and P. G. Duke, 267–80. Walnut Creek, CA: Left Coast Press, 2007.

Sandoval, Chela. "U.S. Third World Feminism: The Theory and Method of Oppositional Consciousness in the Postmodern World." *Genders* 10 (1991): 1–24.

Sedgwick, Eve. *Epistemology of the Closet.* Berkeley: University of California Press, 1990.

Seifert, Donna J. "Within Sight of the White House: The Archaeology of Working Women." *Historical Archaeology* 24, no. 4 (1991): 82–108.

Seifert, Donna J., Elizabeth Barthold O'Brien, and Joseph Balicki. "Mary Ann Hall's First-Class House: The Archaeology of a Capital Brothel." In *Archaeologies of Sexuality*, ed. Schmidt and Voss, 117–28. New York: Routledge, 2000.

Sider, Gerald. "Identity as History: Ethnohistory, Ethnogenesis, and Ethnocide in the Southeastern United States." *Identities* 1, no. 1 (1994): 109–22.

Smith, Matt. "Queering the Museum." In *Contemporary Clay and Museum Culture: Ceramics in the Expanded Field*, edited by Christine Brown, Julian Stair, and Clare Twomey, 196–208. New York: Routledge, 2016.

Sofaer, Joanna, and Marie Stig Sørensen. "Death and Gender." In *The Oxford Handbook of the Archaeology of Death and Burial*, edited by Sarah Tarlow and Liv Nilsson Stutz, 527–42. Oxford: Oxford University Press, 2013.

Spector, Janet. *What This Awl Means: Feminist Archaeology at a Wahpeton Dakota Village*. St. Paul: Minnesota Historical Society Press, 1993.

Spencer-Wood, Suzanne M. "A Feminist Framework for Analyzing Powered Cultural Landscapes in Historical Archaeology." *International Journal of Historical Archaeology* 14, no. 4 (2010): 498–526.

———. "A Feminist Theoretical Approach to the Historical Archaeology of Utopian Communities." *Historical Archaeology* 40, no. 1 (2006): 152–85.

Springate, Megan E. "Double Consciousness and the Intersection of Beliefs in an African American Home in Northern New Jersey." *Historical Archaeology* 48, no. 3 (2014): 125–43.

———. "A Note About Intersectionality, LGBTQ Communities, History, and Place." In *Queer Identities and Place*, edited by Crawford-Lackey and Springate. New York: Berghahn Books, 2019.

———. "Respectable Holidays: The Archaeology of Capitalism and Identities at the Crosbyside Hotel (c. 1870–1902) and Wiawaka Holiday House (mid-1910s–1929), Lake George, New York." Ph.D. diss., Department of Anthropology, University of Maryland College Park, 2017.

Springate, Megan E., ed. *LGBTQ America: A Theme Study of Lesbian, Gay, Bisexual, Transgender, and Queer History*. Washington, DC: National Park Foundation and National Park Service, 2016.

Springate, Megan E., and Caridad de la Vega. "Nominating LGBTQ Places to the National Register of Historic Places and as National Historic Landmarks: An Introduction." In *LGBTQ America: A Lesbian, Gay, Bisexual, Transgender, and Queer History* (Washington, DC: National Park Foundation and National Park Service, 2016). https://www.nps.gov/articles/lgbtqtheme-nominating.htm.

Stottman, M. Jay, ed. *Archaeologists as Activists: Can Archaeologists Change the World?* Tuscaloosa: University of Alabama Press, 2010.

Terendy, Susan, Natasha Lyons, and Michelle Janse-Smekal, eds. *Que(e)rying Archaeology: Proceedings of the Thirty-Seventh Annual Chacmool Confer-

ence, University of Calgary. Calgary: Chacmool Archaeological Association, 2009.

Thomas, Julian, and David Bruno, eds. *Handbook of Landscape Archaeology*. Walnut Creek, CA: Left Coast Press, 2008.

Truth, Sojourner. "Ain't I a Woman." Speech delivered December 1851 at the Woman's Convention in Akron, Ohio.

Tully, Gemma. "Community Archaeology: General Methods and Standards of Practice." *Public Archaeology* 6, no. 3 (2007): 155–87.

Van Buren, Mary, and Kristin A. Gensmer. "Crib Girls and Clients in the Red-Light District of Ouray, Colorado: Class, Gender, and Dress." *Historical Archaeology* 51, no. 2 (2017): 218–39.

Vidales, Lylliam Posadas. "We Want In on This: Contemporary Queer Archaeology and the Preservation of Queer Cultural History." Poster presented at the Society for American Archaeology, San Francisco, 2015.

Voss, Barbara L. *The Archaeology of Ethnogenesis: Race and Sexuality in Colonial San Francisco*. Berkeley: University of California Press, 2008.

———. "Colonial Sex: Archaeology, Structured Space, and Sexuality in Alta California's Spanish Colonial Missions." In *Archaeologies of Sexuality*, edited by Schmidt and Voss, 35–61. New York: Routledge, 2000.

———. "Engendered Archaeology: Men, Women, and Others." In *Historical Archaeology*, edited by Martin Hall and Stephen W. Silliman, 107–26. Malden, MA: Blackwell, 2006.

———. "Looking for Gender, Finding Sexuality: A Queer Politic of Archaeology, Fifteen Years Later." In *Que(e)rying Archaeology*, edited by Terendy, Lyons, and Janse-Smekal, 29–39. Calgary, Alberta, Canada: Chacmool Archaeological Association, 2009.

———. "Sexual Effects: Postcolonial and Queer Perspectives on the Archaeology of Sexuality and Empire." In *The Archaeology of Colonialism*, edited by Voss and Casella, 11–28. New York: Oxford University Press, 2012.

———. "Sexuality Studies in Archaeology." *Annual Review of Anthropology* 37 (2008): 317–36.

———. "Sexual Subjects: Identity and Taxonomy in Archaeological Research." In *Archaeology of Plural and Changing Identities: Beyond Identification*, edited by Eleanor C. Casella and Chris Fowler, 55–77. New York: Kluwer/Plenum, 2005.

Voss, Barbara L., and Eleanor Conlin Casella, eds. *The Archaeology of Colonialism: Intimate Encounters and Sexual Effects*. New York: Cambridge University Press, 2012.

Voss, Barbara L., and Richard A. Schmidt. "Archaeologies of Sexuality: An Introduction." In *Archaeologies of Sexuality*, edited by Schmidt and Voss, 1–32. New York: Routledge, 2000.

Voutaski, S. "Agency and Personhood at the Onset of the Mycenaean Period." *Archaeological Dialogues* 17, no. 1 (2010): 65–92.

Walley, Meghan. "Queering the Inuit Past: Archaeology as LGBTQ Allyship." Paper presented at the annual meeting for the Society for American Archaeology, Vancouver, 2017.

Weeks, Jeffrey. *Sex, Politics, and Society: The Regulation of Sexuality since 1800.* New York: Longman, 1981.

Weik, Terrance M. "The Archaeology of Ethnogenesis." *Annual Review of Anthropology* 43 (2014): 291–305.

———. "The Archaeology of Maroon Societies in the Americas: Resistance, Cultural Continuity, and Transformation in the African Diaspora." *Historical Archaeology* 31, no. 2 (1997): 81–92.

Weiss, Lindsay. "The Currency of Intimacy: Transformations of the Domestic Sphere on the Late-Nineteenth Century Diamond Fields." In *The Archaeology of Colonialism*, edited by Voss and Casella, 49–66. New York: Cambridge University Press, 2012.

White, Carolyn L., and Mary C. Beaudry. "Artifacts and Personal Identity." In *The International Handbook of Historical Archaeology*, edited by Teresita Majewski and David Gaimster, 209–25. New York: Springer, 2009.

Wilke, Laurie A. *Creating Freedom: Material Culture and African American Identity at Oakley Plantation*. Baton Rouge: Louisiana State University Press, 2000.

———. "The Other Gender: The Archaeology of an Early 20th Century Fraternity." *Proceedings of the Society for California Archaeology* 11 (1998): 7–11.

Wilke, Laurie A., and Katherine H. Hayes. "Engendered and Feminist Archaeologies of the Recent and Documented Pasts." *Journal of Archaeological Research* 14, no. 3 (2006): 243–64.

Yamin, Rebecca, and Karen B. Metheny, eds. *Landscape Archaeology: Reading and Interpreting the American Historical Landscape*. Knoxville: University of Tennessee Press, 1996.

CHAPTER 5

Interpreting LGBTQ Historic Sites

Susan Ferentinos

LGBTQ America: A Theme Study of Lesbian, Gay, Bisexual, Transgender, and Queer History, published by the National Park Service and the National Park Foundation in 2016, is raising awareness of LGBTQ history and historic preservation.[1] Hopefully, many of these sites will be not only designated but also interpreted to the public.[2] In addition to these properties with their primary significance in LGBTQ history, many other historic sites, designated for primary reasons other than their LGBTQ connections, still have stories to tell on this topic. Still others may have been working with LGBTQ interpretation for some time, but seek new approaches for reaching wider audiences. With this chapter, I offer some suggestions for sharing LGBTQ stories with a public audience, while also respecting the nuances and diversity of these experiences. I begin by discussing the importance of this work, move on to exploring some conceptual issues, and conclude by providing some concrete first steps to interpretive planning.[3]

Why Interpret LGBTQ History?

Evidence of same-sex love and desire, and of gender crossing, exists throughout the recorded history of North America (and elsewhere), and yet these topics are rarely included in discussions of U.S. history, whether in classrooms, in mainstream media, or at museums and historic sites. This leaves a hole in our national narrative and erases part of the story. The most obvious reason for historic sites to share their LGBTQ stories is that doing so creates a more inclusive and accurate telling of the national past.

At the same time, the process of uncovering LGBTQ history is more than simply an exercise in inclusivity. Studying cultural outsiders not only reveals insight into their experiences, but also sheds light on the experiences of the mainstream. The question of what behavior is and is not considered normal in a particular historical era, the explanations given for those delineations, and the punishments meted out to those who violate these cultural boundaries all reveal information to help us understand the unspoken assumptions and anxieties of a given age.

For example, historian John Murrin—observing that in the New England colonies, charges of sexual deviance were brought disproportionately against adolescent males, while charges of witchcraft were brought disproportionately against older, unmarried women—concluded that these accusations reveal an abiding Puritan anxiety about community members who lived outside of the control of the patriarchal family. Historian Siobhan Somerville has noted that a medical definition of homosexuality developed in an era—the turn of the twentieth century—when science and medicine were also actively seeking scientific proof of white superiority, and she has explored how these various delineations provided a sense of order for native-born white elites amid a rapidly changing society. More recently, in the 1970s, Anita Bryant's anti-gay "Save Our Children" campaign coincided with the growing independence of American women as a result of second-wave feminism and a skyrocketing divorce rate. As these examples illustrate, when we add LGBTQ experiences to our historical narrative, we gain a richer understanding, both by considering a greater range of experiences and by glimpsing new information about stories we thought we already knew.[4]

In addition, as historic sites expand their interpretation, they will likely expand their audiences. An inclusive approach to the past will draw attention. It sends a welcoming message to potential visitors who are accustomed to being spurned and who, in turn, may be less likely to venture to new places until they are clearly welcomed. Interpretation that includes LGBTQ stories also offers something new for all visitors; curiosity and the desire to learn new things will draw many to investigate these sites.

LGBTQ historical interpretation may also improve a site's fulfillment of its mission. Over the past three decades, the role of cultural organizations in U.S. society has changed. Whereas previously these institutions positioned themselves as some of the main conveyers of knowledge, they now more often envision their missions to be about the facilitation of meaning making. This more democratic approach has repositioned historic sites and museums as places of community dialogue, where visitors can explore new topics and draw their own conclusions, as their comfort level allows.[5] Given the current preponderance of LGBTQ issues in the news, sites can offer some historic context to current events and a forum for exploring these connections—by introducing the idea that different eras have understood love between same-sex individuals in different ways, for example. In the process of providing this historical context, these organizations prove their relevance and fulfill their role as sites of public exploration.[6]

Finally, interpreting LGBTQ history can serve as an act of reparation to a group who has historically been slandered, ignored, and erased. Beyond a simple concern about visitor statistics, historic sites can perform a public service by restoring a past to people who quite often have been cut off from their historical identities.[7] Often, as part of claiming an LGBTQ identity, people lose historic connections—to their families of origin, their hometowns, and their religious or ethnic communities. And while LGBTQ subcultures can replace some of these community connections, a desire to relate to the past may still go unfulfilled. As Paula Martinac wrote in the late 1990s, "One thing that historic sites and travel guides never taught me was about a most important part of myself—my heritage as a gay person in this country."[8] Given these circumstances, to actually encounter "their" history included in an official historical narrative can be a profound and moving experience for LGBTQ visitors. As Mark Meinke writes in the prologue to the LGBTQ theme study, encounters with evidence of same-sex-loving and gender-crossing people in the past "provide a perspective peopled with ancestors whose existence reaffirms our existence and whose recognition underpins a feeling that if they matter, we matter."[9]

Conceptualizing the Story

While there are compelling reasons to engage with LGBTQ history, before beginning concrete interpretive planning, sites must lay some initial conceptual groundwork. As with any historical subfield, LGBTQ history carries its own peculiar circumstances that interpreters should be aware of before moving into this territory. Below are some considerations to reflect on in initial efforts to understand LGBTQ stories.

Changing Understandings of Sexuality

Although the topic was hotly debated in the 1990s, scholars now generally agree that sexual identity is socially constructed—that is, it is influenced by time, place, and culture, rather than being immutable. This is an extremely important consideration when approaching same-sex desire and sexual activity in the past. The historical agents being stud-ied may have understood their feelings, identities, and behavior quite differently than we would understand those same circumstances in our own era. Thus, historians need to evaluate source material within the context of the time in which it was created, rather than relying on their own (historically specific) assumptions of meaning.[10] For example, the concept of sexual orientation as a personal characteristic did not be-come firmly entrenched until the turn of the twentieth century. Same-sex sexual activity certainly existed before this, but in earlier eras the emphasis was on behavior, not psychology. Someone might engage in the *sin* or *crime* of sodomy, but that action did not indicate a particular *type* of person, as it would beginning in the twentieth century.[11]

As a result of these changing understandings, the historical record offers many tantalizing hints of activity that, if created in our own time, would seem to be evidence of gay, lesbian, or bisexual desire, behavior, identity, or relationships. The analysis is not that easy, however. These are contemporary labels, and we cannot facilely apply them retrospec-tively to a time period in which such concepts did not exist. For instance, intense, exclusive bonds between members of the same sex—mostly women but also sometimes men—were quite common in the nine-teenth century. Known as "romantic friendships," these relationships in-volved avowals of loyalty and love, pet names, and quite often physical affection. And yet, such bonds carried no stigma and did not preclude their adherents from also entering into marriages with members of the opposite sex.[12] How are we to understand these relationships today? To call them "gay" or "lesbian" assumes a sexual consciousness that quite likely was not present. Such a label also seems somehow to disrespect those who have struggled with or proudly claimed that label in later times. As Victoria Bissell Brown notes when discussing the sexuality of reformer Jane Addams, "I cannot use a word that has purposely erotic meaning in our era to describe the intimate experience of a woman who lived in a very different time. Too many people have fought too hard for modern lesbians' claim to a lusty, erotic life for me to dain-tily retreat to an ahistorical definition of "lesbian" that skirts the blood, sweat, and tears of erotic expression."[13] At the same time, to completely deny the relevance of romantic friendships to LGBTQ history would also be misleading. Surely these bonds lie somewhere on the spectrum of same-sex love and desire; it is the easy use of modern labels that strips these historical trends of their nuance and context.

Shifting the topic from "LGBTQ" to same-sex love and desire ad-dresses some of these issues. This broader category moves away from

Figure 5.1. Portrait of Jane Addams, 1906, by George de Forest Brush. In the collections of the National Portrait Gallery (public domain: Wikimedia Commons).

contemporary labels as well as the modern emphasis on sexual practice and self-identification. Likewise, we can take a similar approach to conceptualizing transgender identity by instead considering the topic of "variant gender expression." Like its companion identities in the label of LGBTQ, transgender identity is a modern concept, with a relatively recent history as an identity distinct from sexual orientation.[14] The past abounds with people who chose to live as a gender opposite to their biological sex. We can certainly speak to that fact, but it is more difficult to presume their motivation for doing so, unless they specifically addressed that question. Once again, it is the modern label, not the topic itself that is problematic.

Vocabulary

Terminology is another issue to keep in mind when beginning to conceptualize the LGBTQ stories related to a site. In addition to the interpretive issues involved in using contemporary labels to describe historical circumstances, sites that interpret the twentieth century—after our modern labels had come into use—face decisions concerning appropriate vocabulary. There is no one universally agreed upon lexicon to describe variant sexuality and gender expression, with preferences varying by generation, subculture, geographic region, and personal inclination. Because of this, some sites choose to devote interpretive space to explaining the connotations and changing meanings of specific words. For instance, *Revealing Queer*, a temporary exhibit at the Museum of History and Industry (MOHAI) in Seattle, dedicated a corner of its thousand-square-foot exhibit space to offering definitions of various labels and providing a space where visitors could record the words they use to identify them-

selves. Regardless of the vocabulary sites choose to employ, site cura-
tors should make this decision carefully and in consultation with local
LGBTQ communities.[15]

Intersectionality

The idea of intersectionality argues that different aspects of one's identity—such as race, class, sexual orientation, gender identity, geographic
region, religion, etc.—intersect to create a particular worldview and thus
require us to approach historical agents as multifaceted beings whose
experience of one condition—sexual orientation, for instance—is informed by all others.[16] Intersectionality is most certainly a factor in conceptualizing LGBTQ stories. There is not one LGBTQ community, one
LGBTQ experience, one LGBTQ past—though we sometimes speak of all
of these. To do true justice to the stories contained in a historic place,
interpreters must consider the intersectionality of identities.[17]

The Underrepresented Nature of Bisexual and Transgender Identities

Although the acronyms GLBT, LGBT, and LGBTQ have been in use for
decades, they do not always deliver equal representation of the identities listed. Gay and lesbian experiences have received far more consideration, generally speaking, than bisexual and transgender experiences.
While one could argue that this is a consequence of greater numbers
and more surviving documentation in the historical record, the neglect
of bisexual and transgender experiences is at least in part an oversight
that warrants redress.

Western culture tends toward the binary. Most of us are quite accustomed to the heterosexual-homosexual binary, or the male-female
binary, and significantly less comfortable with those who blur those
borders, as do both bisexuals and transgender folk. Rather than grapple
with the in-between, many choose simply to ignore those experiences
that complicate the cultural framework. Yet exploring the lives of those
who destabilize cultural categories has the potential to provide new insight; by shifting perspective, we see assumptions that we did not necessarily know existed.

For instance, what are we to make of a heterosexually married person who also left evidence of same-sex desire and behavior?[18] Traditionally, sites may have been inclined to use the fact of a marriage as
a badge of heterosexual acceptability and simply ignore any evidence
that suggested a broader range of interest. Now the pendulum may

have swung too far the other way, and sites might be too quick to assume this hypothetical historical agent was a closeted homosexual, using a socially acceptable marriage as nothing more than a shield against accusations of impropriety. But there is, of course, another possibility. Such a person may have sincerely felt desire for both men and women. In a similar vein, bisexuals have historically shared many of the same experiences as gays and lesbians—fighting for broader protection under the law, being arrested in gay bars, and losing jobs because of perceived "sexual perversion." It might take a second look to find them, even when they are hiding in plain sight.[19]

Along similar lines, transgender identities and same-sex love and desire exist in complicated relation with each other. Today, we understand sexual orientation and gender identity to be two distinct categories, but this has not always been the case. Traditionally, the categories have been conflated in societal understandings. As a result, when delving into the past, interpreters can find opportunities to talk about *both* same-sex love and desire *and* gender transgression.[20] For instance, Alice Austen, a turn-of-the-twentieth-century photographer, challenged gender conventions in much of her work. She also spent fifty years partnered to another woman, Gertrude Tate. Both of these aspects are interpreted at her home, Clear Comfort, which is now a museum.[21] In 2010, the Alice Austen House and its parent organization, the Historic House Trust of New York City, invited photographer Steven Rosen, working with the drag performance troupe Switch 'n' Play, to create contemporary interpretations of some of Austen's more provocative works and thus explore changing attitudes about gender expression and sexual identity. The results were later displayed in an exhibit at the site. While this program was not strictly historical in nature, it does provide an example of museums incorporating innovative programming, highlighting the interrelationship of gender and sexual identity, and encouraging visitors to engage with the past by exploring parallels with (and differences from) their own era.[22]

Considering how variant gender expression has overlapped with variant sexuality in different ways in different eras opens exciting interpretive avenues. But if we unconsciously favor gay and lesbian stories—those that fall neatly into the binary—we run the risk of neglecting other stories also present in historical sources. Staying consciously committed to finding bisexual and transgender stories, as well as gay and lesbian ones, can result in a fuller discussion of the range of ideas and experiences present.

Artifacts

What objects represent the LGBTQ elements of your site's story? The answer will vary with each site, of course, as well as with the period of significance. When interpreting the mid- to late twentieth century, objects may more obviously represent queer experience—mementos from marches or gay bars, for example. Earlier eras may present more of a challenge and may require reviewing your site's collection with new eyes—and possibly engaging the help of a specialist—to discover coded meanings not readily apparent.[23]

Moving Away from Standard Tropes

One could argue that recent efforts to obtain legal recognition for same-sex marriage have fed into a "Queer people are just like us!" mentality. Such thinking obscures the distinct subcultures LGBTQ people have forged. The most successful interpretive efforts will approach LGBTQ experiences on their own terms, as revealed in the surviving sources, rather than crafting a narrative that mimics heterosexual patterns. Indeed, in their role as sex and gender outsiders, many LGBTQ people have worked tirelessly to challenge cultural assumptions about what is and is not "normal," "proper," and "natural." This societal critique—whether it occurred with words or deeds—deserves to be remembered.

A relevant example comes from the *Out in Chicago* exhibit at the Chicago History Museum.[24] The museum convened two separate advisory panels, one comprised of people who identified as LGBTQ and the other comprised of people who identified as straight. Interestingly, when asked what they hoped to get out of an exhibit on Chicago's LGBTQ past, the straight committee said they sought to learn about the ways queer lives were similar to their own, while the LGBTQ committee hoped that their distinct experiences and subcultures would be documented, preserved, and presented to a wider audience. After grappling with the question of how to address the legitimate desires of both groups, the exhibit team decided in the end to privilege the wishes of the LGBTQ stakeholders, who had not had as great an opportunity as the straight stakeholders to see their experiences represented in museum settings.[25]

In addition to moving beyond heterosexual tropes, interpreters should also challenge the "progress narrative." Most likely visitors are accustomed to historical trajectories that move unerringly toward "progress," however defined—expanding democratic freedoms, grow-ing economic strength, lives continually made better by technological innovation and increased access to consumer goods. This device seems particularly prevalent when discussing LGBTQ history, especially when those presentations focus on the question of civil rights.[26]

Historians now understand that, over time, the dangers and free-doms afforded to LGBTQ people expanded and contracted in ways that do not fit neatly into the idea of a steady march toward acceptance and freedom from fear. Examples abound. To take but one, in the revolution-ary period and early nineteenth century, emotional and physical affec-tion between men was seen as a sign of "sensibility," a desired trait in the democratic ideal where empathy, compassion, and thoughtfulness were seen as necessary for exercising the rights of citizenry (at this time restricted to white men). By the twentieth century, however, the emo-tional range considered acceptable for men was greatly constricted, and male-male bonds of affection were derided and strictly policed for fear that they would receive the taint of the then-common taboo of male love for another man (regardless of sexual component).[27]

When conceptualizing the LGBTQ stories to be told, the issue of sexual content is likely to arise, and here, too, I encourage interpreters to challenge their assumptions about what is and is not appropriate. Many authors have written about the role of museums in enforcing heteronormativity—the assumptions that heterosexuality and the nu-clear family are the societal "norm," and hence do not need to be an-alyzed, while all other desires and social arrangements are "abnormal" and thus troubled.[28] Heteronormativity can often slip into historical in-terpretation when LGBTQ experiences are deemed to be too "sexual" to discuss, while analogous heterosexual experiences are present. For instance, think how ubiquitous erotic female nudes (generally created by male artists) are in Western art. These pieces fill art galleries and his-toric homes and seldom receive any critical comments for being there. Would it be more challenging for staff and visitors if erotic depictions of nude men were displayed in the historic home of a lifelong bachelor? Likewise, the fact that Paul Revere fathered sixteen children with two wives is a regular part of the tour at the Paul Revere House. Yet this in-formation is certainly no more or less sexual than the fact that author Willa Cather shared numerous residences and thirty-eight years with her female companion, Edith Lewis.[29]

All of the tendencies described in this section are reasonable as-sumptions to make, given larger societal forces. Nevertheless, truly nuanced historical interpretation needs to push beyond societal assumptions in order to get ever closer to accurately documenting the realities of past experiences.

Accept That You Won't Have All the Answers

Thus far, I have discussed numerous conceptual gray areas—the use of contemporary labels to describe historical experiences, the subtle connotations of language, the intersectionality of identity, the nonbinary nature of bisexual and transgender identities, and historical nuance that doesn't fit neatly into standard cultural tropes. It would be understandable if readers began to feel that uncovering the LGBTQ past were a moving target, one that eludes clear conclusions. And to some extent, such feelings would be correct. Historical inquiry often reveals more questions than answers. This is the core of its power. We don't have to have all the answers in order to engage in a conversation about the past with visitors; the very fact that we do *not* know everything we wish we knew invites the visitor to interact with the past as opposed to merely consuming a historical product. Yet, admitting uncertainty may be new territory for seasoned interpreters accustomed to taking a more definitive stance when sharing the past with visitors. While it may require a change of thinking, or perhaps additional training, this challenge once again points to the potential of this type of interpretation, revealing more clearly to a wide audience that history is not just a collection of known facts. It involves piecing together shards of evidence, grappling with conflicting points of view, and drawing conclusions as best we can. And, in particular, with regard to the queer past, ideas about sexuality change over time: previous prejudice against LGBTQ identities result in a dearth of surviving objects and documents in our own time; past eras were as complicated as our own, with competing interpretations and so very much that went unspoken.

In fact, within the field of public history, there is a growing trend to "pull back the curtain" and reveal historians' work to visitors. Rather than presenting interpretation of established fact, this line of thinking encourages sites to reveal the historical process by presenting evidence and context to visitors and asking them to draw their own conclusions. Uncertainty itself can be an interpretive tool.[30] The Jane Addams Hull-House Museum puts these ideas into practice in interpreting Addams's sexuality. Although historians know that the reformer had an intense bond with her friend Mary Rozet Smith that spanned over thirty years, the couple's correspondence was destroyed (at Addams's request), so questions remain about the specific nature of their relationship. The museum interprets Addams's personal life—including her bond with Smith—in the reformer's bedroom, and is quite open about the fact that the evidence is unclear about Addams's sexual identity. Visitors encounter the evidence that survives and a description of the relevant historical context—that the late nineteenth century saw many life-long pairings between educated, professional women, and the historical circumstances that supported such behavior. However, the museum does not draw conclusions from the evidence, instead providing visitors the opportunity to perform their own analyses.[31]

Interpretive Planning

At some point in the process of uncovering LGBTQ stories, it will be time to move from the conceptual to the concrete, to the specific steps of interpretive planning. While such steps are likely quite familiar to those who work in this area, below I mention a few issues that either are particularly important when beginning LGBTQ interpretation or carry specific implications when approaching these populations.

Buy-In from Stakeholders

As is true of all interpretive efforts, buy-in from stakeholders—including funders—early in the planning process will help ensure that the effort goes smoothly. You might be surprised at how easy this is to achieve. Regardless of individual opinions about LGBTQ current events and legal protections, it would be difficult to find many people in the United States today who deny that LGBTQ people exist and have been productive members of society. As a result of this cultural shift, resistance to LGBTQ historical interpretation is becoming increasingly rare when the information is based on historical evidence and avoids using modern labels to describe past circumstances. What's more, in the last few years there has been a sea change within corporate America. Many major companies in the United States have moved to the forefront of advocating for LGBTQ acceptance, a trend witnessed in the 2015 controversy in Indiana over the state's Religious Freedom Restoration Act, where corporations such as Eli Lilly and Company, Angie's List, Anthem, and Salesforce played a significant role in pressuring lawmakers to amend the law.[32] These events suggest that many corporate funders would welcome the opportunity to support LGBTQ historical interpretation. Nevertheless, it is best to build donor, board, and staff support early in the planning process, rather than face unpleasant surprises later on.

Community Alliances and Partnerships

Seeking input on interpretive development from a wide range of community advisors will assist in creating programming that is relevant and respectful. Advisors can include straight stakeholders as well as representatives of LGBTQ communities, but in selecting advisors, sites should keep in mind that there is not one single cohesive LGBTQ "community." Care must be taken to ensure gender, class, racial, and generational diversity, as well as representation of all the different categories within the LGBTQ label.

When cultivating relationships among LGBTQ advisors, site personnel should be prepared to encounter some distrust and resistance. Mainstream institutions have historically served as agents of oppression for LGBTQ people in this country. Laws criminalized their self-expression; police harassed them; doctors told them they were sick; popular culture portrayed them as depraved; educational materials denied their existence; the military gave them dishonorable discharges; and the federal government's glacial response to the AIDS epidemic led to the deaths of hundreds of thousands of gay and bisexual men and transgender women, among others. These historical realities are fading, but they have created scars that lead many LGBTQ people to assume the worst about the powers that be. Within the museum world, this is most often seen as a reluctance to grant oral history interviews, share lived experiences, or donate material. Community advisors from relevant populations can serve as bridge builders, communicating the organization's goals and objectives and serving as watchdogs against unintended gaffes in interpretation. Historic sites should be prepared, however, to exercise patience when building trust and legitimacy within this area.

In addition to specific individuals serving as community advisors, organizational partnerships can address similar issues, providing content expertise and advice on outreach. The Minnesota Historical Society had an established Summer History Immersion Program (SHIP) teaching first-generation college-bound high school students the skills of college-level historical research. The organization partnered with the University of Minnesota's Jean-Nickolaus Tretter Collection in Gay, Lesbian, Bisexual, and Transgender Studies when looking to expand its program into the field of LGBTQ history. Similarly, the National Constitution Center, Independence National Historical Park, and the William Way LGBT Community Center cosponsored a special exhibit in summer 2015 to commemorate the fiftieth anniversary of the "Annual Reminder" protests for gay and lesbian rights that were held each Independence Day from 1965 to 1969 outside Independence Hall in Philadelphia.[33] The key to creating solid partnerships is mutual assistance. Seek ways to support these organizations as a means of building trust and strengthening relationships.[34]

To assist with these outreach efforts, in 2016 the American Alliance of Museums released a series of LGBTQ welcoming guidelines for museums. This document, freely available online, intentionally aligns with the organization's *National Standards and Best Practices for U.S. Museums* and draws widely from resources on supporting LGBTQ individuals at work, at school, and in the community.[35]

Staffing and Sustainability

Although familiarity with local LGBTQ realities provides an important perspective to LGBTQ site interpretation, historical and interpretive expertise is also important. Thus, choices about what staff to assign to the development of new interpretation should be made with an eye toward expertise rather than personal identification with the subject. While LGBTQ staff members will likely support the organization's efforts in this area, effective interpretation requires the engagement of all staff with relevant skills.

In addition, the issue of sustainability is important to consider from the outset. Will the interpretative changes become part of permanent programming? Or will they be temporary (special events or occasional themed tours, for instance)? If the latter, how will you maintain the new visitors' interest and the audience enthusiasm your efforts are likely to produce? LGBTQ interpretation can send a message of welcome and inclusion, but this message will be met with expectations. How will the organization continue to create a welcoming environment for diverse audiences? How will it avoid tokenism?

Stacia Kuceyeski, director of outreach at the Ohio History Connection (which serves as an institutional partner to the Gay Ohio History Initiative) urges organizations to make LGBTQ projects and outreach a designated part of someone's job, rather than an unevaluated labor of love or collateral duty for a particular staff member, performed above and beyond their assigned job duties. With responsibilities clearly assigned and part of articulated performance goals, Kuceyeski argues,

LGBTQ interpretive efforts are protected from the vagaries of staff turnover or loss of momentum.[36]

Choosing Specific Interpretive Methods

Historic sites have introduced LGBTQ stories to visitors in a variety of ways. Beauport, the home of early-twentieth-century designer Henry Davis Sleeper, discusses Sleeper's sexual identity in their standard visitor tour. They have also hosted lectures on LGBTQ-related topics and an evening reception and private tour specifically for a gay meet-up group.[37] Staff at Rosie the Riveter / World War II Home Front National Historical Park, realizing that they needed more documentation before beginning to interpret LGBTQ stories, launched an oral history project complete with a confidential phone line where people interested in learning more about the project could do so while still preserving their anonymity.[38] The John Q Ideas Collective has staged "discursive memorials," which might also be described as historically informed site-specific theater, at sites throughout Atlanta that hold relevance to the LGBTQ past.[39] The Gay Ohio History Initiative, in partnership with the Ohio History Connection, erected a historical marker in Dayton to author Natalie Clifford

Figure 5.2. Beauport, the Sleeper-McCann House, Gloucester, Massachusetts, 1979. Photo by J. David Bohl, from the National Historic Landmark nomination.

Barney, who partnered with a woman (painter Romaine Brooks) for fifty years, as well as a marker to Cleveland's historic LGBTQ community.[40] An LGBTQ history group in Roanoke, Virginia, has organized a historic bar crawl, where participants visit the sites of former gay bars and learn the history of these sites while sharing a drink.[41] Indianapolis and Minneapolis have each taken a city-wide approach to interpreting LGBTQ history, developing mobile phone apps that map and interpret relevant sites throughout their cities.[42] And the National Park Service and the California Historical Society are among those sponsoring and managing crowd-sourced Historypin projects where the public can upload their memories and photos of LGBTQ-related sites.[43]

The relative newness of LGBTQ historical interpretation means that the field remains particularly open to new ideas and methods. Sites have engaged with this history using both established and experimental interpretive methods, and many sites unfolded their LGBTQ interpretation in stages, beginning with lectures or other one-time programming and eventually moving into more detailed interpretation. A combination of creative thinking and respectful consultation with stakeholders holds the possibility of producing meaningful and engaging content.

Preparing for a Range of Reactions

LGBTQ historical interpretation is still a rare enough phenomenon that many visitors likely will be encountering this subject matter for the first time. Some will be thrilled to find it; others will be challenged. As with any new interpretive effort, it is wise to prepare for a range of reactions. The literature on this subject contains numerous mentions of visitors crying; this can be a hard history to bear witness to. Visitors who have experienced violence, discrimination, and loss because of their LGBTQ identities may have such traumatic memories triggered by this interpretation. People may need a place to reflect and process what they've encountered. They may want to share stories. Some may be angry at encountering this topic; others may be frustrated that the interpretation does not go further. Consider a range of possibilities and prepare for them.

As part of planning for visitor reactions, sites may want to add participatory elements to their interpretation. Providing these kinds of opportunities—video booths or reaction boards, for example—gives visitors a chance to reflect on what they have encountered in an environment where they feel they will be heard. Another approach would be to invite audience members to take on the role of historian, "pulling back the curtain" and analyzing the evidence for themselves.

Ensuring that the nation's historic sites represent a full and inclusive past is an ongoing challenge. As LGBTQ history permeates the national consciousness and becomes increasingly evident in official historical narratives, examples of LGBTQ interpretation at historic sites will increase. And, as with all historical topics, our understanding and interpretation will become more nuanced over time. The key at this moment is to begin.

Dr. Susan Ferentinos is a public history consultant in Bloomington, Indiana.

Notes

1. Megan E. Springate, ed. *LGBTQ America: A Theme Study of Lesbian, Gay, Bisexual, Transgender, and Queer History* (Washington, DC: National Park Foundation and National Park Service, 2016), available at https://www.nps .gov/subjects/tellingallamericansstories/lgbtqthemestudy.htm.
2. In this chapter, I use "interpretation" to mean the ways museums and historic sites engage their visitors with the past. Interpretation can include museum exhibits, site tours, special events, and programming.
3. For more detail, see Susan Ferentinos, *Interpreting LGBT History at Museums and Historic Sites* (Lanham, MD: Rowman & Littlefield, 2015).
4. John M. Murrin, "'Things Fearful to Name': Bestiality in Colonial America," *Pennsylvania History* 65 (January 1, 1998): 8–43; Siobhan B. Somerville, *Queering the Color Line: Race and the Invention of Homosexuality in American Culture*, Series Q (Durham NC: Duke University Press, 2000); and Ian Lekus, "Up They Come Again: The Rise of Family Values Politics," *Ultimate History Project*, accessed 5 November 2015, http://ultimatehistoryproject .com/marriage-lgbt.html.
5. Bill Adair, Benjamin Filene, and Laura Koloski, eds., *Letting Go? Sharing Historical Authority in a User-Generated World* (Philadelphia: Pew Center for Arts & Heritage [distributed by Left Coast Press], 2011); Graham Black, *Transforming Museums in the Twenty-First Century: Developing Museums for Visitor Involvement* (Hoboken, NJ: Taylor & Francis, 2011), 202–40; and Nina Simon, *The Participatory Museum* (Santa Cruz, CA: Museum 2.0, 2010).
6. Guidance for navigating the relevance of past experiences to current events can be found through the International Coalition of Sites of Conscience, www.sitesofconscience.org.
7. This process has similarities to previous efforts by historic sites to respectfully interpret the histories of other underrepresented groups, such as Na-

tive Americans and African Americans. As with LGBTQ history, these earlier efforts were aided by National Park Service theme studies.

8. Paula Martinac, *The Queerest Places: A National Guide to Gay and Lesbian Historic Sites* (New York: Henry Holt & Co, 1997), ix. See also David W. Dunlap, "Library's Gay Show Is an Eye-Opener, Even for Its Subjects," *New York Times*, 6 September 1994, http://www.nytimes.com/1994/09/06/arts/library-s-gay-show-is-an-eye-opener-even-for-its-subjects.html; Kelly Farrell, "Exposing the Soul: An Unexpected Encounter with Community-Based Interpretation," *Legacy: The Journal of the National Association of Interpretation*, February 2010, 20–23; and Alison Oram, "Going on an Outing: The Historic House and Queer Public History," *Rethinking History* 15, no. 2 (June 2011): 193.

9. Mark Meinke, "Prologue: Why LGBTQ Historic Sites Matter," in *LGBTQ America: A Theme Study of Lesbian, Gay, Bisexual, Transgender, and Queer History*, ed. Megan E. Springate (Washington, DC: National Park Foundation and National Park Service, 2016), https://www.nps.gov/articles/lgbtqtheme-prologue.htm.

10. John D'Emilio and Estelle B. Freedman, *Intimate Matters: A History of Sexuality in America*, 3rd ed. (Chicago: University of Chicago Press, 2012), 30–31; Leila J. Rupp, *A Desired Past: A Short History of Same-Sex Love in America* (Chicago: University of Chicago Press, 1999), 27–35; and Kenneth Turino and Susan Ferentinos, "Entering the Mainstream: Interpreting GLBT History," *AASLH History News*, Autumn 2012. Staff at historic sites should understand, however, that although historians now agree that sexuality is socially constructed, the wider public—including interpretive guides—may find this to be a challenging notion. The concept warrants explanation, both in staff training and in interpretation. Indeed, establishing that different historical time periods understood sexual identity and expression differently may end up being one of your site's main interpretive goals.

11. Thomas A. Foster, ed., *Long before Stonewall: Histories of Same-Sex Sexuality in Early America* (New York: New York University Press, 2007), 8–9; and Molly McGarry and Fred Wasserman, *Becoming Visible: An Illustrated History of Lesbian and Gay Life in Twentieth-Century America* (New York: Penguin Studio, 1998), 39. The emphasis before this shift most definitely was on sodomy—most often defined as male sexual penetration of another male. Women's sexual activity with other women was largely off the radar of social commentators until the development of the medical model known as homosexuality.

12. Leila Rupp, "Romantic Friendships," in *Modern American Queer History*, ed. Allida Mae Black (Philadelphia: Temple University Press, 2001), 13–23; Carroll Smith-Rosenberg, "The Female World of Love and Ritual: Relations between Women in Nineteenth-Century America," *Signs: Journal of Women in Culture and Society* 1, no. 1 (1975): 1–29; Anthony Rotundo, "Romantic Friendship: Male Intimacy and Middle-Class Youth in the Northern United

States, 1800–1900," *Journal of Social History* 23 (1989): 1–26; and D'Emilio and Freedman, *Intimate Matters*, 125–29.

13. Victoria Bissell Brown, "Queer or Not: What Jane Addams Teaches Us about Not Knowing," in *Out in Chicago: LGBT History at the Crossroads*, ed. Jill Austin and Jennifer Brier (Chicago: Chicago History Museum, 2011), 67.

14. Originally, the medical model of homosexuality conflated sexual desire for the same sex with the gender identification of the opposite sex (known at the time as "inversion"). See Jennifer Terry, *An American Obsession: Science, Medicine, and Homosexuality in Modern Society* (Chicago: University of Chicago Press, 1999), 40–73; Jonathan Katz, *The Invention of Heterosexuality* (New York: Dutton and Company, 1995), 51–55; and Vern L. Bullough, *Science in the Bedroom: A History of Sex Research* (New York: Basic Books, 1994), 35–40.

15. Ferentinos, *Interpreting LGBT History*, 5–7, 153–54.

16. See Megan E. Springate, "A Note about Intersectionality, LGBTQ Communities, History, and Place," in *Identities and Place: Changing Labels and Intersectional Communities of LGBTQ and Two-Spirit People in the United States*, ed. Katherine Crawford-Lackey and Megan E. Springate (New York: Berghahn Books, 2019).

17. Mieke Verloo, "Intersectional and Cross-Movement Politics and Policies: Reflections on Current Practices and Debates," *Signs* 38, no. 4 (2013): 893–915; Cornelia H. Dayton and Lisa Levenstein, "The Big Tent of U.S. Women's and Gender History: A State of the Field," *Journal of American History* 99, no. 3 (2012): 793–817; and Nan Alamilla Boyd, "Same-Sex Sexuality in Western Women's History," *Frontiers: A Journal of Women Studies* 22, no. 3 (2001): 13.

18. One such person is Ogden Codman Jr., associated with the Codman House (The Grange), 34 Codman Road, Lincoln, Massachusetts, http://www.historicnewengland.org/historic-properties/homes/codman-estate. However, in the discussion that follows, I am not talking specifically about Codman, but hypothetically. For more on Codman, see Kenneth C. Turino, "Case Study: The Varied Telling of Queer History at Historic New England Sites," in *Interpreting LGBT History*, ed. Ferentinos, 135–36. The Grange was listed on the NRHP on 18 April 1974.

19. Lorraine Hutchins, "Making Bisexuals Visible," in *Identities and Place*.

20. Paul Gabriel, "Why Grapple with Queer When You Can Fondle It? Embracing Our Erotic Intelligence," in *Gender, Sexuality and Museums: A Routledge Reader*, ed. Amy K. Levin (New York: Routledge, 2010), 71–79; Susan Stryker, *Transgender History* (Berkeley, CA: Seal Press: Distributed by Publishers Group West, 2008), 150–53.

21. Clear Comfort (The Alice Austen House) at 2 Hylan Boulevard, Staten Island, New York, was listed on the NRHP on 29 July 1970 and designated an NHL on 19 April 1993. On 23 March 2017 the NRHP nomination was amended to include discussion of Alice Austen's gender and sexual expression.

22. Frank D. Vagnone, "A Note from Franklin D. Vagnone," [executive director], *Historic House Trust Newsletter*, Fall 2010; and Lillian Faderman and Phyllis Irwin, "Alice Austen and Gertrude Tate: A Boston Marriage on Staten Island," *Historic House Trust Newsletter*, Fall 2010.

23. Jill Austin et al., "When the Erotic Becomes Illicit: Struggles over Displaying Queer History at a Mainstream Museum," *Radical History Review* 113 (2012): 187–97; and Ferentinos, *Interpreting LGBT History*, 110–15.

24. The Chicago History Museum is located at 1601 North Clark Street, Chicago, Illinois.

25. Jill Austin and Jennifer Brier, "Case Study: Displaying Queer History at the Chicago History Museum," in *Interpreting LGBT History*, ed. Ferentinos, 119–29.

26. Robert Mills, "Queer Is Here? Lesbian, Gay, Bisexual and Transgender Histories and Public Culture," *History Workshop Journal* 62 (2006): 253–63; Robert Mills, "Theorizing the Queer Museum," *Museums & Social Issues* 3, no. 1 (2008): 41–52; and Stuart Frost, "Are Museums Doing Enough to Address LGBT History?" *Museums Journal* 111, no. 1 (2011): 19.

27. Rotundo, "Romantic Friendship"; Clare A. Lyons, *Sex among the Rabble: An Intimate History of Gender and Power in the Age of Revolution, Philadelphia, 1730–1830* (Chapel Hill, NC: Published for the Omohundro Institute of Early American History and Culture, Williamsburg, Virginia, by the University of North Carolina Press, 2006), 123–27; Richard Godbeer, *The Overflowing of Friendship: Love between Men and the Creation of the American Republic* (Baltimore, MD: Johns Hopkins University Press, 2009); and William Benemann, *Male-Male Intimacy in Early America: Beyond Romantic Friendships* (New York: Harrington Park Press, 2006).

28. Mills, "Theorizing the Queer Museum"; Joshua G. Adair, "House Museums or Walk-In Closets? The (Non)Representation of Gay Men in the Museums They Called Home," in *Gender, Sexuality, and Museums*, ed. Amy K. Levin, 269; Kevin Coffee, "Cultural Inclusion, Exclusion and the Formative Roles of Museums," *Museum Management & Curatorship* 23, no. 3 (2008): 261–79; John Fraser and Joe E. Heimlich, "Where Are We?," *Museums & Social Issues* 3, no. 1 (2008): 5–14; Stuart Frost, "Secret Museums: Hidden Histories of Sex and Sexuality," *Museums & Social Issues* 3, no. 1 (2008): 29–40; James H. Sanders III, "The Museum's Silent Sexual Performance," *Museums & Social Issues* 3, no. 1 (2008): 15–25; Patrik Steorn, "Curating Queer Heritage: Queer Knowledge and Museum Practice," *Curator* 55, no. 3 (2012): 355–65; and Jennifer Tyburczy, "All Museums Are Sex Museums," *Radical History Review* 113 (2012): 199–211.

29. Isabella Caruso, "Willa Cather North by Northeast: Cather Related Site-Seeing North of New York City and East of Ohio," ed. Andrew Jewell, Willa Cather Archive, University of Nebraska-Lincoln, 2003, http://cather.unl.edu/community.tours.new_york.html. Possibly the only surviving residence of this couple, where they lived from 1908–1913, is an apartment in Green-

wich Village, New York City, New York. Willa Cather's childhood home on the corner of Third Avenue and Cedar Street, Red Cloud, Nebraska was listed on the NRHP on 16 April 1969 and designated an NHL on 11 November 1971.

30. Susan Ferentinos, "Lifting Our Skirts: Sharing the Sexual Past with Visitors," Digital Content, May 2014 Issue, *Public History Commons: The Public Historian*, 1 July 2014, http://ncph.org/history-at-work/lifting-our-skirts; Robert R. Weyeneth, "What I've Learned along the Way: A Public Historian's Intellectual Odyssey," *Public Historian* 36, no. 2 (2014): 9–25. The *Public History Commons* website ran a series of articles on this idea of "pulling back the curtain." The series is located at http://ncph.org/history-at-work/tag/pulling-back-the-curtain.

31. Ferentinos, "Lifting Our Skirts." The Jane Addams Hull-House Museum, located at 800 South Halsted, Chicago, Illinois, was listed on the NRHP on 15 October 1966 and designated an NHL on 23 June 1965.

32. Jeff Swiatek and Tim Evans, "Nine CEOs Call on Pence, Legislature to Modify 'Religious Freedom' Law," *Indianapolis Star*, 31 March 2015, http://www.indystar.com/story/money/2015/03/30/nine-ceos-call-pence-legislature-modify-religious-freedom-law/70689924.

33. Kyle Parsons and Stewart Van Cleve, "Case Study: Interpreting for the Next Generation," in *Interpreting LGBT History*, ed. Ferentinos, 141–49; and *Speaking Out for Equality: The Constitution, Gay Rights, and the Supreme Court*, National Constitution Center exhibit, http://constitutioncenter.org/experience/exhibitions/feature-exhibitions/speaking-out-for-equality-the-constitution-gay-rights-and-the-supreme-court. Independence Hall, where these protests took place, is at 520 Chestnut Street, Philadelphia, Pennsylvania. It was designated as part of the Independence National Historical Park NHL District on 15 October 1966 and became part of the NPS on 27 June 1948.

34. Brian O'Neill, "Twenty-One Partnership Success Factors," *AASLH History News* 69, no. 4 (2014): 17–21.

35. American Alliance of Museums LGBTQ Alliance, *Welcoming Guidelines for Museums*, 2016, http://aam-us.org/docs/default-source/professional-networks/lgbtq_welcome_guide.pdf.

36. Joe Heimlich and Judy Koke, "Gay and Lesbian Visitors and Cultural Institutions: Do They Come? Do They Care? A Pilot Study," *Museums & Social Issues* 3, no. 1 (2008): 93–104; Donna Mertens, John Fraser, and Joe Heimlich, "M or F?: Gender, Identity, and the Transformative Research Paradigm," *Museums & Social Issues* 3, no. 1 (2008): 81–92; Stacia Kuceyeski, "The Gay Ohio History Initiative as a Model for Collecting Institutions," *Museums & Social Issues* 3, no. 1 (2008): 125–32; and Stacia Kuceyeski, director of outreach at the Ohio History Connection and liaison to the Gay Ohio History Initiative, in phone interview with the author, 3 April 2014.

37. Turino, Case Study, 132–35. Beauport was listed on the NRHP and designated an NHL on 27 May 2003.

38. Rosie the Riveter/ World War II Home Front National Historical Park, "Seeking LGBT Stories from WWII Home Front," National Park Service Website, http://www.nps.gov/rori/planyourvisit/seeking-lgbt-stories-from-wwii-home-front.htm; and Elizabeth Tucker, lead park ranger at Rosie the Riveter/ World War II Home Front National Historical Park, in phone interview with the author, 29 April 2014.

39. Julia Brock, "Embodying the Archive (Part 1): Art Practice, Queer Politics, Public History," *History@Work* (blog), 5 April 2013, http://ncph.org/history-at-work/brock-johnq-intro; Julia Brock, "Embodying the Archive (Part 2): Lineages, Longings, Migrations," *History@Work* (blog), 12 April 2013, http://ncph.org/history-at-work/crichton-brock-intro; and Wesley Chenault, Andy Ditzler, and Joey Orr, "Discursive Memorials: Queer Histories in Atlanta's Public Spaces," *Southern Spaces*, 26 February 2010, http://www.southernspaces.org/2010/discursive-memorials-queer-histories-atlantas-public-spaces.

40. Becki Trivison, "Marking Ohio's LGBT History," *GOHI: The Gay Ohio History Initiative*, 2017, http://gohi.org/marking-ohios-lgbt-history/. The historical marker dedicated to Barney was dedicated in 2009 and is located on East Second Street in Dayton, Ohio, in Cooper Park. The Cleveland LGBT Community marker, dedicated 1 June 2017, is located at 1418 West Twenty-Ninth Street, Cleveland, Ohio.

41. Gregory Rosenthal, "Make Roanoke Queer Again: Community History and Urban Change in a Southern City," *Public Historian* 39, no. 1 (2017): 35–60.

42. *Discover Indiana*, https://indyhist.iupui.edu/; Kirsten Delegard, "Yester-Queer," *The Historyapolis Project* (blog), 25 June 2014, http://historyapolis.com/yesterqueer.

43. "California Pride: Mapping LGBTQ Histories," *Historypin*, https://www.historypin.org/project/469-california-pride/; "LGBTQ America," *Historypin*, https://www.historypin.org/en/lgbtq-america/.

Bibliography

Adair, Bill, Benjamin Filene, and Laura Koloski, eds. *Letting Go? Sharing Historical Authority in a User-Generated World*. Philadelphia: Pew Center for Arts & Heritage, 2011.

Adair, Joshua G. "House Museums or Walk-In Closets? The (Non)Representation of Gay Men in the Museums They Called Home." In *Gender, Sexuality, and Museums*, edited by Amy K. Levin, 264–78. Abingdon: Routledge, 2010.

Austin, Jill, and Jennifer Brier. "Case Study: Displaying Queer History at the Chicago History Museum." In *Interpreting LGBT History at Museums and Historic Sites*, edited by Susan Ferentinos, 119–29. Lanham, MD: Rowman & Littlefield, 2015.

Austin, Jill, Jennifer Brier, Jessica Herczec-Konecny, and Anne Parsons. "When the Erotic Becomes Illicit: Struggles over Displaying Queer History at a Mainstream Museum." *Radical History Review* 113 (2012): 187–97.

Benemann, William. *Male-Male Intimacy in Early America: Beyond Romantic Friendships*. New York: Harrington Park Press, 2006.

Black, Graham. *Transforming Museums in the Twenty-First Century: Developing Museums for Visitor Involvement*. Hoboken, NJ: Taylor & Frances, 2011.

Boyd, Nan Alamilla. "Same-Sex Sexuality in Western Women's History." *Frontiers: A Journal of Women Studies* 22, no. 3 (2001): 13–21.

Brock, Julia. "Embodying the Archive (Part 1): Art Practice, Queer Politics, Public History." *History@Work*, 5 April 2013. http://ncph.org/history-at-work/brock-johnq-intro.

———. "Embodying the Archive (Part 2): Lineages, Longings, Migrations." *History@Work*, 12 April 2013. http://ncph.org/history-at-work/crichton-brock-intro.

Brown, Victoria Bissell. "Queer or Not: What Jane Addams Teaches Us about Not Knowing." In *Out in Chicago: LGBT History at the Crossroads*, edited by Jill Austin and Jennifer Brier, 63–75. Chicago: Chicago History Museum, 2011.

Bullough, Vern L. *Science in the Bedroom: A History of Sex Research*. New York: Basic Books, 1994.

Caruso, Isabella. "Willa Cather North by Northeast: Cather Related Site-Seeing North of New York City and East of Ohio," edited by Andrew Jewell, Willa Cather Archive, University of Nebraska–Lincoln, 2003. http://cather.unl.edu/community.tours.new_york.html.

Chenault, Wesley, Andy Ditzler, and Joey Orr. "Discursive Memorials: Queer Histories in Atlanta's Public Spaces." *Southern Spaces*, 26 February 2010. http://www.southernspaces.org/2010discursive-memorials-queer-histories-atlantas-public-spaces.

Coffee, Kevin. "Cultural Inclusion, Exclusion and the Formative Roles of Museums." *Museum Management & Curatorship* 23, no. 3 (2008): 261–79.

Dayton, Cornelia H., and Lisa Levenstein. "The Big Tent of U.S. Women's and Gender History: A State of the Field." *Journal of American History* 99, no. 3 (2012): 793–817.

Delegard, Kirsten. "YesterQueer." *The Historyapolis Project*, 25 June 2014. http://historyapolis.com/yesterqueer.

D'Emilio, John, and Estelle B. Freedman. *Intimate Matters: A History of Sexuality in America*, 3rd ed. Chicago: University of Chicago Press, 2012.

Dunlap, David W. "Library's Gay Show is an Eye-Opener, Even for Its Subjects." *New York Times*, 6 September 1994. http://www.nytimes.com/1994/09/06/arts/library-s-gay-show-is-an-eye-opener-even-for-its-subjects.html.

Faderman, Lillian, and Phyllis Irwin. "Alice Austin and Gertrude Tate: A Boston Marriage on Staten Island." *Historic House Trust Newsletter*, Fall 2010.

Farrell, Kelly. "Exposing the Soul: An Unexpected Encounter with Community-Based Interpretation." *Legacy: The Journal of the National Association of Interpretation*, February 2010, 20–23.

Ferentinos, Susan. "Lifting Our Skirts: Sharing the Sexual Past with Visitors." *Public History Commons: The Public Historian*, 1 July 2014. http://ncph.org/history-at-work/lifting-our-skirts.

——, ed. *Interpreting LGBT History at Museums and Historic Sites*. Lanham, MD: Rowman & Littlefield, 2015.

Foster, Thomas A., ed. *Long before Stonewall: Histories of Same-Sex Sexuality in Early America*. New York: New York University Press, 2007.

Fraser, John, and Joe E. Heimlich. "Where Are We?" *Museums & Social Issues* 3, no. 1 (2008): 5–14.

Frost, Stuart. "Are Museums Doing Enough to Address LGBT History?" *Museums Journal* 111, no. 1 (2011): 19.

——. "Secret Museums: Hidden Histories of Sex and Sexuality." *Museums & Social Issues* 3, no. 1 (2008): 29–40.

Gabriel, Paul. "Why Grapple with Queer When You Can Fondle It? Embracing Our Erotic Intelligence." In *Gender, Sexuality and Museums: A Routledge Reader*, ed. Amy K. Levin, 71–79. New York: Routledge, 2010.

Godbeer, Richard. *The Overflowing of Friendship: Love between Men and the Creation of the American Republic*. Baltimore: Johns Hopkins University Press, 2009.

Heimlich, Joe, and Judy Koke. "Gay and Lesbian Visitors and Cultural Institutions: Do They Come? Do They Care? A Pilot Study." *Museums & Social Issues* 3, no. 1 (2008): 93–104.

HistoryPin. "California Pride: Mapping LGBTQ Histories." *HistoryPin*. https://www.historypin.org/project/469-california-pride/.

——. "LGBTQ America." *HistoryPin*. https://www.historypin.org/en/lgbtq-america/.

Hutchins, Lorraine. "Making Bisexuals Visible." In *Identities and Place: Changing Labels and Intersectional Communities of LGBTQ and Two-Spirit People in the United States*, edited by Katherine Crawford-Lackey and Megan E. Springate. New York: Berghahn Books, 2019.

Katz, Jonathan. *The Invention of Heterosexuality*. New York: Dutton and Company, 1995.

Kuceyeski, Stacia. "The Gay Ohio History Initiative as a Model for Collecting Institutions." *Museums & Social Issues* 3, no. 1 (2008): 125–32.

Lekus, Ian. "Up They Come Again: The Rise of Family Values Politics." *The Ultimate History Project*. http://ultimatehistoryproject.com/marriage-lgbt.html.

Lyons, Clare A. *Sex among the Rabble: An Intimate History of Gender and Power in the Age of Revolution, Philadelphia, 1730–1830*. Chapel Hill: University of North Carolina Press for the Omohundro Institute of Early American History and Culture, Williamsburg, VA, 2006.

Martinac, Paula. *The Queerest Places: A National Guide to Gay and Lesbian Historic Sites*. New York: Henry Holt & Co., 1997.

McGarry, Molly, and Fred Wasserman. *Becoming Visible: An Illustrated History of Lesbian and Gay Life in Twentieth-Century America*. New York: Penguin Studio, 1998.

Meinke, Mark. "Prologue: Why LGBTQ Historic Sites Matter." In *LGBTQ America: A Theme Study of Lesbian, Gay, Bisexual, Transgender, and Queer History*, edited by Megan E. Springate, chapter 1. Washington, DC: National Park Foundation and National Park Service, 2016.

Mertens, Donna, John Fraser, and Joe Heimlich. "M or F?: Gender, Identity, and the Transformative Research Paradigm." *Museums & Social Issues* 3, no. 1 (2008): 81–92.

Mills, Robert. "Queer is Here? Lesbian, Gay, Bisexual and Transgender Histories and Public Culture." *History Workshop Journal* 62 (2006): 253–63.

———. "Theorizing the Queer Museum." *Museums & Social Issues* 3, no. 1 (2008): 41–52.

Murrin, John M. "Things Fearful to Name: Bestiality in Colonial America." *Pennsylvania History* 65 (1998): 8–43.

National Constitution Center. *Speaking Out for Equality: The Constitution, Gay Rights, and the Supreme Court*. National Constitution Center exhibit. http://constitutioncenter.org/experience/exhibitions/feature-exhibitions/speaking-out-for-equality-the-constitution-gay-rights-and-the-supreme-court.

O'Neill, Brian. "Twenty-One Partnership Success Factors." *AASLH History News* 69, no. 4 (2014): 17–21.

Oram, Alison. "Going on an Outing: The Historic House and Queer Public History." *Rethinking History* 15, no. 2 (2011): 189–207.

Parsons, Kyle, and Stewart Van Cleve. "Case Study: Interpreting for the Next Generation." In *Interpreting LGBT History at Museums and Historic Sites*, ed. Susan Ferentinos, 141–49. Lanham, MD: Rowman & Littlefield, 2015.

Rosenthal, Gregory. "Make Roanoke Queer Again: Community History and Urban Change in a Southern City." *Public Historian* 39, no. 1 (2017): 35–60.

Rosie the Riveter / World War II Home Front National Historical Park. "Seeking LGBT Stories from WWII Home Front." National Park Service website. http://www.nps.gov/rori/planyourvisit/seeking-lgbt-stories-from-wwii-home-front.htm.

Rotundo, Anthony. "Romantic Friendship: Male Intimacy and Middle-Class Youth in the Northern United States, 1800–1900." *Journal of Social History* 23 (1989): 1–26.

Rupp, Leila J. *A Desired Past: A Short History of Same-Sex Love in America*. Chicago: University of Chicago Press, 1999.

———. "Romantic Friendships." In *Modern American Queer History*, edited by Allida Mae Black, 13–23. Philadelphia: Temple University Press, 2001.

Sanders, James H., III. "The Museum's Silent Sexual Performance." *Museums & Social Issues* 3, no. 1 (2008): 15–25.

Simon, Nina. *The Participatory Museum*. Santa Cruz, CA: Museum 2.0, 2010.

Smith-Rosenberg, Carroll. "The Female World of Love and Ritual: Relations between Women in Nineteenth Century America." *Signs: Journal of Women in Culture and Society* 1, no. 1 (1975): 1–29.

Somerville, Siobhan B. *Queering the Color Line: Race and the Invention of Homosexuality in American Culture*. Durham, NC: Duke University Press, 2000.

Springate, Megan E. "A Note About Intersectionality, LGBTQ Communities, History, and Place." In *Identities and Place: Changing Labels and Intersectional Communities of LGBTQ and Two-Spirit People in the United States*, edited by Crawford-Lackey and Springate. New York: Berghahn Books, 2019.

———, ed. *LGBTQ America: A Theme Study of Lesbian, Gay, Bisexual, Transgender, and Queer History*. Washington, DC: National Park Foundation and National Park Service, 2016.

Steorn, Patrik. "Curating Queer Heritage: Queer Knowledge and Museum Practice." *Curator* 55, no. 3 (2012): 355–65.

Stryker, Susan. *Transgender History*. Berkeley, CA: Seal Press, 2008.

Swiatek, Jeff, and Tim Evans. "Nine CEOs Call on Pence, Legislature to Modify 'Religious Freedom' Law." *Indianapolis Star*, 31 March 2015. http://www.indystar.com/story/money/2015/03/30/nine-ceos-call-pence-legislature-modify-religious-freedom-law/70689924.

Terry, Jennifer. *An American Obsession: Science, Medicine, and Homosexuality in Modern Society*. Chicago: University of Chicago Press, 1999.

Trivison, Becki. "Marking Ohio's LGBT History." *GOHI: The Gay Ohio History Initiative*. 2017. http://gohi.org/marking-ohios-lgbt-history/.

Turino, Kenneth C. "Case Study: The Varied Telling of Queer History at Historic New England Sites." In *Interpreting LGBT History at Museums and Historic Sites*, edited by Susan Ferentinos, 135–36. Lanham, MD: Rowman & Littlefield, 2015.

Turino, Kenneth C., and Susan Ferentinos. "Entering the Mainstream: Interpreting LGBT History." *AASLH History News*, Autumn 2012.

Tyburczy, Jennifer. "All Museums are Sex Museums." *Radical History Review* 113 (2012): 199–211.

Vagnone, Frank D. "A Note from Franklin D. Vagnone" [executive director]. *Historic House Trust Newsletter*, Fall 2010.

Verloo, Mieke. "Intersectional and Cross-Movement Politics and Policies: Reflections on Current Practices and Debates." *Signs* 38, no. 4 (2013): 893–915.

Weyeneth, Robert R. "What I've Learned along the Way: A Public Historian's Intellectual Odyssey." *Public Historian* 36, no. 2 (2014): 9–25.

CHAPTER 6

Teaching LGBTQ History and Heritage

Leila J. Rupp

Imagine a world in which students could visit not just Civil War battle-fields that raise the profound issues of slavery and what it means for states to be united, but also buildings that housed places that came to feel like home to people marginalized because of sexuality and gender, places that were important enough to defend against onslaughts by the police. That is the possibility that teaching the lesbian, gay, bisex-ual, transgender, and queer (LGBTQ) past through historic sites offers. The houses where famous and lesser known lesbian, gay, bisexual, and transgender people lived, the commercial establishments they patron-ized and defended, and even places that mark a history of discrimina-tion and violence offer the opportunity to make LGBTQ history a part of U.S. history in a way that makes a difference for students, wherever they are learning history.

A more inclusive history certainly matters to LGBTQ students, who suffer not just from bullying and other forms of discrimination but also from being deprived of a past. Many years ago, I was teaching an in-troductory U.S. history course when I ran into a student from the class who was working in the local gay restaurant. He told me that he had never heard of Stonewall until I talked about it in a lecture on social movements of the 1960s. He was so excited to hear a mention of the gay past in a history class that he told his roommate about it. He also came out, since they had never discussed their sexual identities, and then the roommate came out to him. The student described the mo-ment as life-changing.

Robert King, a high school teacher interviewed by historian Daniel Hurewitz, tells a similar story about Jack Davis, a student in his class at Palisades Charter High School in Southern California. King included LGBTQ content in just one part of one day's lecture on civil rights movements. After a discussion of Stonewall, Davis raised his hand and came out to the class. In an essay he published later, Davis wrote that he had been looking for a way to come out, and the mention of Stonewall opened a door. His classmates applauded, got up out of their seats, and hugged him. He described it as an amazing experience, and the class as "the most defining moment of my coming out." Walking out of the classroom, he felt the weight of the world lifted from his shoulders.[1]

And it is not just LGBTQ students who benefit from a more complete history. I had another experience in a class I taught on the history of same-sex sexuality that made that clear. One self-identified straight male student, who must have signed up for the class simply because it was at a convenient time, started the course expressing strongly homophobic views he argued were based on the Bible. The main paper for the class was the analysis of an interview the students had to conduct with an LGBTQ individual, placing the interviewee's story in the context of the history we had been learning. This student chose to interview a gay coworker, and just hearing about a gay man's life and his struggles and his relationships and his views—including his religious views—completely transformed the student's attitude. Research has shown that knowing an LGBTQ person can change someone's position on political issues connected to sexuality, and in this case, a face-to-face conversation—simply seeing a gay man as a person—was transformative.[2]

This chapter addresses the ways that historic sites can be mobilized in the project of teaching about LGBTQ history in high schools, colleges, and universities, as well as in other contexts. I begin by considering what can be gained by teaching courses on queer history or integrating queer history into U.S. history courses. I then address some of the challenges involved in this undertaking. In the bulk of the chapter, I provide an overview of existing and potential historic sites that illustrate the main themes in the field, with suggestions for ways to bring LGBTQ history into the classroom. I end with a brief conclusion emphasizing why teaching LGBTQ history and heritage matters and what historic sites can bring to the project.

Why Teach LGBTQ History?

Lesbian, gay, bisexual, transgender, and queer history developed as a field within the historical discipline as a result of the LGBTQ movement. As with African American, Asian American, Latinx, Native American, and women's history, it was social movement activism that stimulated a desire to learn and teach about people too often left out of the main-stream historical narrative, and to incorporate those histories into a transformed and inclusive story of the past. In recent years, information about LGBTQ lives has moved into mainstream discourse, thanks to the inclusion of LGBTQ characters in film and television, the coming out of prominent public figures, and debate about—and the rapid change in public opinion on—the issue of same-sex marriage, culminating in the 2015 Supreme Court decision opening marriage to same-sex couples throughout the country. Yet there is little knowledge out there about queer history beyond the famous Stonewall uprising, so notions about the LGBTQ community exist in a vacuum. Official recognition of this state of affairs was behind California's pioneering legislation, the Fair, Accurate, Inclusive, and Responsible (FAIR) Act, the nation's first leg-islation requiring public schools to teach about LGBTQ history. The 2011 law amended the language of the state's education code, add-ing "lesbian, gay, bisexual, and transgender Americans," as well as dis-abled Americans, to the list of those, including "men and women, Native Americans, African Americans, Mexican Americans, Asian Americans, Pacific Islanders, European Americans ... and members of other eth-nic and cultural groups" whose contributions must be considered in classroom instruction and materials.[3] How pioneering this legislation is can be measured by the heated debate in the Tennessee legislature of the Classroom Protection Act, known as the "Don't Say Gay Bill," that, if passed, would have prevented teachers from discussing LGBTQ topics.[4] Or the 1992 attack on a New York City curriculum for first graders, called "Children of the Rainbow," for including references to children's books on lesbian and gay families, including *Heather Has Two Mommies*.[5]

So the first answer to the question of why teach LGBTQ history is that it makes for better history. Over the course of the twentieth and twenty-first centuries, history at all levels of education has moved from the story of wars and the men in power to a more complex depiction of the ways that all the people of a society play a part in history. Black history, Native American history, Asian American history, Latinx history, working-class history, women's history, the history of disability—all of these fields of study within the discipline of history have transformed how we understand the U.S. past. That is what the extensive literature on LGBTQ history has done as well. Cultural attitudes toward same-sex sexuality and gender transformation and expression tell us a great deal about the sexual and gender systems of Native Americans, European colonists, and the new "Americans."[*] Same-sex sexuality is part of the story of the evolution of regional differences and the growth of cities.

Struggles over civil liberties and the role of government in the lives of individuals are central to LGBTQ history, and the collective resistance of sexual minorities is as much a part of U.S. history as the struggles of other marginalized groups, whose histories intersect and overlap with queer history. We come to understand history differently when we recognize it not as the single story of a dominant group but as the convergence of multiple histories.

The second answer to the question of why teach LGBTQ history is that it matters to students, of whatever age, because of the widespread phenomenon of bullying, harassment, discrimination—or worse—of LGBTQ people. At the university level, the case of Tyler Clementi, the Rutgers University student who killed himself in 2010 after his roommate secretly videotaped him in a same-sex sexual encounter, attracted national attention. At the secondary school level, the Gay, Lesbian & Straight Education Network's (GLSEN) 2013 National School Climate Survey documents the ways that a hostile school climate affects LGBTQ students.[6] In 2011, the National Center for Lesbian Rights and the Southern Poverty Law Center, supported by the U.S. Justice Department, filed a lawsuit against the Anoka-Hennepin School District in Minnesota over a gag order forbidding discussion of LGBTQ issues after the suicides of four gay or bisexual students. The successful suit cited a California study that showed that any mention of LGBTQ people or issues in the curriculum increased student safety and improved the climate for students.[7] The GLSEN survey also shows that an inclusive curriculum, along with other resources, makes a difference. In high school, college, and university classrooms and in community centers and other places, there are students who identify or have siblings or parents or children or friends or coworkers or neighbors who identify as lesbian, gay, bisexual, transgender, or queer. Teaching an inclusive U.S. history makes better history for all of them.

But It Isn't Easy

Teaching LGBTQ history is important, but it is not always easy. The process begins with introducing students to the social constructionist perspective, which emphasizes that sexuality is historically contingent. That is, societies, through religion, law, science, medicine, and other institutions, shape sexual behavior and identities in very different ways across time and space. Given that the reigning assumption in our society is that sexuality is purely biological and the fact that, in part because it is an easier sell in the struggle for legal equality, the LGBTQ movement has tended to embrace the notion that people are born gay, it can be difficult to teach from a social constructionist perspective. Students tend to experience their sexual desires and identities as innate and to misread social constructionism as an indication that sexuality can be easily changed. So the first task in any class is to show the ways that sexual desire, behavior, and identities vary across time and in different cultures. Such an approach calls for looking carefully at the evidence we have of what people felt, did, and thought, and using language that refers to identities with sensitivity to the times. Historical evidence of different ways that sexuality has been organized can help students understand that experiencing desire for someone of the same sex or engaging in a sexual act with someone of the same sex did not always and everywhere mean that someone was gay or lesbian or bisexual in the way we understand those terms today. Even after reading about all the different ways that societies have shaped sexuality in the past, students often remain firmly convinced that, in Lady Gaga's words, they were "Born This Way." The challenge is to help them see that their desires and behaviors could have quite different meanings and consequences in other times and places.[8]

As a result of this perspective, it can be difficult to identify who belongs in LGBTQ history. Although there are historians who argue that we can identify gay, lesbian, bisexual, and transgender people in societies (including our own past) in which no such categories existed, most historians would insist that we cannot. As a result, the very question of what LGBTQ history includes is a complex one. Does Eleanor Roosevelt's love for journalist Lorena Hickok make her part of LGBTQ history? In terms of historic sites, should the White House be included? And what about a complex figure such as J. Edgar Hoover, who used the FBI to target those suspected of homosexuality at the same time that he was in a long-term intimate relationship with Clyde Tolson? Is Hoover a part of LGBTQ history?[9] It is important in identifying sites not to convey the message that everyone associated with them can be identified as lesbian or gay or bisexual or transgender or queer in our contemporary sense.

It is essential to attend to the intersections of multiple identities shaped not only by sexuality and gender but race, ethnicity, class, nationality, age, disability, and more. As the U.S. history curriculum adds to the diversity of individuals and groups included as worthy of study, it is important that LGBTQ history not focus only on white people, or urban dwellers, or men, or the middle class. Taking inspiration from the title of a classic work in Black women's history, *All the Women are White, all the Blacks are Men, But Some of Us are Brave*, we need to make sure that not all the lesbian, gay, bisexual, transgender, and queer people are white, urban, and middle class.[10]

And then there is the challenge of transforming, rather than just adding a few queer individuals to, the curriculum. The language of the FAIR Act in California calls for the inclusion of the contributions of LGBTQ individuals. If all we can do is sprinkle in a few people who might have desired, loved, or had sex with others with biologically alike bodies, or who might have thought of themselves as a gender different from the one assigned to them at birth, then we will add little to our understanding of sexuality and gender in the past. Our goal should be a transformational approach that, through considering the forces that have structured the lives of LGBTQ people, opens up new perspectives on families, communities, social practices, and politics.[11] As does ethnic, working-class, and women's history, a transformational LGBTQ history changes what we know about the agency and impact of people not in the seat of power, and about how power operates in complex ways. It changes history.

Teaching with Historic Sites

Historic sites provide the opportunity to bring LGBTQ history alive for students of all ages. All over the country there are places—houses, commercial establishments, public spaces, neighborhoods, and locations of significant events—that connect to the kind of transformational history that integrates sexuality and gender into the story of the past. It is possible to connect lessons to local and nearby (at the very least, state-level) LGBTQ historic sites, making this history directly relevant to where students live.

Teaching with these sites is not without its own challenges. For one thing, there is an unavoidable imbalance of recent history, given the more public nature of LGBTQ history in the last century. The national memorial with the earliest identified LGBTQ significance is the Fort Caroline National Memorial where René Goulaine de Laudonnière and Jacques Le Moyne in the 1650s described two-spirit Timucua Indians.[12] In this case, they were male-bodied individuals who took on the dress and social roles of women, but there are also examples of female-bodied two-spirit people in the historical record (see Roscoe, "Sexual and Gender Diversity in Native America and the Pacific Islands"). The vast majority of LGBTQ historic places are associated with the twentieth century, and this has the potential to reinforce a view of LGBTQ history as an uplifting story of progress. As discussed above, the difficulty of determining who and what is legitimately part of LGBTQ history before the sexological definition of homosexuality and the emergence of the identities of lesbian, gay, bisexual, transgender, and queer makes it tricky to avoid an essentializing approach to some of these sites. For example, another early site, Kealakekua Bay in Hawaii, has a connection to LGBTQ history because a member of the James Cook expedition reported talking with a man named Palea who described himself as *aikane*, a term now interpreted as "friend" that may have then referred to a male sexual companion (see Roscoe, "Sexual and Gender Diversity in Native America and the Pacific Islands").[13] Were the two-spirit people in Florida transgender? Was Palea gay? These are questions that cannot be answered simply, as Native American understandings of two-spirit fall outside our Euro-American concept of a sex and gender binary. These questions require acceptance that what we can know about sexual subjectivity in the past is limited, and recognition that we need to be sensitive about the use of contemporary terms to describe people in the past. Yet another challenge is that many sites, especially the homes of individuals, have the potential to stop at the contribution level of LGBTQ history that emphasizes what a few individuals did rather than moving on to a transformational approach that changes how we view history.

But all of these challenges can be met head on, and a variety of different historic sites can help to breathe life into the study of the past. Whether or not students have the opportunity to visit sites in person, historic places can be brought into the classroom through photographs, and some can be linked to documentary films, oral histories, fiction, or community histories. Students can be encouraged to explore places in their own communities that have significance for LGBTQ history. The key to teaching with these sites is to connect them to the big themes of LGBTQ and U.S. history.

So what might a class—either specifically on LGBTQ history, or a U.S. survey incorporating LBGTQ history—that makes use of historical sites look like? I sketch out here some ways that different kinds of sites can evoke a complex and transformational history. Some of these places are already recognized as historical sites, a few by the National Park Service and some by local or state agencies. Some are recognized in connection to LGBTQ history, some for other reasons. Pre-twentieth-century sites have the potential to open up a discussion of how we understand people's desires, sexual acts, and intimate relationships in different cultures and in times before the naming of homosexuality, and to undermine a simple progress narrative of U.S. history. This is the case for sites connected to European contact with two-spirit Native Americans and Hawaiian *aikane*, including (in addition to Fort Caroline and Kealakekua Bay) Fort Wingate in New Mexico, where a two-spirit Zuni named We'Wha was imprisoned in 1892.[14] Another recognized site, the Little Bighorn Battlefield National Monument, is depicted in a ledger drawing of Cheyenne two-spirit warriors leading the victory dance after Custer's defeat in 1876.[15] Students might compare the role of two-spirit people with the case of a female-assigned individual, Mary Henly, who wore men's clothing and was charged in colonial Massachusetts with behavior "seeming to confound the course of nature."[16] Contrasting the acceptance of gender-nonconformity among some Native American cultures with the secret gender-crossing of individuals in European and American culture illustrates for students the ways that societies view gender in vastly different ways.

The homes of nineteenth-century women who lived with other women open up the question of how we think about the intense, loving, and committed relationships known as "romantic friendships." Because of the sex-segregated domestic world of "love and ritual" in which white, middle- and upper-class women lived, romantic friendships between women (and, although in a somewhat different way, between young men) flourished.[17] As middle-class women gained entry to professions such as teaching and social work, romantic friends could choose to forego marriage and make a life with each other in what were known as "Boston marriages." Hull House in Chicago, home to Jane Addams and Mary Rozet Smith, illustrates the role of settlement houses in fostering such Boston marriages (figure 6.1).[18] Likewise, Mary Dreier and Frances Kellor, active in the labor and social reform movements, lived together for fifty years in their New York City residence located near the Museum of Modern Art. Women's colleges were another location for long-term marriage-like relationships between women. Katherine Bates, feminist author of "America the Beautiful" and English professor, lived in Wellesley, Massachusetts, with Katherine Coman, professor of history and economics and later dean of Wellesley College, for twenty-five years. Looking at the homes that women made together, students might consider how the ideology of separate spheres for women and men—with women assigned the domestic sphere of love and care and men the public sphere of work and rationality—created the conditions for romantic friendships. Boston marriages, in turn, provided women, freed from the necessity of marriage, the support to enter into the professions of social work and higher education.

Figure 6.1. Hull House, Chicago, Illinois, 2010. Photo by Zagalejo (public domain: Wikimedia Commons).

The connection between romantic friendships and Boston marriages and emerging lesbian subjectivity can be illustrated through such sites as Clear Comfort, the home of Alice Austen (1866–1952), who lived for fifty years with another woman, Gertrude Tate, and who photographed women dancing together, embracing in bed, and cross-dressing.[19] Students might consider the persistence into the twentieth century of Boston marriages such as Austen's and Tate's, as well as relationships such as that of Eleanor Roosevelt with Lorena Hickok, even as public awareness of the new category of "lesbian" grew.[20] Austen's photographs and Eleanor Roosevelt's love letters to Hickok might be set against texts that warned against the danger of "schoolgirl friendships" or masculine "inverts" out to seduce innocent women.[21]

A variety of homes of individuals can be used to illustrate LGBTQ lives in the nineteenth and early twentieth centuries. The poetry of Walt Whitman (1819–1892), whose Camden home is a recognized historical site, calls attention to the complexity of male love and homoeroticism in the nineteenth century, since Whitman's love for men did not lead him to claim an identity as homosexual.[22] Equally important for LGBTQ history is the hospital where Whitman, along with Dr. Mary Walker, who dressed in men's clothing, cared for soldiers wounded in the Civil War.[23]

The exuberance of Whitman's appreciation of male friendship and American democracy in his poetry opens up for students the connections between masculinity and U.S. industrial and urban growth in the nineteenth century. Students might consider his *Leaves of Grass* alongside photographs of men and letters written between male friends to bring alive a world in which male friendship was valued.[24]

The Murray Hall Residence in New York City is where a gender-crossing female-born New York City politician (ca. 1840s–1901) lived. His secret came out after twenty-five years when he developed breast cancer and his physician shocked the world by sharing the news of Hall's anatomical sex. Students can follow the publicity about Hall and consider how people might have thought about him at the time. Outhistory. org, the premier source for LGBTQ history on the web, includes material about Hall as well as the memoir of Earl Lind, also known as Ralph Werther, also known as Jennie June, a person who considered themself both male and female.[25] The stories of Hall and Lind continue a consideration of how we think about gender-nonconforming individuals in periods before the concept of transgender and the possibility of sex reassignment surgery. The transition to a period in which changing one's bodily sex became possible is marked by the Dawn Pepita Simmons House in Charleston, South Carolina, the home of one of the first transsexual women in the United States. Born Gordon Langley Hall, Dawn Pepita Simmons (1922–2000) had gender-affirming surgery at Johns Hopkins Hospital in 1968.[26] She lived in Charleston, where she married her much younger Black male servant, John-Paul Simmons. Theirs was the first legal interracial marriage in South Carolina. Publicity about the case connects gender, sexuality, race, and class, allowing students to consider a whole range of issues, from the power dynamics involved in a white woman assigned male at birth marrying a Black servant, to the history and legacy of miscegenation laws in the South, to the variety of ways in which legal and social restrictions have policed intimacy.

Historic sites also include commercial establishments catering to LGBTQ people, illustrating the emergence across time of queer communities and the struggle for the right to gather in public. The Ariston Hotel Baths in New York City, which men interested in sex with other men patronized as early as 1897, was the site of the first recorded police raid on a gay bathhouse in 1903.[27] There are many other sites from the days before the emergence of gay liberation, including Café Lafitte in Exile in New Orleans, operating as a gay bar since 1933; Finocchio's in San Francisco, from 1933 to 1999 a famous drag club and tourist destination; the Jewel Box Lounge in Kansas City, opened in 1948 and Missouri home of the touring Jewel Box Revue that featured male and female imper-sonators, including the famous Stormé DeLarverie; and the Shamrock in Bluefield, West Virginia, opened in 1964 as a gay bar at night in what was a straight diner during the day.[28] The variety of clubs and their spread across the country speaks to the importance of LGBTQ people having access to spaces where they were welcome. Students learning about the variety of LGBTQ commercial spaces—not just in New York and San Francisco—can come to understand how much industrialization and geographical mobility loosened the hold of the family and facilitated the emergence of new subcultures, both heterosexual and homosexual.

The importance of commercial establishments to the LGBTQ move-ment can be seen in the connections that developed between culture and politics. Bars and clubs both facilitated collective identity, which is the foundation of social movements, and served as central commu-nity spaces. A good example is Jewel's Catch One, which opened in 1972, the country's first Black gay and lesbian disco. Catch One was also associated with a community center, nonprofit medical clinic, and the first residential home for homeless women and children with HIV/AIDS.[29] Another example is Julius's Bar, a straight bar where, in 1966, Mattachine members held a "Sip-in," ordering drinks and announcing they were gay, in that way challenging the law against serving alcohol to homosexuals.[30]

The connection between commercial LGBTQ spaces and resistance becomes even clearer when we consider the kinds of activism that pre-ceded the iconic response to a police raid at the Stonewall Inn in New York City, traditionally considered the launch of the gay liberation cycle of the LGBTQ movement.[31] In San Francisco, often considered the na-tion's premier LGBTQ city, the sites of such protests include the Black Cat Club, where José Sarria, famous drag entertainer who ran for the San Francisco Board of Supervisors in 1961, performed; California Hall, where activists responded to a police raid of a drag ball in 1964; and Compton's Cafeteria, scene of a riot by young gay and transgender cus-tomers against police repression in 1966 (figure 6.2).[32] In Los Angeles, customers demonstrated against a police crackdown at Cooper's Do-nuts in 1959 and the Black Cat Tavern in 1966.[33] Many of these early protesters were people of color, and their actions make clear that the streets themselves in some places are historic sites. Like the more gen-teel Mattachine "Sip-in," these street protests show how important phys-ical spaces were to diverse members of the LGBTQ community. The film *Screaming Queens: The Riot at Compton's Cafeteria* can be used to illustrate the impact of these pre-Stonewall protests and to raise the

GENE COMPTON'S CAFETERIA RIOT 1966

HERE MARKS THE SITE OF GENE COMPTON'S CAFETERIA WHERE A RIOT TOOK PLACE ONE AUGUST NIGHT WHEN TRANSGENDER WOMEN AND GAY MEN STOOD UP FOR THEIR RIGHTS AND FOUGHT AGAINST POLICE BRUTALITY, POVERTY, OPPRESSION AND DISCRIMINATION IN THE TENDERLOIN. WE, THE TRANSGENDER, GAY, LESBIAN AND BISEXUAL COMMUNITY, ARE DEDICATING THIS PLAQUE TO THESE HEROES OF OUR CIVIL RIGHTS MOVEMENT.

DEDICATED JUNE 22, 2006

Figure 6.2. Historical marker commemorating the fortieth anniversary of the Compton's Cafeteria Riot, San Francisco, California, 2006. Photo by Saylesf (public domain: Wikimedia Commons).

question of why certain events come to stand for the beginning of movements or the transition to a new historical period.[34]

As the number of locations connected to resistance to police raid suggests, there are many historical sites that document repression and discrimination against LGBTQ people. The Willard Asylum for the Chronic Insane in Ovid, New York, one of the many institutions where gay, lesbian, and gender-nonconforming people were locked up under "sexual psychopath laws," is already on the National Register of Historic Places.[35] The YMCA in Boise, Idaho, gained national attention in 1955 for the arrest of sixteen men accused of homosexual activity.[36] The home where transman Brandon Teena was murdered in Humboldt, Nebraska, in 1993 illustrates the widespread violence against transgender people, as does the site of the murder of African American transwoman Rita Hester in her apartment in Allston, Massachusetts, in 1998. Her murder inspired the annual Transgender Day of Remembrance. The intersection of Pilot Peak and Snowy View Roads in Laramie, Wyoming, is another site of violence as the place where gay youth Matthew Shepard was beaten and left to die in 1998. A discussion of such cases can be set in the history of other forms of violence, such as the lynching of Black people, as an extreme form of social control. Violence can also be linked to school bullying, not just of LGBTQ people but, for example, in the form of slut-shaming directed at women.

More empowering are the wide variety of sites that document the emergence of the homophile movement, gay liberation, and lesbian feminism in the early 1970s, and the bisexual and transgender movements in the 1980s and 1990s. The earliest, albeit short-lived, organization dedicated to gay rights was the Society for Human Rights, launched out of the Henry Gerber House in the Old Town Triangle neighborhood of Chicago in 1924.[37] The Harry Hay House overlooking the Silver Lake Reservoir in Los Angeles marks the spot where Hay and some friends launched the Mattachine Society, the first lasting organization committed to civil rights for homosexuals, in 1950. The Daughters of Bilitis headquarters in San Francisco illustrates the growth of the homophile movement as lesbians began to organize separately from gay men.[38] The Dr. Franklin E. Kameny Residence in the northwest of the District of Columbia is important because Kameny was a central figure in the emergence of homophile militancy in the 1960s, fighting the federal government after he was fired for being gay. Students are often astonished to learn that there was a social movement fighting for the rights of LGBTQ people in the 1950s, so teaching about the homophile movement contributes to a rethinking of the supposedly conformist and domestic post–World War II period. Analyzing the factors that gave rise to the homophile movement—wartime geographic mobility, response to the postwar crackdown on homosexuals in government, the spread of information about gay men and lesbians—helps students to think broadly about the motor forces in history.

Frank Kameny was one of the figures who bridged the largely assimilationist homophile movement and the emergence of a more militant gay liberation movement. The Gay Liberation Front emerged in New York City shortly after Stonewall, and the Gay Activists Alliance Firehouse in New York City was the center for an important group that split from the Gay Liberation Front.[39] A range of other sites throughout the country housed short-lived gay liberation organizations in the early 1970s. Castro Camera, the location of Harvey Milk's shop, apartment, and campaign headquarters, is one of only a very few city-recognized LGBTQ historical sites in San Francisco, despite the city's prominence in queer history.[40] One site that marks the impact of HIV/AIDS on the LGBTQ movement in the 1980s is the Gay Men's Health Crisis headquarters in New York City.[41]

Emerging out of gay liberation and the resurgent women's movement in the early 1970s, lesbian feminism is associated with a variety of places throughout the country. Its regional reach can be illustrated through such sites as the 31st Street Bookstore in Baltimore, a women's bookstore with a strong lesbian feminist presence, which opened in 1973; the home of the newspaper *Ain't I a Woman* in Iowa City, published out of an apartment by the Women's Liberation Front; the Furies Collective House in the southeast of the District of Columbia, home of the influential newspaper *The Furies*; and Olivia Records, founded by members and associates of the Furies Collective, which calls attention to the lesbian feminist goal of creating an alternative culture.[42]

For those close enough to visit, the Lesbian Herstory Archives—originally housed in founder Joan Nestle's Upper West Side Manhattan apartment—is a valuable resource for the study of the lesbian past and illustrates the importance of history to the LGBTQ movement.[43] Hesperia, Michigan, the site of the Michigan Womyn's Music Festival from 1977 to 1981, illustrates the strong connection between culture and politics in the lesbian feminist movement. The struggle over the policy of the festival to admit only "womyn-born womyn," and the subsequent founding by transwomen of Camp Trans outside the festival gates, is illustrative of the ongoing tension about boundaries and belonging within the LGBTQ movement.

Learning about internal struggles over who belongs calls attention to a process at work in all social movements. Students can trace the addition of "lesbian" and then "bisexual," "transgender," and "queer" to "gay" in the name of the movement as a way to consider the expansion of boundaries. Marking that transition are sites connected to bisexual and transgender mobilization, such as the Bisexual Resource Center in Boston, founded in 1985, which grew out of the first national conference of bisexuals, who oftentimes met hostility from gay men and lesbians who assumed they were just avoiding coming out.[44] The Erickson Educational Foundation in Baton Rouge, Louisiana, was where transman Reed Erickson funded research and activism on behalf of transgender rights. Pier 45 in New York City has been, since the 1970s, a gathering place for gay men, drag queens, transgender youth, and other members of the African American ballroom community.[45] Illustrating the inclusion of those beyond what Gayle Rubin calls the "charmed circle" are sites including the Leather Archives and Museum in Chicago, documenting the leather community's role within the LGBTQ world.[46]

The history of the LGBTQ movement in all of its cycles can be easily connected to the story of the other social movements of the 1960s and beyond. Kurt Dearie, a public high school teacher in Southern California, organizes a unit on civil rights that compares the goals, strategies, and support for the civil rights, women's, Native American, Latinx, Asian American, LGBTQ, and disability movements. The students write a paper evaluating what they see as the most effective movement strategies.[47] In this way, students learn about social movement processes in general and can apply what they learn to thinking about the contemporary issues they see in the news.

As the expansion of the letters in LGBTQ illustrates, a number of historic sites show the diversity of LGBTQ life. Bayard Rustin's childhood home in West Chester, Pennsylvania, can be used in a discussion of the Quaker values that Rustin brought to the civil rights movement and the difficulties he encountered in that movement as a gay man. The A. Billy

S. Jones Home in northwestern District of Columbia calls attention to Jones (who identifies as bisexual) as the cofounder of the National Coalition for Black Lesbians and Gays and key organizer of the first LGBTQ people of color conference in association with the first Gay and Lesbian March on Washington in 1979. Black lesbian feminist poet and scholar Audre Lorde's home with her partner, Frances Clayton, on Staten Island, New York, recalls the central role Lorde played in the movement. Identifying locations that mark the contributions of African Americans, Latinx, Asian Americans, and Native Americans to LGBTQ history beyond the ones mentioned here are a priority for celebrating a complete story of the LGBTQ past.

In all of these ways, then, recognized historic sites and those that might become part of our official heritage can be utilized to teach about LGBTQ history, either in discrete courses or as part of a survey of U.S. history. Sites connected to just one individual or one event can be used to open up a broad consideration of the queer past, as I have pointed out above. And important developments in LGBTQ history, in turn, connect to themes that are part of the mainstream narrative of U.S. history. The encounters between Native two-spirit people and European explorers and settlers, for example, provide insight into the deep impact of colonialism. Romantic friendships and Boston marriages illustrate the ways that economic structures and social organization shape intimate relationships. The flourishing of commercial establishments catering to people with same-sex desires ties in with the growth of cities and the importance of social spaces to the building of communities and movements. The history of the homophile, gay liberation, lesbian feminist, and contemporary LGBTQ movements add to the story of organizing to end discrimination and win basic civil rights in the post–World War II period.

Conclusion

Recognizing LGBTQ history as one thread in the fabric of the U.S. past makes for better history: better for all students, who can see how historically contingent sexuality is, and better because it is more complete and more complex. A variety of social justice and multicultural education organizations use the metaphor of mirrors and windows to describe the relationship between students and those who people the history they are studying. When history is about great white men, then elite white male students see themselves as in a mirror. Other students are looking through windows from the outside, viewing a history of which they are not a part. Our goal should be to provide mirrors and windows for everyone so students learn about the histories of their families, communities, and worlds, as well as those of others from different genders, races, ethnicities, classes, sexualities, and abilities. At the same time, we need to problematize the concept of mirrors so that students—in this case, LGBTQ students—do not think that women who loved other women, or men who had sex with other men, or individuals who presented in a gender different than the one they were assumed to be at birth, are just like them.

A history enriched by an understanding of how concepts of sexuality and gender, in conjunction with race, ethnicity, class, disability, age, and other categories of difference, have changed over time is a better history. Such a history fuels new ways of thinking about contemporary debates, including same-sex marriage; gay, lesbian, and transgender people in the military; immigration; and citizenship. What a historical perspective brings is a deeper understanding of why change has happened, why some things have not changed, and how change is not always progress. Legal, social, political, urban, and cultural history lend multiple dimensions to thinking about the LGBTQ past and present, and, in turn, the history of same-sex sexuality and gender nonconformity expands our understanding of all of these facets of history. The central narratives of U.S. history speak to queer lives and, just as important, vice versa.

What teaching with historic sites can do is to help make the past come alive. Houses, official buildings, neighborhoods, commercial establishments, and the scenes of historic protests can make concrete the idea that there is a lesbian, gay, bisexual, transgender, and queer past, that what it means to have same-sex desires or to love someone of the same sex or to cross the lines of gender has changed over time, and that LGBTQ history is not a simple story of progress from the bad old days to the liberated new ones. From the representation of Cheyenne two-spirit people leading a victory dance at the Little Bighorn Battlefield National Monument to Hull House, to the Willard Asylum for the Chronic Insane to Compton's Cafeteria, and to Castro Camera, the places where diverse people lived their lives and struggled and made history have the potential to enrich our understanding of the past. In a society in which bullying, hate crimes, homelessness, and suicides are all too common in the lives of LGBTQ youth, teaching about queer history embodied in historic sites can inspire young minds to imagine and work for a more open and accepting future society. That is my hope.

Dr. Leila J. Rupp is Distinguished Professor of Feminist Studies and associate dean of the Division of Social Sciences at the University of California, Santa Barbara.

Notes

1. Quoted in Daniel Hurewitz, "Putting Ideas into Practice: High School Teachers Talk about Incorporating the LGBT Past," in *Understanding and Teaching U.S. Lesbian, Gay, Bisexual, and Transgender History*, 2nd edition, ed. Leila J. Rupp and Susan K. Freeman (Madison: University of Wisconsin Press, 2017), 74.
2. Mary Bernstein, "Paths to Homophobia," *Sexuality Research and Social Policy* 1, no. 2 (2004): 41–55; Andrew R. Flores, "National Trends in Public Opinion on LGBT Rights in the United States," Williams Institute, https://williamsin stitute.law.ucla.edu/wp-content/uploads/POP-natl-trends-nov-2014.pdf; Gregory M. Herek and John P. Capitanio, "'Some of My Best Friends': Intergroup Contact, Concealable Stigma, and Heterosexuals' Attitudes toward Gay Men and Lesbians," *Personality and Social Psychology Bulletin* 22, no. 44 (1996): 412–24; Gregory M. Herek and Eric K. Glunt, "Interpersonal Contact and Heterosexuals' Attitudes toward Gay Men: Results from a National Survey," *Journal of Sex Research* 30 (1993): 239–44.
3. Quoted in Susan K. Freeman and Leila J. Rupp, "The Ins and Outs of U.S. History," in *Understanding and Teaching*, 5. Some of this chapter is drawn from our introduction to this volume. For more information, see the FAIR education website, http://www.faireducationact.com.
4. Shannon Weber, "Teaching Same-Sex Marriage as U.S. History," in *Understanding and Teaching*, 306.
5. Steven Lee Myers, "Ideas and Trends; How a 'Rainbow Curriculum' Turned into Fighting Words," *New York Times*, 13 December 1992.
6. Joseph G. Kosciw et al., *The 2013 National School Climate Survey: The Experiences of Lesbian, Gay, Bisexual and Transgender Youth in Our Nation's Schools* (New York: GLSEN, 2014), https://www.glsen.org/sites/default/files/2013%20National%20School%20Climate%20Survey%20Full%20Report_0.pdf.
7. Freeman and Rupp, *Understanding and Teaching*, 6.
8. The concepts of essentialism and social constructionism, along with the poststructuralist concept of sexuality and gender as performative categories characterized by fluidity, are complex and beyond the scope of this chapter. What is important is for students to grasp the notion that sexuality has a history.
9. For a sensitive and nuanced consideration of Roosevelt and Hoover in the context of LGBTQ history, see Claire Potter, "Public Figures, Private Lives: Eleanor Roosevelt, J. Edgar Hoover, and a Queer Political History," in *Understanding and Teaching*, 199–212.

10. Gloria T. Hull, Patricia Bell Scott, and Barbara Smith, *All the Women Are White, All the Blacks Are Men, But Some of Us Are Brave: Black Women's Studies* (Old Westbury, NY: The Feminist Press, 1982).

11. See Don Romesburg, Leila J. Rupp, and David M. Donahue, *Making the Framework FAIR: California History-Social Science Framework Proposed LGBT Revisions Related to the FAIR Education Act* (San Francisco: Committee on Lesbian, Gay, Bisexual, and Transgender History, 2014).

12. Fort Caroline National Memorial is located at 12713 Fort Caroline Road, Jacksonville, Florida. It was designated a National Memorial on 16 January 1953 and listed on the NRHP on 15 October 1966.

13. Kealakekua Bay is located along Napo'opo'o Road, Hawaii. It was listed on the NRHP on 12 December 1973.

14. Fort Wingate Historic District was listed on the NRHP on 26 May 1978.

15. The Little Bighorn Battlefield National Monument is located at 7756 Battlefield Tour Road, Crow Agency, Montana. It was first preserved as a U.S. National Cemetery in 1879 and designated a National Monument on 22 March 1946. It was listed on the NRHP on 15 October 1966. For more information on two-spirit people, see Will Roscoe, "Sexual and Gender Diversity in Native America and the Pacific Islands," in *Identities and Place: Changing Labels and Intersectional Communities of LGBTQ and Two-Spirit People in the United States*, ed. Katherine Crawford-Lackey and Megan E. Springate (New York: Berghahn Books, 2019).

16. Quoted in Genny Beemyn, "Transforming the Curriculum: The Inclusion of the Experiences of Trans People," in *Understanding and Teaching*, 115.

17. Carroll Smith-Rosenberg, "The Female World of Love and Ritual: Relations between Women in Nineteenth-Century America," *Signs: Journal of Women in Culture and Society* 1, no. 1 (1975): 1–29.

18. Hull House is located at 800 South Halsted, Chicago, Illinois. It was listed on the NRHP on 15 October 1966 and designated an NHL on 23 June 1965.

19. Clear Comfort is located at 2 Hylan Boulevard, Staten Island, New York. It was listed on the NRHP on 28 July 1970 and designated an NHL on 19 April 1993. An amendment that includes a discussion of the LGBTQ history of Clear Comfort was added to the NRHP nomination on 23 March 2017.

20. Eleanor Roosevelt's home at Val-Kill in New York State is an NPS property, part of the Eleanor Roosevelt National Historic Site, established in 1977.

21. See Leila J. Rupp, *Sapphistries: A Global History of Love between Women* (New York: New York University Press, 2009).

22. Whitman's Camden home was listed on the NRHP on 15 October 1966 and designated an NHL on 29 December 1962.

23. The site is the Old Patent Office Building, Ninth and F Streets NW, Washington, DC. The building is now the location of the National Portrait Gallery. It was listed on the NRHP on 15 October 1966 and designated an NHL on 12 January 1965.

24. See David A. Doyle Jr., "Nineteenth-Century Male Love Stories and Sex Stories," in *Understanding and Teaching*, 132–42.

25. The use of plural pronouns for gender-nonconforming individuals is one alternative to the use of gendered pronouns. On Outhistory, see Catherine O. Jacquet, "Queer History Goes Digital: Using Outhistory.org in the Classroom," in *Understanding and Teaching*, 359–71.

26. Johns Hopkins Hospital Complex, 601 North Broadway, Baltimore, Maryland, was listed on the NRHP on 24 February 1975.

27. The baths were located in the basement of the Ariston Hotel, Broadway and 55th Street, New York City, New York.

28. Café Lafitte in Exile is located at 901 Bourbon Street, New Orleans, Louisiana; it is located in the Vieux Carré NHL District, designated on 21 December 1965. Finocchio's was located at 506 Broadway, San Francisco, California. The Jewel Box Lounge was located at 3219 Troost, Kansas City, Missouri; for the early days of the Jewel Box Revue, see Julio Capó Jr., "Locating Miami's Queer History," in *Communities and Place: A Thematic Approach to the Histories of LGBTQ Communities in the United States*, edited by Katherine Crawford-Lackey and Megan E. Springate (New York: Berghahn Books, forthcoming). The Shamrock was located at 326 Princeton Avenue, Bluefield, West Virginia.

29. Jewel's Catch One was located at 4067 West Pico Boulevard, Los Angeles, California. It was the last Black-owned gay club in Los Angeles when it closed in 2015.

30. Julius's Bar is located at 159 West Tenth Street, New York City, New York. It was added to the NRHP on 21 April 2016.

31. The Stonewall Inn is located at 51–53 Christopher Street, New York City, New York. Stonewall was listed on the NRHP on 28 June 1999, designated an NHL on 16 February 2000, and designated Stonewall National Monument (an NPS unit) on 24 June 2016.

32. The Black Cat Club is located at 710 Montgomery Street, San Francisco, California; it is a contributing property (though not for its LGBTQ history) to the Jackson Square Historic District, listed on the NRHP on 18 November 1971. California Hall is located at 625 Polk Street, San Francisco, California. Compton's Cafeteria was located at 101 Taylor Street, San Francisco, California; this building is a contributing property to the Uptown Tenderloin Historic District, listed on the NRHP on 5 February 2009.

33. Cooper's Donuts was located at 553 or 557 South Main Street, Los Angeles, California, between two gay bars. The Black Cat Tavern was located at 3909 West Sunset Boulevard, Los Angeles, California.

34. *Screaming Queens: The Riot at Compton's Cafeteria*, directed by Susan Stryker and Victor Silverman (San Francisco: Frameline, 2005).

35. The Willard Asylum for the Chronic Insane in Ovid, New York, was listed on the NRHP on 7 June 1975.

36. The YMCA was located at Tenth and Grove, Boise, Idaho.

37. The Henry Gerber House was designated an NHL on 19 June 2015.
38. The Daughters of Bilitis Headquarters were at 165 O'Farrell Street, San Francisco, California.
39. The Gay Activists Alliance Firehouse is located in the SoHo-Cast Iron Historic District (listed on the NRHP and designated an NHL District on 29 June 1978) at 99 Wooster Street, New York City, New York.
40. Castro Camera was located at 573–575 Castro Street, San Francisco, California.
41. The Gay Men's Health Crisis was founded at 318 West 22nd Street, New York City, New York.
42. The 31st Street Bookstore was located at 425 East Thirty-First Street, Baltimore, Maryland. Olivia Records operated out of 4400 Market Street, Oakland, California. The Furies Collective operated out of a row house in the Capitol Hill neighborhood of Washington, DC. The Furies Collective house was added to the NRHP on 2 May 2016.
43. The Lesbian Herstory Archives is currently located at 484 Fourteenth Street, Brooklyn, New York, within the Park Slope Historic District, listed on the NRHP on 21 November 1980.
44. The Bisexual Resource Center is located at 29 Stanhope Street, Boston, Massachusetts.
45. The body of transgender and gay rights pioneer Marsha P. Johnson was recovered from the waters off New York City's Pier 45 in the 1990s.
46. Gayle Rubin, "Thinking Sex: Notes for a Radical Theory of the Politics of Sexuality," in *Pleasure and Danger: Exploring Female Sexuality*, ed. Carole S. Vance (Boston: Routledge and Kegan Paul, 1984), 267–319. The Leather Archives and Museum is located at 6418 North Greenview Avenue, Chicago, Illinois.
47. See Daniel Hurewitz, "Putting Ideas into Practice: High School Teachers Talk about Incorporating the LGBT Past," in *Understanding and Teaching*, 47–76.

Bibliography

Beemyn, Genny. "Transforming the Curriculum: The Inclusion of the Experiences of Trans People." In *Understanding and Teaching U.S. Lesbian, Gay, Bisexual, and Transgender History*, edited by Leila J. Rupp and Susan K. Freeman, 2nd edition, 111–22. Madison: University of Wisconsin Press, 2017.

Bernstein, Mary Bernstein. "Paths to Homophobia." *Sexuality Research and Social Policy* 1, no. 2 (2004): 41–55.

Capó, Julio, Jr. "Locating Miami's Queer History." In *Communities and Place: A Thematic Approach to the Histories of LGBTQ Communities in the United States*, edited by Katherine Crawford-Lackey and Megan E. Springate. New York: Berghahn Books, forthcoming.

Doyle, David A., Jr. "Nineteenth-Century Male Love Stories and Sex Stories." In *Understanding and Teaching U.S. Lesbian, Gay, Bisexual, and Transgender History*, edited by Rupp and Freeman, 132–42. Madison: University of Wisconsin Press, 2017.

Flores, Andrew R. "National Trends in Public Opinion on LGBT Rights in the United States." Williams Institute. https://williamsinstitute.law.ucla.edu/wp-content/uploads/POP-natl-trends-nov-2014.pdf.

Freeman, Susan K., and Leila J. Rupp. "The Ins and Outs of U.S. History: Introducing Students to a Queer Past." In *Understanding and Teaching U.S. Lesbian, Gay, Bisexual, and Transgender History*, edited by Rupp and Freeman, 3–16. Madison: University of Wisconsin Press, 2017.

Herek, Gregory M., and John P. Capitanio. "'Some of My Best Friends': Intergroup Contact, Concealable Stigma, and Heterosexuals' Attitudes toward Gay Men and Lesbians." *Personality and Social Psychology Bulletin* 22, no. 44 (1996): 412–24

Herek, Gregory M., and Eric K. Glunt. "Interpersonal Contact and Heterosexuals' Attitudes toward Gay Men: Results from a National Survey." *Journal of Sex Research* 30 (1993): 239–44.

Hull, Gloria T., Patricia Bell Scott, and Barbara Smith. *All the Women Are White, All the Blacks Are Men, But Some of Us Are Brave: Black Women's Studies*. Old Westbury, NY: The Feminist Press, 1982.

Hurewitz, Daniel. "Putting Ideas into Practice: High School Teachers Talk about Incorporating the LGBT Past." In *Understanding and Teaching U.S. Lesbian, Gay, Bisexual, and Transgender History*, edited by Rupp and Freeman, 47–76. Madison: University of Wisconsin Press, 2017.

Jacquet, Catherine O. "Queer History Goes Digital: Using Outhistory.org in the Classroom." In *Understanding and Teaching U.S. Lesbian, Gay, Bisexual, and Transgender History*, edited by Rupp and Freeman, 359–71. Madison: University of Wisconsin Press, 2017.

Kosciw, Joseph G., Emily A. Greytak, Neal A. Palmer, and Madelyn J. Boesen. *The 2013 National School Climate Survey: The Experiences of Lesbian, Gay, Bisexual and Transgender Youth in Our Nation's Schools*. New York: GLSEN, 2014. https://www.glsen.org/sites/default/files/2013%20National%20School%20Climate%20Survey%20Full%20Report_0.pdf.

Potter, Claire Bond. "Public Figures, Private Lives: Eleanor Roosevelt, J. Edgar Hoover, and a Queer Political History." In *Understanding and Teaching U.S. Lesbian, Gay, Bisexual, and Transgender History*, edited by Rupp and Freeman, 199–212. Madison: University of Wisconsin Press, 2017.

Romesburg, Don, Leila J. Rupp, and David M. Donahue. *Making the Framework FAIR: California History-Social Science Framework Proposed LGBT Revisions Related to the FAIR Education Act*. San Francisco: Committee on Lesbian, Gay, Bisexual, and Transgender History, 2014.

Roscoe, Will. "Sexual and Gender Diversity in Native America and the Pacific Islands." In *Identities and Place: Changing Labels and Intersectional Com-*

munities of LGBTQ and Two-Spirit People in the United States, edited by Katherine Crawford-Lackey and Megan E. Springate. New York: Berghahn Books, forthcoming.

Rubin, Gayle. "Thinking Sex: Notes for a Radical Theory of the Politics of Sexuality." In *Pleasure and Danger: Exploring Female Sexuality*, edited by Carole S. Vance, 267–319. Boston: Routledge and Kegan Paul, 1984.

Rupp, Leila J. *Sapphistries: A Global History of Love between Women*. New York: New York University Press, 2009.

Smith-Rosenberg, Carroll. "The Female World of Love and Ritual: Relations between Women in Nineteenth-Century America." *Signs: Journal of Women in Culture and Society* 1, no. 1 (1975): 1–29.

Stryker, Susan, and Victor Silverman, dirs. *Screaming Queens: The Riot at Compton's Cafeteria*. San Francisco: Frameline, 2005.

Weber, Shannon. "Teaching Same-Sex Marriage as U.S. History." In *Understanding and Teaching U.S. Lesbian, Gay, Bisexual, and Transgender History*, edited by Rupp and Freeman, 297–312. Madison: University of Wisconsin Press, 2017.

CHAPTER 7

San Francisco
Placing LGBTQ Histories in the City by the Bay

Donna J. Graves and Shayne E. Watson

Introduction

San Francisco is internationally recognized as a magnet and place of pilgrimage for lesbian, gay, bisexual, transgender, and queer (LGBTQ) people and a critical proving ground for advancements in queer culture, politics, and civil rights. The city has also pioneered efforts to identify, document, and preserve LGBTQ historic sites, and San Francisco was the site of foundational efforts to bring LGBTQ concerns into the preservation agenda. Those efforts are the focus of this chapter, as we outline our experience preparing a citywide historic context statement for LGBTQ history in San Francisco, which was carried out from 2013 to 2016. We conclude with a summary of some of the key themes in San Francisco's LGBTQ history and examples of historic properties associated with those themes. It is our hope that this chapter may inspire other towns and cities throughout the country to develop LGBTQ heritage preservation programs, as well as serve as an example of how the documentation of sites associated with LGBTQ heritage can be organized from conceptualization to implementation.

San Francisco's first city-level LGBTQ landmark, Harvey Milk's residence and Castro Camera store, was designated in 2000.[1] The following year, the first national conference on LGBTQ historic preservation was organized in San Francisco by the grassroots LGBTQ preservation group Friends of 1800, the Gay, Lesbian, Bisexual, Transgender (GLBT) Historical Society, and the James C. Hormel Gay and Lesbian Center of the San Francisco Public Library.[2] In 2004, the Friends of 1800 sponsored the nation's first historic context statement for LGBTQ history, titled *Sexing the City: The Development of Sexual Identity–Based Subcultures in San*

Francisco, 1933–1979, authored by Damon Scott.[3] *Sexing the City* was groundbreaking as the first LGBTQ heritage documentation report in the country. It was, however, intended to be a framework for future research, not a broad and inclusive study.

In 2013, we secured funding to develop a more comprehensive historic context statement for San Francisco's LGBTQ history, spanning the Native American period through the AIDS epidemic in the 1990s. The *Citywide Historic Context Statement for Lesbian, Gay, Bisexual, Transgender and Queer History in San Francisco* (hereafter referred to as the *LGBTQ Historic Context Statement*) presents historical background on nine historic themes and pays particular attention to incorporating the place-based histories of underdocumented groups within the LGBTQ communities, including lesbians, bisexuals, transgender people, and LGBTQ people of color.[4] In 2015, San Francisco's Historic Preservation Commission formally adopted the context statement; the final version of the report, including revisions responding to public comments, was accepted by the San Francisco Planning Department in March 2016 and is available online.[5]

Crafting a Citywide LGBTQ Historic Context Statement

Context statements are place-based research documents that identify historic resources within a specific theme, geographic area, and/or time period, providing a foundation for future planning and development decisions that affect cultural heritage. Until recently, context statements and historic designations in San Francisco have generally focused on architectural characteristics such as building type or style, or a geographic target such as a neighborhood, rather than a thematic focus on aspects of social or cultural history. To date, three citywide historic context statements have focused on some of the social and cultural aspects of San Francisco's diverse past, including African American, LGBTQ, and Latina/o histories.

The preparation of the *LGBTQ Historic Context Statement* was supported by an extraordinarily talented and diverse advisory committee made up of academics, preservation professionals, independent scholars, and community activists.[6] These individuals reviewed document drafts and shared specific areas of expertise. They also offered advice on strategies to tap community-based knowledge in order to create a document that recognizes the diverse and intersectional experiences of LGBTQ people in San Francisco. Even with the richness of San Francisco's LGBTQ archives, the majority of primary sources reflect the experiences of white, gay, and middle-class men. Connecting with people who had important knowledge of underrepresented communities was an essential task and included numerous individual interviews.[7] This research into otherwise underrepresented members of San Francisco's LGBTQ communities must be ongoing.

Creating a framework for the plethora of potential themes in San Francisco's *LGBTQ Historic Context Statement* was the first task and prompted discussions with archivists and key advisors on organizing important topics, events, sites, and periods into a cohesive and comprehensive document. The overarching theme of the *LGBTQ Historic Context Statement* is the development of LGBTQ communities in San Francisco. The structure of the historical narrative is roughly chronological and is organized around the following nine subthemes:

- Early Influences on LGBTQ Identities and Communities (Nineteenth Century to 1950s)
- Development of LGBTQ Communities in San Francisco (Early Twentieth Century to 1960s)
- Policing and Harassment of LGBTQ Communities (1933 to 1960s)
- Homophile Movements (1950s to 1965)
- Evolution of LGBTQ Enclaves and Development of New Neighborhoods (1960s to 1980s)
- Gay Liberation, Pride, and Politics (1960s to 1990s)
- Building LGBTQ Communities (1960s to 1990s)
- LGBTQ Medicine (1940s to 1970s)
- San Francisco and the AIDS Epidemic (1981 to 1990s)

In addition to a growing library of secondary sources, historians of LGBTQ San Francisco have two invaluable local archives from which to draw: the GLBT Historical Society (established in 1985) and the James C. Hormel Gay & Lesbian Center at the San Francisco Public Library (established in 1996).[8] These archives provided crucial information for tracing the social and physical history of LGBTQ communities in San Francisco. Materials at these repositories include hundreds of oral history interviews, a database of over thirteen hundred sites associated with LGBTQ history, historic photographs and documents, collections related to individuals and organizations, and ephemera associated with sites throughout the San Francisco Bay Area.[9]

Establishing a public presence and lines of communication between the project team and LGBTQ communities was essential in launching the endeavor. We created a project email address, an informational page on the city's Planning Department website, and used a Facebook page, "Preserving LGBT Historic Sites in California," to create a space for people to offer their knowledge, share research findings, and ask questions of community members.[10] Social media and press helped us inform the community about the project and invite questions and information about LGBTQ sites. We also conducted in-person outreach at events, meetings, and conferences of neighborhood associations, LGBTQ groups, preservation organizations, and historical societies.[11]

San Francisco's *LGBTQ Historic Context Statement* was written and organized to be as reader-friendly as possible, guide nonpreservationists through the process of nominating properties for designation as local, state, and federal landmarks, and support future place-based educational and interpretive projects. The report begins with an illustrated narrative history and concludes with a "Step-by-Step Guide to Evaluating LGBTQ Properties in San Francisco," which presents directions for evaluating, documenting, and designating historic LGBTQ properties.

One of the challenges the San Francisco *LGBTQ Historic Context Statement* addresses is that local, state, and national registers of historic places have historically privileged well-maintained buildings or high-style architecture, commonly associated with middle- and upper-class individuals, usually white and male, who could afford to live, work, and socialize within them. Buildings with rich histories but poor integrity have often been overlooked or rejected for landmarking. The importance placed on integrity—requiring that the structure retain a substantial amount of original physical fabric related to its historical significance—can present major obstacles when trying to designate sites associated with marginalized communities such as LGBTQ. Many aspects of LGBTQ history unfolded in San Francisco's less privileged neighborhoods or in areas that were in flux or slated for redevelopment. In many cases, the physical spaces are no longer extant or have undergone major changes. Important events or organizational meetings were often held in restaurants, bars, or storefronts that continually changed over time due to shifting economic and cultural realities in a dynamic city. All of these factors have led to diminished integrity of physical spaces, which historically has left properties vulnerable to substantive change or demolition and therefore ineligible for formal recognition or for historic preservation tax credits.

We assert that loss of integrity should not affect determination of a property's historical significance if that significance is rooted in cultural or social, rather than architectural, histories. The San Francisco *LGBTQ*

Historic Context Statement presents a strong argument and suggestions for recognizing properties that have poor integrity but significant histories.[12] Properties no longer extant or that have undergone physical change can still retain powerful meaning for communities and remain important cultural sites.

In addition to suggesting designation of more individual landmarks and historic districts associated with LGBTQ histories, the *LGBTQ Historic Context Statement* acknowledges that preservation of buildings alone is not sufficient in conveying this important aspect of San Francisco's history. The report's recommendations discuss the importance of interpretation and education at LGBTQ historic sites, and of supporting critical aspects of San Francisco's existing LGBTQ communities, such as historic LGBTQ businesses that are still in operation, and ongoing community events, such as the annual San Francisco Pride Celebration & Parade, the Dyke and Trans Marches, and the Pink Triangle memorial on Twin Peaks. San Francisco is pioneering strategies to protect such manifestations of what is known as "intangible cultural heritage," including the 2015 creation of a "Legacy Business Program" intended to preserve longstanding neighborhood-defining commercial and nonprofit establishments, and a new "cultural heritage district" tool that is being applied to two neighborhoods with significant historical and contemporary meanings to LGBTQ people: a Transgender Cultural District around the site of the 1966 Compton's Cafeteria riot in the Tenderloin, and a Leather Cultural District in the South of Market neighborhood.[13]

By creating a broader and more inclusive picture of the development and establishment of the LGBTQ communities in San Francisco, the *LGBTQ Historic Context Statement* helps community members, city planners, and elected officials make better-informed decisions regarding the protection and stewardship of physical and intangible LGBTQ cultural resources. Furthermore, the *LGBTQ Historic Context Statement* was adopted in the midst of a period of rapid redevelopment in San Francisco and a seemingly constant stream of proposals to demolish socially and culturally significant places. The more than three hundred properties documented in the context statement now stand a chance of being protected under California Environmental Quality Act (CEQA) laws related to historic preservation, which mandate municipalities to consider the impacts of redevelopment on historic properties. Perhaps most importantly, state historic preservation laws afford tremendous power to public opinion during environmental review processes, providing LGBTQ communities an opportunity to use their collective voice to oppose projects that would destroy the historic fabric of San Francisco's LGBTQ enclaves.[14]

Sampling of Historic Themes in the San Francisco *LGBTQ Historic Context Statement* and Associated Properties

The sections that follow illustrate several of the key themes covered in San Francisco's *LGBTQ Historic Context Statement* and a sampling of the types of historic properties associated with them.

Early Influences on LGBTQ Identities and Communities (Nineteenth Century to the 1950s)

Recognizing early expressions of what we now term LGBTQ identities was an important part of the *LGBTQ Historic Context Statement*, even though documentary sources are scarce and our insights into previous lives is limited by our current understanding of sexual identity. The narrative history begins in the Native American period when two-spirit people lived among the San Francisco Bay Area indigenous groups, the Ohlone.[15] When Europeans arrived in California in the 1700s to establish presidios (military garrisons), Catholic missions, and pueblos (secular townships), their contact with two-spirit people was often cruel and punishing.[16] At Mission Santa Clara, a former Ohlone settlement, Spanish soldiers imprisoned two-spirit people, stripped them of their clothes, and humiliated them by forcing them to sweep the plaza (traditionally women's work).[17]

When gold was discovered in California's mountains in 1848, the state's nonindigenous population exploded and San Francisco grew from a tiny village into an "instant city."[18] Californios (the Spanish-speaking descendants of the Spanish and Mexican colonizers, now American citizens), Sonoran Mexicans, Chileans, Peruvians, French, Chinese, Americans, and others flooded into San Francisco before heading to the goldfields. The disparity of men to women (12.2 to 1 in 1850) was extraordinary and opened a space for men to form homosocial and (likely) homosexual relationships.[19] Early forms of non-Native LGBTQ expression in California were born in this period, including cross-dressing and cross-gender entertainment.[20] During the Gold Rush and subsequent decades when women continued to be scarce, men wore traditionally female clothing to play the role of women at all-male parties known as stag dances.[21] During the same period, men performed in cross-gender roles in San Francisco's minstrel and vaudeville theaters.[22] One of the city's famous early female impersonators was Ah Ming, who in the 1890s had a contract at a Chinatown theater and was making $6,000 a year (the equivalent of $159,000 in 2016). Ming's obituary notes, "As a female impersonator ... Ming led all of his countrymen" and was rumored to have performed for the "crowned head of China."[23] In the bawdy saloons and dance halls of entertainment districts such as the Barbary Coast on Pacific Avenue, female impersonators performed on stage but also engaged in the sex trade.[24] One of the most documented early cases of cross-gender performers engaging in homosexual sex occurred at the Dash, one of the largest dance halls built after the 1906 earthquake.[25] In 1908, the Dash became notorious when it was reported that male patrons could purchase sex from cross-gender performers for a dollar.[26] These early cases of cross-dressing and cross-gender entertainment formed what theater historian Laurence Senelick calls a "queer and transgender demi-monde," an early underground LGBTQ community that was able to thrive because of its connection to mainstream cross-gender entertainment.[27] In the Barbary Coast and later the Tenderloin, explains historian Nan Alamilla Boyd, "female impersonators transported the language and gestures of a nascent queer culture to the popular stage" and "enabled audiences to negotiate the boundaries of a changing sexual landscape."[28]

Other subthemes presented in the first chapter of the *LGBTQ Historic Context Statement* are Nineteenth and Early Twentieth Century Sex Laws and Policing, Progressive Era Women's Reform Movements, and Bohemianism. Some of the highlights from these early histories include a highly publicized police sting in 1918 known as the Baker Street Scandal, which uncovered an underground gay community in San Francisco involving dozens of servicemen and civilian men;[29] pioneering female architect Emily Williams and metal artist Lillian Palmer, who shared a life together in the home that Williams designed for them in 1913;[30] Charles Warren Stoddard, one of the first writers in the United States to speak relatively openly about his homosexuality, who in 1903 published an autobiographical novel with homosexual themes set in San Francisco;[31] and lesbian poet and San Francisco resident Elsa Gidlow, who in 1923 published *On a Grey Thread*, a book of lesbian-centric poems that literary historians recognize as the first book of openly lesbian poetry published in North America.[32]

Early Development of LGBTQ Communities in San Francisco (Early Twentieth Century to the 1960s)

The central place of bars and sex-commerce establishments to LGBTQ history in both public memory and scholarship is well established.[33] This important aspect of LGBTQ history was included in San Francisco's

LGBTQ Historic Context Statement, particularly for more recent decades when people could share their memories of places in which they gathered for social life, community organizing, and intimacy.

The repeal of Prohibition in 1933 was a watershed in LGBTQ history, and LGBTQ bars and nightclubs subsequently opened all over the country.[34] Queer spaces thrived in San Francisco in large part because of the highly lucrative tourism industry based on sexualized and racialized nightclub performances.[35] The post-Prohibition nightclub provided a space in which San Francisco's historic cross-gender entertainment model was revived, and the city's tourism industry, which thrived on exoticized entertainments, encouraged the renaissance.[36]

From 1933 through 1965, the North Beach neighborhood was one of San Francisco's most popular tourist destinations, with over twenty venues catering to LGBTQ communities opening during this period.[37] The sexually charged cross-gender performances at nightclubs such as Finocchio's, Mona's 440 Club, and the Black Cat Café drew huge crowds and allowed San Francisco's nascent LGBTQ communities to blend easily with tourists and develop seemingly under the radar.[38]

One of the earliest known LGBTQ spaces in San Francisco was Finocchio's nightclub in the North Beach neighborhood.[39] Finocchio's female impersonation shows began during Prohibition and later featured some of the country's most famous female impersonators, such as Walter Hart, billed as the "Male Sophie Tucker," and Lucian Phelps, the "Last of the Red Hot Papas."[40] Finocchio's was popular with both tourists and members of the city's LGBTQ communities. Since many of the Finocchio's performers were LGBTQ, gay men especially were drawn to the nightclub and viewed the drag queens as heroines because of their overt and unabashed queerness.[41]

San Francisco's first lesbian nightclub was Mona's 440 Club in North Beach.[42] Open from 1938 through 1952, Mona's was known for its cross-gender entertainment featuring tuxedoed male-impersonating performers. As the only lesbian-centric space in San Francisco through World War II, Mona's became famous throughout the country as a fun, safe, and welcoming space where women could find love and friendship.[43] One of the most well-known performers at Mona's was African American singer Gladys Bentley, billed as the "Brown Bomber of Sophisticated Songs."[44]

The Black Cat Café opened in 1933 in Jackson Square near the former Barbary Coast district.[45] Early patrons were a broad mix of bohemians, intellectuals, dockworkers, and North Beach residents. The bar always attracted a clientele described as a cross-section of class, race, and sexuality, but the Black Cat became a popular gay hotspot in the 1950s when it began hosting politically infused drag operas starring gay rights pioneer José Julio Sarria.[46] The Black Cat was at the center of an important court case in 1951 when owner Sol Stoumen, after having his liquor license repeatedly revoked for catering to homosexuals, appealed to the Supreme Court of California and won. The decision in Stoumen v. Reilly essentially legalized gay and lesbian bars in California—the first state in the country to do so, and at the peak of McCarthyism and anti-homosexual policy making.[47] In 1961, the Black Cat served as headquarters for José Sarria's campaign for city supervisor, the first time an openly gay candidate anywhere in the world ran for public office.[48]

Highlights of other important LGBTQ bars, nightclubs, and restaurants documented in San Francisco's *LGBTQ Historic Context Statement* include the Old Crow in the Tenderloin, one of the first gay-friendly bars to open after Prohibition and one of the longest-running LGBTQ bars in the city (open ca. 1935–1980).[49] The Paper Doll in North Beach (open 1947–1961) was one of the first restaurants catering to the queer community in San Francisco and provided a public alternative to nightclubs and bars.[50] Popular with both gay men and lesbians (and presumably bisexual and transgender people), the Paper Doll was one of the earliest spaces in San Francisco that functioned as an informal community center where "gay, lesbian, and transgendered people could make friends, find lovers, get information, or plan activities."[51] The Beige Room in North Beach (open 1951–1958) was a lower-budget but decidedly queerer version of Finocchio's, famous for its female-impersonation shows by performers such as Lynne Carter, a white man known for impersonating African American singers Pearl Bailey and Josephine Baker.[52] Unlike Finocchio's, which followed a stringent hiring process, the Beige Room was more of an "underworld operation . . . with a lot more freedom in [whom] they hired."[53] Many of the performers were openly queer, giving the Beige Room an "insider's appeal," according to Nan Alamilla Boyd.[54] "Female impersonators at the Beige Room both legitimized queer culture and set the standard for flamboyant drag performance . . . the Beige Room was the place where San Francisco's drag culture flourished."[55]

Bathhouses, streets, parks, restrooms, beaches, and other public spaces where cruising and hustling took place allowed vast, but discreet, sex-based communities to develop in San Francisco.[56] "Because *all* sex acts between men were . . . illegal," writes historian Allan Bérubé, "gay men were forced to become sexual outlaws . . . experts at stealing moments of privacy and at finding the cracks in society where they could meet and not get caught."[57]

One of San Francisco's longest-running gay bathhouses was Jack's Turkish Baths, open from the mid-1930s through the 1980s in the Tenderloin.[58] Jack's was popular with gay servicemen during World War II and was known to be more upscale than other gay bathhouses.[59] Another important sex and community space in San Francisco was the Sutro Bath House, open from 1974 through the 1980s in the Mission-Valencia and South of Market neighborhoods.[60] Sutro was one of the only sex clubs that welcomed lesbians and bisexuals. Equally significant was Osento, opened in Mission-Valencia in 1980, the only bathhouse in San Francisco that catered exclusively to women.[61]

Beginning in 1984, as the number of San Franciscans with AIDS grew to unprecedented numbers, bathhouses began to close, primarily a result of business loss as patrons began to fear contracting AIDS.[62] The City of San Francisco ordered bathhouses to close later that year. Osento survived the bathhouse closures and operated until 2008, presumably because it prohibited sex of any kind: "Unlike the men's bathhouses, [Osento] really was a place for bathing .... [T]he rules were no sex (not even with yourself), and privacy was respected. But if you couldn't touch, you could look: it was a place to experience the myriad beauty of real women."[63]

Two of the earliest gay cruising and hustling areas in San Francisco were lower Market Street, as early as the 1920s, and the Tenderloin, a center for gay and transgender sex beginning in at least the 1930s.[64] The Tenderloin intersection of Mason, Turk, and Market Streets became known as the "Meat Market" for the amount of gay hustling that took place there. Other popular public sex spaces throughout the twentieth century were Union Square;[65] the northeast waterfront, especially at the Embarcadero YMCA;[66] the Presidio of San Francisco, with ties to a gay sex scene as early as the 1910s;[67] and all of the city's parks, especially Golden Gate Park, Buena Vista Park in the Haight-Ashbury neighborhood, and Dolores Park in the Mission District.[68]

Policing and Harassment of LGBTQ Communities (1933 to the 1960s)

The history of anti-homosexual and anti-transgender hostility, including manifestations in policing and harassment, is crucial to understanding LGBTQ history and essential to documenting the rise of places of queer resistance. While new queer spaces continued to appear in San Francisco in the 1940s and 1950s, and communities coalesced around them, governmental agencies became intent on reversing this progress. Policing of queer people intensified during this period for a confluence of reasons. World War II brought hundreds of thousands of young men and women to the Bay Area, prompting the military to set boundaries as a form of social control. McCarthyism and the federal anti-gay witch hunt known as the Lavender Scare cast a pall on all things related to "sexual deviancy." New state legislation in the 1950s and homophobic politicians radically changed the way queer people and places were policed in California. Consequently, increased negative media coverage of queer people led to growing public pressure to crack down on queer communities.

Throughout World War II, the armed forces went to great lengths to control the enormous population of military personnel in San Francisco.[69] Military and local police joined forces to monitor queer spaces and people in the city. Policing intensified after World War II when Governor Earl Warren oversaw sweeping changes to California's sodomy laws and punishments for sex crimes, essentially allowing for a conviction for homosexual acts to result in life in prison.[70] This led to an uptick of homosexual-related arrests in San Francisco in the mid-1950s.[71] Dozens of bars were permanently shuttered or had their liquor licenses repeatedly revoked. Countless LGBTQ people were harassed, arrested, imprisoned, institutionalized, and had their lives permanently altered or destroyed by harassment and oppression.

One of the most publicized police raids in San Francisco history occurred on 8 September 1954, when officers raided Tommy's Place / 12 Adler Place in North Beach—at that time the only queer space in the city owned and operated by lesbians.[72] The bars and restaurant were run by entrepreneur Eleanor "Tommy" Vasu, along with her girlfriend, Jeanne Sullivan, and bartenders Grace Miller and Joyce Van de Veer. Police arrested Miller and Van de Veer on suspicion of supplying narcotics to minors. The next morning, photographs of the two women leaving jail appeared in the newspaper under the headline "Arrested."[73] Their ages and home addresses were included in nearly every article reporting on the case. After a long and very public legal battle, the jury found Grace Miller guilty of selling alcohol to minors and sentenced her to serve six months in the county jail. Media attention and public pressure in the wake of the Tommy's / 12 Adler raid forced the two bars to close.[74]

The largest raid of an LGBTQ establishment in San Francisco occurred in August 1961 at a late-night coffee house called the Tay-Bush Inn.[75] Over one hundred people, mostly lesbians, were arrested for disorderly conduct and taken to jail.[76] The Tay-Bush Inn raid is significant not only for the number of patrons arrested, but also because the media coverage of the Tay-Bush raid, unlike previous raids, was somewhat

sympathetic toward the men and women arrested. The resulting spir-
ited public dialogue about the rights of gay men and lesbians to congre-
gate in bars marked a turning point in San Francisco citizens' perception
of gay and lesbian spaces.[77]

Homophile Movements (1950s to the 1960s)

San Francisco is a site of national and international significance for its
role in the rise of mid-twentieth-century homophile movements. The
homophile groups that organized in the United States in the 1950s were
the radical first phase of the gay and lesbian rights movement.[78] By publishing newsletters and organizing national conferences, homophile organizations educated LGBTQ communities and the public about what it
meant to be gay or lesbian in mid-twentieth-century America—and by
doing so made significant steps toward LGBTQ people achieving fundamental rights as citizens.[79] Some of the country's most influential and
enduring homophile organizations were founded in San Francisco in
the 1950s and 1960s.

The country's first nationwide homophile group, the Mattachine
Society, was founded in 1950 by Harry Hay and others in Los Angeles.[80]
The founding premise of the Mattachine Society was to instill a positive
"group consciousness" in homosexuals, urging members to take pride
in their minority status and "forge a unified movement of homosexuals ready to fight against their oppression."[81] The organization educated
members through meetings, conferences, and a newsletter, the *Mattachine Review*. Within a few years, the organization had expanded to
include chapters throughout California, almost exclusively consisting of
white, middle-class gay men. While women were welcome in name,
their participation was limited, with the group focusing predominantly
on men's issues. The first Mattachine Convention was held at San Francisco's Japanese YWCA in 1954; following forced removal and incarceration of Japantown residents, the American Friends Service Committee
leased the building and made it available for a variety of organizations
and campaigns for social justice.[82] After a series of schisms and shifts,
the Mattachine Society reorganized and by 1957 had established its national headquarters in San Francisco's Williams Building in the South of
Market area.[83]

The Daughters of Bilitis (DOB), the nation's first lesbian rights organization, was founded in San Francisco in 1955. Similar to the Mattachine
Society, DOB membership was comprised predominantly of white and
middle-class women. The first meetings were attended by a group of

lesbian couples at the home of Filipina Rose Bamberger and Rosemary Sliepan in the Bayview neighborhood. Two of the cofounders were gay rights pioneers Del Martin and Phyllis Lyon. The DOB was initially a lesbian social organization, but the group's focus soon shifted to LGBTQ advocacy and education with a focus on women's issues. The DOB's first national headquarters was established in 1956 in a space shared with the Mattachine Society in the Williams Building.[84] That same year, the organization began publishing the first national lesbian newsletter, the *Ladder*. The DOB hosted the first of many biennial conventions in San Francisco in 1960 at the Hotel Whitcomb.[85] It was the largest public gathering of lesbians in the country up to that point. The DOB expanded to include local chapters in cities throughout the country. By the mid-1970s, there were twenty chapters throughout the United States. The San Francisco chapter of the DOB closed in 1978.

The Society for Individual Rights (SIR), which eventually became the largest homophile organization in the country, was formed in San Francisco in September 1964.[86] SIR was started during the period when gay and lesbian activism was becoming more militant and more inclusive of all members of queer communities.[87] In April 1966, SIR opened the first LGBTQ community center in the country in the South of Market area, offering job referrals, legal aid, financial advice, and health and wellness services.[88] The organization ceased operations in the late 1970s.

The Council on Religion and the Homosexual (CRH), the first homophile organization in the United States with religious affiliation, was founded in San Francisco in 1964. In 1962, Glide Memorial Methodist Church in the Tenderloin hired clergymen to staff and operate the Glide Urban Center, a pioneering community organizing center that operated out of the church (figure 7.1).[89] Glide hired Reverend Ted McIlvenna to oversee a young-adult program focused on the Tenderloin neighborhood's growing population of homeless youth.[90] Soon after arriving at Glide, McIlvenna discovered that many of the program's youth were young gay men "driven to street hustling by the hostility and ostracism of their parents and peers."[91] Because McIlvenna was heterosexual and unfamiliar with LGBTQ issues, he turned to local homophile organizations for help. In late May 1964, McIlvenna, with sponsorship from the Glide Urban Center, organized a three-day conference attended by twenty Protestant clergymen and over a dozen members of the homophile movement, including representatives from the DOB, Mattachine Society, SIR, and the Tavern Guild.[92] For many of the ministers in attendance, the "face-to-face confrontation" with the homophile activists was "the first time they had ever knowingly talked with a homosexual

Figure 7.1. Glide Memorial Church, 2017. Photo by Shayne E. Watson.

or a lesbian."[93] Del Martin wrote of the retreat, "San Francisco was the setting for the historic birth of the United Nations in 1945. And again, in 1964, San Francisco provided the setting for the re-birth of Christian fellowship . . . to include all human beings regardless of sexual proclivity."[94] The CRH was founded as an outgrowth of the conference. It was the first organization in the country to have "homosexual" in its name.

The CRH sponsored one of the most significant events in LGBTQ history in San Francisco: the Mardi Gras Ball on 1 January 1965 at California Hall.[95] Organized as a fundraiser for the newly founded CRH, over five hundred guests purchased tickets for the event. CRH leaders anticipated some form of police harassment and negotiated with city officials to obtain the proper permits. In spite of this, the police turned out in full force, illuminating Polk Street with klieg lights and photographing everyone who entered the event. After a scuffle with police, six attendees were arrested, including two attorneys retained to prevent harassment. The following morning at a press conference, CRH clergymen called to end police harassment of gay and lesbian communities in San Francisco, marking one of the first times in U.S. history that religious leaders spoke publicly for LGBTQ rights.[96] The ministers' outrage provoked unprecedented public support, and homophile groups mobilized to combat police oppression.

While the New Year's Mardi Gras Ball incident later came to be known as San Francisco's "Stonewall," a much closer parallel event to the 1969 New York rebellion occurred in 1966, in what became known as the Compton's Cafeteria Riot. For several days in August 1966, transgender women, drag queens, and young male hustlers demonstrated militant resistance in the face of police harassment at a favorite late-night Tenderloin establishment, Gene Compton's Cafeteria.[97] Part of a local chain, Compton's Cafeteria at the corner of Turk and Taylor Streets was considered a relatively safe space for transgender women, who often scraped together a living by working as street prostitutes. Cheap residential hotels in the Tenderloin were among the very few places that would rent rooms to them. Protests in San Francisco—such as the Compton's Riot, as well as others by CRH and Vanguard, the first queer youth group founded in 1966—illustrated a new era of gay radicalism that preceded the now far-better-known events at New York's Stonewall Inn of June 1969.

LGBTQ Medicine (1940 to the 1990s)

San Francisco became an important center for the study of gender and sexuality in the 1940s and 1950s through the work of the Langley Porter Clinic at the University of California San Francisco (UCSF).[98] Opened in March 1943, the clinic's founding director, Dr. Karl Bowman, had taught and practiced psychiatry in New York City. During World War II, Bowman conducted research on gay men held in the psychiatric ward of the U.S. Naval Hospital on Treasure Island in the San Francisco Bay after their sexuality had been discovered while in uniform.[99]

One of Bowman's key collaborators was Louise Lawrence, who had been living full-time as a transgender woman since 1942. Lawrence lectured on transgender topics at UCSF and created an expansive international network of transgender people, some of whom stayed with her at her home in the Haight-Ashbury neighborhood, a residence Susan Stryker describes as a "waystation for transgender people from across the country who sought access to medical procedures in California."[100] Lawrence's carefully compiled data supported medical research and treatment by the most prominent doctors dealing with transgender issues, including Alfred Kinsey, Karl Bowman, and Harry Benjamin.[101] Benjamin was a German-born endocrinologist who popularized the term transsexual and publicly defended homosexual rights and the rights of such individuals to medical support rather than psychiatric "cures."[102]

New York–based Benjamin kept a medical office in San Francisco during the summer from the 1930s to the 1970s.[103]

Later, San Francisco's international reputation as a place that challenged gender norms made it the birthplace of the first intersex rights organization. Cheryl Chase, who had been designated male at birth, was later raised as a girl after doctors changed their decision and performed surgery on her at the age of eight.[104] Her discovery as an adult of these childhood manipulations of her gender identity led Chase to move to San Francisco and form the Intersex Society of North America in 1993.[105] In its early years, the Society operated out of Chase's home in the Twin Peaks neighborhood, and early meetings were held at the Institute for Advanced Study of Human Sexuality, where Chase was a student.[106] Within a few years, the organization was providing peer support to approximately four hundred people around the world, educating medical providers about treating people with ambiguous genitalia, and providing education about intersexuality to the general public.[107]

Gay Liberation, Pride, and Politics (1960s to the 1990s)

New York's Stonewall Inn is often cited as the "birthplace" of the gay rights movement in the United States, yet San Francisco and other cities such as Los Angeles, Philadelphia, and Boston played major roles in advancing civil rights for LGBTQ people. Scholars Elizabeth Armstrong and Suzanna Crage argue that the focus on the Stonewall rebellion in 1969 as the starting point of LGBTQ liberation has obscured earlier key moments in LGBTQ history, including the Mardi Gras Ball.[108] The San Francisco *LGBTQ Historic Context Statement* used archival materials and interviews of participants active in San Francisco from the 1960s through the 1980s to identify sites associated with the myriad organizations and events that shaped queer politics, culture, and identity in those pivotal decades.

The radical youth movement of the late 1960s and early 1970s shaped gay liberation organizations that emerged after the homophile period. Bay Area activist Carl Wittman's "A Gay Manifesto" (1970) was an influential and widely distributed essay that linked the fate of gays and lesbians to other oppressed groups and viewed sexual liberation "as merely one aspect of a broader social transformation."[109] Wittman described San Francisco as "a refugee camp for homosexuals," and wrote, "We have fled here from every part of the nation, and like refugees elsewhere, we came not because it is so great here, but because it was so bad where they are."[110] Historian John D'Emilio writes that within a few years of the Manifesto's publication, "San Francisco had become, in comparison with the rest of the country, a liberated zone for lesbians and gay men. It had the largest number and widest variety of organizations and institutions."[111]

Younger people shifted the terms and tactics of the movement for gay rights; as Charles Thorpe, the keynote speaker at the 1970 National Gay Liberation Front Student Conference held at the SIR Community Center, noted, "It is the young that are aware and aware is synonymous with desperate. That means a new culture, a new society, and a new education. This has scared the don't-rock-the-boat older gays."[112] San Francisco's Bay Area Gay Liberation (BAGL, 1975–1978) was among the groups who advocated a radical agenda for LGBTQ rights.[113] Organizational meetings and special events were held at the SIR Community Center and at the gay community centers that followed in San Francisco's Civic Center neighborhood.[114] BAGL activities included protests supporting the Gay Teachers Coalition; against police repression on Polk Street, an area that housed a concentration of gay-owned and oriented businesses; and against the Club Bath's practice of turning away customers who were effeminate, elderly, or African American.[115]

By the mid-1970s, the sheer numbers of LGBTQ people in San Francisco allowed for the emergence of groups organized along various axes of race, ethnicity, and sexual/gender identity. In 1967, transgender women activists formed Conversion Our Goal (COG), which has been described as "probably the first formal organization of self-defined transsexuals in the world."[116] COG met twice monthly at Glide Memorial Church to offer mutual support to its members and call publicly for freedom from police harassment, legal rights to medical care for transition, job opportunities, and fair housing.[117] Bisexual rights pioneer Marguerite "Maggi" Rubenstein helped to found the Bisexual Center, the nation's first specifically bisexual organization in 1976. The center offered counseling and support services to Bay Area bisexuals and published a newsletter, the *Bi Monthly*, from 1976 to 1984.[118]

Recognizing that their concerns were often not reflected in groups dominated by white gay men, LGBTQ people of color formed new organizations beginning in the mid-1970s. The Gay Latino Alliance was founded in 1975 with approximately fifty men and women attending its second meeting at the SIR Center. The same year, Randy Burns and Barbara Cameron founded Gay American Indians, the first reported organization for queer Native Americans. The Black Gay Caucus organized in 1976 and met every two weeks at the Gay Community Center on Page Street. Gay Asian Support Group, formed in 1977, which appears to be the first formal Asian Pacific Islander American organization for LGBTQ people, also held bimonthly meetings at the Page Street community center "to rap, socialize, do outreach work, get into politics, develop ourselves more, make new friends and/or develop relationships."[119]

Many lesbians also began to see the gay liberation movement as reproducing oppressive patterns that privileged men's voices and issues. Del Martin voiced the objections of lesbians who had felt sidelined or condescended to by gay activists in an influential manifesto titled "If That's All There Is," which appeared in the October 1970 issue of *Vector*. "I've been forced to the realization that I have no brothers in the homophile movement," Martin wrote; "Fifteen years of masochism is enough."[120] Lesbians of color stood in complex relation to both the women's movement and gay and lesbian rights organizations. Bay Area lesbian writers Cherrie Moraga and Gloria Anzaldúa helped shape discussion of these issues with their influential 1981 anthology *This Bridge Called My Back: Writings by Radical Women of Color*. The Latina, African American, Asian American, and Native American writers represented in the book—many of them from San Francisco—challenged claims of sisterhood made by white feminists and explored the links between race, class, feminism, and sexuality.[121]

Although not an exclusively lesbian organization, the Women's Building in the Mission District is one of the anchors of the history of women, feminists, lesbians, and queer and progressive groups more generally in San Francisco (figure 7.2).[122] In 1978, a core group of women from the San Francisco Women's Centers, an incubator for women's rights organizations, began looking into purchasing a building. A sympathetic realtor pointed them toward the Sons of Norway's Dovre Hall, built in 1910, which was no longer active except for a ground-floor bar. Negotiations moved forward, and the Women's Building opened in the fall of 1979.[123] Within its first year, the building held a memorial service for assassinated leader Harvey Milk, meetings of Lesbians Against Police Violence, a slide lecture by Allan Bérubé that benefited the San Francisco Lesbian and Gay History Project, and "Becoming Visible"—a conference of African American lesbians. Since then, a remarkable number and range of events and meetings important to LGBTQ history have been held at the Women's Building, which continues to function as a community space.[124]

San Francisco and the AIDS Epidemic (1981 to the 1990s)

San Francisco, New York, and Los Angeles were the first American cities to face the AIDS crisis; a pathologist at UCSF identified the first diagnosis

Figure 7.2. The Women's Building, north facade, 2016. Photo by Donna J. Graves.

of Kaposi's sarcoma in April 1981.[125] Two months later, the Centers for Disease Control (CDC) released a report describing an alarming new disease in a handful of gay and bisexual men. Within a few weeks of the CDC's announcement, clinicians, public health officials, and other medical professionals in San Francisco realized the potential tsunami. The San Francisco Department of Public Health quickly established a system for reporting and registering cases; the reporting network grew over the years to include major hospitals and private clinics.[126]

In December 1981, the San Francisco *Sentinel* published an article in which Bobby Campbell became the first Kaposi's sarcoma patient to publicly announce his illness. Declaring himself the "KS Poster Boy," Campbell convinced Star Pharmacy, a drugstore in the heart of the Castro neighborhood, to allow him to put up posters in their storefront windows warning about the "gay cancer."[127] Campbell's physician, Dr. Marcus Conant, shared his alarm and in 1982 approached activist Cleve Jones about creating an organization to mobilize the gay community and pressure the government for additional funds. The resulting Kaposi's Sarcoma Research and Education Foundation (later renamed the San Francisco AIDS Foundation) initially operated from folding tables covered with flyers and leaflets at the corner of Eighteenth and Castro Streets. Within a few months, it opened the first agency specifically addressing the new disease.[128] In October 1983, the KS/AIDS Foundation offices received national attention when a Florida hospital flew a critically ill AIDS patient to San Francisco and had him dumped at the organization's front door.[129]

By 1984, San Francisco's rate of HIV infection was the highest per capita in the nation. Community members, doctors, public health workers, and others debated their concerns over public health and civil liberties for over a year; in the meantime, nearly a third of the city's twenty bathhouses had closed, primarily because business was down as a result of patrons' fear of contracting AIDS.[130] The City of San Francisco ordered bathhouses to close in October 1984. One bathhouse, the 21st Street Baths, refused to comply but ultimately gave in and closed in 1987 when threatened with a lawsuit by the city. It was the last licensed gay bathhouse in the city.[131]

The first dedicated inpatient AIDS ward in the world, at San Francisco General Hospital's Ward 5B, opened in July 1983 with an innovative program of integrated treatment, care, and support services for patients, partners, friends, and family members.[132] In addition to pioneering patient care, San Francisco was the location for a number of important studies of AIDS prevention and treatment. San Franciscans also established the field of organized end-of-life AIDS care. In 1987, the defunct convent of Most Holy Redeemer Church in the Castro became Coming Home Hospice, reportedly the first AIDS hospice in the nation.[133]

Because public funds to combat AIDS were so scarce, the widely heralded "San Francisco model" of AIDS care developed based on volunteer labor and charitable giving.[134] A plethora of local community groups emerged, made up of individuals who cared for the sick, researched treatment options, raised funds, and pressured government agencies to do more. Because these organizations usually formed as small grass-roots efforts and evolved with the crisis, their space needs and locations shifted over time. Much of the focus of early AIDS organizations was on the Castro, a neighborhood that was predominately white and relatively wealthy. LGBTQ people of color argued that they needed to develop services within their communities that were not being met by the more mainstream organizations such as the San Francisco AIDS Foundation and Shanti Project. From the mid-1980s on, LGBTQ people of color formed numerous HIV/AIDS organizations to serve their communities and to advocate on their own behalf.

As the numbers of the dead grew with no cure on the horizon, many San Franciscans turned their anger and frustration into direct action protests and civil disobedience. In May 1983, thousands walked from the Castro to the Civic Center behind a banner "Fighting for Our Lives" in the AIDS Candlelight March—the first major demonstration against AIDS.[135] Under Mobilization Against AIDS, this event grew to become an annual, international vigil of protest and commemoration. [136] In what has been described as the first use of civil disobedience against the AIDS epidemic anywhere in the world, several protestors chained themselves to the doors of the federal building housing the regional office of Health and Human Services on 27 October 1985.[137] The ARC/AIDS Vigil became an encampment that occupied a lawn in United Nations Plaza twenty-four hours a day for ten years.[138]

San Francisco is the birthplace of two of the nation's most visible and enduring memorials to AIDS: the NAMES Project AIDS Memorial Quilt and the National AIDS Memorial Grove. Conceived by longtime San Francisco gay rights activist Cleve Jones in November 1985, the NAMES Project rallied volunteers to a storefront along Market Street.[139] First shown as forty panels at the 1987 Lesbian & Gay Freedom events in San Francisco, the project soon began accepting a growing flood of panels contributed from across the country. It became an international tool to illustrate the devastating impact of AIDS and to humanize its victims.[140] In 1988, another group of friends began discussing the creation of a public memorial garden in San Francisco to the victims of the AIDS epidemic. Beginning in 1991, monthly workdays brought together diverse Bay Area residents affected by the pandemic who reclaimed a former derelict site in Golden Gate Park. In 1994, the City of San Francisco signed a ninety-nine-year lease with the AIDS Memorial Grove, and two years later it was designated the only national AIDS memorial authorized by Congress and the president.[141]

Conclusion

The *Citywide Historic Context Statement for Lesbian, Gay, Bisexual, Transgender, and Queer History in San Francisco* is the most comprehensive research yet conducted on LGBTQ historic sites in an American city. Yet it is by no means complete. The project points to the need for intensive and detailed studies to fill in the gaps in queer histories, as well as the promise of creative approaches to documentation and interpretation. Our intention is that this information will not only provide a platform for better recognition of LGBTQ heritage in San Francisco, but also serve as a guide and inspiration for similar efforts and nominations across the country.

Ms. Donna J. Graves is a public historian and cultural planner in California.

Ms. Shayne E. Watson is an architectural historian in Mill Valley, California.

Notes

1. Harvey Milk's residence and Castro Camera were located at 573–575 Castro Street, San Francisco, California. Since 2000, two more San Francisco buildings have received local recognition for their LGBTQ significance: the Jose Theatre / Names Project Building at 2362 Market Street and the Twin Peaks Tavern at 401 Castro Street. In 1996, the National AIDS Memorial Grove in San Francisco's Golden Gate Park was designated a National Memorial.
2. The conference Looking Back and Forward: Significant Places of the GLBT Community was held 21–22 June 2001 at the Hotel Bijou (111 Mason Street, extant) and the San Francisco Public Library (100 Larkin Street, extant).
3. Damon Scott with Friends of 1800, *Sexing the City: The Social History of San Francisco's Sexual Subcultures, 1933–1980* (San Francisco: Friends of 1800, 2004). The study can be accessed online at http://www.friendsof1800.org/context_statement.pdf. The Friends of 1800 is a nonprofit organization dedicated to preserving the architectural heritage of San Francisco with a special interest in the identification and recognition of issues and sites important to LGBTQ history and culture. The Friends of 1800 was founded to prevent the demolition of the Fallon Building at 1800 Market Street, an 1894 Victorian that embodies many layers of San Francisco history. The group was successful in preventing the demolition, and the Fallon Building was incorporated into the construction of the LGBT Center (1800 Market Street).

4. Donna J. Graves and Shayne E. Watson, *Citywide Historic Context Statement for Lesbian, Gay, Bisexual, Transgender and Queer History in San Francisco* (San Francisco: San Francisco Planning Department, March 2016). The report can be accessed online at http://sf-planning.org/lgbt-historic-context-statement. The *LGBTQ Historic Context Statement* was funded by a grant from the City's Historic Preservation Fund Committee, with fiscal sponsorship from the GLBT Historical Society, which also provided enthusiastic support as a partner and resource. Since 2005, the San Francisco Historic Preservation Fund Committee has provided grants to preservation-related projects. These grants are drawn from a fund established as a result of civil action pursuant to an unlawful demolition of a landmark building. See http://oewd.org/index.aspx?page=176. Los Angeles' Office of Historic Resources commissioned a similar document, "Survey LA: LGBT Historic Context Statement," completed by GPA Consulting in September 2014 and accessible online at http://preservation.lacity.org/sites/default/files/LGBT%20Historic%20Context%209-14.pdf. Also recently completed by GPA Consulting is the "San Diego Citywide LGBTQ Historic Context Statement" (2016), available online at https://www.sandiego.gov/sites/default/files/san_diego_lgbtq_historic_context_final.pdf.

5. The GLBT History Museum (4127 Eighteenth Street) in the Castro neighborhood has been curating and exhibiting LGBTQ history in San Francisco since its opening in 2010. San Francisco has a long history of interpretive projects honoring significant LGBTQ individuals and events, including the placement of interpretive plaques at the Black Cat Café (710 Montgomery Street), Compton's Cafeteria (101 Taylor Street), the home of gay veteran and activist Leonard Matlovich (along Eighteenth Street in the Castro neighborhood); the renaming of streets and parks to honor gay-rights pioneer José Sarria (José Sarria Court), founder of the Gay Games Dr. Tom Waddell (Dr. Tom Waddell Place), transgender performer and activist Vicki Marlane (Vicki Mar Lane), lesbian businesswoman and activist Rikki Streicher (Rikki Streicher Field), and the Pink Triangle Park in the Castro neighborhood, a memorial to honor LGBTQ people who were persecuted, imprisoned, and/or killed during and after the Nazi regime; and the creation of the Rainbow Honor Walk in the Castro neighborhood, a series of sidewalk plaques honoring LGBTQ individuals.

6. See Graves and Watson, *Citywide Historic Context Statement*, for the list of advisory committee members.

7. Toward the end of the project, Graves and Watson established a partnership with the national oral history collecting project, StoryCorps, which has a recording station at the main branch of the San Francisco Public Library at 100 Larkin Street. A workshop called "Our Stories" gathered video interviews with elders and youth. One of the challenges presented was how to utilize and share these recorded interviews. Digital technologies have reduced barriers to gathering people's memories in audio and video format—but

without expertise and funding to edit the recollections and a platform to share them, the potential of these resources is yet to be tapped.

8. The GLBT Historical Society is located at 989 Market Street. The James C. Hormel Center is located at 100 Larkin Street. Other important LGBTQ archives in California include the ONE National Gay & Lesbian Archives at the University of Southern California and the June Mazer Lesbian Archives at UCLA and in West Hollywood.

9. Some of the materials in these archives were compiled and donated by scholars and historians such as Allan Bérubé, Nan Alamilla Boyd, Martin Meeker, Susan Stryker, and Don Romesburg, whose articles, books, and exhibitions were also critical resources for development of San Francisco's *LGBTQ Historic Context Statement*.

10. Preserving LGBT Historic Sites in California can be found at https://www.facebook.com/PreservingLGBTHistory.

11. The project team organized two community workshops to introduce the project and gather information. The first workshop drew approximately sixty community members who enthusiastically shared their memories in small working groups, facilitated by note-taking volunteers. A subsequent workshop, called "Our Stories," had two purposes: to capture information about sites important to elders in underdocumented communities, including people of color and people who identify as bisexual or transgender; and to foster intergenerational dialogue with youth from the Lavender Youth Recreation and Information Center (LYRIC) summer internship program.

12. Work by historian Raymond W. Rast and architectural historian Elaine Brown Stiles was especially helpful in framing arguments about integrity and significance. Raymond W. Rast, "A Matter of Alignment: Methods to Match the Goals of the Preservation Movement," *Forum Journal* 28, no. 3 (2014): 13–22; Elaine Brown Stiles, "Integrity Considerations in Evaluating LGBTQ Historic Sites," unpublished paper, Arcus Internship, College of Environmental Design, University of California, Berkeley, 2014.

13. See San Francisco Heritage website, "Sustaining San Francisco's Living History: Strategies for Conserving Cultural Heritage Assets," http://www.sfheritage.org/cultural-heritage, 2014; San Francisco Planning Department memo: "Draft Preservation Element: Cultural Heritage Discussion," 24 June 2015.

14. Within two years of its publication, the LGBTQ Historic Context had been used multiple times by the San Francisco Planning Department to assess potential negative effects of redevelopment projects on LGBTQ-associated properties. The results of these studies include identification of California Register of Historical Resources–eligible LGBTQ historic districts in the Tenderloin and South of Market neighborhoods. For examples, see Shayne E. Watson, "Historic Resources Evaluation, 280–282 7th Street, San Francisco," prepared for the San Francisco Planning Department, 20 July 2017; and Shayne E. Watson, "Historic Resources Evaluation, 229 Ellis Street, San

Francisco," prepared for the San Francisco Planning Department, 23 August 2017.

15. Malcolm Margolin, *The Ohlone Way: Indian Life in the San Francisco-Monterey Bay Area* (Berkeley, CA: Heyday Books, 1978), 84. For more about two-spirit peoples, see Will Roscoe, "Sexual and Gender Diversity in Native America and the Pacific Islands," in *Identities and Place: Changing Labels and Intersectional Communities of LGBTQ and Two-Spirit People in the United States*, ed. Katherine Crawford-Lackey and Megan E. Springate (New York: Berghahn Books, 2019).

16. San Francisco's mission (Mission San Francisco de Asís, also known as Mission Dolores) and presidio were constructed in 1776. Important remnants of the Spanish period in California are the extensive manuscripts left by the early explorers and later the Franciscan missionaries and military governors. Firsthand accounts by soldiers and missionaries make it clear that the Spanish wanted to eradicate two-spirits among the indigenous people. The Mission San Francisco de Asís, listed on the NRHP on 16 March 1972, is located at 320 Dolores Street. The Presidio, listed on the NRHP on 15 October 1966, designated an NHL on 13 June 1962, and incorporated into the NPS—part of the Golden Gate National Recreation Area—on 1 October 1994, is at the northern tip of the San Francisco peninsula.

17. Francisco Palóu, *Palóu's Life of Fray Junípero Serra*, trans. and ed. Maynard J. Geiger, O.F.M. (Washington, DC: American Academy of Franciscan History, 1945), 198–99.

18. Roger Lotchkin, *San Francisco, 1846–1856: From Hamlet to City* (New York: Oxford University Press, 1974), xxxvii.

19. Susan Lee Johnson, *Roaring Camp: The Social World of the California Gold Rush* (New York: W.W. Norton, 2000), 174.

20. Historians generally describe three primary motivations for cross-dressing during this period: cross-gender identification (before the concepts of transgender and transsexual existed); cross-dressing for comfort or for access to gender-restricted work; and cross-dressing as a form of entertainment. When discussing cross-gender identities in the nineteenth century, historians caution against applying labels such as gay, lesbian, bisexual, and transgender because it is difficult to know if the men and women identified in these ways, especially in a period before the terminology existed and before the social roles in question were clearly distinguished from one another. See Peter Boag, *Re-Dressing America's Frontier Past* (Berkeley: University of California Press, 2011).

21. A stag dance held on 4 July 1849 on the *Panama*, a ship bound for San Francisco, featured a "fancy dress ball" for which some of the young men dressed in calico gowns. See Boag, *Re-Dressing America's Frontier Past*, 64.

22. Male-to-female cross-dressers were more common than their female-to-male counterparts, but women performing as men also appeared in minstrel troupes. In August 1863, famous American stage performer Adah

Isaacs Menken played a Tartar prince in *Mazeppa* at Maguire's Opera House, Washington and Montgomery Streets (now demolished). The show drew a huge audience that waited outside for hours on opening day and filled the theater every night of the series. Newspapers described Menken's performances as venturing "out of the common run" and creating an "idealized duality of sex"; see Ben Tarnoff, *The Bohemians: Mark Twain and the San Francisco Writers Who Reinvented American Literature* (New York: Penguin Press, 2014), 57. In the 1860s, Salle Hinckley of the Buislay Troupe performed as "Don Guzman" at San Francisco's Metropolitan Theatre, Montgomery and Washington Streets (now demolished). Grace Leonard, billed as "Stageland's Most Artistic Male Impersonator" and "The Ideal American Boy," performed at the Empress, 965 Market Street (now demolished) in 1912. Information on Hinckley and Leonard from various advertisements and articles in the *San Francisco Call*.

23. *San Francisco Call*, 27 November 1892.

24. For more on LGBTQ history in the Barbary Coast district, see Nan Alamilla Boyd, *Wide Open Town: A History of Queer San Francisco to 1965* (Berkeley: University of California Press, 2003). The Barbary Coast was San Francisco's principal entertainment district from the Gold Rush through the 1910s, stretching west along Pacific Avenue from the waterfront to Montgomery Avenue (now Columbus) with branches down Kearny Street and Broadway. The streets were lined with saloons, concert and dance halls, gaming houses, and brothels. The Barbary Coast was home to a mix of ethnicities, with American, Irish, German, and African American saloonkeepers and patrons of many nationalities. The area also was a draw for soldiers stationed at the Presidio and merchant marines arriving at the port of San Francisco. As San Francisco neighborhoods continued to develop to the south and west through the end of the nineteenth century, the Barbary Coast and other northern environs were neglected and cut off from the major streetcar lines leading to the Market Street hub, adding to the district's reputation as a desolate wasteland.

25. The Dash was located at 574 Pacific Avenue, San Francisco, California. The building is extant and is a contributor to the Jackson Square Historic District, listed on the NRHP on 18 November 1971, and the San Francisco Article 10 Jackson Square Historic District.

26. The Dash was short-lived and closed soon after opening. The Dash is often called San Francisco's "first gay bar," but likely it was one of many early examples of a typical entertainment-district saloon featuring female impersonators engaging in homosocial or homosexual activity—either with the intention to deceive or to meet a demand for nonnormative sex. "Dive Men Officials for Cook," *San Francisco Call* 104, no. 142 (October 20, 1908); cited in Boyd, *Wide Open Town*, 25.

27. Laurence Senelick, "Boys and Girls Together: Subcultural Origins of Glamour Drag and Male Impersonation on the Nineteenth-Century Stage,"

in *Crossing the Stage: Controversies on Cross-Dressing*, ed. Lesley Ferris (London: Routledge, 1993), 85. Senelick is quoted in Boyd, *Wide Open Town*, 34.

28. Ibid.

29. The Baker Street Scandal was centered on a residence along Baker Street near the Presidio (the building is partially extant at the rear).

30. The residence in the Nob Hill neighborhood of San Francisco is extant. Williams and Palmer met in 1898 and lived together at various residences until Williams's death in 1942. They are buried together in Los Gatos Memorial Park Cemetery in San Jose, California. For more on Emily Williams, see Inge S. Horton, *Early Women Architects of the San Francisco Bay Area: The Lives and Careers of Fifty Professionals, 1890–1951* (Jefferson, NC: McFarland & Co., 2010).

31. Stoddard formed an intimate relationship with Japanese poet Yone Noguchi in the late 1890s. See Amy Sueyoshi, "Intimate Inequalities: Interracial Affection and Same-Sex Love in the 'Heterosexual' Life of Yone Noguchi, 1897–1909," *Journal of American Ethnic History* 29 (2010): 26. See also Amy Sueyoshi, "Remembering Asian Pacific American Activism in Queer History," in *Identities and Place*.

32. Elsa Gidlow lived at 150 Joice Street (now demolished) near Chinatown in San Francisco for thirteen years (ca. 1924–1937). After that, she moved to the Haight-Ashbury neighborhood, first to 1158 Page Street (now demolished) and later a few blocks away, also on Page Street (extant). Gidlow lived for thirteen years in a former summer cottage in Fairfax, Marin County, before moving to Druid Heights in Muir Woods. Druid Heights is now part of the Muir Woods National Monument, added to the NPS on 9 January 1908 and listed on the NRHP on 9 January 2008. Gidlow died at Druid Heights in 1986.

33. For a broader discussion, see Jen Jack Gieseking, "The Geographies of LGBTQ Lives: In and Beyond Cities, Neighborhoods, and Bars," in *Communities and Place*, ed. Katherine Crawford-Lackey and Megan E. Springate (New York: Berghahn Books, forthcoming); Tracy Baim, "Sex, Love, and Relationships," in *LGBTQ America: A Theme Study of Lesbian, Gay, Bisexual, Transgender, and Queer History*, ed. Megan E. Springate (Washington, DC: National Park Foundation and National Park Service, 2016), https://nps.gov/articles/lgbtqtheme-love.htm; Christina B. Hanhardt, "Making Community: The Places and Spaces of LGBTQ Collective Identity Formation," in *Communities and Place*; and David K. Johnson, "LGBTQ Business and Commerce," in *LGBTQ America: A Theme Study*.

34. Little documentation exists about queer spaces in San Francisco during and prior to Prohibition, but certainly there were spaces frequented by the nascent LGBTQ communities. Finocchio's, discussed later in this section, started out as a speakeasy, and after Prohibition became famous for its cross-gender performances.

35. For a detailed explanation of how and why queer spaces thrived in San Francisco as part of a tourist economy after Prohibition, see Nan Alamilla Boyd's *Wide Open Town*.

36. Boyd, *Wide Open Town*, 15.

37. Ibid., 245. A substantial number of LGBTQ spaces opened in the Tenderloin during the same period, including the Old Crow at 962 Market Street (extant), opened ca. 1935, and the Silver Rail at 974 Market Street (partially extant), opened ca. 1942.

38. Ibid.

39. Finocchio's was originally a restaurant owned by heterosexual couple Marjorie and Joseph Finocchio. It opened in the late 1920s or early 1930s at 441 Stockton Street (extant) near Union Square. Sometime in the mid-1930s, Finocchio's moved to the second floor of a two-story building at 406 Stockton Street near Sutter Street (now demolished). In the late 1930s, Finocchio's moved to 506 Broadway Street near Kearny (extant). Finocchio's closed at this location in 1999. For more on the history of Finocchio's, see Boyd, *Wide Open Town*, 52.

40. Clyde Evans, interview by Allan Bérubé and Eric Garber, 12 April 1983, GLBT Historical Society Oral History Collection, The Gay, Lesbian, Bisexual, Transgender Historical Society; Eric Garber, "Finocchio's: A Gay Community Landmark," *Newsletter of the San Francisco Bay Area Gay & Lesbian Historical Society* 3, no. 4 (1988): 1.

41. Esther Newton, *Mother Camp: Female Impersonators in America* (Englewood Cliffs, NJ: Prentice-Hall, 1972), cited in Garber, "Finocchio's: A Gay Community Landmark."

42. A heterosexual, self-described bohemian named Mona Sargent is credited for operating San Francisco's first lesbian bar, Mona's 440 Club, at 440 Broadway in the North Beach neighborhood. Sargent opened her first bar in 1933 in a small storefront at 451 Union Street (now demolished) on Telegraph Hill above North Beach. The bar was short-lived and closed after two years. In 1936, Sargent opened her second bar in the basement space at 140 Columbus Avenue (extant). Known as Mona's Barrel House, the space became a draw for lesbians when Sargent featured male-impersonating waitresses as entertainment. For more on the history of Mona Sargent's lesbian bars, see Boyd, *Wide Open Town*, 68.

43. Mona (Sargent) Hood, interview by Nan Alamilla Boyd, 25 July 1992, GLBT Historical Society Oral History Collection, Gay, Lesbian, Bisexual, Transgender Historical Society.

44. Boyd, *Wide Open Town*, 76. For more on Gladys Bentley, see Boyd.

45. The Black Cat Café building at 710 Montgomery Street remains extant. It is a contributor to the Jackson Square Historic District, listed on the NRHP on 18 November 1971. Austrian holocaust survivor and libertarian heterosexual Solomon "Sol" Stoumen purchased the Black Cat in 1945 and operated the bar until it closed in 1963. For more on the history of the Black Cat Café, see Boyd, *Wide Open Town*, 56.

46. Gerald Fabian, interviewed by Willie Walker, 30 November 1989 and 23 January 1990, Gay, Lesbian, Bisexual, Transgender Historical Society. José Sarria was born in San Francisco to a Colombian mother and a Nicaraguan father. Sarria also cofounded several homophile organizations, including the League for Civil Education, the Tavern Guild, and the Society for Individual Rights. In 1964, he founded the Imperial Court System, which became an international association of charitable organizations and the second largest LGBTQ organization in the world.

47. Christopher Lowen Agee, *The Streets of San Francisco: Policing and the Creation of a Cosmopolitan Liberal Politics, 1950–1972* (Chicago: University of Chicago Press, 2014), 85.

48. Had he won, Sarria also would have been the first Latino to win a supervisor's seat in San Francisco; see Boyd, *Wide Open Town*, 60.

49. The Old Crow at 962 Market Street (extant) and another gay bar, the Silver Rail at 974 Market Street (extant at front, demolished at rear), were located in the same building at the corner of Market, Turk, and Mason Streets, an area known as the Meat Market, a hot spot for gay hustling and prostitution. Turk Street from Jones to Mason was one of the main drags for cruising and hustling from the 1940s to the 1980s. The Old Crow and the Silver Rail were known gay hustler pick-up spots.

50. The Paper Doll was located at 524 Union Street (extant).

51. Boyd, *Wide Open Town*, 61.

52. The Beige Room was located at 831 Broadway (extant).

53. Gerald Fabian, interviewed by Willie Walker, 1989 and 1990.

54. Boyd, *Wide Open Town*, 130

55. Ibid., 130, 132.

56. The experiences of gay men and transgender women are the focus of this section; for a variety of reasons, those populations were more inclined to seek sex in public and to form communities around sexual activity.

57. Allan Bérubé, "The History of the Baths," *Coming Up!* (San Francisco), December 1984. Historian George Chauncey, in his groundbreaking *Gay New York: Gender, Urban Culture, and the Makings of the Gay Male World, 1890–1940* (New York: Basic Books, 1994), argues that cruising and hustling on city streets and sex in public spaces mirrored, or blended with, the sexualized street culture of urban working-class heterosexual neighborhoods in the first half of the twentieth century.

58. Jack's Baths opened at 1052 Geary Boulevard near Van Ness Avenue in the mid-1930s, according to San Francisco city directories; the building is extant. In 1941, Jack's Turkish Baths moved one block away to 1143 Post Street, where it remained until it closed in the 1980s (extant).

59. Bérubé, "The History of the Baths"; and Gerald Fabian, interviewed by Willie Walker, 1989 and 1990.

60. Sutro Bath House opened at 312 Valencia Street in 1974 and moved to 1015 Folsom Street ca. 1977. Both buildings are extant.

61. The building that housed Osento is extant in the Mission District, and is

now a private residence. Osento was reportedly very strict about not allow-ing sexual activity among its patrons.

62. John-Manuel Andriote, *Victory Deferred: How AIDS Changed Gay Life in America* (Chicago: University of Chicago Press, 1999), 78.

63. Stephanie J. Rosenbaum, "Osento, 1980–2008," *The Adventures of Pie Queen* (blog), 20 August 2008, http://piequeen.blogspot.com/2008/08/osento-1980-2008.html.

64. The portion of Lower Market that was popular for gay hustling and cruising stretched from the Embarcadero to Fifth and Mason Streets. One reason for the popularity of this strip was that it served as a connection between the waterfront and the Tenderloin, and it was an entertainment corridor dotted with movie theaters, restaurants, bars, and all-night cafeterias. See Susan Stryker and Jim Van Buskirk, *Gay by the Bay: A History of Queer Culture in the San Francisco Bay Area* (San Francisco: Chronicle Books, 1996), 24.

65. Union Square in downtown San Francisco is bordered by Geary, Powell, Post, and Stockton Streets.

66. The Embarcadero YMCA was built in 1926 at 169 Steuart Street between Mission and Howard and is still extant and in operation. By World War II, the Embarcadero YMCA had become a favorite spot for gay sexual activ-ity. Alfred Kinsey called it the "most notorious Y in the states"; Kinsey cited in Justin Spring, *Secret Historian: The Life and Times of Samuel Steward, Professor, Tattoo Artist, and Sexual Renegade* (New York: Farrar, Straus and Giroux, 2010), 180.

67. Stryker and Van Buskirk, *Gay by the Bay*. In the 1930s, gay rights pioneer Harry Hay was involved in a gay sex network associated with the Presidio. Hay describes a guardhouse off of one of the Geary-side gates (likely the Presidio Gate) that was headquarters for the network. See Harry Hay, "Gay Sex before Zippers," interview with Chris Carlsson (San Francisco: Shaping San Francisco, 1995), https://archive.org/details/ssfHAYBVDCT. Part of the Golden Gate National Recreation Area (as of 1 October 1994), the Presidio of San Francisco was listed on the NRHP on 15 October 1966 and desig-nated an NHL on 13 June 1962.

68. Golden Gate Park, located on the west side of the city, was listed on the NRHP on 15 October 2004.

69. Allan Bérubé, *Coming Out under Fire: The History of Gay Men and Women in World War Two* (New York: Free Press, 1990), 113.

70. William N. Eskridge Jr., *Dishonorable Passions: Sodomy Laws in America, 1861–2003* (New York: Viking, 2008), 88–91. Warren was governor of Cali-fornia from 1943 to 1953.

71. Boyd, *Wide Open Town*, 92.

72. Tommy's Place and 12 Adler Place were located in the same building with addresses at 529 Broadway Street and downstairs at the rear at 12 Adler Place (both extant). For detailed discussion of the raid on Tommy's Place / 12 Adler Place, see Boyd, *Wide Open Town*, 91.

73. "Arrested," *San Francisco Call-Bulletin*, September 1954, Grace Miller Papers, San Francisco Public Library. See also Boyd, *Wide Open Town*.

74. "2 Girls Tell Visits to Tommy's Place," *San Francisco Examiner*, 2 December 1954, Grace Miller Papers, San Francisco Public Library. See also Boyd, *Wide Open Town*.

75. The Tay-Bush Inn (now demolished) was located at 900 Bush Street at the corner of Bush and Taylor Streets between Union Square and Nob Hill.

76. Eskridge, *Dishonorable Passions*, 97.

77. Boyd, *Wide Open Town*, 213–15.

78. John D'Emilio, *Sexual Politics, Sexual Communities: The Making of a Homosexual Minority in the United States, 1940–1970* (Chicago: University of Chicago Press, 1983), 3. For a detailed history of homophile movements in San Francisco, see D'Emilio, *Sexual Politics, Sexual Communities*; and Martin Meeker, *Contacts Desired: Gay and Lesbian Communications and Community, 1940s–1970s* (Chicago: University of Chicago Press, 2006).

79. San Francisco's first homophile organizations were generally focused on lesbians and gay men. Bisexual and transgender organizing was largely separate and started in the 1960s.

80. The group was originally called the Mattachine Foundation and had their first meetings in the homes of Harry Hay and his mother in the Silver Lake and Hollywood Hills neighborhoods of Los Angeles. The first homophile group in the United States was the Society for Human Rights, founded by Henry Gerber and others in Chicago, Illinois, in 1924.

81. D'Emilio, *Sexual Politics, Sexual Communities*, 58, 65–66.

82. The first Mattachine Convention was held at 1830 Sutter Street, San Francisco, built originally as the Japanese YWCA in 1932; Donna Graves, draft nomination for 1830 Sutter Street to the National Register of Historic Places (2017).

83. The Williams Building, located at 693 Mission Street in the South of Market neighborhood is extant. The Mattachine Society stayed at the Williams Building through ca. 1967, when the organization moved to Adonis Books at 348 Jones Street; Meeker, *Contacts Desired*, 53. The Williams Building was also the location of offices of the Daughters of Bilitis and Pan Graphic Press, one of the first small gay presses in the United States, responsible for publishing issues of both the *Mattachine Review* and the *Ladder*.

84. Del Martin and Phyllis Lyon, *Lesbian/Woman* (San Francisco: Glide Publications, 1972), 11.

85. The Hotel Whitcomb is extant at 1231 Market Street. See "1st National Convention (1960)—San Francisco," Box 7, Phyllis Lyon and Del Martin Papers (1993-13), Gay, Lesbian, Bisexual, Transgender Historical Society.

86. SIR was founded in the basement of a residential building in the Haight-Ashbury neighborhood of San Francisco. "Society for Individual Rights," José Sarria papers, Gay, Lesbian, Bisexual, Transgender Historical Society.

87. D'Emilio, *Sexual Politics, Sexual Communities*, 190.

88. The building is extant at 83 Sixth Street and, although no longer a queer space, continues to operate as a community center.

89. Glide Memorial Methodist Church is extant at 330 Ellis Street.

90. D'Emilio, *Sexual Politics, Sexual Communities*, 192.

91. Ibid, 191–92.

92. The retreat was held at the extant Ralston L. White Memorial Retreat at 2 El Capitan in Mill Valley, California. The retreat center is a residence designed by Bay Area architect Willis Polk. See Agee, *The Streets of San Francisco*, 103; and Marcia Gallo, *Different Daughters: A History of the Daughters of Bilitis and the Rise of the Lesbian Rights Movement* (New York: Carroll & Graf Publishers, 2006), 105.

93. D'Emilio, *Sexual Politics, Sexual Communities*, 193.

94. Gallo, *Different Daughters*, 106.

95. California Hall is extant at 625 Polk Street and is a San Francisco Article 10 Landmark.

96. Gallo, *Different Daughters*, 108.

97. Gene Compton's Cafeteria was located at 101 Taylor Street (extant). A smaller, but similar "riot" occurred in 1959 at Cooper's Doughnuts in Los Angeles. See Lillian Faderman and Stuart Timmons, *Gay L.A.: A History of Sexual Outlaws, Power Politics, and Lipstick Lesbians* (New York: Basic Books, 2006), 1. Neither event received wide press coverage, which has contributed to the erasure of these events from popular understanding of LGBTQ history. See Susan Stryker, "Transgender History in the United States and the Places that Matter," in *Identities and Place*.

98. The UCSF Medical School and the California Department of Institutions, which oversaw the state's psychiatric hospitals, founded the clinic in 1941 as a joint venture creating California's first "psychiatric institute where several specialties in medicine, especially neurology and neurosurgery, would collaborate in a true multi-discipline approach to mental illness." Bowman's tenure ended in 1956. Mariana Robinson, *The Coming of Age of the Langley Porter Clinic: The Reorganization of a Mental Health Institute*, ICP case series (Indianapolis, IN: Bobbs-Merrill Co., 1962), 2–3, 8. The Clinic, later known as the Langley Porter Neuropsychiatric Institute, was located at 401 Parnassus Avenue (extant).

99. Susan Stryker, *Transgender History*, Seal Studies (Berkeley, CA: Seal Press, 2008), 41–42.

100. Ibid., 44.

101. Stryker, *Transgender History*, 44.

102. Joanne Meyerowitz, *How Sex Changed: A History of Transsexuality in the United States* (Cambridge, MA: Harvard University Press, 2002), 144. Susan Stryker, "Dr. Harry Benjamin," GLBTQ Encyclopedia.com, 2015, http://www.glbtqarchive.com/ssh/benjamin_h_S.pdf.

103. Benjamin organized Magnus Hirschfeld's tour of the United States in 1930; see Meyerowitz, *How Sex Changed*, 44. His office was located at 450 Sutter Street, extant. The building was added to the NRHP on 22 December 2009.

104. Vernon A. Rosario, "An Interview with Cheryl Chase." *Journal of Gay and Lesbian Psychotherapy* 10, no. 2 (2006): 93–104.

105. Natalie Angier, "Intersexual healing," *New York Times*, 4 February 1996, http://www.nytimes.com/1996/02/04/weekinreview/ideas-trends-inter sexual-healing-an-anomaly-finds-a-group.html.

106. Bo Laurent (formerly Cheryl Chase), electronic communication with Donna Graves, 23 July 2014. The Institute for Advanced Study of Human Sexuality, founded in 1976, is located at 1523 Franklin Street.

107. Cheryl Chase, "Surgical Progress is Not the Answer to Intersexuality," *Journal of Clinical Ethics* 9, no. 4 (1998): 385–92; Susan Stryker, *Transgender History*, 138. The Intersex Society of North America (ISNA) closed in 2006 and turned its mission over to Accord Alliance; see http://www.isna.org.

108. Elizabeth A. Armstrong and Suzanna M. Crage, "Movements and Memory: The Making of the Stonewall Myth," *American Sociological Review* 71, no. 4 (2006): 724–51.

109. Elizabeth A. Armstrong, *Forging Gay Identities: Organizing Sexuality in San Francisco, 1950 to 1994* (Chicago: University of Chicago Press, 2002), 2.

110. Carl Wittman, "A Gay Manifesto," in *Out of the Closets: Voices of Gay Liberation*, ed. Karla Jay and Allen Young (New York: Douglas Book Corp, 1972), 332–42.

111. John D'Emilio, "Gay Politics, Gay Community: San Francisco's Experience," in *Making Trouble: Essays on Gay History, Politics, and the University*, ed. John D'Emilio (Hoboken, NJ: Taylor and Francis, 2014), 87.

112. Charles P. Thorpe, "I.D., Leadership and Violence," in *Out of the Closets*, 352.

113. Christina B. Hanhardt described BAGL's platform as "based on a multi-issue critique of capitalism and the state"; see "Butterflies, Whistles and Fists: Gay Safe Streets Patrols and the New Gay Ghetto, 1976–1981," *Radical History Review* 100 (2008): 65.

114. San Francisco had a small succession of gay community centers in the 1970s and 1980s: 32 Page Street operated from ca. 1976–1978 (extant) and a larger center at 330 Grove Street operated ca. 1977–1981 (now demolished). In 1982, many of the organizations from 330 Grove moved to a former convent at 890 Hayes Street (extant); Groups Ephemera Collection GLBT Historical Society; Christina B. Hanhardt, *Safe Space: Gay Neighborhood History and the Politics of Violence* (Durham, NC: Duke University Press, 2013), 98.

115. The Club Baths was located at 201 Eighth Street (extant).

116. Meyerowitz, *How Sex Changed*, 230.

117. Ibid.

118. Clare Hemmings, *Bisexual Spaces: A Geography of Sexuality and Gender* (New York: Routledge, 2002), 156. The Bisexual Center operated first out of offices at 544 Market Street and later from the North Panhandle neighborhood home of cofounder David Lourea; initial Bisexual Center meetings were held at Rubenstein's home just south of Glen Park. For more on the

bisexual rights movement, see Loraine Hutchins, "Making Bisexuals Visible," in *Identities and Place*.

119. Gay Asian Support Group (GASP) Newsletter, 22 September 1977, in GLBT Historical Society Newsletters. See also Will Roscoe, "Sexual and Gender Diversity in Native American and the Pacific Islands," in *Identities and Place*; Amy Sueyoshi, "Remembering Asian Pacific American Activism in Queer History," in *Identities and Place*; and Deena J. González and Ellie D. Hernandez, "Latina/o Gender and Sexuality," in *Identities and Place*.

120. Josh Sides, *Erotic City: Sexual Revolutions and the Making of Modern San Francisco* (New York: Oxford University Press, 2009), 114. She expanded on this observation in *Lesbian/Woman*, coauthored in 1972 with her partner Phyllis Lyon, and originally produced by the publications arm of Glide Memorial Church.

121. Cherrie Moraga and Gloria Anzaldúa, eds, *This Bridge Called My Back: Writings by Radical Women of Color* (Watertown, MA: Persephone Press, 1981).

122. The Women's Building is located at 3543 Eighteenth Street, San Francisco, California.

123. Sushawn Robb, *Mothering the Movement: The Story of the San Francisco Women's Building* (Denver: Outskirts Press, 2012), 47–48.

124. Many organizations initially supported by the Women's Building went on to form their own nonprofits, such as Lesbian Visual Artists, the San Francisco Network for Battered Lesbian and Bisexual Women, Older Lesbian Organizing Committee, and the Lavender Youth Recreation and Information Center.

125. Randy Shilts, *And the Band Played On: People, Politics and the AIDS Epidemic* (New York: St. Martin's Griffin, 2007), 60.

126. Sides, *Erotic City*, 177. The Department of Health was headquartered at 101 Grove Street (extant).

127. Ibid., 10–108. Star Pharmacy was located at 498 Castro Street (extant).

128. Shilts, *And the Band Played On*, 161. For the initial address of 520 Castro Street, see San Francisco AIDS Foundation website, "The View from Here: Cleve Jones and Dr. Marcus Conant," 2011, http://www.sfaf.org/hiv-info/hot-topics/from-the-experts/the-view-from-here-cleve-jones-marcus-co nant-2011.html. The first offices of the San Francisco AIDS Foundation were at 520 Castro Street (extant).

129. Mark Thompson, ed., *Long Road to Freedom: The Advocate History of The Gay and Lesbian Movement* (New York: St. Martin's Press, 1994), 240.

130. John-Manuel Andriote, *Victory Deferred*, 78. By spring 1984, The Cauldron, Cornholes, Liberty Baths, Sutro Baths, and Bulldog Baths had all closed according to Rodger Streitmatter, *Unspeakable: The Rise of the Gay and Lesbian Press in America* (Boston: Faber and Faber, 1995), 257.

131. "14 San Francisco Sex Clubs Told to Close to Curb AIDS," *New York Times*, 10 October 1984, http://www.nytimes.com/1984/10/10/us/14-san-francisco-sex-clubs-told-to-close-to-curb-aids.html; and Johnny Miller, "Last Gay

Bathhouse in S.F. Shut Down over AIDS," *San Francisco Chronicle*, 13 May 1987, http://www.sfgate.com/entertainment/article/Last-gay-bathhouse-in-S-F-shut-down-over-AIDS-3549850.php. The 21st Street Baths were located at 3244 Twenty-First Street (now demolished).

132. Andriote, *Victory Deferred*, 116; and Carol Pogash, *As Real as It Gets: The Life of a Hospital at the Center of the AIDS Epidemic* (New York: Birch Lane Press, 1992), 21. San Francisco General Hospital is located at 1001 Potrero Avenue. Pogash describes AIDS treatment at S.F. General starting in the seven-story main building constructed in the 1970s and moving to an older brick structure late in 1982.

133. Donal Godfrey, *Gays and Grays: The Story of the Gay Community at Most Holy Redeemer Catholic Church* (Lanham, MD: Lexington Books, 2007), 89. The Hartford Street Zen Center purchased 61 Hartford Street in 1988. David Schneider, *Street Zen: The Life and Work of Issan Dorsey* (New York: Da Capo Press, 2000), 174–75. Coming Home Hospice was located at 115 Diamond Street (extant).

134. Stryker and Van Buskirk, *Gay by the Bay*, 93.

135. The Civic Center Historic District was added to the NRHP on 10 October 1978 and designated an NHL on 27 February 1987.

136. Mobilization Against AIDS brochure, 1986. Mobilization Against AIDS file, Groups Ephemera Collection, Gay, Lesbian, Bisexual, Transgender Historical Society. Other ephemera in this collection indicate that the first meeting of MOB was held at 647-A Castro Street, and by 1986 offices were located at 2120 Market Street, Suite 106.

137. Libby Ingalls, "AIDS/ARC Vigil 1985–1995," Found SF website, http://foundsf.org/index.php?title=AIDS/ARC_Vigil_1985-1995. Health and Human Services was located in the Federal Building, 50 United Nations Plaza (extant), a contributing element to the Civic Center Historic District (see note 135).

138. ARC = AIDS-Related Conditions.

139. The NAMES Project first met and had their first home at 2362 Market Street (extant, San Francisco Landmark No. 241).

140. The quilt had grown to nearly two thousand panels when it was displayed four months later on the National Mall in Washington, DC, during the Second National March on Washington for Lesbian and Gay Rights. The NAMES Quilt was nominated by Representative Nancy Pelosi for a Nobel Peace Prize in 1989, the same year that San Francisco filmmakers Rob Epstein and Jeffrey Friedman won an Academy Award for the documentary film, *Common Threads: Stories from the Quilt* (San Francisco: Telling Pictures Films, 1989). Cleve Jones with Jeff Dawson, *Stitching a Revolution: The Making of an Activist* (San Francisco: Harper One, 2000).

141. By 1990 the Grove Steering Committee had received Recreation and Parks Department permission to use de Laveaga Dell in Golden Gate Park. Volunteers who reclaimed the formerly derelict site saw it as a metaphor for resilience and the power of community. See Bruner Foundation, *Na-*

tional AIDS Memorial Grove, 1999 Silver Medal Winner (Cambridge, MA: Bruner Foundation, 2000), 70–71, http://www.brunerfoundation.org/rba/pdfs/1999/03_NationalGrove.pdf.

Bibliography

Abbot, Alysia. *Fairyland: A Memoir of My Father*. New York: W.W. Norton & Co., 2014.

Agee, Christopher Lowen. *The Streets of San Francisco: Policing and the Creation of a Cosmopolitan Liberal Politics, 1950–1972*. Chicago: University of Chicago Press, 2014.

Andriote, John-Manuel. *Victory Deferred: How AIDS Changed Gay Life in America*. Chicago: University of Chicago Press, 1999.

Angier, Natalie. "Intersexual Healing." *New York Times*, 4 February 1996. http://www.nytimes.com/1996/02/04/weekinreview/ideas-trends-intersexual-healing-an-anomaly-finds-a-group.html.

Armstrong, Elizabeth A. *Forging Gay Identities: Organizing Sexuality in San Francisco, 1950–1994*. Chicago: University of Chicago Press, 2002.

Armstrong, Elizabeth A., and Suzanna M. Crage. "Movements and Memory: The Making of the Stonewall Myth." *American Sociological Review* 71, no. 4 (2006): 724–51.

Baim, Tracy. "Sex, Love, and Relationships." In *LGBTQ America: A Theme Study of Lesbian, Gay, Bisexual, Transgender, and Queer History*, edited by Megan E. Springate. Washington, DC: National Park Foundation and National Park Service, 2016. https://nps.gov/articles/lgbtqtheme-love.htm.

Berube, Allan. *Coming Out under Fire: The History of Gay Men and Women in World War Two*. New York: Free Press, 1990.

———. "The History of the Baths." *Coming Up!* (San Francisco), December 1984.

Boag, Peter. *Re-Dressing America's Frontier Past*. Berkeley: University of California Press, 2011.

Boyd, Nan Alamilla. *Wide Open Town: A History of Queer San Francisco to 1965*. Berkeley: University of California Press, 2003.

Bruner Foundation. *National AIDS Memorial Grove, 1999 Silver Medal Winner*. Cambridge, MA: Bruner Foundation, 2000. http://www.brunerfoundation.org/rba/pdfs/1999/03_NationalGrove.pdf.

Chase, Cheryl. "Surgical Progress Is Not the Answer to Intersexuality." *Journal of Clinical Ethics* 9, no. 4 (1998): 385–92.

Chauncey, George. *Gay New York: Gender, Urban Culture, and the Making of the Gay Male World, 1890–1940*. New York: Basic Books, 1994.

D'Emilio, John. "Gay Politics, Gay Community: San Francisco's Experience." In *Making Trouble: Essays on Gay History, Politics, and the University*, edited by John D'Emilio, 74–95. Hoboken, NJ: Taylor and Francis, 2014.

———. *Sexual Politics, Sexual Communities: The Making of a Homosexual Minority in the United States, 1940–1970*. Chicago: University of Chicago Press, 1983.

Epstein, Rob, and Jeffrey Friedman, dirs. *Common Threads: Stories from the Quilt*. San Francisco: Telling Pictures Films, 1989.

Eskridge, William N., Jr. *Dishonorable Passions: Sodomy Laws in America, 1861–2003*. New York: Viking, 2008.

Faderman, Lillian, and Stuart Timmons. *Gay L.A.: A History of Sexual Outlaws, Power Politics, and Lipstick Lesbians*. New York: Basic Books, 2006.

Gallo, Marcia. *Different Daughters: A History of the Daughters of Bilitis and the Rise of the Lesbian Rights Movement*. New York: Carroll & Graf Publishers, 2006.

Garber, Eric. "Finocchio's: A Gay Community Landmark." *Newsletter of the San Francisco Bay Area Gay & Lesbian Historical Society* 3, no. 4 (1988): 1, 4–5.

Gieseking, Jen Jack. "The Geographies of LGBTQ Lives: In and Beyond Cities, Neighborhoods, and Bars." *Communities and Place: A Thematic Approach to the Histories of LGBTQ Communities in the United States*, edited by Katherine Crawford-Lackey and Megan E. Springate. New York: Berghahn Books, forthcoming.

Godfrey, Donal. *Gays and Grays: The Story of the Gay Community at Most Holy Redeemer Catholic Church*. Lanham, MD: Lexington Books, 2007.

Gonzalez, Deena J., and Ellie D. Hernandez. "Latina/o Gender and Sexuality." In *Identities and Place: Changing Labels and Intersectional Communities of LGBTQ and Two-Spirit People in the United States*, edited by Katherine Crawford-Lackey and Megan E. Springate. New York: Berghahn Books, 2019.

GPA Consulting. *San Diego Citywide LGBTQ Historic Context Statement*. San Diego: City of San Diego, 2016. https://www.sandiego.gov/sites/default/files/san_diego_lgbtq_historic_context_final.pdf.

———. *Survey LA: LGBT Historic Context Statement*. Los Angeles: Los Angeles Office of Historic Resources, September 2014. http://preservation.lacity.org/sites/default/files/LGBT%20Historic%20Context%209-14.pdf.

Graves, Donna J., and Shayne E. Watson. *Citywide Historic Context Statement for Lesbian, Gay, Bisexual, Transgender and Queer History in San Francisco*. San Francisco: San Francisco Planning Department, March 2016. https://sf-planning.org/project/lgbt-historic-context-statement.

Hanhardt, Christina B. "Butterflies, Whistles and Fists: Gay Safe Streets Patrols and the New Gay Ghetto, 1976–1981." *Radical History Review* 100 (2008): 61–85.

———. "Making Community: The Places and Spaces of LGBTQ Collective Identity Formation." In *Communities and Place: A Thematic Approach to the Histories of LGBTQ Communities in the United States*, edited by Crawford-Lackey and Springate. New York: Berghahn Books, forthcoming.

———. *Safe Space: Gay Neighborhood History and the Politics of Violence*. Durham, NC: Duke University Press, 2013.

Hay, Harry. "Gay Sex before Zippers," interview with Chris Carlsson. San Francisco: Shaping San Francisco, 1995. https://archive.org/details/ssfHAYBVDCT.

Hemmings, Clare. *Bisexual Spaces: A Geography of Sexuality and Gender*. New York: Routledge, 2002.

Horton, Inge S. *Early Women Architects of the San Francisco Bay Area: The Lives and Careers of Fifty Professionals, 1890–1951*. Jefferson, NC: McFarland & Co., 2010.

Hutchins, Loraine. "Making Bisexuals Visible." In *Identities and Place: Changing Labels and Intersectional Communities of LGBTQ and Two-Spirit People in the United States*, edited by Crawford-Lackey and Springate. New York: Berghahn Books, 2019.

Ingalls, Libby. "AIDS/ARC Vigil 1985–1996." *FoundSF*. http://foundsf.org/index.php?title=AIDS/ARC_Vigil_1985-1995.

Johnson, David K. "LGBTQ Business and Commerce." In *LGBTQ America: A Theme Study of Lesbian, Gay, Bisexual, Transgender, and Queer History*, edited by Springate. Washington, DC: National Park Foundation and National Park Service, 2018. https://nps.gov/articles/lgbtqtheme-business.htm.

Johnson, Susan Lee. *Roaring Camp: The Social World of the California Gold Rush*. New York: W.W. Norton, 2000.

Jones, Cleve, with Jeff Dawson. *Stitching a Revolution: The Making of an Activist*. San Francisco: Harper One, 2000.

Lotchkin, Roger. *San Francisco, 1846–1856: From Hamlet to City*. New York: Oxford University Press, 1974.

Margolin, Malcolm. *The Ohlone Way: Indian Life in the San-Francisco-Monterey Bay Area*. Berkeley, CA: Heyday Books, 1978.

Martin, Del, and Phyllis Lyon. *Lesbian/Woman*. San Francisco: Glide Publications, 1972.

Meeker, Martin. *Contacts Desired: Gay and Lesbian Communications and Community, 1940s–1970s*. Chicago: University of Chicago Press, 2006.

Meyerowitz, Joanne. *How Sex Changed: A History of Transsexuality in the United States*. Cambridge, MA: Harvard University Press, 2002.

Miller, Johnny. "Last Gay Bathhouse in S.F. Shut Down over AIDS." *San Francisco Chronicle*, 13 May 1987. http://www.sfgate.com/entertainment/article/Last-gay-bathhouse-in-S-F-shut-down-over-AIDS-3549850.php.

Moraga, Cherrie, and Gloria Anzaldua, eds. *This Bridge Called My Back: Writings by Radical Women of Color*. Watertown, MA: Persephone Press, 1981.

Newton, Esther. *Mother Camp: Female Impersonators in America*. Englewood Cliffs, NJ: Prentice-Hall, 1972.

New York Times. "14 San Francisco Sex Clubs Told to Close to Curb AIDS." *New York Times*, 10 October 1984. http://www.nytimes.com/1984/10/10/us/14-san-francisco-sex-clubs-told-to-close-to-curb-aids.html.

Palóu, Francisco. *Palóu's Life of Fray Junípero Serra*, translated and edited by Maynard J. Geiger, O.F.M. Washington, DC: American Academy of Franciscan History, 1945.

Pogash, Carol. *As Real as It Gets: The Life of a Hospital at the Center of the AIDS Epidemic*. New York: Birch Lane Press, 1992.

Rast, Raymond W. "A Matter of Alignment: Methods to Match the Goals of the Preservation Movement." *Forum Journal* 28, no. 3 (2014): 13–22.

Robb, Sushawn. *Mothering the Movement: The Story of the San Francisco Women's Building*. Denver: Outskirts Press, 2012.

Robinson, Mariana. *The Coming of Age of the Langley Porter Clinic: The Reorganization of a Mental Health Institute*. Indianapolis, IN: Bobbs-Merrill Company, 1962.

Rosario, Vernon A. "An Interview with Cheryl Chase." *Journal of Gay and Lesbian Psychotherapy* 10, no. 2 (2006): 93–104.

Roscoe, Will. "Sexual and Gender Diversity in Native America and the Pacific Islands." In *Identities and Place: Changing Labels and Intersectional Communities of LGBTQ and Two-Spirit People in the United States*, edited by Crawford-Lackey and Springate. New York: Berghahn Books, 2019.

Rosenbaum, Stephanie J. "Osento, 1980–2008." *The Adventures of Pie Queen*, 20 August 2008. http://piequeen.blogspot.com/2008/08/osento-1980-2008 .html.

San Francisco AIDS Foundation. "The View from Here: Cleve Jones and Dr. Marcus Conant." San Francisco AIDS Foundation, 2011. http://www.sfaf.org/ hiv-info/hot-topics/from-the-experts/the-view-from-here-cleve-jones-ma rcus-conant-2011.html.

San Francisco Call. 27 November 1892.

———. "Dive Men Officials for Cook." *San Francisco Call* 104, no. 142 (20 October 1908).

San Francisco Call-Bulletin. "Arrested." *San Francisco Call-Bulletin,* September 1954.

San Francisco Examiner. "2 Girls Tell Visits to Tommy's Place." *San Francisco Examiner*, 2 December 1954.

San Francisco Heritage. "Sustaining San Francisco's Living History: Strategies for Conserving Cultural Heritage Assets." *San Francisco Heritage*, 2014. http:// www.sfheritage.org/cultural-heritage.

Schneider, David. *Street Zen: The Life and Work of Issan Dorsey*. New York: Da Capo Press, 2000.

Scott, Damon, and Friends of 1800. *Sexing the City: The Social History of San Francisco's Sexual Subcultures, 1933–1980*. San Francisco: Friends of 1800, 2004. http://www.friendsof1800.org/context_statement.pdf.

Senelick, Laurence. "Boys and Girls Together: Subcultural Origins of Glamour Drag and Male Impersonation on the Nineteenth-Century Stage." In *Crossing the Stage: Controversies on Cross-Dressing*, edited by Lesley Ferris, 82–96. London: Routledge, 1993.

Shilts, Randy. *And the Band Played On: People, Politics, and the AIDS Epidemic*. New York: St. Martin's Griffin, 2007.

Sides, Josh. *Erotic City: Sexual Revolutions and the Making of Modern San Francisco*. New York: Oxford University Press, 2009.

Spring, Justin. *Secret Historian: The Life and Times of Samuel Steward, Professor, Tattoo Artist, and Sexual Renegade*. New York: Farrar, Straus and Giroux, 2010.

Stiles, Elaine Brown. "Integrity Considerations in Evaluating LGBTQ Historic Sites." Unpublished paper, Arcus Internship, College of Environmental Design, University of California Berkeley, 2014.

Streitmatter, Rodger. *Unspeakable: The Rise of the Gay and Lesbian Press in America*. Boston: Faber and Faber, 1995.

Stryker, Susan. "Dr. Harry Benjamin." GLBTQ Encyclopedia.com, 2015. http://www.glbtqarchive.com/ssh/benjamin_h_S.pdf.

———. "Transgender History in the United States and the Places that Matter." In *Identities and Place: Changing Labels and Intersectional Communities of LGBTQ and Two-Spirit People in the United States*, edited by Crawford-Lackey and Springate. New York: Berghahn Books, 2019.

———. *Transgender History*. Berkeley, CA: Seal Press, 2008.

Stryker, Susan, and Jim Van Buskirk. *Gay by the Bay: A History of Queer Culture in the San Francisco Bay Area*. San Francisco: Chronicle Books, 1996.

Sueyoshi, Amy. "Remembering Asian Pacific American Activism in Queer History." In *Identities and Place: Changing Labels and Intersectional Communities of LGBTQ and Two-Spirit People in the United States*, edited by Crawford-Lackey and Springate. New York: Berghahn Books, 2019.

———. "Intimate Inequalities: Interracial Affection and Same-Sex Love in the 'Heterosexual' Life of Yone Noguchi, 1897–1909." *Journal of American Ethnic History* 29 (2010): 22–44.

Tarnoff, Ben. *The Bohemians: Mark Twain and the San Francisco Writers Who Reinvented American Literature*. New York: Penguin Press, 2014.

Thompson, Mark, ed. *Long Road to Freedom: The Advocate History of the Gay and Lesbian Movement*. New York: St. Martin's Press, 1994.

Thorpe, Charles P. "I.D., Leadership and Violence." In *Out of the Closets: Voices of Gay Liberation*, edited by Karla Jay and Allen Young, 352–62. New York: Douglas Book Corp., 1972.

Wittman, Carl. "A Gay Manifesto." In *Out of the Closets: Voices of Gay Liberation*, edited by Jay and Young, 332–42. New York: Douglas Book Corp., 1972.

Preservation of LGBTQ Historic and Cultural Sites

A New York City Perspective

Jay Shockley

For over two decades, New York City has been in the forefront nationally in the historic preservation of LGBTQ historic and cultural sites. Beginning in the early 1990s, a number of historic preservationists, historians, and artists began documenting LGBTQ history and worked on projects to bring official commemoration and public awareness to significant LGBTQ sites.

Given that New York is the largest American city in population and has a dense urban building fabric, and also that New York LGBTQ communities have been so prominent in LGBTQ rights and other social movements nationwide as well as in all aspects of American arts and culture, it is no surprise that there are many notable sites. The city has long been a magnet for many people associated with the arts, as well as those longing for freedom of expression in all its forms. New York City is also extraordinarily fortunate in having had strong historic preservation protections since 1965. Many neighborhoods and sites associated with LGBTQ history remain extant through landmark and historic district designations, even if their LGBTQ histories have often not been officially recognized. Greenwich Village, in particular, has multiple historic districts that have thus far protected many sites. The Village is one of the earliest neighborhoods in the city that allowed, and gradually accepted, an open gay and lesbian presence in the early twentieth century, resulting in its emergence as a nationally significant LGBTQ enclave.

A number of strategies have been employed to bring these "hidden histories" to light: identifying previously unknown sites and reinterpreting historic sites through maps, guidebooks, walking tours, public talks, online guides, and street-marking projects; weaving LGBTQ history into documentation of individual landmark and historic district designations; and using a variety of tools to advocate for official recognition of significant representative sites. Unlike the City of San Francisco, for instance, which recently commissioned a four-year-long project to produce a context statement for its LGBTQ history and associated sites, New York City has not yet had an officially sanctioned overall survey of LGBTQ sites, despite extensive documentation within city landmarks designation reports. The currently evolving, independent New York City LGBT Historic Sites Project, founded in 2014, is doing this through a comprehensive survey, documentation, evaluation of LGBTQ-associated properties in all five boroughs of the city, and an interactive website.[1] Below is a chronology of these documentation and preservation efforts over the past twenty-five years, as well as a case history of LGBTQ Greenwich Village.

New York City Landmarks Preservation Commission Designation Reports (1992 on) and Pride Month Website Slide Shows (2013–2017)

In 1992, Andrew S. Dolkart in *Guide to New York City Landmarks*, the official guidebook to the New York City Landmarks Preservation Commission's designated landmarks and historic districts, included for the first time several LGBTQ sites, including the Stonewall Inn.[2] Also beginning that year, staff members of the commission's research department began to include LGBTQ history, where appropriate, in official designation reports for projects to which they were assigned.[3] The commission did not undertake an effort to locate significant LGBTQ historic sites, so this staff effort was rather random and in no way reflected an ordering of the most important LGBTQ sites or the diversity of the city in terms of boroughs or race or other criteria. However, as a result of these staff efforts and research, New York City has far more official landmark designation reports that document LGBTQ history and specific extant sites than any other American city. Despite this extensive documentation, New York lagged behind at least five other cities in designating landmarks specifically for their LGBTQ associations. In June 2015, after years of staff and public advocacy, the NYC Landmarks Preservation Commission designated the Stonewall as New York City's first landmark recognized for its LGBTQ history.[4]

Many of the LGBTQ-related sites documented by staff and designated by the commission happened to be in the greater Greenwich Village area of Manhattan (see case study below), though there were some chance and surprise discoveries in the rest of the city. On occasion, there was the opportunity to introduce an LGBTQ context in a discussion of, for instance, a building type. The Wilbraham is a prime example of a bachelor flats building, a type of residential hotel that developed in the late nineteenth century exclusively for men. At that time, nearly half of men over the age of fifteen in the city were unmarried, and housing options were severely limited for single men, who were seen as a threat to marriage and traditional gender roles. Historian George Chauncey, in his pioneering book *Gay New York: Gender, Urban Culture, and the Making of the Gay Male World, 1890–1940*, recognized these apartments as significant early private spaces for some upper-middle-class and professional gay men.[5]

Another Landmarks Preservation Commission research staff effort has been the reinterpretation of already designated landmarks and buildings in historic districts all over the city from an LGBTQ perspective. These have been made publicly available via slide shows posted on the commission's official website for Pride Month in June of 2013 through 2017.[6] The selection of the following sites, from the mid-nineteenth century to the present and representing the diversity of NYC's LGBTQ history, included associations with African Americans, women, and the boroughs other than Manhattan.

Bethesda Fountain, Central Park

Sculptor Emma Stebbins (1815–1882) designed her masterpiece *Angel of the Waters* in the 1860s while living in Rome with her lover Charlotte Cushman, a leading actress of the American and British stages. Stebbins was but one of a number of lesbian artists who formed a circle around Cushman. This fountain is the earliest public artwork by a woman in New York City and was the only sculpture sanctioned as part of the early design and construction phase of Central Park.[7]

"Clear Comfort" (Alice Austen House)

Alice Austen (1866–1952) lived for much of her life in this early family farmhouse on Staten Island. A photography pioneer most active from the 1880s to the 1920s, she produced about eight thousand images. Among these are Austen and friends dancing together, embracing in bed, and cross-dressing, photographs that were unique for their time and have become iconic for the LGBTQ community (figure 8.1). In 1899,

Figure 8.1. "Julia Martin, Julia Bredt, and self: dressed up," 1891. Photo by Alice Austen. From the Collection of Historic Richmond Town.

Austen formed an intimate relationship with Gertrude Amelia Tate (1871–1962), who came to live here from 1917 until they were evicted from the property in 1945. The women were later forced to live separately—Austen in an institution, and Tate with her family (who would not accept Austen). The house became a public museum in 1975, and for decades the real story of the owners' lives was actively discouraged in the museum's interpretation. In recent years, the Historic House Trust has reversed this policy.[8]

Oliver Smith House

This Brooklyn Heights residence was purchased in 1953 by Oliver Smith (1918–1994), one of the most famous theatrical designers of his day and a twenty-five-time Tony Award nominee. He created the original sets for such Broadway shows as *Guys and Dolls*, *West Side Story*, *My Fair Lady*, *The Sound of Music*, *Hello Dolly!*, and such ballets as *Rodeo* and *Fancy Free*. Smith was associated with an influential group of gay writers, artists, and intellectuals, and, perhaps influenced by his time at February House (a noted gay commune that once stood at 7 Middagh Street, since demolished), he established his own home as a center of gay culture in Brooklyn. From around 1955 to 1965, he rented the garden apartment to Truman Capote (1924–1984).[9]

Paul Rudolph Apartments

Paul Rudolph (1918–1997), architect and chairman of the Department of Architecture at Yale University, began renting an apartment in 1961 by the East River in Midtown. After purchasing the building in 1976, he converted it into apartments and added a remarkable sculptural penthouse completed in 1982. This work is emblematic of the architectural contribution of the LGBTQ community to American architecture and Rudolph's acclaim as one of America's most innovative twentieth-century architects. From 1922 to 1951, this had been the home of "First Lady of the Theater" Katharine Cornell and her husband, director-producer Guthrie McClintic, who had one of the most famous Broadway "lavender marriages" of their day.[10]

Audre Lorde House

The acclaimed Black lesbian feminist writer and activist Audre Lorde (1934–1992) resided on Staten Island from 1972 to 1987 with her partner, psychology professor Frances Clayton. During her time here, Lorde held professorships at Hunter and John Jay Colleges and wrote several books of poetry and essays, as well as her renowned autobiographical works, *The Cancer Journals* (1980) and *Zami: A New Spelling of My Name* (1984).[11]

Lesbian Herstory Archives

Celebrating its fortieth anniversary in 2014, the Archives houses the world's largest collection of materials by and about lesbians and their communities. Established in the Manhattan apartment of Joan Nestle and Deborah Edel, the Archives moved in 1993 to Brooklyn. A combined research facility, museum, and community center, it owns a vast library of books and journals, subject and organizational files, unpublished papers, conference proceedings, reference tools, audiovisual materials, art, and ephemera.[12]

OLGAD Map, REPOHistory, and *Gay New York* (1994)

In 1994, the year of the twenty-fifth anniversary of the Stonewall Rebellion in New York City, a group of eight historic preservationists and one architect participated in the short-lived Organization of Lesbian + Gay Architects and Designers (OLGAD) and produced one of the first known public attempts in the United States to introduce LGBTQ preservation and historic sites.[13] One of the group's members, Ken M. Lustbader, had recently broached this topic in his Columbia University historic preservation thesis, "Landscape of Liberation: Preservation of Gay and Lesbian History in Greenwich Village."[14] OLGAD's map, "A Guide to Lesbian & Gay New York Historical Landmarks," was intended as a sampling of LGBTQ-related sites, with walking tours of Greenwich Village, Harlem, and Midtown, displaying a wide range of extant buildings. These included well-known landmarks, such as hotels and theaters, listed for their LGBTQ connections, as well as bars and social meeting places, residences of notable people, and gay rights movement locations. This map led the Municipal Art Society and others to begin sponsoring LGBTQ walking tours.

Many of the sites were located in Greenwich Village, which had the largest map. Another map was of Harlem, one of New York's most significant African American neighborhoods and another early LGBTQ enclave. Just one of the significant sites featured was the famous Apollo Theater, where nearly every important African American entertainer played during its heyday from the 1930s into the 1970s as a showcase for Black performers. Gay, lesbian, and bisexual luminaries such as Bessie Smith, Alberta Hunter, Ethel Waters, Jackie "Moms" Mabley, Little Richard, Johnny Mathis, Alex Bradford, and James Cleveland appeared there. During the 1960s, a popular attraction was the drag Jewel Box Revue, America's first traveling troupe of gender impersonators featuring a racially integrated cast of twenty-five men and one woman, Master of Ceremonies Stormé DeLarverié.[15]

The OLGAD map was not the only project that sought to recognize important LGBTQ sites as part of Stonewall's twenty-fifth anniversary. REPOHistory, an activist group of visual and performance artists, writers, filmmakers, and historians who sought to publicly repossess aspects of history that had generally been ignored, undertook a Queer Spaces project. They designed pink triangle signs giving the LGBTQ history of nine Manhattan locations, which they then erected on street signposts.[16] George Chauncey's *Gay New York*, also published that year, was an immensely important contribution to raising awareness of the incredibly rich LGBTQ history of late nineteenth- and early twentieth-century New York City. Two subsequent guidebooks that listed many LGBTQ sites in New York in 1997 were *The Queerest Places: A Guide to Gay and Lesbian Historic Sites* and *Stepping Out: Nine Tours through New York City's Gay and Lesbian Past*.[17]

Effort to Have the Stonewall Declared a National Historic Landmark (1994)

In connection with the twenty-fifth anniversary of Stonewall, OLGAD members worked to have the Stonewall Inn declared a National Historic Landmark (NHL).[18] The designation did not happen at this time for two crucial reasons: the lack of building owner support, which was necessary in order to proceed, and the lack of precedence. Since there had never been any prior LGBTQ NHL historic context or theme study developed, much less any attempt to have an LGBTQ property federally recognized, the Department of the Interior deemed it impossible to determine the Stonewall's significance. Further, the successes of the gay rights movement were seen as too recent and too limited at that point; a street riot was questioned as the most worthy site for commemoration; Stonewall was not considered a defining moment or event for the LGBTQ community's "basic humanity" to be demonstrated (or commemorated) to American society; and written gay history was misinterpreted as too "lacking" to provide sufficient historical background.[19]

Thirtieth Anniversary of Stonewall—National Register of Historic Places (1999) and National Historic Landmark (2000)

Just four years later, the nomination of Stonewall to the National Register of Historic Places (NRHP) became a priority. This was initiated by Department of the Interior staff and facilitated by openly gay John Berry, who was serving as assistant secretary for policy, management and budget, Department of the Interior.[20] Sponsored by the Greenwich Village Society for Historic Preservation, the nomination was fast-tracked for listing on the New York State Register and then the NRHP in 1999, and Stonewall was designated an NHL in 2000.[21] The nomination focused solely on the significance of Stonewall to LGBTQ history, since it was already part of the listed Greenwich Village Historic District, and included the surrounding streets and Christopher Park where the Stonewall Rebellion took place. The inclusion of the park and streets was promoted by Kathleen LaFrank, of the New York State Historic Preservation Office, who suggested Civil War battlefields as a boundary precedent. In order to address the issue of the NRHP fifty-year threshold, the nomination extensively quoted from contemporary newspapers and journals, personal reminiscences, scholarly books, and historians' statements, which established Stonewall's "exceptional significance" due to its impact on the history of civil rights both nationally and internationally. The Stonewall was the first and only specifically LGBTQ-related listing on the NRHP until the Dr. Franklin E. Kameny Residence was added in 2011, and was the only LGBTQ NHL until the Henry Gerber House was designated in 2015.[22] Stonewall was designated a National Monument in 2016.

New York City LGBT Historic Sites Project (2014–2018)

In 2011, three former OLGAD members, Jay Shockley, Andrew S. Dolkart, and Ken M. Lustbader, wishing to raise the discussion of LGBTQ historic preservation to a national level, led the session "Beyond Stonewall: Recognizing Significant Historic Sites of the Lesbian, Gay, Bisexual & Transgender Community" at the National Trust for Historic Preservation Conference in Buffalo, New York. When the Department of the Interior, in 2014, announced the National Park Service Historic Preservation Fund Grants to Underrepresented Communities, for projects broadening the diversity of sites on the NRHP and as NHLs, the three men submitted an LGBTQ grant application through the New York State Historic Preservation Office. The New York City LGBT Historic Sites Project was awarded a federal grant of $49,999.00, and it subsequently leveraged additional foundation support. It received a second Underrepresented Communities federal grant in 2017.

The New York City LGBT Historic Sites Project is currently surveying, documenting, and evaluating previously unknown and undocumented properties associated with LGBTQ historic and cultural themes in all five boroughs of the city, as well as reevaluating those already locally designated or listed on the NRHP for LGBTQ connections. A publicly accessible website presenting such sites has been created, using outreach and input from professionals, organizations, archives, and community members. Although New York City has been a national leader in the LGBTQ rights movement, no survey or comprehensive documentation previously existed of sites associated with LGBTQ history. The project provides context and baseline documentation for New York City's LGBTQ history and extant sites, establishes a resource for future scholarship and preservation efforts, and is producing new and amended NRHP nominations. The first NRHP nomination by the project was Julius' Bar, which was listed on the NRHP in April 2016.[23] The project's amended Alice Austen House NRHP nomination was accepted in March 2017; its Caffe Cino nomination was accepted in November 2017; and its Earl Hall, Columbia University nomination was accepted in March 2018.

Greenwich Village: An LGBTQ Historic Preservation and Cultural Case History

Within greater Greenwich Village, including the East Village and also a few sites in the immediately adjacent SoHo and Union Square neighborhoods, there are numerous, disparate extant sites representing the history of the LGBTQ community from the 1850s to the present. These include bars, popular meeting places, cultural institutions, housing accommodations, theaters, residences of noted persons, and sites associated with LGBTQ civil rights. Greenwich Village was one of the first neighborhoods in New York City that allowed, and gradually accepted, an open gay, lesbian, and bisexual presence. This resulted in its emergence as an early and nationally significant LGBTQ enclave, attracting many like-minded residents and visitors.

The following discussion is not meant to be a definitive history of the LGBTQ community in Greenwich Village or New York, or of the various communities within the larger community. It represents a partial narrative of New York's first "gay" neighborhood based solely on extant sites drawn from the various New York documentation and preservation projects mentioned above. In particular, much of this site-based history is documented in official city landmark designation reports, a fact which is unique nationally. These sites demonstrate the long chronology and breadth of the history of the LGBTQ community here. New York City is fortunate that so many LGBTQ-associated sites are protected by historic district designations. In Greenwich Village alone there are six such historic districts. (In contrast, Harlem has lost many of its significant sites through demolition over the decades.)

Early Known Gay and Lesbian Life from the 1850s to the 1890s

The period from the 1850s to the 1890s is the first recorded emergence in Greenwich Village of what would now be regarded as LGBTQ spaces, a number of which remain extant. The earliest currently known is Pfaff's, operated from 1859 to 1864 by German-born proprietor Charles Igna-tius Pfaff, a Rathskeller-like beer/wine cellar restaurant in the Coleman House Hotel, extending into the sidewalk vaults (basement area below the sidewalk). It became a favorite haunt of the Bohemians of the 1850s, including artists, writers, and actors. Walt Whitman, iconic in the United States and Europe as one of the first people to openly express the con-cept of men loving men via his poetry, was a central figure among this group from 1859 to 1862. During his Pfaff's period, around 1859, Whit-man wrote twelve famously homoerotic "Calamus" poems that were included in the 1860 edition of *Leaves of Grass*. A portion of Pfaff's was known as a place for men looking for other men. Although Pfaff's vault space has been destroyed, the basement, along with the rest of the ho-tel, survives.[24]

In *Gay New York*, Chauncey identified the 1890s as one of the ear-liest periods in the city when one very specific, and "notorious," aspect of the emerging gay male community—the subculture of flamboyantly effeminate "fairies"—became noticed by a wider public. He posited that this subculture was more fully and publicly integrated into work-ing-class than middle-class culture.[25] While the Bowery, Lower East Side, and Tenderloin were the most notorious New York centers for "commercialized vice" and "homosexual rendezvous" at this time, there were also such spots on Bleecker Street in Greenwich Village. Upper-middle-class men in particular, and some women, were attracted to downtown in part to witness the "depravity" of the lower classes and thus to be scandalized or titillated (or both). For example, the Slide was popularly identified in 1890 as "New York's 'worst dive' because of the fairies ... gathered there."[26] A "slide," in prostitutes' jargon of the time, was "an establishment where male homosexuals dressed as women and solicited men."[27] Contemporary newspapers, purporting to be defend-ing the public's morals, spotlighted the most sensational aspects of this underworld. The Slide was closed by police in 1892, and the proprietor convicted of keeping a "disorderly house."[28] Another "dive," the Black Rabbit, was personally raided in 1900 by Anthony Comstock of the So-ciety for the Suppression of Vice. Of this establishment, he fumed "that he [had] never before raided a place so wicked, and that 'Sodom and Gomorrah' would blush for shame at hearing to what depths of vice its habitués had descended."[29]

On the opposite side of the social spectrum were a number of LGBTQ individuals who operated within the spheres of upper New York society, politics, and culture. The Victorian lesbian power couple Elsie de Wolfe, often credited as America's first professional interior designer, and Elisabeth Marbury, one of the world's leading and pioneering female theatrical producers, lived in a house near Union Square between 1892 and 1911. They first met in 1887, and their relationship lasted nearly forty years. Their Sunday afternoon salons, held in their home, were attended by notables connected with the worlds of the arts, society, and politics. By coincidence, the house next door was, according to a 1914 biography, a place where the great gay Irish wit and writer Oscar Wilde lodged while touring America in 1882.[30]

Murray H. Hall (1840–1901) was a Tammany politico who lived as a man for decades without his gender being questioned. Following Hall's death, however, the *New York Times* reported that Hall's "true sex" was revealed by the doctor. As an early instance of a gender-nonconforming person in New York, this attracted worldwide attention, including that of pioneering English sexual psychologist Havelock Ellis. In 1872, Hall married Cecilia Florence Lowe, a school teacher, and by 1874 Hall had established an employment agency chiefly representing domestic help. The couple moved several times but remained close to the Jefferson Market Police Court since Hall was also a bail bondsman. Hall's last home office was an apartment on Sixth Avenue. As a Tammany figure, Hall played poker and pool with city and state officials and other political leaders and was often able to secure appointments for friends.[31]

The Gay, Lesbian, and Bisexual Presence in the 1910s and 1920s

After a period of decline as a desirable residential neighborhood, Greenwich Village became known, prior to World War I, not only for its historic and picturesque qualities and affordable housing, but also for the diversity of its population and their social and political ideas. In the 1910s, gay men and lesbians frequented the many cheap Italian restaurants, cafeterias, and tearooms that the Village became known for. After the war and increasingly in the 1920s, they appropriated their own spaces, despite some opposition from fellow Villagers. This represented the first instance in New York City of covert middle-class gay and lesbian commercial enterprises, and started the Village's reputation as its most famous gay neighborhood. As Chauncey wrote, "The Village . . . came to represent to the rest of the city what New York as a whole represented to the rest of the nation: a peculiar social territory in which the normal social constraints on behavior seemed to have been suspended and where men and women built unconventional lives outside the family nexus."[32]

In 1914, the block of MacDougal Street just south of Washington Square emerged as a cultural and social center of the Bohemian set, with the Liberal Club, radical feminist Heterodoxy Club, and Washington Square Bookshop. The Provincetown Playhouse was, from 1916 to 1929, a serious amateur theater, and though most famous in this period for playwright Eugene O'Neill, it was also associated with figures prominent in the gay, lesbian, and bisexual community, including Edna St. Vincent Millay, Djuna Barnes, Katharine Cornell, Tallulah Bankhead, and Eva Le Gallienne.[33] Washington Square Park was by the early twentieth century a popular cruising ground for gay men, and its west side became known as the "meat rack."[34] While West Third and Fourth Streets had housed some of the speakeasies and tearooms run by and/or catering to New York's burgeoning lesbian and gay community after the war, this block of MacDougal became an important LGBTQ nucleus, especially after a series of police crackdowns on spots elsewhere in the Village in 1924 and 1925.

One such place on this block was Eve Adams' tearoom, a popular after-theater club run in 1925 and 1926 by Polish-Jewish lesbian émigré Chawe Zlocsewer (with other variations, such as Eva Kotchever or Eva Czlotcheber), with a sign that read "Men are admitted but not welcome." A Village columnist in 1931 reminisced that her club was "one of the most delightful hang-outs the Village ever had."[35] After a police raid, Zlocsewer was convicted of obscenity (for *Lesbian Love*, a collection of her short stories) and disorderly conduct, and was deported.[36] The Black Rabbit (unrelated to the earlier Bleecker Street establishment with the same name), another of "the Village's gay stamping grounds,"[37] was closed by the police around 1929.

Webster Hall, one of New York's most historically and culturally significant large nineteenth-century assembly halls, has been the venue for countless events, including conventions and political and union rallies, particularly for the working-class and immigrant populations of the Lower East Side. In the 1910s and '20s, it became famous for its Bohemian masquerade balls. It was significant as a gathering place for the city's early twentieth-century lesbian, gay, and bisexual community, who felt welcome to attend the balls in drag, and then sponsored their own events by the 1920s. Among the many notables who attended events here at this time were artist Charles Demuth and writer Djuna Barnes.[38]

The Village attracted a large number of artistic and socially progressive residents, among them many gay men, lesbians, and bisexuals. One of the most notable and enduring Village cultural institutions is the Little Red School House, often considered the city's first progressive school, founded by lesbian reform educator Elisabeth Irwin (1880–1942). As early as 1912, Irwin worked at revising public school curriculum, and started her progressive "Little Red School House" curriculum in 1921. With the threat of public funding cuts, she was urged to found her own private, independent primary school. In 1932, the school moved to Bleecker Street, and a high school (now Elisabeth Irwin High School) was added in 1940.[39] Irwin continued to direct the school until her death. Her partner of thirty years was Katharine Anthony, a social researcher and feminist biographer. They lived nearby and were members of the Heterodoxy Club.[40]

Author Willa Cather, then an editor at *McClure's Magazine*, lived on Washington Square from about 1908 to 1913, with her partner Edith Lewis. Edna St. Vincent Millay was the first woman to win the Pulitzer Prize for poetry (1923), and "Vincent" had a number of relationships with women before her marriage. One of Millay's many Village residences was on Bedford Street in 1923–1925.[41]

LGBTQ Social and Cultural Life, 1930s to the 1950s

From the 1930s, and particularly after World War II, the area of Greenwich Village south of Washington Square continued as the location of many known bars and clubs that catered to, welcomed, or merely tolerated the LGBTQ community. Reflecting the not wholly hospitable climate of the postwar period, even in this neighborhood, many of these bars (largely lesbian) were located in the shadow of the elevated train that ran along West Third Street. Louis' Luncheon (1930s–1940s) was a hangout popular with gay men and lesbians, writers, and chorus girls. Tony Pastor's Downtown (1939–1967) had a mixed clientele of lesbians and tourists, some gay men, and female impersonators. Raided on morals charges in 1944 for permitting lesbians to "loiter" on the premises, Pastor's survived apparently with mob backing. The New York State Liquor Authority, however, revoked its liquor license in 1967 because, in the homophobic language of the agency, it had "become disorderly in that it permitted homosexuals, degenerates and undesirables to be on the license premises and conduct themselves in an offensive and indecent manner."[42] Among the numerous other lesbian bars nearby were Swing Rendezvous (1938–1965), also a jazz club; Ernie's Restaurant/ Three Ring Circus (ca. 1940–1962), mostly heterosexual but also attracting working-class lesbians; Mona's (ca. late 1940s–early 1950s); and Pony Stable Inn (1945–1970). Both the Swing Rendezvous and the Pony

Stable Inn are remembered by African American lesbian poet Audre Lorde in *Zami: A New Spelling of My Name*.[43]

The San Remo Cafe (ca. 1925–1967) was a working-class bar that became a famous Bohemian hangout that attracted in the late 1940s and early 1950s, among its most prominent patrons, many gay artists and writers. These included Tennessee Williams, Gore Vidal, James Baldwin, Allen Ginsberg, William Burroughs, W. H. Auden, Harold Norse, John Cage, Larry Rivers, Frank O'Hara, and Merce Cunningham. The Music Box (ca. 1950–1972) was one of the places listed in a 1955–1956 FBI investigative report of "notorious types and places of amusement" in the Village that stated, "A majority of the bars and restaurants in this area cater to lesbians and homosexuals, quite a few of whom reside in the area and are not inhibited in the pursuit of their amorous conquests. In the bars and restaurants there will also be found a segment of the tourist trade who go to the Village to observe the lesbians and queers at play and to enjoy the atmosphere of the 'gay life.'"[44]

Farther west in the Village, the Stewart (later Life) Cafeteria opened in 1933, and quickly became a popular haunt for lesbians and gay men. Its plate-glass windows allowed visitors to the Village to gawk at the homosexuals inside, frequently attracting crowds.[45] In today's East Village, the Mafia-controlled 181 Club (1945–1953), called "the homosexual Copacabana," was one of the most luxurious gay and lesbian clubs in the United States and featured lavish shows of female impersonators.[46]

Greenwich Village continued to attract many notable LGBTQ residents. First Lady Eleanor Roosevelt had key associations with Village women beginning in the 1920s. An apartment building on West Twelfth Street housed many influential women between 1920 and 1950, including lesbians of note: political radical Polly Porter; Democratic Party leader Mary Dewson; artist Nancy Cook; and educator Marion Dickerman, who organized the Todhunter School on the Upper East Side, and the Val-Kill furniture factory in partnership with Roosevelt on her property near Hyde Park, New York. From 1933 to 1942, Roosevelt rented an apartment "haven" in the East Eleventh Street house of two close friends, writer Esther Lape and attorney Elizabeth Read. The couple, who lived there for over two decades, were influential suffragists, political reformers, and founders of the League of Women Voters. Roosevelt maintained her own apartment on Washington Square from 1942 to 1949.[47]

Photographer Berenice Abbott (1898–1991) and her partner Elizabeth McClausland (1899–1965) lived and worked in two flats they shared in a Village loft building from 1935 to 1965. An influential art critic and historian, McClausland wrote the text for Abbott's classic photographic series *Changing New York*, published in 1939. Djuna Barnes was a long-time resident of a modest row house on Patchin Place after the publication of her lesbian novel *Nightwood* in 1936.[48] St. Luke's Place with its stately houses has long been a favored address for leaders in the arts and entertainment industry. Among its famous residents were painters Paul Cadmus (1904–1999) and Jared French (1905–1988), lovers when they moved there in 1935. Jared French married artist Margaret Hoening in 1937 and they continued to share their home with Cadmus, who was joined after World War II by a new lover, painter George Tooker (1920–2011). In 1948, their friend George Platt Lynes photographed them here. Another close friend, British author E. M. Forster, was their houseguest in 1947 and 1949, and other visitors included Tennessee Williams, Cadmus's brother-in-law Lincoln Kirstein, and Andy Warhol.[49]

In the 1950s, the celebrated African American authors, civil rights activists, friends, and early gay-rights pioneers James Baldwin (1924–1987) and Lorraine Hansberry (1930–1965) moved to the Village. Baldwin was openly gay and many of his works centered on gay or bisexual characters and frankly explored issues of identity, race, and homosexuality.[50] Calling himself a "transatlantic commuter," he lived much of his life abroad while maintaining a series of residences in New York. From 1958 to 1961, he rented a Village apartment. Hansberry, meanwhile, moved into an apartment on Bleecker Street in 1953, shortly after she married Robert B. Nemiroff. She joined the Daughters of Bilitis homophile organization in 1957, around the time the couple separated, and penned several essay-length letters about such topics as sexual identity, feminism, and homophobia that were printed in its publication, the *Ladder*. In 1960, using a portion of the profits from her wildly successful play *A Raisin in the Sun* (1959), she purchased a residence near Washington Square. Hansberry became involved with one of the building's tenants, Dorothy Secules, and the two remained partners until Hansberry's premature death from cancer.[51]

The LGBTQ community has had a disproportionately significant and immeasurable impact on the cultural life of Greenwich Village and all of New York City, particularly in its theaters, which have featured the work of LGBTQ actors, directors, playwrights, and the various associated professions, as well as performers in its cafes and clubs, and as patrons of all of these venues. In the 1950s, Greenwich Village and the East Village became the cradle of what became the off-Broadway and off-off-Broadway theater movements. The former Jaffe Art Theater, one of the most tangible reminders of the heyday of Yiddish theater in twentieth-century New York, was particularly renowned as the Phoenix Theater from 1953 to 1961. Founded by Norris Houghton and T. Edward Hambleton, it featured the work of such directors as Tony Richardson and such performers as Montgomery Clift, Will Geer, Farley Granger, Eva Le Gallienne, and Roddy McDowall.[52] In 1955, actress-manager Julie Bovasso established and directed the Tempo Playhouse in the East Village, where she is credited with the American premieres of works by Jean Genet, including *The Maids*, as well as Gertrude Stein's *In a Garden* and *Three Sisters Who Are Not Sisters*.[53]

Caffe Cino is widely recognized as the birthplace of off-off-Broadway theater and is also significant in the pioneering of gay theater. In 1958, Joe Cino (1931–1967) rented a ground-story commercial space, originally intending to operate a coffeehouse with art exhibits. He then allowed patrons to stage small avant-garde theatrical performances. His partner Jon Torrey worked as the electrician and, in the early years, as the lighting designer. Many of its early productions featured gay characters or subject matter. The staging of Lanford Wilson's *The Madness of Lady Bright* in 1964 was both the café's breakthrough hit and an early play to deal explicitly with homosexuality. Caffe Cino provided an important platform for newly emerging gay playwrights such as Doric Wilson, H. M. Koutoukas, Bob Heide, William Hoffman, Lanford Wilson, Tom Eyen, Jeff Weiss, David Starkweather, Charles Stanley, and Robert Patrick. The coffeehouse itself also became an important gay meeting spot, offering an alternative to bars and bathhouses. It closed in 1968, a year after Cino's suicide following Torrey's accidental death.[54] Another important venue for avant-garde performances was the activist Judson Memorial Church on Washington Square, which sponsored Judson Poets Theater and Judson Dance Theater under playwright/associate minister Al Carmines after 1962.[55]

1960s–Early 1970s: The Early LGBTQ Rights Movement and Cultural Influence

Inevitably, Greenwich Village has many of the sites most associated with the struggle for LGBTQ rights in New York City, and nationally, over the decades. Julius' Bar by the 1960s attracted a gay clientele, despite the treatment they received. With the New York State Liquor Authority's (SLA) regulations against serving liquor to "disorderly" patrons, and its interpretation that homosexuals were in that category, the bar's management pursued a policy of not encouraging the presence of gay men. On 21 April 1966, members of the New York Mattachine Society staged what became known as a "Sip-In" at Julius' to challenge SLA regulations. The tactic was that men would enter the bar, declare their sexual orientation, and order a drink—knowing that they would be turned away. The publicity attracted favorable public support and the attention of the New York City Commission on Human Rights, and caused the SLA to publicly disavow its policy. This was a hugely significant pre-Stonewall assertion of LGBTQ rights and paved the way for the right of gay people to peacefully assemble and the legalization of gay bars.[56] That same year, Mayor John Lindsay's administration's attempt to "clean up" Washington Square and the police policy of entrapment of gay men was challenged at a meeting at Judson Memorial Church, which was used in the 1960s–70s for lesbian and gay political gatherings.[57] In 1967, gay activist Craig Rodwell opened the Oscar Wilde Memorial Bookshop on Mercer Street, which was the nation's first lesbian and gay bookstore. It became a community meeting center as well.[58]

The Stonewall Inn is considered one of the most significant sites associated with LGBTQ history in New York City and the entire country. In June 1969, a routine police raid on this bar resulted in active resistance, setting off days of confrontation and demonstrations, with unprecedented cries for "gay pride" and "gay power." The Stonewall Rebellion (also known as the Stonewall Riot) sparked a new phase of the gay liberation movement, which involved more radical political action during the 1970s, and also inspired the LGBTQ pride movement. The first anniversary of the uprising was commemorated in June 1970 as Christopher Street Gay Liberation Day, the main event being a march from Greenwich Village to Central Park.

In the immediate aftermath of Stonewall, one of the earliest organizations formed was the Gay Liberation Front (GLF). Though of brief duration, the Gay Community Center was located from 1970 to 1971 on West Third Street (in the location formerly housing Tony Pastor's Downtown). GLF had Sunday meetings and dances here, and this was also the headquarters of Radicalesbians, spun off of the male-dominated GLF in 1970, and the meeting place of Gay Youth, for GLF members under the age of eighteen.[59] A former firehouse in SoHo served as the headquarters of Gay Activists Alliance (GAA) (figure 8.2) from 1971 to 1974. Formed in 1969 when a number of members broke away from the more radical GLF, GAA was primarily a political activist organization whose exclusive purpose was to advance LGBTQ civil and social rights. It lobbied for the passage of local civil rights laws, the banning of police entrapment and harassment, the creation of fair employment and housing legislation, and the repeal of sodomy and solicitation laws. Many of the

Figure 8.2. Gay Activists Alliance Firehouse, 99 Wooster Street, New York City, ca. 1972. Photo by John Barrington Bayley. Courtesy of the New York City Landmarks Preservation Commission.

group's activities were planned at the Firehouse, including sit-ins and picket lines. Perhaps the most famous GAA tactic was the "zap," a direct, public confrontation with a political figure regarding LGBTQ rights designed to gain media attention. The Firehouse also served as an important community center and hosted numerous social events, particularly Saturday night dance parties and Firehouse Flicks, a movie series selected by activist and film buff Vito Russo.[60]

During the 1960s, the influence of the LGBTQ community on off- and off-off-Broadway theater continued as strongly as before. The Provincetown Playhouse, in a later incarnation, housed Edward Albee's first play *The Zoo Story* (1960).[61] The Cherry Lane Theater, formed in 1924–1926 as an experimental theater by veterans of the Provincetown Playhouse, developed a close association with Albee in the early 1960s, presenting *The American Dream*, *The Sandbox*, and *The Death of Bessie Smith*. In 1969, the theater featured a retrospective look at the life and career of Lorraine Hansberry, *To Be Young, Gifted and Black*.[62] La MaMa Experimental Theatre Club in the East Village was founded in 1961 by Ellen Stewart and opened in its current location in 1969. Today, it is widely considered the oldest surviving, most influential, and most prolific of all the off-off-Broadway stages. Though commercial theater has never been its focus, a number of La MaMa plays achieved success on Broadway, including Harvey Fierstein's three plays later combined as *Torch Song Trilogy*, and its resident director, Tom O'Horgan, later produced the influential hit *Hair*. Among the many notable playwrights and directors associated with La MaMa have been Jean-Claude van Itallie, Tom Eyen, Lanford Wilson, William Hoffman, Charles Ludlam, Terrence McNally, Joseph Chaikin, John Vaccaro, Marshall Mason, and Meredith Monk.[63]

1970s to the Present

While the LGBTQ bar and social scene in Greenwich Village had emerged around MacDougal Street in the 1910s–1920s and remained centered in the South Village through the 1960s, there was also a migration northwest, to venues on Greenwich Avenue by the 1960s. Christopher Street became one of the best-identified LGBTQ locations in the world after Stonewall, and the popularity of the thoroughfare was sustained into the 1980s by many gay-owned and gay-friendly bars and businesses. Gay men had traversed to the western terminus of Christopher for decades, to the piers along West Street, for sexual encounters. By the early

1970s, the western end of Christopher Street and adjacent blocks along West Street, long established with seamen-oriented waterfront taverns, had become a nucleus for bars catering to a gay clientele. Six of the fourteen buildings that comprise the Weehawken Street Historic District have housed gay bars from that time to the present.[64] While the waterfront and piers have limited historic physical reminders of its LGBTQ past, they remain important public spaces for LGBTQ people, especially queer youth and queer young adults of color.

North of Christopher Street, in the meatpacking district (today's Gansevoort Market Historic District), another type of LGBTQ nightlife—very late and usually sexual—emerged. The *New York Times* in 1995 described its varied activities:

> Nightspots lie scattered, often tucked away, among the frigid warehouses of beef, pork, veal and poultry .... The meatpacking district runs around the clock, and throughout, there are marked shifts in what goes on .... Burly men in stained white overalls often unload meat trucks in the predawn hours just as club kids and bikers emerge from late-night hangouts .... The district has always had a vibrant gay and lesbian night scene.[65]

The first of the new businesses (other than clubs) in the district was Florent Restaurant, opened in 1985 by Florent Morellet in a 1949 diner, which became quite popular as an all-hours spot and performance venue.[66]

Two of New York's most famous LGBTQ clubs opened in the East Village. The Pyramid Club (1979–present) became a defining venue in the 1980s for avant-garde music and "politicized" drag performers such as Lypsinka, Lady Bunny, and RuPaul, and sponsored early benefit concerts for AIDS. The Saint (1980–1988), owned by gay entrepreneur Bruce Mailman and located in the former Commodore Theatre (later Fillmore East), was one of the most spectacular and expensive dance clubs the city had ever seen.[67]

Numerous LGBTQ notables in the arts have continued to reside and work in the Village. The Merce Cunningham Dance Studio, one of America's most influential dance companies, was located in a penthouse of Westbeth Artists' Housing (former Bell Telephone Laboratories) along the Hudson River waterfront from 1971 until 2010.[68] Star chef James Beard and his partner, architect Gino Cofacci, purchased a house on West Twelfth Street in 1973. The ground-floor interior was redesigned for the kitchen, site of Beard's famous classes and cooking demonstrations, and the building later became home of the James Beard Foundation.[69] After the front portion of the Jaffe Art Theater was converted into apartments, residents included Jackie Curtis ("superstar" in Andy Warhol films), photographer Peter Hujar (1973–1987), and artist David Wojnarowicz (1980–1992).[70] The last apartment of iconic artist Keith Haring (1958–1990) was on LaGuardia Place, near his art studio at 676 Broadway. Author/playwright Paul Rudnick, who lived in the 1990s in the former apartment of actor John Barrymore, wrote the play *I Hate Hamlet* (1991), which was set in this apartment and featured the ghost of Barrymore.[71]

As New York's longest-established gay neighborhood, the Village remained the location of a number of significant institutions. From 1975 to 2016, Congregation Beit Simchat Torah, the city's first LGBTQ synagogue (established 1973), worshiped at Westbeth. The congregation has been led by Rabbi Sharon Kleinbaum since 1992.[72] The Lesbian & Gay Community Services Center (now Lesbian, Gay, Bisexual & Transgender Community Center) was organized in 1983 and took title to a former school building in 1984. A focal point for LGBTQ activities in the metropolitan area, each year the Center welcomes more than three hundred thousand visitors and is used by over four hundred community groups to host meetings, social and cultural events, and health-based programs. The Center witnessed the founding of GLAAD (formerly Gay & Lesbian Alliance Against Defamation) in 1985 and ACT UP (AIDS Coalition to Unleash Power) in 1987. The important community service group SAGE (Services & Advocacy for Gay, Lesbian, Bisexual & Transgender Elders) also met here for over twenty years. In 1988, it housed the Quilt Workshop to create panels for the NAMES Project AIDS Memorial Quilt. For Stonewall's twentieth anniversary in 1989, the Center presented *Imaging Stonewall*, a site specific installation of fifty artworks that included the mural *Once Upon A Time*, by Keith Haring, in the second floor men's room (restored 2012).[73] In 1990, the LGBT Community Center Archive was established under the curatorship of Rich Wandel and now houses thousands of papers, periodicals, correspondence, and photographs donated by individuals and organizations. The Center continues to serve as a major forum for politicians and gathering place for political groups, an important center for cultural events, and a gathering place for the LGBTQ community in times of trouble and celebration.[74] The former Rectory of St. Veronica's Roman Catholic Church was selected by the Catholic Church to become a hospice for homeless AIDS patients, and the facility opened in December 1985. From 1993 to 2003, the New York City Gay and Lesbian Anti-Violence Project and Empire State Pride Agenda were located in the meatpacking district.[75]

Finally, one former restaurant location has taken on historic significance in light of the path-breaking Supreme Court decision in *United States v. Windsor* in 2013. Portofino (ca. 1959–1975) was an Italian restaurant in the South Village that was a discreet meeting place frequented on Friday evenings by lesbians. The case that overturned the federal Defense of Marriage Act had its roots in the date here in 1963 of Edith S. Windsor and Thea Clara Spyer. The couple eventually married in Canada in 2007. Windsor challenged the Defense of Marriage Act after receiving a large tax bill from inheriting Spyer's estate.[76]

Summary

New York City, with the largest population of any American city, has played a prominent role in the LGBTQ rights and other social movements, and is recognized as one of the most important centers for all aspects of American arts and culture. There are many known extant historic and cultural sites of import to the LGBTQ community and nation. Since the early 1990s, various efforts toward their documentation, recognition, and commemoration have placed New York in the forefront nationally in LGBTQ historic preservation. Greenwich Village is an example of an early and historic "gay" neighborhood that can be analyzed for its significant sites. However, much work remains to be done in New York—such as further research and evaluation of known sites, uncovering currently unknown ones, and, above all, representing the great diversity of all of the communities within the greater LGBTQ community in all five boroughs of the city. The New York City LGBT Historic Sites Project, among many other efforts, will hopefully accomplish these tasks and continue to provide inspiration for other projects around the nation.

Mr. Jay Shockley is an architectural/cultural historian and historic preservationist in New York City.

Notes

1. New York City LGBT Historic Sites Project, https://www.nyclgbtsites.org/.
2. Andrew S. Dolkart, *Guide to New York City Landmarks* (Washington, DC: Preservation Press, 1992).
3. This was led primarily by Jay Shockley and Gale Harris.

4. Jay Shockley began to publically advocate for the Stonewall to be designated as an individual NYC landmark in 2009 when he was invited to speak on LGBTQ preservation by the Greenwich Village Society for Historic Preservation (GVSHP). Under Andrew Berman, GVSHP became a political force for LGBTQ preservation after the loss in 2012 of the building at 186 Spring Street, which had been home to a number of early LGBTQ rights leaders. The Stonewall, located at 51–53 Christopher Street, was designated as part of the Greenwich Village Historic District (GVHD) on 29 April 1969, just months before the uprising. It was the first LGBTQ site listed on the NRHP (28 June 1999), the first LGBTQ NHL (16 February 2000), and the first LGBTQ National Monument (24 June 2016). It was designated a NYC Landmark on 23 June 2015.

5. George Chauncey, *Gay New York: Gender, Urban Culture, and the Making of the Gay Male World, 1890–1940* (New York: Basic Books, 1994). The Wilbraham, located at 1 West Thirtieth Street, remains a residential building; Landmarks Preservation Commission (LPC), *The Wilbraham Designation Report* (New York: City of New York, 2004), researched and written by Jay Shockley.

6. This was done by Jay Shockley, Gale Harris, and Christopher D. Brazee.

7. Central Park was designated an NHL on 23 May 1963, listed on the NRHP on 15 October 1966, and designated an NYC Scenic Landmark on 16 April 1974.

8. The Historic House Trust Newsletter (Fall 2010) included contemporary re-creations of several of Alice's images by photographer Steven Rosen. The Austen House is located at 2 Hylan Boulevard, Staten Island. It was designated an NYC Landmark on 2 August 1967, added to the NRHP on 28 July 1970, and designated an NHL on 19 April 1993. The NRHP nomination was amended on 23 March 2017 to include Austen's longtime relationship with Tate. This amendment was produced by the NYC LGBT Historic Sites Project.

9. Capote wrote portions of *Breakfast at Tiffany's* (published 1958) and *In Cold Blood* (published 1966) during his time living here. The Smith House is located in the Brooklyn Heights Historic District, which was designated an NHL on 12 January 1965, designated by NYC on 23 November 1965, and added to the NRHP on 15 October 1966.

10. The term "lavender marriage" usually refers historically to a marriage between a gay man and a lesbian, often done for social and professional reasons. The Rudolph Apartments were designated a NYC Landmark on 16 November 2010.

11. The Lorde House is located in the St. Paul's Avenue-Stapleton Heights Historic District, Staten Island, designated by NYC on 22 June 2004.

12. The Archives is located at 484 Fourteenth Street in the Park Slope Historic District, Brooklyn, designated by NYC on 17 July 1973, and added to the NRHP on 21 November 1980.

13. Joan C. Berkowitz, Don L. Dinkel Jr., Andrew S. Dolkart, Gale Harris, Mary Jablonski, Ken M. Lustbader, Tom Reynolds, and Jay Shockley.

14. Ken M. Lustbader, "Landscape of Liberation: Preservation of Gay and Lesbian History in Greenwich Village," master's thesis, Columbia University, 1993.
15. The Apollo Theater is located at 253 West 125th Street. It was designated a NYC Landmark and NYC Interior Landmark on 28 June 1983, and listed on the NRHP on 17 November 1983. Organization of Lesbian + Gay Architects and Designers (OLGAD), "A Guide to Lesbian & Gay New York Historical Landmarks" (1994); LPC website, Pride Month slide show (PMSS), 2014, http://www.nyc.gov/landmarks.
16. These included the site of the first ACT UP demonstration at Trinity Church, 74 Trinity Place, listed on the NRHP and designated an NHL on 8 December 1976; Everard Baths, 28 West Twenty-Eighth Street; Julius' Bar, 159 West Tenth Street; and a headquarters of the Daughters of Bilitis.
17. Paula Martinac, *The Queerest Places: A Guide to Gay and Lesbian Historic Sites* (New York: Henry Holt & Co., 1997); and Daniel Hurewitz, *Stepping Out: Nine Tours through New York City's Gay and Lesbian Past* (New York: Henry Holt & Co., 1997).
18. This effort was led by OLGAD member Gale Harris.
19. Memorandum, 4 March 1994, NPS, Department of the Interior.
20. Stephen Morris, Chris Thomson, and Jim Gasser, members of Gay, Lesbian or Bisexual Employees (GLOBE), began meeting about the Stonewall in 1998; *Interior GLOBE News* (Spring 2000).
21. The nomination was written by Andrew S. Dolkart with Jay Shockley, using, in part, research later published in David Carter, *Stonewall: The Riots That Sparked the Gay Revolution* (New York: St. Martin's Press, 2004).
22. The Dr. Franklin E. Kameny Residence, in the Palisades neighborhood of Northwest Washington, DC, was added to the NRHP on 2 November 2011. The Gerber House, in the Old Town Triangle neighborhood of Chicago, was designated an NHL on 19 June 2015.
23. Julius at 159 West Tenth Street, New York City, was added to the NRHP on 21 April 2016.
24. The Coleman House Hotel, 645–647 Broadway, is located in the NoHo Historic District, designated by NYC on 29 June 1999. LPC, PMSS, 2014. The only other known extant New York City location associated with Whitman is his house in Wallabout, Brooklyn, where he was living when the 1855 edition of *Leaves of Grass* was published.
25. Chauncey, *Gay New York*, 34.
26. Ibid, 37.
27. Ibid, 68. Chauncey suggested that the Slide, in a row house basement, was so named to specifically announce its character, even though its "fairies" did not in fact dress as women.
28. The Slide was located at 157 Bleecker Street in the South Village Historic District (SVHD); "The Lesbian, Gay, Bisexual and Transgender (LGBT) Community's Presence in the South Village," in LPC, *South Village Historic District Designation Report* (New York: City of New York, 2013), researched and written by Jay Shockley.

29. "Black Rabbit Club is Closed Forever," *New York Herald*, 15 March 1899, 12; and "Raid on 'The Black Rabbit,'" *New York Times*, 6 October 1900, 2. The Black Rabbit was located at 183 Bleecker Street in the SVHD.

30. LPC, *East 17th Street/Irving Place Historic District Designation Report* (New York: City of New York, 1998), researched and written by Gale Harris and Jay Shockley; and LPC, PMSS, 2013.

31. According to one source, Hall (née Mary Anderson) was born in Scotland and at about age sixteen began dressing as a man, taking the name John Anderson. Anderson married young, but had a roving eye and an angry wife who disclosed Anderson's gender to the police. Fearing arrest, Anderson fled to America in 1870 and assumed the name Murray H. Hall; "Murray Hall Fooled Many Shrewd Men," *New York Times*, 19 January 1901, 3; GVHD; and LPC, PMSS, 2014.

32. Chauncey, *Gay New York*, 237, 243–44.

33. Washington Square Bookshop was located at 135 MacDougal Street, the Liberal and Heterodoxy Clubs at No. 137, and the Provincetown Playhouse at No. 139. Of these locations, only a portion of the facade of the playhouse survives.

34. GVHD; OLGAD, *A Guide*.

35. Chauncey, *Gay New York*, 242.

36. Ibid, 240. Allegedly, "the police had received many complaints about objectionable persons visiting the tea room." "Sentenced for Giving Book," *New York Times*, 3 July 1926, 13. Eve Adams' tearoom was located at 129 MacDougal Street. LPC, *129 MacDougal Street House Designation Report* (New York: City of New York, 2004), researched and written by Jay Shockley; SVHD.

37. Chauncey, *Gay New York*, 241. The Black Rabbit was located at 111 MacDougal Street in the SVHD.

38. Webster Hall is located at 119–125 East Eleventh Street. LPC, *Webster Hall and Annex Designation Report* (New York: City of New York, 2008), researched and written by Jay Shockley.

39. The Little Red School House is located at 196 Bleecker Street in the SVHD. The Irwin High School is located in the Charlton-King-Vandam Historic District, designated by NYC on 16 August 1966, and added to the NRHP on 20 July 1973.

40. Their house on Bank Street is in the GVHD; Martinac, *The Queerest Places*, 112–13.

41. Cather's apartment was at 82 Washington Place West. This building and Millay's residence are in the GVHD. OLGAD, *A Guide*.

42. "Liquor License is Revoked at Tony Pastor's Night Spot," *New York Times*, 18 March 1967, 15.

43. Audre Lorde, *Zami: A New Spelling of My Name* (Trumansburg, NY: Crossing Press, 1982). Louis' Luncheon was located at 116 MacDougal Street. Tony Pastor's Downtown was located at 130 West Third Street. Swing Rendezvous was located at 117 MacDougal Street. Ernie's Restaurant/Three Ring

Circus was located at 76 West Third Street. Mona's was located at 135 West Third Street. All of these buildings are in the SVHD.

44. FBI, "Notorious Types and Places of Amusement" (April 1956), cited by the OutHistory website, October 2013, http://www.outhistory.org. The San Remo was located at 93 MacDougal Street, and the Music Box at 121 West Third Street. Both buildings are in the SVHD.

45. The Stewart Cafeteria was located at 116 Seventh Avenue South, in the GVHD; OLGAD, *A Guide*.

46. The 181 Club was located in the former Louis N. Jaffe Art Theater, 181–189 Second Avenue; LPC, *Louis N. Jaffe Art Theater Designation Report* (New York: City of New York, 1993), researched and written by Jay Shockley; and LPC, PMSS, 2014. The building was listed on the NRHP as the Yiddish Art Theatre on 19 September 1985.

47. The apartment building at 171 West Twelfth Street, house on East Eleventh Street, and apartment building at 29 Washington Square West are located in the GVHD; OLGAD, *A Guide*.

48. Abbott and McClausland resided on Commerce Street. This building and Patchin Place are located in the GVHD; LPC, PMSS, 2013 and 2014; OLGAD, *A Guide*.

49. The Cadmus-French-Tooker residence is located in the GVHD. Playwright-screenwriter-director Arthur Laurents (1917–2011) also bought a house on St. Luke's Place around 1960 and resided there until his death in 2011, for most of the time with his partner Tom Hatcher (d. 2006). Over that long period, Laurents wrote the screenplays for *The Way We Were* (1973) and *The Turning Point* (1977) and won Tony Awards for his book for *Hallelujah, Baby!*, his direction of *La Cage aux Folles* (1984), and a revival of *Gypsy* (2009); LPC, PMSS, 2013 and 2014; OLGAD, *A Guide*.

50. These included his second novel *Giovanni's Room* (1956), *Another Country* (1962), and *Tell Me How Long the Train's Been Gone* (1968).

51. Baldwin's apartment on Horatio Street and Hansberry's residences on Bleecker Street and Waverly Place are all located in the GVHD; LPC, PMSS, 2014.

52. The Phoenix Theater was located at 181–189 Second Avenue; LPC, *Louis N. Jaffe Art Theater Designation Report*.

53. The Tempo Playhouse was located on St. Mark's Place. In 1964 this location also became a venue for the showing of early avant-garde "underground" films by the Film-Makers' Cooperative under Jonas Mekas, then film critic of the *Village Voice* and editor-publisher of *Film Culture* magazine. The work of the Kuchar Brothers was introduced here, including the premiere of *Lust for Ecstasy*. The district attorney's office raided the theater, seizing Jack Smith's allegedly "obscene" film *Flaming Creatures* and arresting Mekas, and he was again arrested for showing Genet's *Un Chant d'Amour*; LPC, *Hamilton-Holly House Designation Report* (New York: City of New York, 2004), researched and written by Jay Shockley.

54. Caffe Cino was located at 31 Cornelia Street; LPC, *Greenwich Village Historic District Extension II Designation Report* (New York: City of New York, 2010), researched and written by Olivia Klose Brazee, Marianne Percival, and Virginia Kurshan; and LPC, PMSS, 2013. It was listed on the NRHP on 9 November 2017.
55. Judson Memorial Church, 55 Washington Square South, was designated an NYC Landmark on 17 May 1966, and listed on the NRHP on 16 October 1974; OLGAD, *A Guide*.
56. Julius' Bar, which remains in operation, is located at 159 West Tenth Street, in the GVHD; LPC, PMSS, 2013 and 2014. It was listed on the NRHP on 21 April 2016.
57. OLGAD, *A Guide*.
58. The first location of the shop was at 291 Mercer Street in an apartment building. From 1973 to 2009 when it closed for good, the bookshop was located at 15 Christopher Street, in the GVHD; OLGAD, *A Guide*; and LPC, PMSS, 2014.
59. The Gay Community Center was located at 130 West Third Street, in the SVHD.
60. The Firehouse, at 99 Wooster Street, was designated as part of the SoHo–Cast Iron Historic District by NYC on 14 August 1973, while GAA still occupied the building and their lowercase lambda symbol was displayed on the facade. The district was designated an NHL on 29 June 1978, and listed on the NRHP on 29 June 1978; LPC, PMSS, 2013 and 2014.
61. SVHD.
62. The Cherry Lane Theater, at 38 Commerce Street, is in the GVHD; OLGAD, *A Guide*.
63. La MaMa is located at 74 East Fourth Street; LPC, *AschenbroedelVerein (later Gesangverein Schillerbund/now La Mama Experimental Theatre Club) Building Designation Report* (New York: City of New York, 2009), researched and written by Jay Shockley.
64. These included West Beach Bar & Grill, 388–390 West Street (ca. 1970–1980); Choo Choo's Pier, 392–393 West Street (ca. 1972); Peter Rabbit, 396–397 West Street (ca. 1972–1988); Ramrod, 394–395 West Street (ca. 1973–1980); Sneakers, 392–393 West Street (ca. late 1970s–1999); Badlands, 388–390 West Street (ca. 1983–1991); and Dugout/RockBar, 185 Christopher Street (ca. 1985–present); LPC, *Weehawken Street Historic District Designation Report* (New York: City of New York, 2006), researched and written by Jay Shockley.
65. "Shifting Shadows and the Multiple Personality of the Meatpacking District," *New York Times*, 5 February 1995. The earliest gay club here was the Zoo, 421–425 West Thirteenth Street, in 1970. This was followed by Cycle/Den/Zodiac/O.K. Corral/Mineshaft, 835 Washington Street (1970–1985); Triangle/Barn/Attic/Sewer/J's Hangout/Hellfire, 669–685 Hudson Street (1971–2002); Clit Club/Mother/Jackie 60, 859–877 Washington Street (1990s); Lure, 405–409 West Thirteenth Street (1995–2003); and Locker Room/Mike's Bar, 400

West Fourteenth Street (1990–1993); LPC, *Gansevoort Market Historic District Designation Report* (New York: City of New York, 2003), researched and written by Jay Shockley. The Gansevoort Market Historic District (GMHD) was listed on the NRHP on 30 May 2007.

66. It was located at 69 Gansevoort Street, in the GMHD.

67. The Pyramid Club is located at 101 Avenue A, and the Saint was located at 105 Second Avenue; LPC, *East Village/ Lower East Side Historic District Designation Report* (New York: City of New York, 2012), researched and written by Christopher D. Brazee.

68. The Cunningham Dance Studio was located at 55 Bethune Street; LPC, *Bell Telephone Laboratories Complex Designation Report* (New York: City of New York, 2011), researched and written by Jay Shockley. Bell Telephone Laboratories was listed on the NRHP on 15 May 1975. It was listed again as Westbeth on 8 December 2009.

69. The James Beard Foundation, at 167 West Twelfth Street, is in the GVHD; OLGAD, *A Guide*.

70. The former Jaffe Art Theater is located at 181–189 Second Avenue; LPC, *Louis N. Jaffe Art Theater Designation Report*.

71. Haring's and Rudnick's apartments were located in the SVHD.

72. The synagogue was located at 57 Bethune Street; LPC, *Bell Telephone Laboratories Complex*; and LPC, PMSS, 2014.

73. See Tara Burk, "LGBTQ Art and Artists," in *Communities and Place: A Thematic Approach to the Histories of LGBTQ Communities in the United States*, ed. Katherine Crawford-Lackey and Megan E. Springate (New York: Berghahn Books, forthcoming).

74. The Center is located at 208 West Thirteenth Street, in the GVHD; LPC, PMSS, 2014.

75. The Rectory of St. Veronica's Roman Catholic Church was located at 657 Washington Street; LPC, *Greenwich Village Historic District Extension Designation Report* (New York: City of New York, 2006), researched and written by Jay Shockley. The Anti-Violence Project and Empire State Pride Agenda were located at 647 Hudson Street, in the GMHD.

76. Portofino was located at 206 Thompson Street, in the SVHD.

Bibliography

Brazee, Christopher D. *East Village / Lower East Side Historic District Designation Report*. New York: New York City Landmarks Preservation Commission, 2012.

Brazee, Olivia Klose, Marianne Percival, and Virginia Kurshan. *Greenwich Village Historic District Extension II Designation Report*. New York: New York City Landmarks Preservation Commission, 2010.

Burk, Tara. "LGBTQ Art and Artists." In *Communities and Place: A Thematic Approach to the Histories of LGBTQ Communities in the United States*, edited by Katherine Crawford-Lackey and Megan E. Springate. New York: Berghahn Books, forthcoming.

Carter, David. *Stonewall: The Riots that Sparked the Gay Revolution*. New York: St. Martin's Press, 2004.

Chauncey, George. *Gay New York: Gender, Urban Culture, and the Making of the Gay Male World, 1890–1940*. New York: Basic Books, 1994.

Department of the Interior Gay, Lesbian, or Bisexual Employees (GLOBE). *Interior GLOBE News* (Spring 2000).

Dolkart, Andrew S. *Guide to New York City Landmarks*. Washington, DC: Preservation Press, 1992.

Harris, Gale, and Jay Shockley. *East 17th Street / Irving Place Historic District Designation Report*. New York: New York City Landmarks Preservation Commission, 1998.

Historic House Trust. *Historic House Trust Newsletter* (Fall 2010).

Hurewitz, Daniel. *Stepping Out: Nine Tours through New York City's Gay and Lesbian Past*. New York: Henry Holt & Co., 1997.

Lorde, Audre. *Zami: A New Spelling of My Name*. Trumansburg, NY: Crossing Press, 1982.

Lustbader, Ken M. *Landscapes of Liberation: Preservation of Gay and Lesbian History in Greenwich Village*. Master's thesis, Columbia University, 1993.

Martinac, Paula. *The Queerest Places: A Guide to Gay and Lesbian Historic Sites*. New York: Henry Holt & Co., 1997.

New York City Landmarks Preservation Commission. Pride Month Slide Show, 2013.

———. Pride Month Slide Show, 2014. http://www.nyc.gov/landmarks.

New York Herald. "Black Rabbit Club Is Closed Forever." *New York Herald*, 15 March 1899.

New York Times. "Murray Hall Fooled Many Shrewd Men." *New York Times*, 19 January 1901.

———. "Liquor License is Revoked at Tony Pastor's Night Spot." *New York Times*, 18 March 1967.

———. "Raid on 'The Black Rabbit.'" *New York Times*, 6 October 1900.

———. "Sentenced for Giving Book." *New York Times*, 3 July 1926.

———. "Shifting Shadows and the Multiple Personality of the Meatpacking District." *New York Times*, 5 February 1995.

Organization of Lesbian + Gay Architects and Designers (OLGAD). "A Guide to Lesbian & Gay New York Historical Landmarks." New York: OLGAD, 1994.

Shockley, Jay. *129 MacDougal Street House Designation Report*. New York: New York City Landmarks Preservation Commission, 2004.

———. *Aschenbroedel Verein (later Gesangverein Schillerbund / now La Mama Experimental Theatre Club) Building Designation Report*. New York: New York City Landmarks Preservation Commission, 2009.

———. *Bell Telephone Laboratories Complex Designation Report*. New York: New York City Landmarks Preservation Commission, 2011.

———. *Gansevoort Market Historic District Designation Report*. New York: New York City Landmarks Preservation Commission, 2003.

———. *Greenwich Village Historic District Extension Designation Report*. New York: New York City Landmarks Preservation Commission, 2006.

———. *Hamilton-Holly House Designation Report*. New York: New York City Landmarks Preservation Commission, 2004.

———. "The Lesbian, Gay, Bisexual and Transgender (LGBT) Community's Presence in the South Village." *South Village Historic District Designation Report*. New York: New York City Landmarks Preservation Commission, 2013.

———. *Louis N. Jaffe Art Theater Designation Report*. New York: New York City Landmarks Preservation Commission, 1993.

———. *Webster Hall and Annex Designation Report*. New York: New York City Landmarks Preservation Commission, 2008.

———. *Weehawken Street Historic District Designation Report*. New York: New York City Landmarks Preservation Commission, 2006.

———. *The Wilbraham Designation Report*. New York: New York City Landmarks Preservation Commission, 2004.

CHAPTER 9

Tradition, Community, and Grungy Secret-ness

What Preservationists Can Learn from the Story of Phase One

Ty Ginter

> Every day I saw others like me in this city—enough of us to populate our own town. But we only acknowledged each other with a furtive glance, fearful of calling attention to ourselves. . . . We didn't seem to have any of our own places to gather in community, to immerse ourselves in our own ways and our own languages.
> —Leslie Feinberg, *Stone Butch Blues*

Introduction

Although this quote from Feinberg's *Stone Butch Blues* arguably describes a narrator on the transgender spectrum discussing the lack of spaces for trans people in New York City during the 1980s[1] it very well could be used to describe how members of the lesbian community in Washington, DC, have felt since the closing of the iconic lesbian bar Phase One.[2] Washington's LGBTQ community is one heavily divided along racial, gender, and socioeconomic lines, highlighting generations of segregation, pay inequity, and discrimination accrued along the intersectional lines of those who make it up. Often overlooked for cities like San Francisco and New York City, the District of Columbia's unique position as the nation's capital provides it a history filled with protest and activism for LGBTQ rights.

In and among that history was Phase One, the longest running LGBTQ bar in Washington, DC, and the longest continually operating lesbian bar in the United States until it closed in February of 2016.[3] Sometimes written "Phase 1" and colloquially known as "The Phase" or simply "Phase," the bar was a staple of the lesbian community in Washington, DC, since it opened in the early 1970s. Like many LGBTQ spaces, its history and significance were never formally documented or written down; once the business was gone and the building sold to a developer, all that was left of the bar were stories (figure 9.1). In this chapter, I explore the preservation of a place based not just on the written record, but through the memories and remembered geographies of those who were there through oral history. I also explore the importance of telling location-based history *and* neighborhood context in the recording of the complete story of LGBTQ locations so that preservationists might move forward with a better understanding of how to preserve LGBTQ history.[4]

The history in this chapter was recorded primarily through oral histories; all names provided in the text are aliases. This chapter was

Figure 9.1. The historic wooden facade of Phase One in March 2018, painted white, black, and red by the new tenant of 525 Eighth Street SE. The business did not last; shortly after this photograph was taken, the facade and door were removed and replaced with a glass and steel storefront, similar to other buildings along Eighth Street. Photo by Ty Ginter.

initially written for my thesis, D.C. Dykaries, which has since evolved into a larger project focused on recording the history of DC lesbian/Sapphic/women's spaces.[5] As the thesis and D.C. Dykaries are ongoing, more information about the Phase and its history will come to light in the future, and thus this should not be considered a complete history of Phase One—just as the history of any space, place, or community should not be considered completely written.

History

In the 1960s, the Eastern Market neighborhood of Washington, DC, was just one area of DC that was the site of major changes. In 1962, the neighborhood—which had already seen many of its middle-class residents move to the suburbs after World War II—was bisected by the Southeast Freeway. At the end of the decade, it was heavily looted after the 1968 riots that followed the assassination of Dr. Martin Luther King Jr. Many of the businesses remained closed, and buildings boarded up, for years afterwards.[6]

It was in this run-down, boarded-up neighborhood that Allen Carroll and Chris Jansen opened Phase One on 29 February 1970.[7] Located at 525 Eighth Street SE just north of the Marine Barracks, the Phase was one of many other gay and lesbian bars that moved into the area: Johnnie's, a gay bar, opened at 500 Eighth Street SE in 1949; Plus One, the first gay bar in DC to offer same-sex dancing, opened at 529 Eighth Street SE in 1968; Jo-Anna's, another lesbian bar, also moved in up the street in 1968 at 430 Eighth Street SE.[8] So many establishments that catered to a gay and lesbian clientele opened on Eighth Street in the 1970s and 1980s that *Polk's Washington*, a city directory for the District, dubbed the street "Gay Way" (figure 9.2).[9] The building Phase One opened in was owned by Delores Plant, described as a straight woman who lived in one of the two apartments over the ground-floor bar.[10]

Soon after its opening, ads for the bar began appearing in the *Gay Blade*, the Washington, DC, gay newspaper, advertising the new bar as "for women." By 1972 Phase was being regularly advertised as a distributor for the *Blade*, and in 1975 Phase was being used as a way-finder landmark for the newly opened women's bookstore in DC's Southeast, Lammas. It was through these ads and word of mouth that seventeen-year-old Dorothy found herself stepping into the "rough neighborhood" that was Eighth Street SE to go to Phase One.[11] "You couldn't really find it," she recalled. The bar's nondescript front made it blend in along a

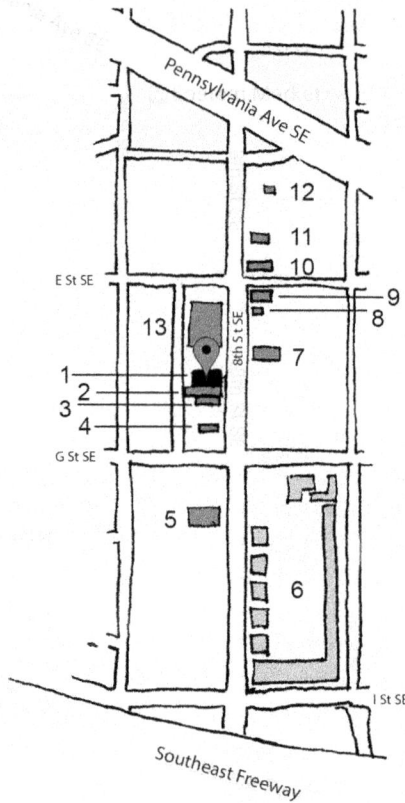

Figure 9.2. Eighth Street SE was considered "Gay Way" because of the over twenty LGBTQ establishments that were located on the street from the late 1960s to 2017. Notable Eighth Street "Gay Way" locations: (1) Phase One, (6) Marine Barracks (non LGBTQ-establishment), (9) Johnnie's. Image by Ty Ginter. Addresses, dates, and gender assignation provided by Rainbow History Project (M = men; W = women).

Key:
(1) 525 Eighth Street SE: Phase One (W; 1970–2016)
(2) 527 Eighth Street SE: Pub 9 (M; 1970–1972)
(3) 529 Eighth Street SE: Plus One (M; 1968–1973)
(4) 539 Eighth Street SE: (a) Wild Oates (MW; 1991–1993); (b) Knickerbocker (M; 1984–?)
(5) 713 Eighth Street SE: Sheridan's Dance Hall and Saloon (MW; 1999–?)
(6) Marine Barracks (non-LGBTQ)
(7) 516 Eighth Street SE: Hill Haven (W; 1989–1993)
(8) 506 Eighth Street SE: (a) Capitol Hill Town Tavern Restaurant (MW; 1971–1978); (b) Michelangelo's Supper Club (MW; 1973?–?); (c) Dot's Town House Restaurant (MW; 1978–?)
(9) 500 Eighth Street SE: (a) Club Madame (W; 1974–1978); (b) Johnnie's (M; 1949–1974); (c) Banana Café (MW; 1996–2017); (d) Bachelor's Mill (M; 1978–1984)
(10) 430 Eighth Street SE: (a) Jo-Anna's (W; 1968–1972, 1973 –1978); (b) Round Up (W; 1978–1979); (c) Horseshoe Saloon (M; 1975?–?)
(11) 424 Eighth Street SE: Ellington's
(12) 406 Eighth Street SE: Millie's (M; 1970–?)
(13) 507–513 Eighth Street: Guild Press (MW; 1965–1974)

street of boarded-up windows and liquor stores; there was no sign, and "back in those days you just found the address and went in."[12]

For Dorothy, like many of the lesbians who came through front door, the Phase was home. "As a young lesbian [in the 1970s] you walked in and you saw your type. There weren't straight people there. There might have been one or two men, definitely gay men, but you could identify this was my tribe. You found a home."[13] In a time where it was legal to be fired for being gay and being gay in and of itself was a felony under DC's sodomy laws, finding a bar like Phase One was important.[14] "We couldn't be ourselves anywhere else. Those kinds of spaces were so precious."[15]

Those precious spaces came with a cost. Because of their location near the Marine Barracks, as well as the marginal nature of the neighborhood, the women who attended Phase took a risk every time they went there. "I was laser focused [in that neighborhood]," J.J. recalled. "You ran to get in the door. The neighborhood wasn't safe [and] there was lots of gay bashing . . . there were always guys out on the street and they would holler stuff and it wasn't pleasant. You would always hear stories of people getting harassed. We were scared and wanted to get inside."[16] In May of 1978, there were a string of assaults, robberies, and rapes outside Phase One, and two women were beaten unconscious outside The Other Side, another lesbian bar also in Southeast DC that same year.[17] Dorothy recalled getting attacked outside of Phase when she had stepped out to smoke a cigarette, and Sam said they were often worried about getting mugged.[18] The rewards, though, of being in a woman-only, lesbian-dominated space were worth it for the many patrons who went to Phase during the 1970s, '80s, and '90s. "I never felt unsafe in the bar itself [but] leaving the bar I *always* felt unsafe. *Always.* . . . You tried to go out with someone else [when you left]. I escorted many a woman to her car because we just watched out for each other."[19]

Phase was not, however, an early haven for every lesbian in Washington, DC In July of 1979, a discrimination complaint was filed against Phase One by the DC Office of Human Rights after "community reports" suggested that "five establishments [including Phase One] are treating Black residents negatively and different from White Residents when they seek admission." These different practices including "carding," instituting dress codes that excluded popular African American attire and those in drag, and lying about crowd capacity regulations as a means of keeping African Americans and transsexuals out of the bars.[20] As a result, in 1984 Black and white activists successfully lobbied the DC Council to pass a bill that allowed the liquor licenses to be pulled and fines to be levied against bars that were found to be using "proof-of-age" carding techniques to discriminate against African American patrons.[21] Despite the new law, the damage was done; LGBTQ African Americans were less inclined to visit Phase One and many other predominantly white gay establishments; instead, they created and patronized their own bars, clubs, restaurants, and private social clubs across the city, such as Nob Hill, as an alternative to the hostile, racist environment they found elsewhere.[22]

Through the years, gay and lesbian bars opened and closed around the city, but Phase stayed a constant. Jo-Anna's, with its crowd of "older, bulldagger dykes," closed in 1972, then reopened in 1973.[23] It closed for the final time five years later in 1978.[24] That same year, on the heels of the closing of Jo-Anna's, Allen Carroll opened a second lesbian bar, the Other Side, at 1345 Half Street SE (now underneath Nationals Park baseball stadium).[25] It had a bigger dance floor than the Phase, and Carroll used it as "a place to hold his drag shows."[26] At the time, young lesbians preferred the Other Side, Tracks, and the Hung Jury (both of which opened in 1984) to Phase. While Phase was all women, all the time, the Other Side, Tracks, and the Hung Jury had mixed gender clientele or were straight bars during the day.[27] While these locations often only had specified "ladies nights," they made up for it with larger large dance floors, better music to dance to, and a younger, more diverse crowd. By the 1980s, reported J.J., "the Phase was seen as more for older women. Where the hot girls were at—you know—they were at Hung Jury, so we would go to Hung Jury."[28]

The fact that most young lesbians went to Tracks, the Other Side, or the Hung Jury didn't stop J.J. from going to Phase in 1983 when her lesbian rugby team, the Washington Furies, wanted to go there for drinks after practice. "We'd go down there . . . and just dance and laugh. The fifty-somethings that would sit at the bar . . . loved to watch us because we were funny. I felt like there were two age groups that hung out there. The fifty-ish age group and [my group] the twenty-five-somethings."[29] Despite the other bars opening and closing all around it, Phase One stayed open. Many people, including Anna and Dorothy, club hopped in Southeast DC. They would start the night at Phase, then move around to the Hung Jury, the Other Side, Tracks, and other bars in the area for dancing and "better music."[30] Sometimes, Anna said, they would catch a nightcap at Phase before heading home. "We always knew we were going to end up at Phase."[31]

In the 1990s, change started on Eighth Street SE. "Families were returning to Capitol Hill," moving back because commuting into the city had lost its appeal. The new residents looked for ways to brighten up their new neighborhoods.[32] Margot Kelly, a local real estate owner and resident, created the Barracks Row Business Alliance (BBA). She collected dues from contributing businesses "to support street cleaning and fancified tree boxes," while organizations such as Community Action Group worked to address the area's homeless population.[33] With Kelly spearheading the effort, the BBA used guidelines laid out by the National Trust for Historic Preservation's Main Street Program to attempt to beautify the street and make it more promising to future shop owners and other "respectable" retail establishments.[34] Gradually, as the perceived safety of the street increased, retail shops moved in and the character of the street began to improve. In 1998, the Shakespeare Theater renovated the abandoned Odd Fellows Hall three buildings north of Phase, and the Barracks Row Main Street Program was launched.[35] By 2003, an $8.5-million-dollar construction project had widened sidewalks, put in new gutters and curbs, replaced trees, installed lighting, and made the entire street more pedestrian friendly.[36] In 2005, the Barracks Row Main Street program was awarded the National Trust for Historic Preservation's Great American Main Street Award for the successful restoration of more than fifty historic facades, the creation of two hundred new jobs, and the attraction of forty new businesses to Eighth Street SE.[37]

This gentrifying neighborhood was the one that Phoebe and C.T. knew when they went to Phase in the early to mid-2000s. Gone were the boarded-up windows, liquor stores, sign shops, and cheap Chinese restaurants that filled the street in the 1970s, '80s, and early '90s. Marines still roamed Eighth Street SE, but fewer of them were "looking to punch out a dyke" than had been just a decade or two earlier.[38] However, there still were aspects of the club that spoke to its age and its history on Eighth Street SE. "At the time [being vetted at the door] felt like a vestige of the past that didn't necessarily feel appropriate anymore," Phoebe said, and C.T. recalled that even once the neighborhood began to gentrify that patrons were still told to "make sure you're leaving together." C.T. mused, "I'm not sure how much of that was Southeast, how much of that was a notion of a white clientele in a non-white neighborhood, [or] how much of it because it was a women-focused [bar] and that is a script you hear a lot of women being told."[39]

"In terms of outings, [Phase] was probably a second or third choice," C.T. said, a sentiment echoed by Phoebe.[40] The two of them would go to the bar at the prompting of friends, but would not go alone—Phoebe would rather have gone to the bars and clubs in Baltimore, if she went out at all, and C.T. preferred to go to the Hung Jury, Apex, and Chaos for their larger dance floors, more racially diverse crowds, and better dance music (in this case, "better music" meant electronic dance music and not the usual fare of Top 40 Hits).[41]

"If we were going to Phase it was for a specific lesbian [or] women's event," said C.T. "Not necessarily drag shows at the time . . . but Phase-Fest." PhaseFest, now PhazeFest, was the creation of Archer Lombardi, Mara Levi, and Riot Grrrl Ink; it started in 2006 as "a platform and safe space for queer rockers," continuing on the tradition of Phase One being a space for lesbian artists to perform.[42] In the 1980s, the Phase hosted Hippocampe and Sweetwater; in August 2007, when PhaseFest started, it welcomed acts like God-des and She, Sick of Sarah, Kaki King, and Hunter Valentine.[43] The music festival, held every year at the end of September at the Phase, continued on at the 9:30 Club after the bar closed.[44]

Around the early 2000s, Phase One became home to its own drag king troupe. Drag kings, also known as male impersonators, are the flip side of drag queens. Kings are usually female-bodied individuals who dress, present, and perform as masculine characters. While drag kings appeared at Phase as early as 1985, it was in 2005 that the DC Kings, a troupe of drag kings in the District, started to regularly perform at Phase One.[45] After another venue, Club Chaos, closed in 2008, the DC Kings moved to performing at Phase One full time.[46] Copeland was one of the drag kings that performed at Phase. "It was the very first stage I had ever performed on in drag. [My drag persona] was born in Phase."[47] Raphael, another DC King and employee at Phase, recalled the basement as "disgusting."[48] The basement, which was off-limits to everyone except employees and performers, was used as a dressing room for shows. It was full of forty-five years of accumulated detritus and flooded often. As a result, it had a permanent musty, moldy odor which rose up into the bar on hot summer days.[49] There was also, according to Raphael, "a blow up sex doll hanging from the ceiling by its neck."[50]

By 2012, when Raphael and Wells, another drag king from DC, started going to Phase, the neighborhood had "gentrified." It was a rich, white neighborhood, where he felt safe going to shows at the Phase. Both Raphael and Wells had mixed feelings about going to Phase "knowing the history of the bar, knowing that it was problematic for trans people and folxs of color, Black folxs."[51] However, there was nowhere else to go for lesbians in the city; at this point, Phase One was the only lesbian bar remaining in the District. "I had friends who wouldn't go in there because there weren't any Black girls in there. . . . I had to step in there consciously [knowing] it was a playground for other [white] people."[52]

While attending Phase, Raphael used his drag king persona as an avenue to explore his gender identity; he came out as transgender. He said that butch lesbians would pick on the trans men like himself, and he was once asked, "Why are you signing away your womanhood?" in reference to his transition.[53] Other trans men, such as Cole, did not feel safe at Phase; Cole was physically assaulted inside the bar and then told to leave because he presented as a man.[54] Raphael added in his interview that he saw transgender women who identified as lesbians openly mocked inside the bar, and asserted that "trans women didn't feel safe [at Phase]."[55]

The Phase closed the first time in January 2015: seven days after New Year's it abruptly shut its doors and announced it would be "closed temporarily" for renovations.[56] To compound the sudden closing, Carroll fired all of the staff, including long-term manager Archer Lombardi. Lombardi had worked for Carroll at Phase One and Phase One Dupont, which Carroll had opened in Dupont Circle in February 2012, for over ten years, and was instrumental in bringing the DC Kings and PhazeFest to the bar; it was the hope of many patrons that Carroll would sell the bar to Lombardi or another lesbian or woman when the time came.[57] Many in the lesbian community in DC took the sudden closure and firing of all the staff as a slight. "The stories I read both online, from the Facebook page, from the *Blade*, for the women who were working there when it went down, I think that was pretty messed up. That's six to ten dykes that don't have jobs, and I think he was kind of squirrely about what he was going to do."[58]

When the bar reopened in March, it opened on a limited Thursday through Saturday night schedule, whereas before it had been open most days and nights of the week.[59] The DC Kings, at that point the "longest, continuously operating Drag King troupe in the world," resumed some performances at the bar, but ultimately stopped performing when founder Kendra "Ken Vegas" Kuliga retired from drag and closed the troupe. The final DC King show was across town at the Bier Baron Tavern in Dupont, not at the Phase; this shift in location indicates that despite the fact the Phase was the home of DC Kings, toward the end of its life the Kings could no longer rely on it as a venue and had to go elsewhere for their final performance.[60]

Phase closed for the second and last time shortly thereafter, in February 2016. Much like the first time, it was abruptly announced on Facebook that Phase would be closed "until further notice."[61] Lombardi and Senait, another long-term staff member at Phase, said that business was the biggest reason Carroll closed the bar. Business "[hadn't] been that great."[62] Even with theme nights and parties, fewer people came to Phase, and after it closed the first time, business got even slower. While Carroll owned the building mortgage-free, he still had to pay property taxes: he paid $4,800 in taxes in 2006, approximately $9,600 in 2010, $23,000 in 2011, and $31,836 in 2014.[63]

The exponential rise in taxes, driven by the neighborhood gentrifying around it, coupled with the decreased business, meant that it was simply not financially feasible for the Phase to continue to stay open. Carroll denied the allegations that the taxes were the reasons for the bar closing, but said that lesbians simply were not going out as much.[64] Whether the reasons were related to assimilation,[65] the rise of social media, or the fact women are paid less than men (and therefore spend less money going out) are anybody's guess; most of the community I interviewed speculates a combination of all three.[66] Much of the Baby Boomer population was simply aging out of going to the Phase, instead preferring house parties or staying at home with partners instead of going to the bars.[67] By June 2016, it was announced that Phase had officially closed for good, and in March of 2017 Carroll sold the bar and the building for $3.3 million.[68]

The loss was felt throughout the community, especially among the older generation of lesbians. "For my generation [the closing of Phase] was very sad," J.J. said. "It felt like the end of an era."[69] The fact that the bar had been around for forty-five years gave it "a sense of tradition [and] . . . security" that other bars did not have.[70] Many were sorry to see it go because it felt like the last remaining vestiges of a disappearing community.[71] Despite being more assimilated into mainstream culture, Dorothy believes very much that lesbian space is still needed. "Yes, I can go out [anywhere and] have a drink, but it's not the same thing . . . . It's not our own space where it's going to be all my like kind. [Purely lesbian space] simply doesn't exist anymore."[72] Wells said that the closing was a "rude awakening" for the white lesbian community, but said "older [people of color] has no illusions of the place being special."[73] Lesbians of color, they explained, were used to their spaces disappearing from the adverse effects of gentrification, assimilation, and technology. "People realized they had taken it for granted, said Wells."[74] Barracks Row Main Street was "sorry to see Phase go" but said that "Allen just got tired" after forty-five years of owning the business and decided to close it rather than pass it on to another owner.[75]

Spatial Analysis

Neighborhood: Transportation

Although Phase was only 0.2 miles (0.03km) from the Eastern Market Metro station, most of the patrons who attended Phase over the years elected to drive instead of take public transportation.[76] The Eastern Market Metro station opened in 1977, but most patrons came into the city from Virginia or Maryland to go to Phase, areas that were not generally Metro accessible (Metro did not extend to Huntington, Virginia, until 1983; Vienna, Virginia, until 1986; Greenbelt, Maryland, until 1993, and Franconia-Springfield, Virginia, until 1997).[77] After Metro did expand, it was dangerous (or perceived to be dangerous) to walk down Eighth Street SE before the year 2000. People who went to Phase therefore mostly drove, because driving was (or was perceived to be) the only, or only safe, option.

Most patrons would approach the bar from Pennsylvania Avenue, turn onto Eighth Street SE, and attempt to park in front of the Phase on Eighth. If parking directly in front of the bar was unavailable, patrons would park on G and I streets, or further down on Eighth in front of the Marine Barracks.[78] "You parked on the street and hoped you got in safe," recalled Dorothy. As the neighborhood gentrified, parking went from parallel to diagonal, and as the neighborhood nightlife grew, parking on the street became "really difficult."[79] Phoebe said that in the mid- to late 2000s, she and her friends would sometimes park on Pennsylvania Avenue and get dinner before going to Phase, or attend an afternoon game at the new Nationals Stadium before getting dinner and then going to the bar.[80]

Neighborhood: Eighth Street SE as "Gay Way"

Eighth Street SE was a vibrant neighborhood for gay and lesbian business in the latter half of the twentieth century. Twelve buildings between Pennsylvania Avenue and the Southeast Freeway housed twenty gay and lesbian bars over the course of approximately fifty years (figure 9.2). Most of the establishments lasted only a few years; some, like Phase One and Johnnie's, lasted longer.[81] The Marine Barracks, also located in this neighborhood, posed problems for many of these establishments. Marines often hassled, harassed, and occasionally assaulted their patrons. When the street gentrified in the early 2000s, most of the gay bars in the neighborhood were driven out. Only the LGBTQ eateries like Banana Café and Phase survived until the Phase closed in 2016 and the Banana Café closed in December 2017. The Marine Barracks remains open and active.

Bar: Approach

Most of Eighth Street SE is comprised of row buildings, between one to three stories tall, with brick facades. The lots are more often longer than they are wide, resulting in clusters of ten to twenty relatively flat, brick storefronts per block. The storefronts form a hard edge along the sidewalk. This repetitious patterning, combined with the Phase's unassuming and relatively unadorned storefront and complete lack of windows, made it inconspicuous. "You couldn't really find it," Dorothy recalled, and patrons often walked right past it without seeing it.[82] "Even as someone who knew where I was going, it was so easy to miss," said Phoebe.[83] Later, signs of various shapes and lettering were added, but the bar was still quite easy to overshoot if one was not paying attention. Phoebe believed that this was "absolutely intentional" because "[Phase] was a place you didn't necessarily want people to [know] you were going .... The whole point was not to have a street presence. It was like going into a speakeasy."[84]

Bar: Clientele

As previously discussed, many people of color and transgender individuals did not feel welcome at Phase. They were not alone: by the time Phase One closed, it had a storied reputation of being a women's only bar that did not allow men. Men were "not welcome," J.J. recalled emphatically.[85] They mostly stayed away, but every once in a while one would make it through the doors. The men who came into the bar often fell into two categories: men who were with women and had been vetted as trustworthy (usually gay men), or men who were looking for trouble.[86] Men who came in to hit on or harass the lesbian clientele were swiftly shown the door by the patrons and staff alike. "We protected our space," said J.J.[87]

Heterosexual couples, or those who appeared to be heterosexual, were also not welcome. Anna recalled a time she and her friend, who was a butch lesbian and looked very masculine, sat at the bar and were not served because the bartender believed them to be a heterosexual couple. It was only when the butch lesbian spoke and the bartender heard her feminine voice that they got service, reported Anna; "She came right over and served us."[88]

This emphasis on not welcoming men or heterosexual couples often made transgender individuals and those that dated them uncomfortable. Trans men like Raphael and Cole were often harassed or physically assaulted for presenting as male in accordance with their gender identity, even if they had previously attended the spaces or been active in the community while identifying as female. Iona, a queer woman who identified as a lesbian before shifting identities to pansexual/bisexual, said that at Phase she didn't feel "super-duper comfortable."[89] In many lesbian bars or "ladies nights," not just at Phase, she and her partner, a trans man, were often met with harsh or unwelcoming attitudes from lesbians and other LGBTQ individuals who believed them to be a straight and cisgender couple invading an LGBTQ space. She went on to say that "lesbian bars are [often] lesbian specific, so if you're a queer women but you're not a lesbian you're not always going to feel welcome in those kinds of spaces. Those are definitely some of the not so great things [about Phase] . . . it wasn't always open to people who were the B and the T [in LGBTQ]."[90]

Bar: Entrance

"When you walked into Phase it felt like you were going into a back-room club," said Sam, a sentiment echoed by every other interviewee in some form or another.[91] Patrons had to pass through a small door with a diamond-shaped window and get vetted by a bouncer before being allowed into the inner sanctum that was the bar itself. Its "speakeasy feel" and dilapidated, dingy dive-bar interior gave it a sort of "grunge-y secret-ness" not found in other lesbian or women's bars in the city.[92] Viewing straight into the bar was impossible because of a movable partition wall; this wall not only blocked the line of site from the street into the bar, but also funneled patrons from the doorway toward the bouncer for vetting. In describing it, Phoebe said, "There is not supposed to be any porosity between [the inside of the bar] and the street."[93] That wall, however, was not always there; Dorothy recalls when she first started going to Phase in 1975, the partition did not exist. It was most likely put up sometime in the late 1970s.[94]

Bar: Layout

The layout of Phase One changed very little in the forty-five years it was open (figure 9.3). It was small, barely over 1,900 sq. ft. (176.5 m²) total. J.J. estimated that excluding the kitchen and bar area, the pub-

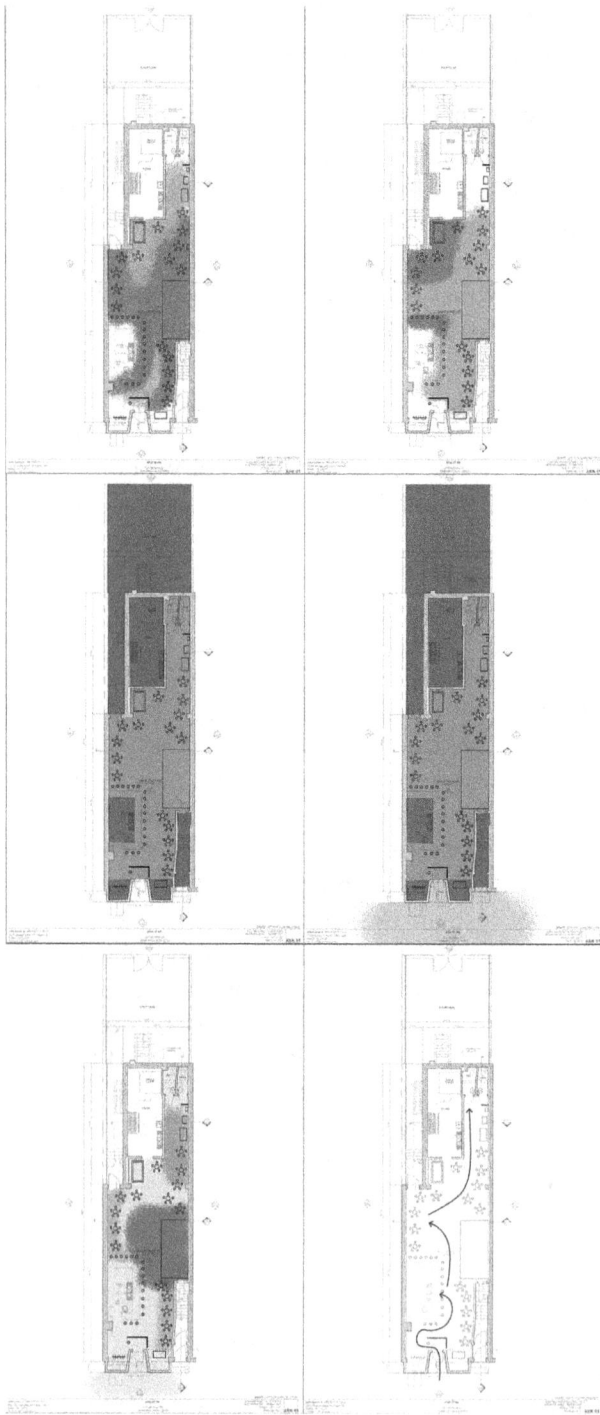

Figure 9.3. Phase One interior use, 1990s/early 2000s. These Phase One diagrams and plans were compiled from memory maps drawn by patrons, staff, and others who attended Phase One, showing their recollections of 1990s/early 2000s furniture placement and use. Compilation image by Ty Ginter. The architectural drawing on which these diagrams were created was authored by John Linan Jr. and provided by Christopher Martin of the Martin Development Company.

Key: *Top left:* gathering space (dark gray = high concentration of people); *top right:* old vs. young gathering space (dark gray = older patron gathering location, light gray = young patron gathering location, white = little/no patron gathering); *middle left:* public vs. private space pre-gentrification (dark gray = most private, indicating staff-only space or space inaccessible by patrons); *middle right:* public vs. private space post-gentrification (dark gray = most private, indicating staff-only space or space inaccessible by patrons); *bottom left:* popular zones in Phase One including the dance floor (dark gray), "wallflower" zone, and "canoodling" hallway (light gray); *bottom right:* patron circulation through the bar.

licly occupiable footprint was closer to 1,200 sq. ft. (111.5 m²).[95] As you walked in, the large wooden bar dominated the left-hand wall; the ten-by-ten-foot raised dance floor located along the right wall, diagonally opposite the bar, never changed in size throughout the bar's life.[96] In the 1970s, there was a "cowboy"-like fence around the dance floor to separate it from the rest of the bar, and large, four-person tables crowded the walkways.[97] In the 1980s, the fence came down and the tables were replaced with smaller cocktail tables that could seat more people.[98] By 2000, many of the cocktail tables and chairs had been replaced with high tops, banquet seating, and booths (figure 3).[99] This layout remained until the bar closed until 2016. The ubiquitous single pool table was a staple of the Phase throughout its life. Although it moved around a bit, it always stayed generally in the southwest corner of the bar, near the entrance to the kitchen and the exit to the courtyard. The table was replaced at least once, and was "smaller than average" in the 1980s.[100] The corner with the pool table was where "butch dykes," older lesbians, and the "tough" crowd gathered; J.J. recalled that to get to the bathrooms one had to pass the table and "get stared down" by the pool players and their girlfriends.[101]

Bar: Circulation, Gathering Spaces, and Separation of Space

The words most often used by interviewees to describe Phase One were "dark," "small," and some variation of "dingy." Many patrons, when entering Phase One for the first time, were struck by how small it was.[102] Raphael, having frequented Phase Dupont before he visited the original Phase in 2012, expected the bar to be much larger because of the stories he had heard and its historic place in the community.[103] When compared to other spaces in the city, including the Hung Jury and Apex/Phase Dupont, Phase was the size of a postage stamp; these other spaces were large and meant for attracting large crowds of people for dancing.[104] At Phase, patrons exchanged the "anonymity" of these larger spaces for the comfort and community that the bar brought.[105] For J.J., that small footprint detracted from the overall experience of going to the bar. "I have mild claustrophobia . . . and I did not feel comfortable [in Phase] for that reason . . . it would get *so crowded* [on the weekends]!" J.J. purposefully avoided Phase when it was crowded and would instead go to larger venues, like Tracks or the Hung Jury.

Being small, the bar filled up quickly, which made circulating, dancing, and even ordering a drink at the bar difficult. C.T. remembered that walking between the bar and the tables that lined the wall, when both the tables and bar were filled, felt like running a gauntlet.[106] The main places for gathering were the bar, the dance floor, and the tables. On crowded nights, the bar itself was often packed with people two or three deep trying to get drinks.[107] There were so few tables that they were usually full by the time J.J. and her friends got there.[108] Patrons on the dance floor often spilled out into the tabled areas, meaning there was no true "dance" area versus a true "hangout" area.[109] Wallflowers lurked near the tables by the bar or on the wall opposite the dance floor, and lovers canoodled in the hallway to the bathroom (figure 9.4).[110] After the neighborhood became safer and smoking was banned indoors, the street outside of the bar became a secondary hangout, away from the crowds and the noise of inside (figures 9.3 and 9.4).[111] Despite the fact the bar had access to a courtyard/patio, it was rarely used by patrons.

The patrons of Phase often self-arranged by age, much as they arranged themselves by different activities. "There was always this one [older lesbian] who always sat at the bar," Ivy recalled.[112] Throughout the life of Phase, older lesbians generally sat at the bar, usually on the corner overlooking the dance floor, or at the tables by the pool table, while younger lesbians had control of the dance floor and all other areas of the bar.[113] While this did not mean there was no intermixing in these zones, older lesbians, according to J.J., were generally content to sit and watch their younger counterparts dance and "be silly."[114]

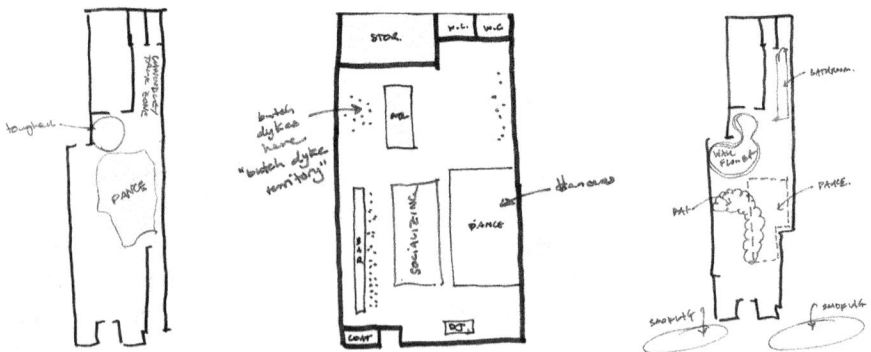

Figure 9.4. Three memory maps drawn by three different patrons with varying levels of assistance; the left and right maps were drawn over an architectural plan of the Phase, while the middle map was drawn from memory alone. The information they provide is essentially the same.

Bar: Materiality

While the exterior of the bar remained mostly the same, the interior of the bar changed several times over Phase One's forty-five-year lifespan. The iconic storefront was at one point windowed, but the windows were covered in vertical wood boards painted a "burnt orange," "brown," or "dark red."[115] The door was set three feet back in the middle of the storefront, accessed by a small ramp up to an unpaneled metal door painted black with a single diamond window installed in it at eye level.[116]

Inside, the decor changed at least five separate times. While the bar always remained wooden, the walls and floor changed. In 1975, when Dorothy first went to Phase, the walls were covered in "yellow [and] silver metallic" wallpaper that Dorothy proclaimed was "hideous."[117] At some point, the bar had "pink and white tile."[118] In the 1980s, the walls and ceiling were painted black, dark carpet was installed, and mirrors were added to the walls in an attempt to make the space seem bigger. There were also, much to J.J.'s amusement, labels on the bathroom doors that designated them as "men's" and "women's" restrooms, despite the nearly all-female clientele.[119]

When Archer Lombardi took over the bar in the early 2000s, he instituted more design changes. Red, black, and corrugated metal made up the main design palate of the bar and gave it a very "leather-and-punk" aesthetic.[120] It was during this time that a major renovation of the bar's bathrooms was done; Sam helped with the March 2007 renovations. "We took all the flooring and floor joists out and . . . rebuilt [the bathrooms] from the basement up. Then we put down new plywood and retiled the floors and painted. I made new wood thresholds for the bar floor to tile floor. [We] put in new sinks and lighting."[121] An existing mural of a woman's face was painted over during the project, something Sam was sad to see covered.

These renovations inadvertently started a trend among younger lesbians of taking selfies in the Phase One bathrooms. These "Red Wall Selfies," thus named for being taken against the newly re-stuccoed and painted walls, offer a fascinating glimpse at lesbian/queer fashion and the growth of selfie culture.[122] Tonya and Ivy took selfies together in the bathroom, as did DC Kings drag performers Sebastian Katz and Rick Shaw.[123] The bathrooms went from "disgusting" and a place in the bar to avoid to a place that was sought out by the younger members of the community.[124] The sheer volume of pictures taken in the Phase One bathrooms between 8 March 2007 when the renovations where completed to when the bar closed in 2016 speaks toward a shift in the community from being hidden and scared to being visible and proud. In the 1970s, taking photographs in bars was prohibited for the same reason the windows of gay and lesbian bars were covered: being gay was for all intents and purposes illegal, and images of people in gay bars could get individuals ostracized from their families, fired from their workplaces, and kicked out of their homes. To be able to take photographs in a gay bar and distribute them online in the age of social media, without fear of retribution, shows how far the community has come in such a short amount of time.

Significance and Conclusions

Phase One's historical significance can be measured through several factors:

- its status as being one of the oldest lesbian bars, if not *the* oldest operating lesbian bar, in the country before its closing in 2016;[125]
- its positioning in one of Washington, DC's oldest neighborhoods, in a building that dates back to 1888;[126]
- the fact that it was part of the "Gay Way" of Washington, DC, and was one of a multitude of LGBTQ businesses in a now mostly defunct "gayborhood";
- the fact it lasted for so long in the gentrifying neighborhood while other gay and lesbian establishments closed around it, and indeed, around the country;[127]
- its role as one of the main performance spaces for the longest-running drag king troupe in the world, as well as PhazeFest;[128]
- and the community of women it served, created, helped sponsor, and gave a home: Phase was not just a bar, but "a meeting place" for women and lesbians—"for women's softball team members, college students, politicos, and feminists"—for over 40 years.[129]

Interviewees state that the fact that Phase was a women-only space, and that men were discouraged from patronizing it, was the main reason for its success. It was an all-women space that was all-women every day of the week, not just one or two days out of the week, month, or year. This made it an attractive place for women and lesbians to go despite its small size, smaller dance floor, and often-crowded capacity. The fact that it promoted female artists and supported lesbian events and groups made it even more popular. Other lesbian spaces and dance halls with better music or more diverse crowds drew some business away over the years, but Phase persisted and became an anchor point and safe space in the community. Its downfall came from a myriad of factors: the fact that lesbian patrons make and spend less money than their cis gay male counterparts, the rise of social media and acceptance in society making lesbian bars less necessary for community survival, the limits of a small building footprint, a rapidly gentrifying neighborhood increasing taxes to a prohibitively expensive amount, an aging business owner, a splintering community with a growing generational and philosophical divide, and simply an inability for the bar to shift with the times and cater to a more diverse modern clientele who were looking for less of a "lesbian" or "women's" space and more of a "queer" space. For many years, Phase adapted as best as it was able, but ultimately it suffered the same fate as many other lesbian and gay spaces before it closed.

Takeaways

The collection and preservation of the history of the Phase is a prime example of the preservation challenges that face LGBTQ preservation. The Phase, despite having been the oldest continually operating lesbian bar in the country, lost its architectural integrity to development. While the building is still standing, protected for now as part of a Historic Main Street, it has lost most of the features that that made it distinctive and recognizable to DC's LGBTQ community. The only history left of the Phase is what can be recorded through oral history interviews, memory maps, and what information has fallen into archives or become part of personal collections over the years. Some of the takeaways from my work with the Phase include the following:

When it comes to recording lost spaces and other aspects of intangible cultural heritage, documentation through oral history interviews, memory maps, and archival research are often the only ways to gather that history and determine significance. Significance goes beyond the fact a building was historically or architecturally significant; in this study, oral histories were vital in determining the importance of the bar to the community. What the Phase meant to people and their lives was simply unable to be articulated through archival material alone. Information found in archives should always supplement, not overwhelm or take precedence over, oral history interviews. Oral historic interviews are key to defining the importance of a place to the community it served be-

yond what preservationists have historically used to determine significance—building age, architectural detailing, and building integrity being
prime examples.

Community members are often reluctant to participate in oral history interviews or give information because they "do not know what
they can provide." Despite their misgivings, community members are
actually able to provide in-depth and useful information about spaces,
included their feelings about them and how they interacted with them.
Getting community members past that first hurdle of realizing they are
an important source of knowledge is difficult, but can be overcome with
persistent in-person engagement and interaction that focuses on aspects of building community and nurturing connection, rather than academic interest. Being a member of the LGBTQ community, and being
referred by community members to other interviewees, helped form
trust, which aided in the interview process.

People's memories are fallible and inconsistent. Interviewees often
conflated bars with one another and sketches drawn from memory
were either very consistent with the actual building's plan or wildly inaccurate. While sketches may not be accurate in terms of architectural
scale, these memory maps can help historians understand how patrons
viewed these spaces, as well as how they gathered in and circulated
through these spaces. These maps may also yield a sense of which parts
of the space were hierarchically important to patrons; areas that were
most important to interviewees (gathering zones, dance floors, and
bars) were often drawn much larger than their actual size, while spaces
deemed less important (bathrooms, coat checks, emergency exists, and
parking lots) were drawn in much smaller scale or forgotten completely.

If architectural accuracy (including furniture placement and materiality) is the goal of these memory maps and diagrams, research *must*
to be done pre-interview to attempt to find floor plans and pictures
of these locations before interviews are conducted so that diagraming
can be done as accurately as possible. However, if such plans or photographs are impossible to find, it is much better to have proportionally
inaccurate memory maps drawn by interviewees than no maps at all.

Spaces are nothing without their context. Understanding the historical, community, and neighborhood context of a space helps implicitly
and explicitly inform the history of the space. Trajectories of culture, development, and sociopolitical movements can aid in the understanding
of space creation, sustainability, and demise on a broader level than just
confining the history of an establishment to the events inside it.

In looking at context, individuals rarely pay attention to the landscape in which the establishment is located. Very few interviewees could say what businesses were on Eighth Street SE beyond the Phase and major landmarks like the Marine Barracks. Thus, neighborhood analysis, including information on shifting local businesses and gentrification, should be based heavily on archival research, historical data, and city records.

In interviews, it was found that white and cisgender individuals are more likely to gloss over uncomfortable issues, including racism and transphobia. The racial makeup of spaces was often heavily inflated by white participants to be inclusive of people of color as compared to descriptions of the racial makeup provided by interviewees of color. Often, white interviewees would simply define racial makeup as "mixed." The racial, gender, and socioeconomic make-up of spaces should be clarified in the interviews with numeric percentages, as "mixed" is simply not accurate enough.

For lesbian/women's spaces in particular: the generational divide between older lesbians and the new "queer" generation is deeper than expected. Fear that an identity (namely lesbian) is disappearing, and a desire to retain "female only" spaces seems to be driving hostility toward the younger generation from older lesbians. Meanwhile, a distaste for the perception that older lesbians hold trans-exclusionary radical feminist and racist ideologies (whether explicit or implicit) causes the younger generation to purposely exclude older lesbians from their new communities. Whether or not this perception is true appears to be irrelevant; the phenomenon is seen in communities outside of Washington, DC, and will both inform and hinder research.[130]

LGBTQ identity is tied heavily to place, as place is where the community gathers. When the Phase closed, the community was without a women's bar for two years; monthly "ladies nights" and drag king shows at gay bars or other venues were not enough to fill the void. Further research needs to be done into how the Phase affected the creation of community and identity in Washington, DC, over the years. The books *Identities and Place* and *Communities and Place* provide a good foundation on how the creation of LGBTQ identities and communities are tied to places and spaces in time.[131]

Ty Ginter is a graduate of the historic preservation master's program at the University of Maryland, College Park. They are the cofounder of

D.C. Dykaries, a project designed to record the history of the District of Columbia's lesbian/sapphic spaces.

Notes

1. Leslie Feinberg, *Stone Butch Blues: A Novel* (Ithaca, NY: Firebrand Books, 1993), 270.
2. This chapter was written before the opening of A League of Her Own and XX+, two new spaces in DC for queer womxn, in the summer of 2018.
3. *Capitol Hill Corner*, "Phase 1: Barracks Row's Iconic Lesbian Bar and Nightclub Looks Closed for Good." *Capitol Hill Corner*, 29 June 2016; Elise Ford, *Night+Day D.C.* (San Francisco: Pulse Guides, 2006), 168.
4. This chapter about Phase One's history was originally written in December 2017, with edits made in fall 2018. Individual oral history interviews combined with memory mapping exercises, along with extensive archival research conducted mostly in the archives of the *Gay Blade* and *Tagg Magazine*, made up the majority of the research. Photographs of the interior and exterior of the building were collected through online archives and personal donations. All names of the interviewees have been changed to respect anonymity and privacy.
5. D.C. Dykaries, https://www.facebook.com/dykaries/.
6. Barracks Row Main Street, "8th Street's History," 24 September 2010, accessed 19 December 2017, http://www.barracksrow.org/index.php/what/history.html; Cultural Tourism DC, "Barracks Row Main Street," 2017, accessed 19 December 2017, https://culturaltourismdc.org/portal/barracks-row-main-street.
7. Will O'Bryan, "40-Year Phase," *Metro Weekly*, 25 February 2010, accessed 19 December 2017, http://www.metroweekly.com/2010/02/40-year-phase/.
8. Rainbow History Project, "Rainbow History Project Places and Spaces," Places & Spaces Database, accessed 19 December 2017, http://www.rainbowhistory.org/?page_id=28.
9. Amber Bailey, "HABS No. DC-883," *Historic American Buildings Survey* (Washington, DC: National Park Service, July 2016).
10. O'Bryan, "40-Year Phase." The building into which Phase One moved is a historic building, dating back to 1888. It is included in the Barracks Row Main Street listing for its architectural history, not its LGBTQ history. Information courtesy of Partner Engineering and Science, "Phase I Environmental Site Assessment" (Report), 6 January 2017.
11. Dorothy MacGregor, Phase One oral history interview by the author in person, 16 December 2017.
12. J.J. Wilder, Phase One oral history interview by the author over the phone, 1 December 2017.
13. Ibid.
14. Rene Sanchez, "D.C. Repeals Sodomy Law," *Washington Post*, 8 April 1993,

accessed 19 December 2017, https://www.washingtonpost.com/archive/politics/1993/04/08/dc-repeals-sodomy-law/41859dbd-e4c7-443e-a99f-7830c9976e35/?utm_term=.9c2e2e9946d6. Under the DC law §22-3502, which was repealed in 1993, sodomy was defined as "Oral-genital, and Anal-genital sexual contact by **any** two people: male-female, male-male, female-female; married as well as single." It was considered a felony and was "penalized by up to 10 years imprisonment and a fine of up to $1,000, when the participants are 16 years of age or older, and by up to 20 years in prison, if involving persons below 16." Consent in the acts was considered "irrelevant."

15. Wilder, Phase One interview.
16. Ibid.
17. Sam Donaldson, Phase One oral history interview by the author in person, 6 December 2017.
18. MacGregor, Phase One interview.
19. Wilder, Phase One interview.
20. Lou Chibbaro Jr., "Gay Bar Loses Bias Suit," *Blade*, 25 October 1979; *Blade*, "D.C. Police to Issue 'Carding' Order," *Blade*, 8 November 1979, 7.
21. Genny Beemyn, *A Queer Capital: A History of Gay Life in Washington D.C.* (New York: Routledge, 2015), 205.
22. Ibid., 204–6.
23. MacGregor, Phase One interview; Rainbow History Project, "Places and Spaces."
24. Rainbow History Project, "Places and Spaces."
25. Donaldson, Phase One interview; Rainbow History Project, "Places and Spaces."
26. MacGregor, Phase One interview.
27. The Other Side was primarily a lesbian bar/club, but it closed in 1988. Carroll opened Ziegfeid's/Secrets, a gay male–focused drag club with a male strip club in the back, in the same location in March 1988. Rainbow History Project, "Places and Spaces."
28. Wilder, Phase One interview.
29. Ibid.
30. MacGregor, Phase One interview.
31. Anna Wyatt, D.C. Dykaries test interview #1 Part 2, interview by author in person, 5 August 2017.
32. Sharon Bosworth, Barracks Row Main Street Program interview by author over the phone, 18 December 2017.
33. Lesley Bain, Barbara Gray, and Dave Rodgers, *Living Streets: Strategies for Crafting Public Space* (Hoboken: John Wiley & Sons, 2012), 257, accessed 14 December 2017, ProQuest Ebook Central; Stephanie Cavanaugh, "Margot Kelly: Hale to the Queen of Barrack's Row," *Capital Community Life*, n.d., 58, http://www.capitalcommunitynews.com/PDF/2011/58-59_RAG_0711.pdf.
34. Cavanaugh, "Margot Kelly," 58–59.

35. Bain, Gray, and Rodgers, *Living Streets*, 258.
36. Ibid., 257–60.
37. Ibid., 260.
38. MacGregor, Phase One interview.
39. Phoebe Clarke, Phase One oral history interview by author in person, 11 November 2017; Washington Metropolitan Area Transit Authority, "WMATA Facts," July 2009; C.T., Phase One oral history interview by author in person, 6 December 2017.
40. C.T., Phase One interview.
41. Ibid.
42. Joey DiGuglielmo, "A New Year, A New PhazeFest," *Washington Blade*, 27 August 2015, http://www.washingtonblade.com/2015/08/27/a-new-year-a-new-phazefest/.
43. Katherine Volin, "Phase in the Music: Lesbian Bar Hosts Its First Queer Arts Festival, Focusing on Diverse Lineup," *Washington Blade*, 10 August 2007.
44. DiGuglielmo, "A New Year": Doug Rule, "Welcome Revival: PhazeFest comes to the 9:30 Club," *Metro Weekly*, June 22, 2017, http://www.metroweekly.com/2017/06/phazefest-2017-930-club/.
45. DC Kings, "About Us," Welcome to the DC Kings, 2015, accessed 19 December 2017, http://dckings.com/about-us/.
46. Rainbow History Project, "Places and Spaces"; Katy Ray, "The DC Kings Retire after 15 Years of Gender-Bending," *Tagg Magazine*, 11 September 2015, https://taggmagazine.com/the-dc-kings-retire-after-15-years/.
47. Tonya Copeland and Ivy Thorne, Phase One oral history interview by author in person, 10 December 2017.
48. Raphael Cortez and N. Wells, Phase One oral history interview by author in person, 10 December 2017.
49. Copeland and Thorne, Phase One interview; Cortez and Wells, Phase One interview.
50. Cortez and Wells, Phase One interview.
51. Ibid.
52. Ibid.
53. Ibid.
54. Trae & Iona, D.C. Dykaries interview by author, 5 August 2018.
55. Ibid.
56. Joey DiGuglielmo, "A Murky Future for Phase 1," *Washington Blade*, http://www.washingtonblade.com/2015/02/05/murky-future-phase-1/.
57. Donaldson, Phase One interview; Clarke, Phase One interview; MacGregor, Phase One interview; Cortez and Wells, Phase One interview; DiGuglielmo, "A Murky Future."
58. MacGregor, Phase One interview.
59. Lou Chibbaro Jr., "Sale of Phase 1 Ends 45-Year Run of Lesbian Bar," *Washington Blade*, 6 April 2017, http://www.washingtonblade.com/2017/04/06/sale-phase-1-ends-45-year-run-lesbian-bar/.

60. Ray, "The DC Kings Retire."
61. Andrew Giambrone, "Iconic D.C. Lesbian Bar Phase 1 Goes on the Market," *Washington City Paper*, 29 June 2016, https://www.washingtoncity paper.com/news/city-desk/blog/20826912/iconic-dc-lesbian-bar-pha se-1-goes-on-the-market.
62. DiGuglielmo, "A Murky Future."
63. Ibid.
64. DiGuglielmo, "A Murky Future"; Joey DiGuglielmo, "Not Just a Phase," *Washington Blade*, 25 February 2010, http://www.washingtonblade.com/2010/ 02/25/not-just-a-phase/.
65. Assimilation refers to lesbians and other LGBTQ people being accepted by and into society because of recent shifts in cultural values, and therefore not necessarily needing spaces of their own to be accepted or to find community.
66. Bonnie J. Morris, *The Disappearing L: Erasure of Lesbian Spaces and Culture* (Albany: SUNY Press, 2017).
67. Wilder, Phase One interview; Donaldson, Phase One interview; Wyatt, D.C. Dykaries test interview; MacGregor, Phase One interview.
68. Chibbaro, "Sale of Phase 1."
69. Wilder, Phase One interview.
70. Donaldson, Phase One interview.
71. MacGregor, Phase One interview; Morris, *The Disappearing L.*
72. MacGregor, Phase One interview.
73. Cortez and Wells, Phase One interview.
74. Ibid.
75. Bosworth, "Barracks Row Main Street."
76. Google Maps. The Eastern Market Metro station is a stop on the Orange/ Blue/Silver lines on DC's mostly underground subway system.
77. Washington Metropolitan Area Transit Authority, "WMATA Facts"; Eugene L. Meyer, "Lukewarm Thrill at End of Line: New Metro Station Fails to Dazzle All in Greenbelt," *Washington Post*, 10 December 1993, http://www.high beam.com/doc1P2-97902.html?refid=easy_hf.
78. C.T., Phase One interview; Donaldson, Phase One interview; MacGregor, Phase One interview.
79. MacGregor, Phase One interview; Clarke, Phase One interview.
80. Clarke, Phase One interview.
81. Rainbow History Project, "Places and Spaces."
82. MacGregor, Phase One interview; C.T., Phase One interview.
83. Clarke, Phase One interview.
84. Ibid.
85. Wilder, Phase One interview.
86. Wyatt, D.C. Dykaries test interview; Wilder, Phase One interview.
87. Wilder, Phase One interview.
88. Wyatt, D.C. Dykaries test interview.

89. Trae & Iona, D.C. Dykaries interview.
90. Ibid.
91. Donaldson, Phase One interview.
92. Cortez and Wells, Phase One interview; Donaldson, Phase One interview.
93. Clarke, Phase One interview.
94. MacGregor, Phase One interview.
95. Wilder, Phase One interview.
96. MacGregor, Phase One interview.
97. Ibid.
98. Donaldson, Phase One interview; Wyatt, D.C. Dykaries test interview; Wilder, Phase One interview.
99. Copeland and Thorne, Phase One interview; Clarke, Phase One interview; Cortez and Wells, Phase One interview.
100. MacGregor, Phase One interview; Donaldson, Phase One interview.
101. Wyatt, D.C. Dykaries test interview; Wilder, Phase One interview; Copeland and Thorne, Phase One interview.
102. Wilder, Phase One interview; Cortez and Wells, Phase One interview; Clarke, Phase One interview.
103. Cortez and Wells, Phase One interview. Phase One Dupont/Phase Dupont (1415 Twenty=Second Street NW), colloquially known as "Phase Two," was opened in Dupont Circle by Allen Carroll in February 2012. It was billed as the club equivalent to Phase One and was open simultaneously to the Capitol Hill venue. Phase One Dupont took over the building that previously housed Apex and Badlands, gay dance clubs that hosted wildly successful 18+ "Liquid Ladies" dance nights and drag king shows. Phase One Dupont closed in 2013.
104. C.T., Phase One interview.
105. Ibid.; Cortez and Wells, Phase One interview.
106. C.T., Phase One interview.
107. Donaldson, Phase One interview.
108. Wilder, Phase One interview.
109. Donaldson, Phase One interview; C.T., Phase One interview.
110. Clarke, Phase One interview; Donaldson, Phase One interview; Copeland and Thorne, Phase One Interview.
111. Cortez and Wells, Phase One interview; Copeland and Thorne, Phase One interview; Clarke, Phase One interview.
112. Copeland and Thorne, Phase One interview.
113. Donaldson, Phase One interview; Clarke, Phase One interview; Copeland and Thorne, Phase One interview; Cortez and Wells, Phase One interview; Wyatt, D.C. Dykaries test interview; MacGregor, Phase One interview.
114. Wilder, Phase One interview.
115. Bailey, "HABS No. DC-883"; Wilder, Phase One interview; Donaldson, Phase One interview.
116. Bailey, "HABS No. DC-883"; Donaldson, Phase One interview.

117. MacGregor, Phase One interview.
118. DiGuglielmo, "Not Just a Phase."
119. Wilder, Phase One interview.
120. Ibid.
121. Donaldson, Phase One interview.
122. Bathroom selfies/portraits were also taken at the Lexington, the last San Francisco lesbian bar, which closed in 2015. Lauren Morrell Tabak, "Saying Goodbye to the Last Lesbian Bar in San Francisco," *Buzzfeed News*, 29 July 2015, https://www.buzzfeed.com/LaurenMorrellTabak/the-last-lesbian-bar-in-san-francisco.
123. Copeland and Thorne, Phase One interview.
124. Wilder, Phase One interview.
125. Bailey, "HABS No. DC-883"; Bosworth, "Barracks Row Main Street."
126. Partner Engineering and Science.
127. Donaldson, Phase One interview; Bailey, "HABS No. DC-883."
128. Ray, "The DC Kings Retire."
129. Bailey, "HABS No. DC-883."
130. Jen Jack Gieseking, "Queering the Meaning of 'Neighbourhood': Reinterpreting the Lesbian-Queer Experience of Park Slope, Brooklyn, 1983–2008," in *Queer Presences and Absences*, ed. Yvette Taylor and Michelle Addison (London: Palgrave Macmillan, 2013), 178–200; Jen Jack Gieseking, "Constellating Queer Spaces," *Urban Omnibus*, 7 February 2018, accessed 30 October 2018, https://urbanomnibus.net/2018/02/constellating-queer-spaces/.
131. Katherine Crawford-Lackey and Megan E. Springate, eds., *Identities and Place: Changing Labels and Intersectional Communities of LGBTQ and Two-Spirit People in the United States* (New York: Berghahn Books, 2019); Katherine Crawford-Lackey and Megan E. Springate, eds., *Communities and Place: A Thematic Approach to the Histories of LGBTQ Communities in the United States* (New York: Berghahn Books, forthcoming).

Bibliography

Bailey, Amber. "HABS No. DC-883." *Historic American Buildings Survey*. Washington, DC: National Park Service, July 2016.

Bain, Lesley, Barbara Gray, and Dave Rodgers. *Living Streets: Strategies for Crafting Public Space*. Hoboken: John Wiley & Sons, 2012. Accessed 14 December 2017. ProQuest Ebook Central.

Barracks Row Main Street. "8th Street's History." 24 September 2010. Accessed 19 December 2017. http://www.barracksrow.org/index.php/what/history.html.

Beemyn, Genny. *A Queer Capital—A History of Gay Life in Washington D.C.* New York: Routledge, 2015.

Blade. "D.C. Police to Issue 'Carding' Order.'" *Blade*, 8 November 1979.

Capitol Hill Corner. "Phase 1: Barracks Row's Iconic Lesbian Bar and Nightclub Looks Closed for Good." *Capitol Hill Corner*, 29 June 2016. Accessed 19

December 2017. https://capitolhillcorner.org/2016/06/29/phase-1-barracks-rows-iconic-lesbian-bar-and-nightclub-looks-closed-for-good/.

Cavanaugh, Stephanie. "Margot Kelly: Hale to the Queen of Barrack's Row." *Capital Community Life*, n.d. http://www.capitalcommunitynews.com/PDF/2011/58-59_RAG_0711.pdf.

Chibbaro, Lou, Jr. "Gay Bar Loses Bias Suit." *Blade*, 25 October 1979.

———. "Sale of Phase 1 Ends 45-Year Run of Lesbian Bar." *Washington Blade*, 6 April 2017. http://www.washingtonblade.com/2017/04/06/sale-phase-1-ends-45-year-run-lesbian-bar/.

Crawford-Lackey, Katherine, and Megan E. Springate, eds. *Communities and Place: A Thematic Approach to the Histories of LGBTQ Communities in the United States*. New York: Berghahn Books, forthcoming.

———. *Identities and Place: Changing Labels and Intersectional Communities of LGBTQ and Two-Spirit People in the United States*. New York: Berghahn Books, 2019.

Cultural Tourism D.C. "Barracks Row Main Street." 2017. Accessed 19 December 2017. https://www.culturaltourismdc.org/portal/barracks-row-main-street.

DiGuglielmo, Joey. "A Murky Future for Phase 1." *Washington Blade*, 5 February, 2015. http://www.washingtonblade.com/2015/02/05/murky-future-phase-1/.

———. "A New Year, A New PhazeFest." *Washington Blade*, 27 August 2015. http://www.washingtonblade.com/2015/08/27/a-new-year-a-new-phazefest/.

———. "Not Just a Phase." *Washington Blade*, 25 February 2010. http://www.washingtonblade.com/2010/02/25/not-just-a-phase/.

DC Kings. "About Us." Welcome to the DC Kings. 2015. Accessed 19 December 2017. http://dckings.com/about-us/.

Eklund, Janice. "Police Arrest Suspect in Capitol Hill Rapes." *Gay Blade*, July 1978.

Feinberg, Leslie. *Stone Butch Blues: A Novel*. Ithaca, NY: Firebrand Books, 1993.

Ford, Elise. *Night+Day D.C.* San Francisco: Pulse Guides, 2006.

Gay Blade. "Gay Blade Advertisement." *Gay Blade*, December 1972.

———. "JoAnna's." *Gay Blade*, January 1973.

———. "Phase One Advertisement." *Gay Blade*, December 1972.

Giambrone, Andrew. "Iconic D.C. Lesbian Bar Phase 1 Goes on the Market." *Washington City Paper*, 29 June 2016. https://www.washingtoncitypaper.com/news/citydesk/blog/20826912/iconic-dc-lesbian-bar-phase-1-goes-on-the-market.

Gieseking, Jen Jack. "Constellating Queer Spaces." *Urban Omnibus*, 7 February 2018. Accessed 30 October 2018. https://urbanomnibus.net/2018/02/constellating-queer-spaces/.

———. "Queering the Meaning of 'Neighbourhood': Reinterpreting the Lesbian-Queer Experience of Park Slope, Brooklyn, 1983–2008." In *Queer Presences and Absences*, edited by Yvette Taylor and Michelle Addison, 178–200. London: Palgrave Macmillan, 2013.

Meyer, Eugene L. "Lukewarm Thrill at End of Line: New Metro Station Fails to Dazzle All in Greenbelt Series. NEIGHBORHOOD Series Number: 4/4." *Washington Post*, 10 December 1993. Accessed 19 December 2017. http://www.highbeam.com/doc/1P2-979021.html?refid=easy_hf.

Morris, Bonnie J. *The Disappearing L: Erasure of Lesbian Spaces and Culture*. Albany: SUNY Press, 2017.

O'Bryan, Will. "40-Year Phase." *Metro Weekly*, 25 February 2010. Accessed 19 December 2017. http://www.metroweekly.com/2010/02/40-year-phase/.

Partner Engineering and Science. "Phase I Environmental Site Assessment" (Report). 6 January 2017. Courtesy of Christopher Martin.

Rainbow History Project. "Rainbow History Project Places and Spaces." Places & Spaces Database. Accessed 19 December 2017. http://www.rainbowhistory .org/?page_id=28.

Ray, Katy. "The DC Kings Retire after 15 Years of Gender-Bending." *Tagg Magazine*, 11 September 2015. https://taggmagazine.com/the-dc-kings-retire-after-15-years/.

Rule, Doug. "Welcome Revival: PhazeFest Comes to the 9:30 Club." *Metro Weekly*, 22 June 2017. http://www.metroweekly.com/2017/06/phazefest-2017-930-club/.

Sanchez, Rene. "D.C. Repeals Sodomy Law." *Washington Post*, 8 April 1993. Accessed 19 December 2017. https://www.washingtonpost.com/archive/politics/1993/04/08/dc-repeals-sodomy-law/41859dbd-e4c7-443e-a99f-7830c9976e35/?utm_term=.9c2e2e9946d6.

Tabak, Lauren Morrell. "Saying Goodbye to the Last Lesbian Bar in San Francisco." *Buzzfeed News*, 29 July 2015. https://www.buzzfeed.com/Lauren MorrellTabak/the-last-lesbian-bar-in-san-francisco.

Volin, Katherine. "Phase in the Music: Lesbian Bar Hosts Its First Queer Arts Festival, Focusing on Diverse Lineup." *Washington Blade*, 10 August 2007.

Washington Blade. "Hippocampe Country Band." *Washington Blade*, 13 February 1987.

——. "Mr. Moe." *Washington Blade*, 7 June 1985.

——. "Sweetwater." *Washington Blade*, 13 February 1987.

Washington Metropolitan Area Transit Authority. "WMATA Facts." July 2009. https://web.archive.org/web/20100113082838/http://wmata.com/about_metro/docs/metrofacts.pdf.

Historic Preservation Activities

Katherine Crawford-Lackey

The following worksheets and activities are based on content covered in the previous chapters. They are intended to prompt readers to think critically about two-spirit, lesbian, gay, bisexual, transgender, and queer (LGBTQ) history and culture and the places associated with these communities. Rooted in public history pedagogy, the activities encourage readers to engage in the practical application of historic preservation, museum management, oral storytelling, public archaeology, and more. These teaching materials are intended for advanced college undergraduate and graduate students and will prompt readers to delve deeper into the topic material by exploring different disciplines within the umbrella of public history. In addition to providing strategies for practically applying the knowledge included in this volume, these activities allow for self-reflection and provide opportunities to connect with others.

Note: similar to this series as a whole, these activities emphasize the use of the National Register of Historic Places as a means of identifying properties worthy of preservation. The activities frequently refer to queer places listed on the National Register and encourage readers to learn about and participate in the process of nominating properties to the National Register. The emphasis on the National Register stems from the book's origins as a product of the National Park Service (NPS) and National Park Foundation. The National Register of Historic Places is a program managed by the National Park Service, and when these chapters were originally written and published online by the National Park Service in 2016, the authors accordingly emphasized the places and processes affiliated with the NPS. The emphasis on the National Register by no means detracts from the importance of using local and state processes for recognizing and preserving historic properties.

Spotlight Local Historic Properties

Documenting and preserving historic places is essential to ensure their survival for future generations. While many historic sites are cared for outside of formal channels, pursuing some type of local, state, or federal designation is a way to help protect these places. There are many ways to recognize the importance of historic places. Because the chapters in this book were written in the context of the National Park Service and its programs, this activity focuses on the process for nominating places to the National Register of Historic Places.

A list of federally recognized sites deemed "worthy of preservation," the National Register of Historic Places helps people identify and evaluate historically significant places.[1] Listing a property on the National Register gives it legitimacy and often makes the public more aware of its historical significance.[2]

Nominated properties are evaluated on several criteria, including historical significance, architectural integrity, and age. To be eligible for listing on the National Register, a property must be associated with notable historical events or figures, must be architecturally significant, or must produce important evidence about the past (in an archaeological context).

The National Register of Historic Places' website provides guidelines for those interested in nominating a property. These guidelines, however, can make it challenging (but not impossible) to nominate properties that are under fifty years old or that do not possess original integrity. There are, however, multiple case studies of how to nominate properties that are less than fifty years old or that have experienced many architectural changes.[3]

As decades of urban development and renewal have caused a loss in historic structures, particularly those of nonheteronormative Americans, preserving the places of lesbian, gay, bisexual, transgender, and queer (LGBTQ) Americans is particularly important. A number of factors, including a lack of financial capital, discriminatory zoning laws and practices, and an increased likelihood of transiency, cause the spaces associated with marginalized communities to often go unrecognized. The National Register criteria does not take into account the added challenges of nominating the places of minority communities and can, as a result, be exclusionary. This should cause professionals to reevaluate how "historical significance" is determined.[4]

With this in mind, how would you evaluate historical significance? In your opinion, what makes a place worth preserving? Why do you think "place" is important?

Activity

Create a blog or podcast about what "historical significance" means to you. Identify some LGBTQ-related sites in your local area that you think are significant and worth preserving. Feature these properties and their history in your blog or podcast.

We recommend exploring some of the following topics in your blog/ podcast:

- Describe the history and function of these places.
- Why are they significant in local, regional, or national history?
- Are these properties owned by the public? Or by private individuals or entities? Does this change the significance of the property? Why or why not?
- What efforts are being taken to preserve and interpret these properties?
- Where are these places located? Describe the surroundings. What other structures are located nearby and how does this impact the significance of the property?

Notes

1. National Register of Historic Places website, National Park Service, accessed 10 October 2017, https://www.nps.gov/subjects/nationalregister/index.htm.
2. It should be noted that while there are advantages to having a property listed on the National Register, there are many other ways to recognize historically significant properties through state and local programs.
3. National Register Bulletin 15, National Park Service, accessed 10 October 2017, https://www.nps.gov/nr/publications/bulletins/nrb15/nrb15_2.htm.
4. In the last several decades, scholars such as urban historian Dolores Hayden and architectural historian and cultural geographer Michael R. Allen have argued that recognizing the spaces of gender and ethnic minorities should not be dependent on an extant structure(s). Their work explores how to memorialize past people and events even when the built environment has been disturbed. Dolores Hayden, *The Power of Place: Urban Landscapes as Public History* (Cambridge, MA: MIT Press, 1995); Michael R. Allen, "What Historic Preservation Can Learn from Ferguson," in *Bending the Future: 50*

Ideas for the Next 50 Years of Historic Preservation in the United States, ed. Max Page and Marla R. Miller (Amherst: University of Massachusetts Press, 2016); for more information about the spaces of transient communities, see Jen Jack Gieseking, "The Geographies of LGBTQ Lives: In and Beyond Cities, Neighborhoods, and Bars," in *Communities and Place: A Thematic Approach to the Histories of LGBTQ Communities in the United States*, ed. Katherine Crawford-Lackey and Megan E. Springate (New York: Berghahn Books, forthcoming).

Explore a Place

Our personal and cultural identities are influenced by place, meaning that we are shaped by the spaces of our past and present—our child-hood home, a local restaurant, our place of worship, the workplace, and more. Part of our individuality is informed by the places where we live, and this context is essential for our own self-expression as well as how we make connections with others on a local and national scale.[1]

Beginning in the late nineteenth century, physical meeting loca-tions afforded opportunities to socialize, protest, mourn, and celebrate. Lesbian, gay, bisexual, transgender, and queer (LGBTQ) communities formed in the mid-to-late twentieth century due in part to the estab-lishment of queer-tolerant public spaces, which facilitated the emer-gence of a collective identity.[2]

Queer meeting spaces were subsequently targeted by the police, and, as a result, these places became sites of resistance. One of the most notable is Stonewall Inn in Greenwich Village, New York City, where in 1969, a group of gay, lesbian, and transgender individuals fought back against police brutality. Many historians consider the Stonewall Uprising the start of the modern gay rights movement. Stonewall continues to serve as a symbolic place for many LGBTQ communities, and, in 2016, President Obama recognized its importance in the larger narrative of American history by designating it a National Monument.

In addition to serving as an invitation to socialize, resist, and re-member, place can also instill a sense of belonging. Urban historian Do-lores Hayden argues that public spaces in particular have the potential to "nurture" a sense of citizenship.[3] Place is powerful because it serves as a tangible link between past, present, and future, allowing us to con-nect more deeply to a shared heritage that strengtheners the bonds of citizenship and civic duty.

Studying history based in place has the power to reach a more di-verse audience by tapping into our emotional connections to space. The National Park Service (NPS) in particular uses this approach in its parks and programs.[4] NPS interpretation aims to discover the untold stories of historically significant places. A new interpretive resource called the "Discovery Journal," created through a collaboration of National Park Service professionals, is one such tool for discovering the many sto-ries of a place. Intended for preservationists, interpreters, educators, and historians both inside and outside the National Park Service, the journal inspires the creation of new interpretation that addresses the untold stories of a place in order to facilitate healing and change.

The heart of this process entails exploring a place from a new perspective. When we become familiar with a place, we often begin to make assumptions and we forget to ask questions about other uses and meanings of the space.[5] The following diagram is intended to inspire new inquiry by encouraging you to think about your place and its connection to larger themes in American history.

Activity

Pick a place that has meaning to you and fill out the diagram.

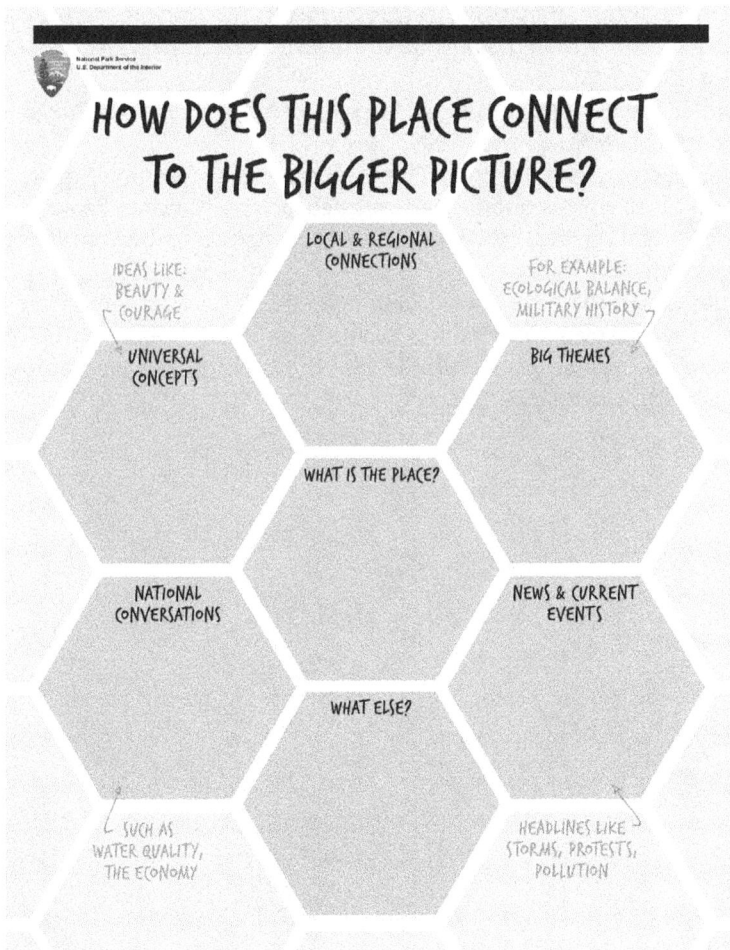

Figure A.1. "How does this place connect to the bigger picture?" National Park Service product. Diagram graphic designed by Mickey Shin. "Discovery Journal: Giving Voice to America's Places," National Park Service, n.d.

Notes

1. Kath Browne and Eduarda Ferreira "Introduction to Lesbian Geographies," in *Lesbian Geographies: Gender, Place and Power*, ed. Kath Browne and Eduarda Ferreira (New York: Routledge, 2016); Kath Browne and Gavin Brown, "An Introduction to the Geographies of Sex and Sexualities," *The Routledge Research Companion to Geographies of Sex and Sexuality* (New York: Routledge, 2016).

2. Gay, lesbian, and transgender citizens would often frequent bars, taverns, and restaurants, and, while not necessarily welcome, gender and sexual minorities usually received service. Genny Beemyn, *A Queer Capital: A History of Gay Life in Washington D.C.* (New York: Routledge, 2015); John D'Emilio, *Sexual Politics, Sexual Communities: The Making of a Homosexual Minority in the United States, 1940–1970* (Chicago: University of Chicago Press, 1983).

3. Dolores Hayden, *The Power of Place: Urban Landscapes as Public History* (Cambridge, MA: MIT Press, 1997), 9.

4. The Teaching with Historic Places program, for example, offers lesson plans based on historic properties listed on the National Register of Historic Places; see https://www.nps.gov/subjects/teachingwithhistoricplaces/index.htm.

5. Katie Crawford-Lackey and Barbara Little, "Exploring American Places with the Discovery Journal: A Guide to Co-Creating Meaningful Interpretation," *George Wright Forum* 34, no. 3 (2017), http://www.georgewright.org/343crawford-lackey.pdf.

Identify LGBTQ Material Culture

Artifact collections are typically associated with museums; however, many other establishments also care for their own collections, including archives, libraries, and historic sites. Any establishment that cares for a collection should have a collections management policy that provides guidance on acquiring, accessioning, preserving, and deaccessioning material culture.

Even an establishment with the most comprehensive collections management policy may not understand the significance of some of their artifacts. Museum professionals are not necessarily trained to recognize queer objects, for example. As a result, much of this material culture is mislabeled and misinterpreted. Queer material culture can be anything from newspapers and letters to buttons, postcards, clothing, flags, and many other objects.[1]

All museums should conduct an inventory of their collections every year. This can be an inventory of the whole collection or part of it. Museums can also conduct random inventories of their collections.[2] Even though this is a time-consuming process, inventorying a collection allows museum professionals to record the current condition of the artifacts and identify any missing objects. An annual inventory is also an opportunity for museum professionals to rediscover the potential significance of some of their collections.

Activity

Create a guide to help museum professionals identify potential lesbian, gay, bisexual, transgender, queer, and two-spirit material culture as they inventory their collections. Providing a list of identifying features can help museums recognize (or at least learn more about) objects that are potentially associated with queer history.

Helpful tip: many museums may already have their collections inventoried in a software program. If they have information about the provenance and date range of the artifacts, this can help establish whether an object is associated with queer history.

Example of collections management policy from the American Association of Museums (AAM): http://www.aam-us.org/docs/default-source/continuum/developing-a-cmp-final.pdf?sfvrsn=4.

Example of a collections inventory from the National Park Service (NPS): https://www.nps.gov/museum/publications/MHII/mh2ch4.pdf.

Notes

1. See Susan Ferentinos's work for more information about identifying queer material culture. Susan Ferentinos, "Interpreting LGBTQ Historic Sites," (this volume); Susan Ferentinos, *Interpreting LGBTQ History at Museums and Historic Sites* (Lanham, MD: Rowman & Littlefield, 2015).
2. For more information about museum inventories, see Hugh H. Genoways and Lynne M. Ireland, *Museum Administration 2.0* (Lanham, MD: Rowan & Littlefield, 2017), 293. The American Alliance of Museums also provides information about the inventory process at their website: http://www.aam-us .org/resources/ethics-standards-and-best-practices/collections-stewa rdship.

Create a Toolkit for Interpreting LGBTQ History

Many museums and historic sites are making efforts to interpret the history of lesbian, gay, bisexual, transgender, and queer (LGBTQ) Americans. Some institutions may find this challenging depending on their geographic location, access to collections, familiarity with content, and level of stakeholder involvement.

Providing a toolkit for interpreting LGBTQ and two-spirit history can encourage museums and historic sites to take steps toward including queer history. A toolkit is a guide to creating and implementing educational content about a topic. Using the information from the book, create a guide for how public institutions can include LGBTQ history in exhibits, programs, and other educational material.

Activity

There are two ways to approach this activity:
1. Create a toolkit in collaboration with a historic site, museum, or organization to address their specific needs.
2. Create a toolkit with a broader framework that can be used by many different places.

Tailoring the toolkit to the needs of a museum or historic site gives you practice collaborating with other professionals. It also gives you an idea for how the consultation process works. On the other hand, creating the toolkit with a broader audience in mind allows you to focus on "big picture" topics.

Creating a toolkit with a museum/historic site	Creating a toolkit for a broader audience
Before you get underway, meet with a representative to establish what the site or organization is trying to accomplish through its interpretation. What is their ultimate goal in incorporating queer history? ➤ Is it to showcase a collection? ➤ Educate the public? ➤ Engage local LGBTQ communities? How can you best aid them in accomplishing their goals?	Sit down with your colleagues and establish several key themes that the toolkit should address. Who is your audience and what do you want them to gain from this toolkit? ➤ Examples of successful LGBTQ-centered interpretation? ➤ Exhibit design ideas? ➤ Strategies for interpreting queer history with diverse audiences? ➤ All of the above?

Consider the following suggestions when creating your toolkit:

Components to discuss in the toolkit:	Why include this?
Introduction to LGBTQ interpretation	An introduction explains why it's important for museums to include LGBTQ history in their interpretation.
Discussion of terminology	Establishes a framework for the terminology the museum or historic site should (or should not) not use in interpretation and why.
Foundational concepts of LGBTQ theory	In order to interpret LGBTQ history, museums must acknowledge several foundational theories—such as the social construction of gender and sexuality. This influences how both museum professionals and the public talk about queer people and queer history. Susan Ferentinos discusses several of these theories in her chapter of this volume.
Strategies for tailoring interpretation for specific audiences	Establishing a target audience is important when interpreting any kind of history. The content of the exhibit, program, or other education material should be accessible to the intended audience.
Strategies for dealing with resistant members of the public	Establish strategies to respond to visitors who express unproductive commentary on the subject of the interpretation. Providing this framework can help museum professionals and historians train their interpreters to respond effectively if such situations arise.

Create a Mental Map

Historians, geographers, cultural anthropologists, and other profession-als are interested in the study of mental maps (and the process of their construction). Urban cultural geographer Jen Jack Gieseking defines a mental map as "the representation of an individual or group's cognitive map, hand sketched and/or computer assisted, in drafting and labeling a map or adding to and labeling an already existing map."[1] Ty Ginter used mental maps in their research on Phase One.[2] Scholars have debated the relationship between mental and physical space for hundreds of years. In the past several decades, scholars have become increasingly interested in studying mental maps, or drawings of physical locations from memory.[3]

The act of mapping is both an exercise of power and a method of preservation. The way one views the world is subjective and inherently biased, and how this world view is translated to paper in the form of a map gives legitimacy to that perspective.[4] While ordinary citizens have little control over the official map-making process, the creation of men-tal maps allows scholars to study and preserve public perceptions of space. The resulting maps give voice to those who have little say in the official representation of the community, the region, and the country.

Understanding the topography of our surroundings allows us to better understand the workings of the physical world, including the nuances of politics, economics, and culture. The creation of mental maps, then, allows scholars to study how individuals perceive the world around them—on the local, regional, national, and even international scale.

Despite the importance of understanding our physical environment, we are not always consciously aware of the world around us. For exam-ple, has anyone ever asked you for directions? What was your response? What imagery came to your head when attempting to answer? Did you describe street names or landmarks? Or did you use cardinal directions? Why did you respond this way?

We often move through space unconsciously, without picturing a map in our minds. Instead, we are able to walk to class or drive to work without ever visualizing the route ahead. When prompted to draw our route, or when asked for directions, we are left thinking more deeply about the spatial layout of our surroundings.[5]

Even though we don't always consciously think about it, we all cre-ate mental pictures of the landscape in our minds. This helps us understand how the world is spatially arranged. The way we perceive and move through space reveals much about our society and our individual places within the culture.[6]

Our world view—our perceptions of class, race, gender, ability, etc.—impact how we form these maps in our heads. Scholars are interested in studying mental maps because they reveal an individual's or group's understanding of the world, including perceptions of social hierarchies, biases toward others, and much more. As a result, the way we mentally construct the physical topography may not be precisely accurate; however, our mental maps depict how we perceive the arrangement of space.[7]

Activity

With your classmates, decide on a physical location and draw individual mental maps of this place. Choose a location you are all familiar with—perhaps a place on campus or an area of the nearby community.

After everyone has drawn this place from memory, compare with an original map. How accurately does your reproduction match up? Were you surprised by the outcome? Why or why not?

Share your map with your classmates.

- How is your mental map similar to and different from those of your classmates? What is the cause of the similarities and differences?
- What does your map reveal about your perceptions of this place? Why do you think that is?
- Do these mental maps reveal any hidden biases? Why or why not?
- What are some way to address the inaccuracies of your maps? Are these inaccuracies inherently negative?

Notes

1. Quoted in Jen Jack Gieseking, "Where We Go from Here: The Mental Sketch Mapping Method and Its Analytic Components," *Qualitative Inquiry* 19, no. 9 (2013): 712–24. Gieseking provides a detailed analysis on the process of making mental maps and the psychology behind it.
2. Ty Ginter, "Tradition, Community, and Grungy Secret-ness: What Preservationists Can Learn from the Story of Phase One" (this volume).

3. Ralph A. Sanders and Philip W. Porter, "Shape in Revealed Mental Maps," *Annals of the Association of American Geographers* 64, no. 2 (1974): 258–67, http://www.jstor.org/stable/2562514.
4. Angèle Smith, "Mapped Landscapes: The Politics of Metaphor, Knowledge, and Representation of Nineteenth-Century Irish Ordinance Survey Maps, *Historical Archaeology* 41, no. 1 (2007): 81–91.
5. Yi-Fu Tuan, *Space & Place: The Perspective of Experience* (Minneapolis: University of Minnesota, 2003), 68–70.
6. Yi-Fu, Tuan, "Images and Mental Maps," *Annals of the Association of American Geographers* 65, no. 2 (1975): 205–13, http://www.jstor.org/stable/2562082.
7. For more information about shared authority and mental map-making in LGBTQ communities, see Michael Brown and Larry Knopp, "Queering the Map: The Productive Tensions of Colliding Epistemologies," *Annals of the Association of American Geographers* 98, no. 1 (2008): 40–58.

Preserve Oral Narratives

Until recently, historians have traditionally relied on written records to study and write about the past. Such an approach limited the diversity of the historical narrative as usually only those who were white, wealthy, and male had the educational background and resources to leave behind written records. Those who had sexual desires or gender preferences that differed from Western societal "norms" usually did not record their thoughts or behavior, making historical study of queer Americans particularly challenging.[1] Scholars are now diversifying the resources they use to learn about queer Americans and others by relying on evidence such as built landscapes, material culture, and oral histories.

Oral stories provide evidence about the past and enhance our understanding of historical events. Oral accounts have historically served as a way for those with marginalized identities to speak about their experiences and challenge majority narratives. These histories continue to serve as a way for people with different backgrounds to document their lived experiences and recall the past on their own terms.

Activity

Participate in the preservation of the past by recording the stories of two-spirit, lesbian, gay, bisexual, transgender, and queer (LGBTQ) colleagues, loved ones, or members of the community. Offer an invitation to meet, talk, and record oral stories. Topics to address include childhood memories, "coming-out" experiences, and navigating heterosexual society as someone who identities as LGBTQ. Use a digital or audio recorder for the interview—this can be as low-tech as using an app on your phone.[2]

Oral interviews are an act of co-creation between the interviewer and the interviewee. You are as much a part of this experience as the person you are interviewing. Your role, however, is to listen! Allow the interviewee plenty of time to respond and expand on their thoughts; try not to interrupt.

Below are a few questions to help you get started. Don't feel obligated to ask every question listed. Instead, concentrate your full attention on what the person is saying and let their conversation guide you to ask informed questions.

Feel free to come up with our own list of questions. Open-ended questions are usually the most successful because they prompt the interviewee to elaborate instead of providing one-word answers. Here are some suggestions to get you started:

- State your full name
- Describe your childhood
- Describe your family and your relationship with them.
- When did you realize you were attracted to the same sex and how did this make you feel?
- Did you feel the need to tell your family and friends? Why or why not?
- What was one of the most pivotal moments in your life?
- Did you experience any discrimination after identifying as LGBTQ? How did you respond to this discrimination?
- What is one of your most vivid memories?
- Describe a time in your life when you were struggling.

After the interview, thank the participant for sharing their story. Write a transcript of the interview to ensure long-term preservation. If you are able and if the interviewee has given permission, work with a university oral history program to archive and store the interview.

Checklist of items to have for your interview:

- ☐ Recording device
- ☐ Plan for how you are going to save, store, and share the digital files
- ☐ Biographical form to fill out about the interviewee*
- ☐ Description form to fill out about interview**
- ☐ List of interview questions
- ☐ Release form or deed of gift signed by interviewee
- ☐ _____
- ☐ _____
- ☐ _____

*The biographical form should include information such as the interviewee's name, address, date of birth, place of birth, additional contact info, etc.
**The description form should include the name of interviewer (you), contact information of interviewer, name of interviewee, date of interview, time period covered in the interview, purpose of interview, how the interview was recorded (type of files), how those files are labeled, overview of what was discussed, etc.

Notes

1. Leisa Meyer and Helis Sikk, "Introduction to Lesbian, Gay, Bisexual, Transgender, and Queer (LGBTQ) History in the United States," in *LGBTQ America: A Theme Study of Lesbian, Gay, Bisexual, Transgender, and Queer History*, ed. Megan E. Springate (Washington, DC: National Park Foundation and National Park Service, 2016). See also Ty Ginter, "Tradition, Community, and Grungy Secret-ness: What Preservationists Can Learn from the Story of Phase One" (this volume), for how oral histories can be integrated into historic preservation.
2. For examples of oral interviews, questions about copyright, and guidance for uploading and sharing these interviews, see the New York City Trans Oral History Project at https://www.nyctransoralhistory.org/.

Explore Archaeological Context

Preservation is often associated with the act of conserving extant structures, yet the authors of this volume demonstrate the importance of studying sites that lack structures in the traditional sense, including archaeological sites and cultural landscapes.

Archaeology is the study of past humans through the examination of material remains. Excavating artifacts is an important part of the archaeological process, as is studying features—human changes to the earth.[1] Physical traces—whether in the form of material objects, built structures, or altered landscapes—allow practitioners to study the culture, traditions, and even the behavior of past societies.[2]

The spatial arrangement of a house or town has the potential to yield information about the nuances of a society's politics, economics, and culture. Over the past several decades, practitioners (including landscape archaeologists, historic preservationists, and public historians) have begun studying how past societies altered the landscape. Examining why sites were chosen for settlement and how they were laid out and developed reveals information about social status, political hierarchies, and religious or spiritual traditions in past societies.[3]

Activity

To explore the archaeological context of your home, consider the following questions:

- What would archaeologists learn about you from looking at your home or neighborhood?
- As you think about the layout of you home, consider the material objects within it.
- How about the possessions you are most proud of? Where do you keep these objects? Why?
- What could someone tell about you based on the objects you own?
- Draw the floor plan of your home.
  - How have you used the space through placement of furniture and other objects?
  - What does this reveal about your intentions?
- Share your map with your peers.
  - How do the floor plans differ? How are they similar?

○ What greater impact does movement through and use of space have on society? For example, do you think that the differences in spatial layout of your home versus that of your peers drastically alters your lived experience? Why or why not?

Notes

1. Douglass T. Price, *Principles of Archaeology* (Boston: McGraw-Hill, 2006), 108.
2. Ian Hodder, *Reading the Past: Current Approaches to the Interpretation of Archaeology* (Cambridge: Cambridge University Press, 1986).
3. Christopher Y. Tilley, *A Phenomenology of Landscape: Places, Paths, and Monuments* (Oxford: Berg, 1994); Matthew Johnson, "Phenomenological Approaches in Landscape Archaeology," *Annual Review of Anthropology* 41 (2012): 269–84; Matthew Johnson, *Ideas of Landscape* (Malden, MA: Blackwell, 2007); Mark P. Leone and Silas D. Hurry, "Seeing: The Power of Town Planning in the Chesapeake," *Historical Archaeology* 34, no. 4 (1998): 34–62.

Begin the Nomination Process
(National Register of Historic Places)

The National Register of Historic Places, managed by the National Park Service, is a list of the country's historic properties deemed "worthy of preservation" by the federal government.[1] While being listed doesn't necessarily preserve a property from demolition, it is an official recognition of the property's significance in American history.[2]

Properties that are nominated are evaluated based on their age, architectural integrity, and historical significance. Those completing a nomination should make a strong case for the property based on these three factors.

Completing an entire National Register nomination can be a long and tedious process, and it usually requires the involvement of historic preservationists, public historians, archaeologists, and other professionals. As a result, this activity does not require the completion of a nomination, which can take months or years. Instead, this activity focuses on the heart of the nomination process—addressing the significance of the property.

To be potentially eligible for listing, a property must retain architectural integrity to its period of significance and meet one of the four criteria listed below:

Criteria A: the property is "associated with events that have made a significant contribution to the broad patterns of our history";

Criteria B: the property is "associated with the lives of significant persons in our past";

Criteria C: the property embodies "the distinctive characteristics of a type, period, or method of construction, or that represent the work of a master, or that possess high artistic values, or that represent a significant and distinguishable entity whose components may lack individual distinction";

Criteria D: the property has "yielded or may be likely to yield, information important in history or prehistory."[3]

The exercise below will prompt you to think about historic places near you and why they should be preserved. It should also inspire you to dig a little deeper into the primary sources to discover the history of your community.

Activity

Identify a historic property that you think is eligible for listing on the National Register of Historic Places. Why is it significant? Does it meet Criteria A, B, C, or D? Is it significant locally or statewide? Or is the property associated with national events and people?

Establish a period of significance and argue a case for preserving the property. This assessment will require additional research at the local library, archive, or historical society.

While you are not focusing on the property's integrity and age, the architecture and date of construction (if an extant structure) may help you support a case for significance.

Consider the following questions as you prepare a case for significance:

- Where is the property located? Does that add to its significance?
- Who were the past owners of the property? The current owners?
- What was the property's function?
- Are there other buildings located on the property?
- What is the period of significance?
- How does the property fit in with its surroundings?
- What other structures and buildings surrounded the property during its period of significance?
- What can this tell you about the history of the area?
- How does this contribute to your property's significance?

Write a case for your property's significance and share with the class.

Notes

1. For more information about the National Register, visit their official website: https://www.nps.gov/nr/.
2. It should be noted that while there are advantages to having a property listed on the National Register, there are many other ways to recognize historically significant properties through state and local programs. The National Register guidelines can be limiting and exclusionary and have in the past favored the histories of wealthy, white, heterosexual American men. A number of factors—including a lack of financial capital, discriminatory zoning laws and practices, and an increased likelihood of transiency—causes the spaces associated with those with marginalized identities to often

go unrecognized. The National Register criteria do not take into account the added challenges when considering the places of minority communities. For more information about the spaces of transient communities, see Jen Jack Gieseking, "The Geographies of LGBTQ Lives: In and Beyond Cities, Neighborhoods, and Bars," in *Communities and Place: A Thematic Approach to the Histories of LGBTQ Communities in the United States*, ed. Katherine Crawford-Lackey and Megan E. Springate (New York: Berghahn Books, forthcoming). For more information on alternative ways to recognize and preserve significant historic places, see Dolores Hayden, *The Power of Place: Urban Landscapes as Public History* (Cambridge, MA: MIT Press, 1995); Michael R. Allen, "What Historic Preservation Can Learn from Ferguson," in *Bending the Future: 50 Ideas for the Next 50 Years of Historic Preservation in the United States*, ed. Max Page and Marla R. Miller (Amherst: University of Massachusetts Press, 2016), 44–48.

3. National Park Service, *How to Apply the National Register Criteria for Evaluation*, National Register Bulletin 15 (Washington, DC: National Park Service, 1997), https://www.nps.gov/nr/publications/bulletins/nrb15/nrb15_2.htm.

Historic Preservation Activities Bibliography

Allen, Michael R. "What Historic Preservation Can Learn from Ferguson." In *Bending the Future: 50 Ideas for the Next 50 Years of Historic Preservation in the United States*, edited by Max Page and Marla R. Miller, 44–48. Amherst: University of Massachusetts Press, 2016.

American Alliance of Museums. "Collections Stewardship." http://www.aam-us .org/resources/ethics-standards-and-best-practices/collections-steward ship.

Beemyn, Genny. *A Queer Capital: A History of Gay Life in Washington, D.C.* New York: Routledge, 2015.

Brown, Michael, and Larry Knopp. "Queering the Map: The Productive Tensions of Colliding Epistemologies." *Annals of the Association of American Geographers* 98, no. 1 (2008): 40–58.

Browne, Kath, and Gavin Brown. "An Introduction to the Geographies of Sex and Sexualities." In *The Routledge Research Companion to Geographies of Sex and Sexuality*, edited by Gavin Brown and Kath Browne, 1–12. New York: Routledge, 2016.

Browne, Kath, and Eduarda Ferreira. "Introduction to Lesbian Geographies." In *Lesbian Geographies: Gender, Place and Power*, edited by Kath Browne and Eduarda Ferreira, 1–28. New York: Routledge, 2016.

Crawford-Lackey, Katie, and Barbara Little. "Exploring American Places with the Discovery Journal: A Guide to Co-Creating Meaningful Interpretation." *George Wright Forum* 34, no. 3 (2017): 335–42.

D'Emilio, John. *Sexual Politics, Sexual Communities: The Making of a Homosexual Minority in the United States, 1940–1970*. Chicago: University of Chicago Press, 1983.

Ferentinos, Susan. "Interpreting LGBTQ Historic Sites." In *Preservation and Place: Historic Preservation by and of LGBTQ Communities in the United States*, edited by Katherine Crawford-Lackey and Megan E. Springate. New York: Berghahn Books, 2019.

———. *Interpreting LGBTQ History at Museums and Historic Sites*. Lanham, MD: Rowman & Littlefield, 2015.

Gieseking, Jen Jack. "The Geographies of LGBTQ Lives: In and Beyond Cities, Neighborhoods, and Bars." In *Communities and Place: A Thematic Approach to the Histories of LGBTQ Communities in the United States*, edited by Katherine Crawford-Lackey and Megan E. Springate. New York: Berghahn Books, forthcoming.

———. "Where We Go from Here: The Mental Sketch Mapping Method and Its Analytic Components." *Qualitative Inquiry* 19, no. 9 (2013): 712–24.

Genoways, Hugh H., and Lynne M. Ireland, *Museum Administration 2.0*. Lanham, MD: Rowman & Littlefield, 2017.

Ginter, Ty. "Tradition, Community, and Grungy Secret-ness: What Preservationists Can Learn from the Story of Phase One." In *Preservation and Place:*

Historic Preservation by and of LGBTQ Communities in the United States, edited by Katherine Crawford-Lackey and Megan E. Springate (New York: Berghahn Books, 2019).

Hayden, Dolores. *The Power of Place: Urban Landscapes as Public History*. Cambridge, MA: MIT Press, 1997.

Hodder, Ian. *Reading the Past: Current Approaches to the Interpretation of Archaeology*. Cambridge: Cambridge University Press, 1986.

Johnson, Matthew. *Ideas of Landscape*. Malden, MA: Blackwell, 2007.

———. "Phenomenological Approaches in Landscape Archaeology," *Annual Review of Anthropology* 41 (2012): 269–84.

Leone, Mark P., and Silas D. Hurry. "Seeing: The Power of Town Planning in the Chesapeake." *Historical Archaeology* 34, no. 4 (1998): 34–62.

Meyer, Leisa, and Helis Sikk. "Introduction to Lesbian, Gay, Bisexual, Transgender, and Queer (LGBTQ) History in the United States." In *LGBTQ America: A Theme Study of Lesbian, Gay, Bisexual, Transgender, and Queer History*, ed. Megan E. Springate. Washington, DC: National Park Foundation and National Park Service, 2016.

National Park Service. *How to Apply the National Register Criteria for Evaluation*, National Register Bulletin 15. Washington, DC: National Park Service, 1997. Accessed 10 October 2017. https://www.nps.gov/nr/publications/bulletins/nrb15/Index.htm

———. National Register of Historic Places website, National Park Service. Accessed 10 October 2017. https://www.nps.gov/nr/.

———. Teaching with Historic Places website, https://www.nps.gov/subjects/teachingwithhistoricplaces/index.htm.

New York City Trans Oral History Project. Website. https://www.nyctransoralhistory.org/.

Price, Douglass T. *Principles of Archaeology*. Boston: McGraw-Hill, 2006.

Sanders Ralph A., and Philip W. Porter. "Shape in Revealed Mental Maps." *Annals of the Association of American Geographers* 64, no. 2 (1974): 258–67.

Smith, Angèle. "Mapped Landscapes: The Politics of Metaphor, Knowledge, and Representation of Nineteenth-Century Irish Ordnance Survey Maps," *Historical Archaeology* 41, no.1 (2007): 81–91.

Tilley, Christopher Y. *A Phenomenology of Landscape: Places, Paths, and Monuments*. Oxford: Berg, 1994.

Tuan, Yi-Fu. "Images and Mental Maps." *Annals of the Association of American Geographers* 65, no. 2 (1975): 205–13.

———. *Space and Place: The Perspective of Experience*. Minneapolis: University of Minnesota, 2003.

Index

www.ingramcontent.com/pod-product-compliance
Lightning Source LLC
Chambersburg PA
CBHW070901030426
42336CB00014BA/2277